TV
(THE BOOK)

...

TWO EXPERTS PICK
THE GREATEST AMERICAN SHOWS
OF ALL TIME

ALAN SEPINWALL
AND
MATT ZOLLER SEITZ

GRAND CENTRAL
PUBLISHING

NEW YORK   BOSTON

Grand Central Publishing
Hachette Book Group
1290 Avenue of the Americas
New York, NY 10104
grandcentralpublishing.com
twitter.com/grandcentralpub

First Edition: September 2016

Grand Central Publishing is a division of Hachette Book Group, Inc.
The Grand Central Publishing name and logo is a trademark of Hachette Book Group, Inc.

The publisher is not responsible for websites (or their content) that are not owned by the publisher.

Some material contained herein is reproduced in part from articles published in the *Star-Ledger, Salon, Slant*, movingimage.us, and Hitfix.com.

Library of Congress Cataloging-in-Publication Data

Names: Sepinwall, Alan, 1973- author. | Zoller Seitz, Matt, author.
Title: TV (the book) : two experts pick the greatest American shows of all time / Alan Sepinwall & Matt Zoller Seitz.
Description: First edition. | New York : Grand Central Publishing, 2016. | Includes index.
Identifiers: LCCN 2016015540 | ISBN 9781455588190 (paperback) | ISBN 9781478912576 (audio download) | ISBN 9781455588206 (ebook)
Subjects: LCSH: Television series—United States—History and criticism. | BISAC: PERFORMING ARTS / Television / Guides & Reviews. | PERFORMING ARTS / Television / History & Criticism.
Classification: LCC PN1992.8.S4 S3985 2016 | DDC 791.45/75—dc23 LC record available at https://lccn.loc.gov/2016015540

ISBNs: 978-1-4555-8819-0 (pbk.), 978-1-4555-8820-6 (ebook)

Printed in the United States of America

LSC-C

10 9 8 7 6 5 4 3

*To Susan Olds and Mark Di Ionno, who had the very good idea
to put these two loud kids on the TV beat together*

◾ CONTENTS ◾

The Introduction

We wanted to write about movies, not TV.

Sure, we *watched* TV—watched it so religiously that we can identify a particular *Brady Bunch* or *Little House on the Prairie* episode in under ten seconds—but growing up, we always expected to be film critics. Movies were an adventure; TV was the thing that everyone said was going to rot our brains. Movies were art; TV was the vast wasteland. There was even a TV show where a couple of film critics talked about the latest releases; good luck trying to get the local multiplex to screen a discussion of whether *The A-Team* was better than *The Dukes of Hazzard*.

For us, the glamour of movie criticism went well beyond Siskel's and Ebert's thumbs. It was in the film reviews we read in magazines while our mothers were shopping. More important, it was in the *books* about movies. There were so many of them at the library, or the local B. Dalton. Some were about a particular movie, or the works of just one actor or director, but the books that always drew us in were those voluminous guides to the world of cinema at large, whether the endless capsules of *Leonard Maltin's Movie and Video Guide* and *Halliwell's Film Guide,* or the longer essays found in collections of Pauline Kael's and Roger Ebert's best reviews. We devoured those, and many more, carrying them in cardboard boxes from childhood homes to college dorms to adult apartments. There was a permanence to them, and a sense of authority. Western literature had its own canon, and, increasingly, so did Western cinema. And we couldn't wait to weigh in on it.

Somehow, though, we both wound up covering television, in what turned out to be the best possible era—and, for multiple reasons, the best possible place—to do so. In the late '90s, we were assigned to share the TV beat for the *Star-Ledger*, New Jersey's biggest daily, and soon to become famous as the paper at the end of Tony Soprano's driveway. It was still a boom time in newspapers, where the *Ledger* could have a half dozen writers and editors primarily focusing on TV, and it was the start of a creative explosion in television—one we had a front seat to watch and write about—that ended the medium's second-class citizenship.

For ten years of the revolution that gave us *The Sopranos*, *The Wire*, and more—which made watching TV from the couch every bit the adventure going to the multiplex had once been—we sat at adjacent desks, shared a column with a logo that made us look like twins conjoined at the shoulder, and each had frequent debates about TV so passionate (or, at least, loud) that nearby copy editors would frequently have to ask us to shut up about *Deadwood*, already.

It's been another decade since we worked together regularly, even though we still talk about TV (at a volume that continues to annoy passersby) constantly, arguing over which shows are the best (and worst) ever, and trying to convince the other to give a second chance to our own pet shows, like Matt's beloved *K Street*.

Our careers have gone in different directions. Alan went to HitFix .com. Matt landed at *New York* magazine and, in a full-circle move, RogerEbert.com, after fifteen years of writing about movies and TV for different outlets simultaneously. Meanwhile, TV's creative and commercial growth continued. In the summer of 2015, the head of FX, the cable channel that's given us new classics like *The Shield* and *Louie*, noted that by the end of that year, more than four hundred original scripted series—many of them good—would have aired in prime time, and suggested we still hadn't reached "Peak TV in America" yet.

Television is better than ever, and yet there have been very few attempts (David Bianculli's *Teleliteracy*, and its companion *Dictionary of Teleliteracy*, to name a couple) to create a TV canon in book form in the spirit of all the good ones about movies, such as Andrew Sarris's *The American Cinema*, David Thomson's *The New Biographical Dictionary of Film*, and Ebert's *The Great Movies* series.

TV (The Book) is our attempt to rectify that, and to capture the spirit of some of our old *Star-Ledger* bull sessions in printed form.

In the ensuing pages, we will identify the one hundred greatest scripted shows in American TV history, explain their greatness in a series of essays, and almost certainly make everyone very angry by ranking some above others and omitting many dozens or hundreds more.

Because there are more hours of good present-day TV to watch during any given year—never mind all the great older shows that you may want to catch up on at some point—than there are hours in which to watch them, this book also tries to boil sixty-plus years of the medium's history down to an essential viewing list, so people can experience some version of a canon without killing themselves.

We knew it was presumptuous to think that any two critics could identify TV's best shows ever, then rank them. Nevertheless, we wanted to see a book like this exist. And with our four combined decades of professional TV knowledge (plus close to that again, if you count our misspent youths), we feel that we know the medium thoroughly enough to make informed judgments.

That said, this project was undertaken with a spirit of humility and invitation. *TV (The Book)* is Matt and Alan's canon at this particular moment; no more, no less. We don't want, much less expect, for it to be treated as the canon for all time (not that it would be) or as an attempt to shut down discussion rather than open it up. We still crack open the Thomsons and Eberts and Maltins on our bookshelves, and every few years we read and argue about canonical film lists published by *Sight & Sound*, *The Village Voice*, *Cahiers du Cinéma*, and other august publications; just as none of those necessarily trump any others, we hope that our TV equivalent will eventually be seen as merely one survey among many.

This is our canon; we look forward to yours.

The Explanation

HOW DOES THIS WORK?

The heart of the book is the Pantheon: a list of the one hundred greatest comedies and dramas.

To create it, we made a list of several hundred candidates for the best shows of all time, allowing for various caveats explained in the following pages.

Then we set about the sensible and not-at-all-controversial task of assigning numerical values to art.

We decided on five categories, to which we eventually added a sixth. Each of us was assigned 10 points per category, for a possible maximum score of 120 if both of us gave a particular series perfect scores. (No show got perfect scores across the board.)

Those categories are:

Innovation. Was the show trying something—in terms of form, subject matter, or both—that felt new, or was it following or embellishing upon tradition? Shows like *All in the Family* and *24* scored highly here because they did things no one in American television had really tried before, whereas an otherwise great show like *Parks and Recreation* had a comparatively low Innovation rating because it largely duplicated a stylistic template its creators had used for *The Office*.

Influence. How much of an impact did the show have either on the medium of television or on the culture at large? Shows like *Hill Street Blues* and *Friends* were copied by many other TV series. *Freaks and Geeks*, a short-lived show that had few obvious imitators, scored highly because of the impact its cast and creators had on the entire comedy business during the past fifteen years. *Will & Grace* (which finished outside the top 100) scored highly here because of the role it played in helping to reshape public attitudes about homosexuality.

Consistency. How much did the quality fluctuate from episode to episode, or season to season? That said, consistency isn't a mark just of smooth sailing from start to finish but of how well a series weathered storms beyond its control, like Nancy Marchand's death after only two seasons of *The Sopranos*, or the constant cast turnover on *Law & Order*.

Performance. This deals not only with how great the actors on the show were but how well-crafted their characters were. So *The Sopranos* did better in this category than *24*, because even if you feel that James Gandolfini and Kiefer Sutherland were giving performances of equal quality, Tony Soprano was just a richer, more complex character than Jack Bauer, and the same was true of supporting characters on each series.

Storytelling. Here we come to the parts of writing beyond characterization, such as tone and structure, not to mention such filmmaking elements as direction, production design, editing, and music. Among the seeming intangibles that come into play are comic timing, suspense, surprise, formal audacity, and its obverse, perfectly executed classicism. *Hannibal*, *Twin Peaks*, and *The Simpsons* prided themselves on doing something different every week, whereas *Cheers* and *The Honeymooners* did more or less the same thing every week. All five scored well in this category because what matters in storytelling isn't just what you're doing but how well you're doing it.

Peak. A late addition, factoring in how great each show was at its absolute best, using a full season, more or less, as our unit of measurement. Other categories were judged against the entirety of television; this was graded on a curve against the rest of the Pantheon: only a few 10s, lots of middling scores, and a few low ones reflecting how that show's best compares to, say, the fourth seasons of *The Wire* or *Seinfeld*.

The breakdown of each show's score can be found in the appendix in the back of the book. You may notice that occasionally, a show was scored by only one of us. That's because we knew certain shows clearly had to be considered, but only one of us had enough history with it to score it with authority. Rather than dismiss these shows from contention, or require the other guy to binge-watch thirty or sixty hours in the space of a few days, we decided to double Matt's or Alan's score for that show and get on with it.

WHAT SHOWS WERE CONSIDERED?

We made the following rules:

1. US television shows only.

Fawlty Towers, *Prime Suspect*, *Space Battleship Yamato* (*Star Blazers*), *Les Revenants* (*The Returned*), both *Kingdom* miniseries, and other beloved imports would rank highly if we opened this book to international series. Ultimately, though, we felt that while there were a few blind spots here and there in our knowledge of TV originating in the States, the gaps became much wider when we factored in shows from other countries. We didn't want to be so foolish as to mistake our knowledge of the relatively paltry handful of British, Mexican, Japanese, Danish, and other foreign shows that have made it to the United States for the totality of international TV. Given US programs' global reach, this might not be as much of an issue for critics in other countries, but there would still be knowledge constraints. If French critics were doing their version of this book and trying to include American series, they'd surely know of *The Sopranos* and *I Love Lucy*, but would they know *Terriers* or *Frank's Place*?

The line between what is and isn't a US-made show can be blurry, and we made what are sure to be considered debatable calls. To use three current examples: *Game of Thrones* is shot all over the world and has an international cast, but it originates on and is funded by HBO, so we counted it as a US series. *Top of the Lake* was shot in New Zealand and cofunded by several international sources, but a good chunk of that money came from Sundance Channel, so we counted it as US. And *Catastrophe* is a hilarious comedy cocreated by and costarring American comedian Rob Delaney, but he and Sharon Horgan made it for the United Kingdom's Channel 4; that it's available to stream here on Amazon makes it no more American than *Sherlock*, which is produced in the UK but airs here on PBS.

Of course there are going to be some borderline cases that we will cop to having included because we liked them and felt confident in writing about them. We might get dinged for inconsistency there, but we're willing to live with it.

2. Completed shows only. Mostly.

If we were writing this book in early 2012, and *Homeland* had been canceled after its first, outstanding season, it might have earned itself a spot somewhere in the top 100. The ensuing seasons, unfortunately, dragged its average down far enough that it finished well outside the running. TV shows can vary wildly in quality from season to season—just look at the roller-coaster ride that was *Friday Night Lights* seasons 1–3—and it felt unfair to make final judgments if a show wasn't complete. You never know when a series is going to pull a *Roseanne* and do something absolutely dire in a later year, or make like *Frasier* or *Scrubs* and return to former glory before the end.

That said, we made exceptions. *The Simpsons* has been on the air for almost thirty seasons, which feels like a large enough sample size to make a judgment about, no matter how good or bad the next few decades of the show may be. (Ditto *South Park* as it finishes its second decade.) We also made space for a few shows like *Curb Your Enthusiasm*, *Arrested Development*, and *Louie*, which could theoretically return at some point but which were on prolonged hiatuses at the time of this book's creation. If more seasons or episodes get produced, great: We'll happily watch and evaluate them. If not, we're comfortable judging them as if they *were* complete.

We decided to consider *Twin Peaks* and *The X-Files* complete despite the existence of recent or upcoming seasons that were announced while we were writing the book. We felt that because so much time has elapsed since the presumed "end" of each series—fourteen years for *The X-Files*; twenty-five-plus years for *Twin Peaks*—that any additional seasons should be considered the beginnings of separate series (or miniseries) that have the same names.

3. Narrative fiction only.

As it is, comparing comedies and dramas—let alone shows from different eras, like trying to decide whether *The Fugitive* is greater than *30*

Rock—was onerous enough without also trying to figure out variables for sketch comedy, talk shows, documentary and news programs, reality TV, sports, and so on. Comedy versus drama is already apples and oranges; to add plantains, tangelos, and star fruit would have been foolish indeed.

We considered anthology shows on a case-by-case basis, deciding that series such as *The Twilight Zone* and *The Outer Limits* fit the larger idea of what we were trying to do, because the episodes each week were linked by style and theme and, often, a common creative team, while something like *Playhouse 90* should be looked at more as an umbrella title for a collection of filmed plays, some of which are cited individually elsewhere in the book. (Ditto the brilliant *Mystery Science Theater 3000*, which consists of maybe 90 percent annotated film-watching and 10 percent character-based comedy.)

We steered away from children's programming because, like international programming, the subject seemed vast enough to merit a second book, and too prone to glaring omissions to consider here. (Our own children protested this choice.) A few series that could be considered kids' shows are cited in the Pantheon and on other lists; they made it in because if, by some chance, you were not in the company of kids when you first stumbled upon them, you might have considered them sophisticated enough to pass muster as grown-up entertainment. *SpongeBob SquarePants* is an absurdist masterpiece that Salvador Dalí and Groucho Marx would have watched together in their smoking jackets, *Samurai Jack* is the greatest action movie that John Woo never made, and *Recess* is *Lord of the Flies* plus *One Flew Over the Cuckoo's Nest*, minus murder.

4. One-season shows are eligible, but with some penalties.

This was the subject of a lot of debate. Is it fair to judge a show like *My So-Called Life*—which made nineteen more or less perfect episodes, then ended before it could enter the kind of decline phase that afflicted *Homeland*—against long-running series that were subjected to the indignities and compromises that come with age? Yes, for the same reason that one could compare the acting virtues of James Dean, who appeared in only three films, and Paul Newman, who appeared in almost sixty.

But once you decide to do that, you need to establish parameters. In an effort to consider one-season wonders while being fair to shows that stuck around longer, we artificially limited their point totals, which means they had to be extra-impressive in their one season to make it into the Pantheon. The most a one-season show could score in each category was a 9, except for consistency—the easiest task to accomplish over only a year—where the highest possible score was a 7.

WHAT'S IN THE BOOK BESIDES THE PANTHEON?

There's a section on some of our favorite current shows—including several that would have been Pantheon contenders if the timing had been a little different—titled "Works in Progress." There are also essays accompanying lists of TV's best miniseries, movies, and televised plays, and terse lists covering such topics as great theme songs, memorable deaths, and the best houses and apartments.

(Some of these other sections and lists feature rankings, while others are just alphabetical. But any rankings done outside the Pantheon were done with less rigor: gut feeling, occasionally augmented by Rock Paper Scissors and cursing contests.)

We also have a separate section called "A Certain Regard," named after Prize Un Certain Regard, a category outside of the main competition at the Cannes Film Festival, established in 1978 to draw the international film community's attention to works of diverse subject matter and style. (In 1998, a prize was attached to it.) This is the section in which we wrote about shows we loved and wanted to praise in the book, even if we couldn't justify goosing their scores enough to move them into the Pantheon, or if they were lacking in key categories (such as Storytelling or Influence), or never had much interest in them to start with.

A Certain Regard is also the place where we honor programs or aspects of programs that are great in pieces but maybe not as a whole, like the outlier second season of *Sons of Anarchy* and the first seasons of *Crime Story* and *Homeland*.

SERIOUSLY, THOUGH: HOW DARE YOU ASSIGN A NUMERICAL VALUE TO ART?

If you treat H. L. Mencken's statement that "criticism is prejudice made plausible" not as a condemnation but as a set of marching orders, you can see how we can rank some shows above others—all of this is subjective. The fact is, some shows are simply better than others. Assigning ten-point scores across six categories isn't a perfect solution to the problem, but it's better than the alternative, which is either (a) a list of one hundred supposedly equally good programs ordered alphabetically, or (b) a list of one hundred programs plucked out of a hat.

Plus, the simple fact of the matter is, when somebody asks you which is better, *CHiPs* or *Barney Miller*, you not only answer *"Barney Miller,"* you know why. Attaching numbers to your feelings only clarifies them.

On top of all that, people ask us **all the time**, "What's the best comedy ever?" "What's the best drama ever?" "What's the best show of all time?" and "What are the best shows on the air right now?" This is our attempt to finally answer those questions. The results may surprise you, just as they surprised us when we were done.

And now, rather than answer every question individually, we can smile cryptically and hand people copies of this volume from the handcrafted leather *TV (The Book)* rucksacks we will carry on our person until the end of our days, then jump feetfirst through the nearest open window while playing the *SpongeBob SquarePants* theme on a slide whistle.

WHY ARE SOME OF THE SHOWS WRITTEN ABOUT IN PAIRS OR GROUPS?

For the most part, each show in the Pantheon gets its own essay, which in bulk tend to decrease in length as we travel further down the list. Every now and then, though, we realized that there was such obvious overlap between the themes of certain essays—say, the changing demographics of sitcom casts, as reflected in *The Golden Girls* and *Friends*—that it made more sense to write about them in tandem.

Whenever we did this, the joint essay appears in the position of the highest-ranked show.

WHY AREN'T THERE MORE OLD SHOWS ON THIS LIST?

We don't believe that TV suddenly became good when *The Sopranos* debuted. But it would be foolish to disregard the fact that for the first twenty, maybe thirty, years of its existence, television was more of an appliance or advertising delivery mechanism than an artistic medium. We don't mean to say that it was impossible to produce art on television; clearly it was. We just mean that the commercial constraints were so severe that shows were lucky to show flashes of artistry, and those that did were occasionally overrated for the same reason that one might declare a sip of dirty water to be the finest beverage in the desert. Most shows of the '50s, '60s, and even into the '70s could be great at one or two things, but it was rare for them to be great at lots of things at the same time, much less demonstrate the kind of audacity that was common in literature, theater, cinema, even popular music.

You will find shows from those early decades in this book—*The Honeymooners*, for instance, and *The Twilight Zone*, and *The Westerner*—but it's fair to say the medium didn't begin to reach its full artistic potential until the '80s, because for the most part, the words "full" and "potential" weren't allowed anywhere near each other. We can't stress enough that much of the fault for this must be laid at the feet of the networks, indeed, the system as a whole, rather than individual artists'. Too often the artists' will to create was thwarted by the networks saying, "No way." There were too many words you couldn't utter, too many topics you couldn't address even obliquely, too many stylistic choices you weren't allowed to make, because executives feared turning off viewers and scaring off advertisers. Once the range of expression expanded—thanks to the advent of cable as well as the broadcast networks' desire to compete with feature films aimed at grown-ups—you were more likely to see expressive and sophisticated and even daring shows amid the usual crud.

Brilliant individual artists played a part in driving the medium's evolution forward, too. There were great gymnasts before Nadia Comăneci, and great boxers before Muhammad Ali, but their greatness was so distinctive, of such a higher order of magnitude than anything that had come before, that it kicked open the doors of possibility to all who came after, and showed there was more to their sports than even the most ardent spectators thought possible. In the same vein, many TV writers, directors, and actors are on record saying they were spurred to innovation by shows from many different eras, everything from *The Ernie Kovacs Show* and *Mary Hartman, Mary Hartman* through *The Larry*

Sanders Show and *True Detective*. We've tried to honor TV's pioneers here, in the context of the shows they helped create and sometimes in self-contained entries.

ARE THERE SPOILERS IN THIS BOOK?

Hell yes.

There's no way to properly express the greatness of these shows without giving away many of the things that happened on them, sometimes all the way to the end. If you haven't seen a particular show and don't want any surprises spoiled, jump to the next entry.

IF MY FAVORITE SHOW ISN'T IN THE BOOK, DOES THAT MEAN IT'S NOT GOOD?

Absolutely not, unless your favorite show is *Work It!*

As we said, there's a lot of TV, past and present. Even if we tried to confine the Pantheon to shows of the twenty-first century, we'd still be leaving a lot of good stuff out. These are just the ones we felt were most impressive artistically, or that we had a soft spot for, or thought were underappreciated or misunderstood.

THE PANTHEON

■ ■ ■

The 100
Greatest Shows Ever

How Do You Pick the Best Show of All Time?

(The authors conducted the following conversation over several days via GChat after their initial attempt to rank the greatest shows of all time resulted in a five-way tie for the top spot.)

Alan Sepinwall: Okay, so we have a five-way tie for first: *The Sopranos*, *Breaking Bad*, *Cheers*, *The Simpsons*, and *The Wire*.

Matt Zoller Seitz: The question is, what do we do about it? They're all excellent in one way or another, they got to their positions on merit, and they're all very different. Maybe we should argue this out.

Alan Sepinwall: Yes. The first thing to do is maybe figure out if any of them should be eliminated from contention straightaway. We started out with this ranking system, where we were assigning scores independently of other shows, but now that we have these five neck and neck, are there any that clearly shouldn't be above the others?

Matt Zoller Seitz: Well, my knee-jerk reaction, which is not necessarily to be trusted, is to prize the most aesthetically daring shows over the others, because that's how I usually roll. That would mean that the greatest show of all time cannot be *Cheers*, which is the summation of everything that had been done in the three-camera sitcom format up until that point, and arguably the greatest thing ever *to* be done in that format, since no other sitcom has quite matched it since.

But as I describe *Cheers*, I find myself appreciating that achievement.

And it is an achievement. To be the best at something that other shows were doing quite well for three decades before your show came down the road: That's nothing to sneeze at.

At the same time, my gut tells me *Breaking Bad* cannot be the greatest TV show of all time. But I don't know why I feel that.

Alan Sepinwall: I was thinking of *Breaking Bad*, too. It's an extraordinary show, and deserving of a high position here. But I can't see myself putting it above *The Sopranos*, and not just because *The Sopranos* was first. *Breaking Bad* is the more consistent show, and the more narratively satisfying one, and yet *The Sopranos* feels like the greater artistic achievement, if that makes sense.

Matt Zoller Seitz: There is something to be said for consistency over time, and "perfection"—defined here, perhaps, by the absence of episodes or seasons that didn't quite work. *Breaking Bad* and *Cheers* have no bad seasons and, I would contend, no bad episodes, only good and great. You can't say that for *The Sopranos* or *The Simpsons* or even *The Wire*.

But I think if I am being true to myself, I have to value the more extravagant, even grandiose achievements of *The Sopranos*, *The Wire*, and *The Simpsons*, even though the downside is that you sometimes end up with stuff like the Columbus Day episode or Vito in New Hampshire, or some of the newspaper stuff in season 5 of *The Wire* that didn't go anywhere.

And *The Simpsons*, as I am sure we'll get into, has a whole other problem, which is that it is still on the air as we write this. That means that, as inventive as it is, it cannot help but repeat itself in some ways, and do variations of things it's done before. We don't want to run the risk of confusing the artists' unwillingness to quit while they're ahead, or their inability to recognize a promising idea that cannot be properly executed, with boldness. Sometimes a part of art is deciding not to do a thing because it's not worth doing, or might not work. You know: judgment.

I'm seesawing here, I know, I know.

Alan Sepinwall: I have a whole elaborate argument about *The Simpsons* that we will, indeed, get to. As for *Cheers*, I would argue that achieving perfection in your form—even if it's ultimately a less artistically challenging form—is just as powerful a statement as aiming higher and mostly hitting the target.

As you say, *Cheers* was the sum total of decades of the medium's most beloved type of series, and the best example of it. I can understand the arguments for why *The Simpsons* and the two HBO shows are simply more important, and might make them myself, but there's nothing wrong with being the best there ever was at something that **many** people—including Ball, Gleason, Reiner, Lear, et cetera—took a crack at over the decades.

Matt Zoller Seitz: Okay, so since we both seem to feel like the greatest show of all time cannot be *Breaking Bad*, maybe we should dig into that one first and see if we change our minds.

For me it comes down to *Breaking Bad*'s very clearly being a descendant of *The Sopranos*. It is more consistently clever, and just more consistent than *The Sopranos*, over nearly the same span of storytelling acreage, and it's funny and entertaining, but I don't feel awed by it in the way I do *The Sopranos*.

Alan Sepinwall: If you were to ask me what is the best hour of dramatic television ever, I would say *Breaking Bad*'s "Ozymandias" and not think twice about it. In terms of consistency, visual flair, and use of the serialized nature of the medium to build narrative, suspense, and character, *Breaking Bad* is better than *The Sopranos*.

But, like you, I feel ever so slightly more pulled in by the emotion and the thematic scope of *The Sopranos*, even as it is much easier to point out story lines, characters, and even entire seasons that are less strong. It's not just that it was first (otherwise, *I Love Lucy* would be here over *Cheers*) but that it was reaching for something much grander.

Which, of course, is the exact opposite of the argument I just made for *Cheers*. This is hard!

Matt Zoller Seitz: Here's what it comes down to for me: If *The Sopranos* and *Breaking Bad* are treading similar thematic terrain, and I believe they are, I then have to ask myself which show explored it more thoughtfully and in a more challenging or surprising way. The answer is *The Sopranos*. No drama in the history of television was more surprising. And I don't just mean reversal of expectations. I count infuriating the audience as a form of surprise. Anticlimax can create surprise, too. So can what I call "double-bluffing": where you think you know what a typical TV series would do, and assume *The Sopranos* won't do it because it's *The Sopranos*, and then they do it, and you're surprised.

I feel like David Chase and his writers and directors had the entire history of television in the backs of their minds as they made that show, and were determined never to do the obvious thing, even if the obvious thing would be the crowd-pleasing thing. There were times when *Breaking Bad* did the obvious, crowd-pleasing thing, in a way that very slightly cheapened the rest of the show's extraordinary achievements for me.

If you compare, say, the way that Walt dealt with the threat from Gus Fring—which was awesome in an action-movie sense—versus the way that Tony dealt with Ralphie Cifaretto on *The Sopranos*, you can see what I mean. The former is a very elegantly laid-out protagonist-versus-antagonist, cat-and-mouse game, which is wonderful on its own terms. But Tony versus Ralphie is about something other than crime or gangsterism. It's about having to work with somebody you hate, and how an organization or business forces you to eat dirt sometimes, and how money talks (Ralphie's a good earner, so the higher-ups keep excusing his loathsomeness). When the end finally comes for Ralphie at the hands of Tony, the context is surprising, and the timing is surprising. You almost assumed it wasn't going to happen, and it happens because Tony's suppressed rage and despair over Ralphie's murder of the stripper Tracee erupts in a different context, over Ralphie burning down the stable where the horse Pie-O-My sleeps. Psychologically, dramatically, thematically, it's five times more complex than anything *Breaking Bad* has done, and the fact that *Breaking Bad* is simply more fun, more exciting, and equally humorous can't quite counter that for me.

And then compare the endings: The finale of *Breaking Bad* is satisfying, in a fan-service way, but people are still arguing about the meaning and intent of the end of *The Sopranos*. Really actively arguing. It makes people angry, still.

So in a head-to-head between *Breaking Bad* and *The Sopranos*, *Breaking Bad* loses. That doesn't mean *Breaking Bad* is a bad show; it just means it is one of the greatest shows of all time, but not *the* greatest. And we're left with the rest.

Alan Sepinwall: I agree. So let's set that one aside and talk about *The Simpsons*.

Matt Zoller Seitz: Please do.

Alan Sepinwall: I feel like the thing that's holding us back from just naming it as the best show of all time is the show's continued existence past its first dozen years or so. I happen to like the later years better than you, but I also think that it's not necessarily fair to hold those years against it.

I'll put it in baseball terms: When Hall of Fame voting time comes around, players who were very obvious Hall of Famers at the peaks of their careers (say, Tim Raines) sometimes get perceived by the voters to be less than that because they stuck around forever, hitting for less power and average, eventually becoming a designated hitter or a platoon player. Because those later years are fresher in the voters' minds, the players get dismissed by some as compilers, who are under consideration in the first place only because they played so long.

Just as a hypothetical, let's pretend that the series ended with "Behind the Laughter," the season 11 finale. No episodes were made after that, and we're thus considering only the years of "Homer the Heretic," "Marge vs. the Monorail," "Last Exit to Springfield," and so on. Is *The Simpsons* your number one show in that case?

Matt Zoller Seitz: I'm not sure. And I say that as somebody who believes, and has argued, that *The Simpsons* was excellent, or at least consistently entertaining with flashes of greatness, through at least season 13, which is incredible when you stop and think about what that entailed, and all the changeovers of writers and producers.

But I want to hold *The Simpsons* in our pocket for now because we need to ask, why not *The Wire*? Why not *Cheers*?

Alan Sepinwall: Well, since I just contradicted myself about my earlier *Cheers* defense with what I wrote about *Breaking Bad*, I'm tempted to set that one aside.

Also, frankly, if you're asking me what the best comedy in TV history is, I'm saying *The Simpsons*. The only way *Cheers* wins that is if there's some kind of "live-action only" qualifier, which we obviously aren't using.

Would you agree that *The Simpsons* is ahead of *Cheers*, and thus Sam and Diane should be watching the rest of this from the sidelines with Walt and Jesse?

Matt Zoller Seitz: I'm torn on that, because there is a case to be made for *Cheers'* near perfection over the long haul, its exquisitely timed moments of human interaction. That sort of thing is often devalued. But we're not making a case here for *Cheers* as a great show. We already did that. That's why it ended up in the top 5.

I think of all the categories we've established as criteria for judging, the one I have to keep coming back to here is "peak." As you put it, at its peak, how good was *The Simpsons*? When it was magnificent, how magnificent was it in relation to other shows on this list?

And here we get into the issue of "better" versus "greater." "Better" is something that can be judged in an almost mathematical way, as weird as that sounds. You can look at a show and go, "Well, it was consistently excellent more often than this other show."

But "peak" is all about greatness, and greatness for me transcends issues of consistency or craft. Greatness suggests magnitude. Awesomeness. Surprise. Delight. And if we're measuring "peak" here, which I'm doing in this final tiebreaker discussion, *The Simpsons* beats *Cheers*. *Cheers* was more consistently entertaining over a longer period of time but under more rigidly circumscribed parameters, which was part of the point of *Cheers*. And that's great. But *The Simpsons* had hundreds of transcendent, awesome, delightful moments, maybe thousands, during half of its run, which was longer than *Cheers'*, and when it did something that you'd never seen before, which was often, it would feel so new, so odd, so right, that you might gasp.

Just tonight I watched the Valentine's Day episode again, with Krusty's special and Ralph Wiggum developing a crush on Lisa and the Presidents' Day pageant at the end; the moment when Ralph's heart breaks in two in freeze-frame on the VCR, the moment where Krusty chastises his younger self, the final shot of the kids on the swing with "Monster Mash" reprising—that's great. It's peak.

Alan Sepinwall: And then...there were three: Tony Soprano versus Homer Simpson versus the city of Baltimore.

We haven't talked at all about *The Wire* yet. The argument for that as the greatest show in TV history is pretty easy. It's got grandeur (five years of its fictionalized Baltimore feels just as densely populated as twenty-five-plus years of Springfield, and with far more complex and well-rounded characters), it's got thematic ambition, it's more tightly plotted than *The Sopranos* while still feeling as emotionally devastating, and though there are issues with that final season, they're no worse than some of the aforementioned *Sopranos* bumps, let alone some of the weaker latter-day *Simpsons* years.

So tell me why we shouldn't just call it a day and go with McNulty and company.

Matt Zoller Seitz: Because of "peak." *The Sopranos* at its peak was greater than *The Wire* at its peak, and even if you accept that their peaks were equally great, though different, *The Sopranos* just had more of them— and they were often more surprising, more daring, more unusual. The frame was just bigger and there was more in the picture aesthetically.

David Simon's show was, as he himself has joked in season 5, Dickensian—the way it showed all levels of society was tough but also compassionate and filled with details that only reporters, or reporters at heart, could provide. And the notion of stacking new narrative structures atop established ones was new, and challenging. By the time we got to the end we were looking at a layer cake, with the cops and drug dealers on the bottom and then all these levels of other institutions stacked on top of that.

But *The Sopranos* had a sense of the characters' interiors—not just through Tony's dreams but also in the way the show was photographed and edited. It was more modern, at times postmodern, even as it delivered traditional storytelling satisfactions; there was a sense in which it was contemplating our relationship to the show even as it was telling the story.

And, Alan, I've said this to you before, but if all things were equal, and you could look at *The Wire* and *The Sopranos* and say, "They are equally good in every area in which one could compare them," I would have to give it to *The Sopranos* just for the ending. When I had to choose between *The Sopranos* and *The Wire* in the Vulture drama derby a few years ago, I went back and forth up until the last possible second. I even went with *The Sopranos*, then changed my mind and chose *The Wire*, but the thumbnail on the page still said the winner was *The Sopranos*, which was funny! But as I thought about that ending again, I began to wish I'd stuck with *The Sopranos*.

Alan Sepinwall: We're going to get yelled at for a lot of things in this book, but I imagine picking *The Sopranos* as number one specifically because of the ending will be the thing we get yelled at about most. (And that's leaving aside that neither of us is a "Tony dies" truther.)

I would counter that while we didn't get to know the interior life of anyone on *The Wire* nearly as well as we got to know Tony's, we got to know everyone else in Baltimore far better than all but a handful of other people in North Jersey. There were different designs for each show. I don't think we should be so quick to dismiss the achievement of creating a fictional world where you could follow any individual character home and it would be fascinating. You just can't say that about a large swath of *Sopranos* country. What *The Wire* may have lacked in aesthetic daring, I think it compensated in breadth and depth.

Matt Zoller Seitz: Fair enough.

Still, I do feel that *The Wire* represents the absolute best of things that have been done before—setting aside the not-at-all-trivial matter of that stacked structure, which was really something. Whereas *The Sopranos* always felt forward-looking, even as it built its story around a familiar core, that of the mob narrative à la *The Godfather* or Scorsese's movies. The fascination with moral relativity, the juxtaposition of extreme violence and complex psychology with almost sitcom-like comedy—this was all new, or at least a new spin, and it was unsettling for many. *The Sopranos* pushed the entire medium forward in a way that I don't think *The Wire* ever did, as much as I love it. And I don't just mean the antihero aspects—which is what some inferior shows latched on to. *The Sopranos* kept innovating and surprising all the way up to its final seconds, confounding whatever you thought you knew about it.

And here again we get into the *Cheers*-versus-*Simpsons* conundrum: If

I devalue a more aesthetically conservative kind of storytelling, am I giving too many bonus points for stuff that's swaggering or being gimmicky?

Alan Sepinwall: And I adore *The Sopranos* and would have no regrets if it winds up as our winner, or simply ranked ahead of *The Wire*. I just want to be sure we aren't overvaluing the swagger.

That stacked structure of *The Wire* is nothing to sneeze at. While David Simon likes to refer to *The Wire* as a novel for television, I really think it's the apex of what TV as a medium allows in terms of serialization. Other shows had told long-form story arcs before (the first *Sopranos* season is magnificent in that regard) but never to this extent, with this many story elements set up and paid off not only within each season, but across five different seasons.

Just look at what they did with Bubbles, and how sixty-odd hours of television were all in service of making the audience weep at the simple, familiar image of a man jogging up the steps to enjoy a family dinner. That's swagger, just of a different sort.

And having said all that, I still feel like we need to take a long, hard look at putting *The Simpsons* ahead of both.

Matt Zoller Seitz: Are you saying *The Wire* should be elevated over *The Sopranos* in this final five ranking?

If so, I think I need a little more convincing.

Let me give you a film example to explain where I'm coming from. If I had to choose which classic '70s drama is altogether greater, *The Godfather* or *All That Jazz*, I would ultimately go with *All That Jazz*, because *The Godfather* represents the apotheosis of classical Hollywood studio narrative, a summation after which little of significance can be added, whereas *All That Jazz* to me does all of that, too, in its way, but it also brings in traditions of abstract or experimental cinema, the "trip" film, European auteur cinema like *8½* and *Hiroshima Mon Amour*, and at the same time it's looking beyond the moment that it was in. That film was the future, and it still is. So I'm an *All That Jazz* man.

See what I mean? *The Wire* isn't lacking for love here; at worst it could end up the fifth-greatest show in the history of American TV, but I still have to put Chase's everything-plus-the-kitchen-sink comedy drama over Simon's *The Wire*, a nineteenth-century novel set in twenty-first-century Baltimore.

Alan Sepinwall: Okay, I am tempted to hide the keys to your TV critic mobile after that *All That Jazz/Godfather* decision. And not just because I'd probably argue for *The Godfather Part II.*

But we're obviously down to a very specific slice of personal preference now. And I would say that it's not necessarily fair to dock *The Wire*, or *The Godfather*, for being a summation of the previous traditions of Western TV or cinema without also bringing in other influences. (And besides, there's at least as much of the blues in *The Wire* as there is jazz in *Tremé.*) *The Sopranos* means an enormous amount to me as a critic, above and beyond our professional attachments to it as the two TV writers from Tony's hometown paper.

But this is close.

Matt Zoller Seitz: Okay, then, let's assume that *The Wire* and *The Sopranos* are tied, whatever place they end up in. We will have to break that tie at some point, but for now we have to concern ourselves only with certain positioning questions, namely, (1) Are *The Sopranos* and *The Wire* greater shows than *Cheers* and *Breaking Bad*? (2) Are *The Wire* and *The Sopranos* greater than *The Simpsons*?

Alan Sepinwall: (1) Yes. I think we're pretty clear on that. (2) I am not at all sure that the two HBO dramas are better than *The Simpsons*, whether or not we are considering all the seasons as opposed to the first dozen or so.

Matt Zoller Seitz: To quote *Pulp Fiction*, that's a bold statement.

Alan Sepinwall: It's about as apples to oranges as you can get, but *The Simpsons* is just as brilliant and savage a commentary on modern America as *The Sopranos* and *The Wire*. It's gone everywhere and done everything you could possibly want or expect a comedy to do (and then done many things beyond that), and it was at its peak for longer (in years and episodes) than the dramas.

Also, given how relatively quickly we were able to dismiss *Cheers* versus the struggle we're having splitting the HBO baby, there's a wider gulf between it and the next-best comedy than there is between whichever drama we pick and the next-best drama.

Why should it not be seriously considered here?

Matt Zoller Seitz: The only answer I can give to that is that while *The Simpsons* is a comedy, and a great one, *The Wire* and *The Sopranos* are simultaneously dramas and comedies. *The Simpsons* has heart, and sometimes "heart," and it creates main characters who are believable as can be, considering the ludicrous situations they find themselves in, but this is not the same as saying that the show *contains* drama in the sense that *The Sopranos* and *The Wire* do. In fact, I think you could make a stronger case for *Cheers* as a sitcom that contains real drama, more so than *The Simpsons*. So to me, what we're doing when we talk about elevating *The Simpsons* over *The Wire* or *The Sopranos* is making a statement that, in effect, *The Simpsons* comedy was so hilarious, so surprising, so innovative, so well-crafted, that its achievement outshines these other two shows, *The Sopranos* and *The Wire*, which contain both comedy *and* drama, and arguably do them both equally well. (And you could tack *Cheers* on there as well if you were so inclined, even though it's a comedy that contains dramatic elements rather than the reverse.)

Alan Sepinwall: First, I think the argument can be made about the comedic achievement of *The Simpsons*. But I also think you are selling the character moments of *The Simpsons*, particularly in the early years, short. Lisa's heartbreak in the episode with Dustin Hoffman as her substitute teacher is every bit as powerful as the funniest moment on *The Wire* or *The Sopranos* is hilarious.

Maybe it didn't go there as often as those shows went to the comic well (or that *Cheers*, in its early years, went to dramatic moments), but there's an awful lot of dramatic meat to the Simpson marriage, and to the relationships between each parent and child over those early years.

Matt Zoller Seitz: I don't know if I can follow you there. That moment with Lisa is great, but it's not as profoundly sorrowful or moving as countless other moments on *The Wire* or *The Sopranos*, where you feel like your heart has been ripped from your chest.

I know that probably sounds like I'm prizing drama over comedy, but I'm really not. I'm just trying to express this feeling that the drama on *The Simpsons* was mostly parenthetical to the comedy, whereas the comedy on *The Wire* and *The Sopranos* was not parenthetical to the drama; they were often equal in any given episode.

And that's all in service of building a case for *The Simpsons*' being great as a comedy, but those other shows' being great as comedies but also great as dramas, which to me is a bit like being equally great at piano and cello, or basketball and swimming. It's really, really hard, and if we're going for "greatness" here, we have to consider that.

Alan Sepinwall: No, I think you're missing my point. I'm saying that the most dramatic *Simpsons* moment is equivalent to the funniest *Sopranos* or *Wire* moment.

Matt Zoller Seitz: Okay, that's a horse of a different color. Elaborate.

Alan Sepinwall: You were making the argument that *The Sopranos* and *The Wire* should be considered ahead of it because they were not only devastating and ambitious as drama but incredibly funny when they wanted to be comic. And my counter is that the Mr. Bergstrom moment is as effective as drama as, say, Omar getting the better of Maury Levy in court is as comedy.

And if you would agree to that, then we are considering whether the comic achievements of *The Simpsons*—and its distance from what we are calling the second-best comedy—are enough to elevate it over the dramatic achievements of either HBO drama.

Does that make sense?

Matt Zoller Seitz: I can't quite accept that the most dramatic *Simpsons* moment is equivalent to the funniest *Sopranos* or *Wire* moment. If I were to just pick, off the top of my head and rather arbitrarily, the funniest moments from *The Sopranos* and *The Wire*—Paulie Walnuts explaining that he can do the time in purgatory standing on his head, and the McNulty and Bunk scene where they're searching an apartment and every word of dialogue is "fuck"—then I would say those funny moments are greater, as comedy, than the Mr. Bergstrom moment is great as drama.

You could possibly convince me that *The Simpsons* is greater than those other shows on the basis of formal daring and comedic invention alone, Alan, but that's a different tack than the one you were taking.

Alan Sepinwall: And I can do that. You just baited me with the suggestion that *The Sopranos* and *The Wire* should get extra credit for being funny. Which they are.

Matt Zoller Seitz: I wouldn't say "extra credit," just credit. I do think both those shows are among the greatest comedies TV has given us, and that if they contained no dramatic situations to speak of, they might still make this book.

Alan Sepinwall: But just imagine *The Simpsons* as a melancholy comedy in the vein of *BoJack Horseman* or *Enlightened*, and that wasn't laugh-out-loud funny. I think Mr. Bergstrom, Bart crying over being stupid, and some of the dicier moments in the Homer-Marge marriage might also get it onto the list.

Matt Zoller Seitz: Okay, you're swinging me around to your point of view. I can imagine that very easily.

Alan Sepinwall: Just look at the sweep of what *The Simpsons* was able to do, and the way a show that was originally a vaguely grounded animated family comedy was able to do things like "Marge vs. the Monorail" or "Deep Space Homer" or "Homer Badman" and have them all feel like part of the same universe. It shouldn't be surprising how elastic the reality on an animated series can be, but it took the various people running this show over the years to truly understand that and exploit it to its fullest.

So you can't only have Lisa reading Mr. Bergstrom's note, but have her singing a Woody Guthrie–style protest song as the power plant goes on strike, *and* go to the future to see her be president, *and* have her meet the creator of Malibu Stacy. Or have Homer essentially turn into Stanley Kowalski one week and befriend God the next.

It's a show that can be anything, and has been. If you want to talk both innovation and influence, it's hard to top. And we've barely even scratched the surface of how damn funny it is.

Matt Zoller Seitz: Where are you going with this? Are you about to mount an argument for *The Simpsons* as greater than *The Wire* or *The Sopranos*? As the greatest American TV series of all time?

Alan Sepinwall: Yes. You can argue for any of these three for best exploiting everything it's possible to do on television, but I think *The Simpsons* has ultimately done more things, and done them spectacularly well, even if you try to allow for its having a vastly longer life span than the other two.

Matt Zoller Seitz: Well, that last part is a stumbling block, admittedly, though maybe less so for me than for others. *The Simpsons* was great, I mean really great, for at best half of its run, probably a third if you want to be strict—though I'd argue that seasons 11 through 14 contained more gems than paste, but I'm probably a bit more forgiving there. But as you've said, if you think of this in terms of a hypothetical contest pitting one athlete against another from a different time period, you can forgive a player for staying in past his or her peak. When I was old enough to really appreciate Muhammad Ali, he was fighting people like Leon Spinks and Ken Norton, and it was kind of pathetic, but that can't take away from the fact that for the space of about ten years, he was the greatest fighter the sport had ever seen.

But if we agree on that, and I think we do, then you've still got the comedy-versus-drama issue in a very specific respect: *The Wire* and *The Sopranos* hit lower notes, deeper notes, and were just generally more harrowing and powerful at their darkest than *The Simpsons* ever was, or was ever inclined to be—although I think you could argue that the Frank Grimes episode was as disturbing in its way, for what it said about human nature, as the grimmest and most wrenchingly tragic episodes of *The Wire* or *The Sopranos*.

This is of course a big leap: to say that what *The Simpsons* was doing at its peak is different from, but equal to, what these other two great series achieved—much of which cannot be achieved in a format like that of *The Simpsons*.

Alan Sepinwall: Sure, but every comparison we are making here—even between two adult HBO dramas like *The Wire* and *The Sopranos*—is to some degree an impossible one. Are you arguing that drama is inherently better (or more important) than comedy, and thus the greatest drama of all time simply has to be ahead of the greatest comedy of all time? Do we really want to say that, for instance, Tony listening to the FBI tapes revealing that his mother plotted his murder is fundamentally more valuable than Homer figuring out how to gain weight so he can go on disability?

Okay, when I write it out like that, I can see the argument for drama's inherent superiority. But then I think of Homer wearing a muumuu and a fat guy hat, and I'm not so sure anymore.

Matt Zoller Seitz: I don't think comedy is inherently inferior to drama, and our final list reflects that we're both opposed to that way of thinking.

But I must admit that as we wrestle our way through the top three I am discovering that the conditioning is more powerful than I imagined.

There is something in me that rebels at placing *The Simpsons* above *The Sopranos*, and it's because moments like, say, Dr. Melfi's rape or the shot of Tony in the stable with Pie-O-My or cradling his son by the edge of the swimming pool keep popping into my head and saying, "Has *The Simpsons* ever affected you as profoundly as these images did?" Same thing with all the stuff with the kids in season 4 of *The Wire*, or Ziggy's arc in season 2, or the second half of the series finale where you see an entire community coming full-circle, one set of people replacing another in roles that are doomed to replicate old patterns rather than reforming. That's all stuff *The Simpsons* can't equal.

Unless, that is, you decide to tear out the wires and reject the conditioning and look at what *The Simpsons* can give you that no other show ever has, like the constant, consistent formal experimentation—modeling episodes on *Thirty-Two Short Films About Glenn Gould* and *Pulp Fiction* at the same friggin' time, and the "Treehouse of Horror" anthologies, to name just two examples. And the mix of different intellectual levels of humor—very low, medium low, middlebrow, highbrow—and also the mix of visual and verbal, and the Easter eggs hidden in scenes that are mainly about something else. All that is amazing.

I think I'm coming around to this idea, Alan, and a big part of the reason why is my belief that "greatest" and "best" are judged by different yardsticks. If you ask me what is the best series, I would probably go for something that demonstrated exquisite judgment throughout and that almost never did anything out of character or beyond the parameters it seemingly had set for itself—something like *Cheers* or *The Larry Sanders Show* or, to go way back in time, *I Love Lucy*, which was a brilliant example of a protean kind of entertainment.

But "greatest," to me, implies something else. It signifies a restlessness, an inability to be happy with wringing variations from a particular set of themes, or within a certain framework. The word "great" is associated with scale. Big. Grand. Immense. Epic.

Most of the shows we've put in our top 100 could plausibly be argued to be the best in a certain category, and they all had moments when they were the finest examples of whatever they incarnated or revamped.

But "great," as subjective and slippery as it is, implies something else. It's a comet passing through the solar system. Like the one the Springfield citizenry is terrified of when they all show up outside of Ned Flanders's fallout shelter. And then they crowd in and the camera tracks past them as they sing "Que Sera, Sera," and oh, dammit, yeah, *The Simpsons* is the greatest.

Alan Sepinwall: Yes, you could be affected more profoundly by something like Melfi's rape or what happens to Randy Wagstaff. But I think the effect comedy has on us is equally profound. In fact, let me quote an exchange from one of the best *Simpsons* episodes of them all, "Bart Sells His Soul," where a worried Lisa reminds Bart that "Pablo Neruda said laughter is the language of the soul." (To which Bart replies, "I am familiar with the works of Pablo Neruda.")

I don't know that I see as clear a best/greatest distinction as you do (to me, it's more like my saying that *Midnight Run* is my favorite movie, even though I know it's far from the best and/or greatest movie ever made), but I see where you're coming from in terms of consistency versus ambition and the ability to achieve that ambition.

As we discussed earlier, *Cheers* or *Breaking Bad*—or, even if we have some issues with season 5, *The Wire*—all have fewer flaws than *The Simpsons* or *The Sopranos* does. And if it was a *Sopranos*-versus-*Wire* debate (which we may have to have next to sort out the order of the top 5), I'm not sure which way I'd lean at this moment.

But in my mind, the fact that *The Simpsons* was able to do so many things, sometimes brilliantly, sometimes oddly, but to keep striving and trying, even now at an absurdly advanced age for any TV show, is an argument for putting it on top. I like the later seasons more than you do, and I would put some of those episodes (like "Eternal Moonshine of the Simpson Mind" or "Holidays of Future Passed") in among the best of that first decade, but even if you want to call the show today a thin shadow of its former self, think about how mind-bogglingly great its former self had to be for so diminished a version to be watchable at all.

Matt Zoller Seitz: So I think we can agree that *The Simpsons* is number one, which leaves the question of where *The Sopranos* and *The Wire* rank.

Alan Sepinwall: *Victory!*

Okay, so do you have a strong feeling about *The Sopranos* vs. *The Wire* for the second-greatest show of all time?

Matt Zoller Seitz: It's tough, because they're not trying to do the same things, and are equally good at what they are respectively doing.

That said, if we consider them, for purposes of argument, as being equal in the first five categories—and I think they are very close—then we're left with "peak." And I think that on peak points, *The Sopranos* wins. In my world, it wins for the audacity of its ending alone. But even if it didn't have that audacious, divisive, totally unexpected finale, I'd still give it to *The Sopranos* on peak points, because it has so many peaks, so many moments when you could not believe what you were seeing and yet it ultimately always felt justified. "College," "University," "Pine Barrens," "Funhouse," "Employee of the Month," "Whoever Did This," "The Test Dream," "Soprano Home Movies"—I could go on.

And then within episodes there were just so many mysterious and somehow wonderfully right moments, moments of poetry and sadness and black humor. It always came at things from a surprising angle. You know that as a formalist that's always going to appeal to me, over and above a demonstration of classical mastery, which *The Wire* had, its layer-cake structure notwithstanding.

That's not to say I have less than total respect for *The Wire*—of course I do, look at how highly it ranked—it's just that my value system gives *The Sopranos* a slight edge overall.

Alan Sepinwall: I'm going to concede.

Matt Zoller Seitz: You are? I'm stunned. Why?

Alan Sepinwall: Because I love those two shows for very different reasons, and they're ultimately a coin-flip, and I feel like I already won by talking you into *The Simpsons* as my top. So if you feel strongly for *The Sopranos*, then by all means, buddy.

Matt Zoller Seitz: So you're benevolently reaching down from the mountaintop and handing me *The Sopranos*?

Alan Sepinwall: Sure.

Matt Zoller Seitz: Motherfucker!

The Inner Circle

The Simpsons (Fox, 1989–present) Total score: 112

If, by some chance, you stumbled across a person who had never seen a frame of *The Simpsons*, and they wanted to know why it was so popular, so respected, so beloved, how would you explain it?

You could start by showing them Sideshow Bob stepping on eight rakes in a row in under thirty seconds. The scene, from the classic season 5 episode "Cape Feare," represents the whole spectrum of humor folded and refolded into a single gag. Layer one is the lowest form of humor, violent slapstick. The sight of Bob stepping on rake after rake after rake is a monument to comic excess, pushing one joke past all reasonable limits—a gag on the same wavelength of Jonathan Winters in *It's a Mad, Mad, Mad, Mad World* systematically destroying an entire gas station with his bare hands, or Laurel and Hardy in *Big Business* repeatedly trying and failing to get a piano up a flight of stairs. At the same time, though, it is also conceptual humor, because it is also about the *idea* of excess. As David Letterman demonstrated on his late-night shows when he repeated the same knowingly lame catchphrase for weeks on end, sometimes a gag is funny the first time, less funny the second, still less funny the third, then ceases to be funny at all, until the audacity of continuing to repeat it wears down your resistance and makes you laugh again. Finally, the rake gag is a bit of character-based humor with actual philosophical overtones: Sideshow Bob, who keeps trying and failing to murder his young nemesis, Bart Simpson, throughout the show's run, fears that the universe is indifferent to his desires, and may even derive joy from watching him suffer. What simpler way to confirm Bob's fears than by topping the lead-up to the gag—Bob being mangled and torn while hanging beneath the Simpsons' station wagon en route to witness protection at Cape Feare Lake—with a series of rakes to the face? That the onslaught of the rakes is so tedious, so basic, so *not personal*, only makes it worse. Everywhere Bob steps, a rake, a rake, another rake. The rakes stand in for every twist of fate that sabotages Bob's plan, every indignity heaped upon him, every eventuality his supposed genius could not foresee, every moment of potential glory snatched from his grasp. And of course the rake is also Bart Simpson: the Road Runner to Bob's Wile E. Coyote, Droopy Dog to Bob's Wolf. Bob's guttural shudders (a brilliant verbal flourish by guest star Kelsey Grammer) are not merely expressions of physical agony but marrow-deep self-disgust. Each time a rake hits Bob in the face, it confirms his secret fear that beneath his educated facade and delusions of omnipotence, he's still an unemployable TV clown, a second banana in his own life, a living embodiment of unmerited hubris and well-deserved failure—all of which, point of fact, he is. This lone gag crystallizes every facet of Bob in relation to the world of *The Simpsons*.

And he's not even a regular character!

That one could write a similarly expansive lead paragraph drawing on any one of dozens of other *Simpsons* gags—maybe hundreds; at the time of this book's publication, Matt Groening's animated sitcom was nearing the end of its third decade—gives some hint of the show's richness.

As conceived by Groening, James L. Brooks, and Sam Simon, and continued by an endlessly repopulated writers' room, with a brilliant voice cast (headed by Dan Castellaneta as Homer, Julie Kavner as Marge, Nancy Cartwright as Bart, Yeardley Smith as Lisa, plus Hank Azaria, Harry Shearer, and other utility infielders, including Pamela Hayden, Tress MacNeille, and the late Phil Hartman), *The Simpsons* is so ambitious, intimate, classical, experimental, hip, corny, and altogether free in its conviction that the imagination should go where it wants, that to even begin to explain all the things *The Simpsons* is, and all the things it does, you would need an immense Venn diagram drawn on a football field, each circle representing different modes of comedy. And even then, summing up *The Simpsons* would be impossible, because the best gags, the best scenes, the best episodes, the best seasons, contain multitudes within multitudes within multitudes, like that rake gag. Trying to identify any one aspect as *the* key to the show's genius would be a folly as unwise as building the monorails that destroyed Ogdenville, Brockway, and North Haverbrook, and nearly ruined Springfield. The show has been on for far too long (so long that it now predates the existence of many of its viewers), done too many amazing things, and been through too many evolutions.

The Simpsons is the greatest show in TV history for all the reasons listed previously, plus so many more, that contemplating them all feels a bit like Homer's daydream about a trip to the Land of Chocolate. It went to more places—tonally and topically as well as geographically—tackled more issues, and told more jokes about more subjects than any comedy has before or since, and at its peak (roughly seasons 3–12) did it better than anyone else. But it also found a deep reservoir of emotion in its depiction of the Simpson family itself, as well as the complicated dynamics between husband and wife, brother and sister, father and daughter, student and teacher, spike-haired brat and gunboat-footed, Gilbert and Sullivan–loving maniac.

Even the question "What kind of show is *The Simpsons?*" is hard to answer without sounding reductive, because it has kept morphing throughout its run. It began as a laugh track–free sitcom in the schlubby dad–harried mom–bratty son–precocious daughter vein, but one that happened to be animated (a mode that Fox's subsequent *King of the Hill* stayed in). But within a few seasons the slapstick had become more extreme, the structural flourishes more brazen (the peak was probably the anthology "22 Short Films About Springfield"), and the pop culture references had become multivalent.

The season 4 finale, "Krusty Gets Kancelled," for instance, contains a scene where the show's resident action-film superstar, the Arnold Schwarzenegger manqué Rainier Wolfcastle, appears on *Springfield Squares*, hosted by newsman Kent Brockman. It is simultaneously a send-up of 1970s game shows (specifically *The Hollywood Squares*); the supposed "newsman" as celebrity (in the 1950s, longtime *60 Minutes* correspondent Mike Wallace was a radio actor and cigarette pitchman at the same time that he gained fame as an interviewer); Schwarzenegger's attempts to remake himself as a star of family comedies like *Twins* and *Junior*; the 1980s craze for comedies about "nerds" (Wolfcastle is on the game show to pitch his latest picture, *Help, My Son Is a Nerd!*, which has the same plot as *Back to School* and, according to him, is "not a comedy"); and the cliché of the resident who won't leave his home during a disaster (when a tsunami approaches, the longtime occupant of a bottom square, Charlie, refuses to leave because he's been there thirty years, and is instantly washed away). This same episode contains references to Judy Collins, Joey Bishop, Elvis Presley's 1968 comeback special, Howdy Doody (via the ventriloquist's dummy Gabbo, whose success shatters Krusty), Cold War–era Eastern European animation (*Worker & Parasite*, the cartoon video Krusty shows when Gabbo steals *Itchy & Scratchy*), and parodies of Johnny Carson's farewell episode of *The Tonight Show* (via Krusty the Clown's comeback special, where Bette Midler serenades Krusty the way she did Johnny as his final guest). Celebrity cameos include Midler, the Red Hot Chili Peppers (who replay a moment when Ed Sullivan asked the Doors to neuter a line from "Light My Fire"), and Carson, who offers Krusty career advice and lifts a Buick over his head.

And yet, despite its nonstop maelstrom of satire, parody, whimsy, and shtick, *The Simpsons* never forgot the family at its core. This is what raises it above so many imitators. Bart's rebellious attitude and catchphrases ("Eat my shorts!") made him the show's initial breakout character, but in time, he and Lisa would both be more memorably deployed to explore the melancholia of childhood: Bart's belief that he's peaked at age ten or the despair he feels after facetiously selling his soul to best friend Milhouse; Lisa's constant fear that she'll never find a place or group where she feels like she belongs. (When jazzman Bleeding Gums Murphy invites Lisa to jam with him, she improvises a song with the lyric, "I'm the saddest kid in grade number two.") Marge, with her frustration at always having to be the responsible parent, provided gravity that became more valuable as the show's plots became more outlandish: Homer joins NASA and goes into space; Bart offends the population of Australia and is sentenced to being kicked by a giant boot; Mr. Burns tries to block the sun's rays from reaching the town. And even though there was only so much that the writers could do with Maggie, who doesn't age and never masters more than one word ("Daddy," spoken by Elizabeth Taylor, of all people), they still managed to establish her as both the wisest and the toughest Simpson (she shoots Mr. Burns and stages a prison break from a totalitarian daycare center).

But it was Homer who would become the show's most important character, and its comic engine. He was the American male—and the American psyche—taken to a logical, hilarious, unnerving extreme: sweet and well-intentioned but also selfish, gluttonous, impulsive, and proud of his ignorance ("Oh, people can come up with statistics to prove anything, Kent—fourteen percent of people know that"). As revolting as Homer can be, he's also a wish-fulfillment object, albeit one who could not be further away from the likes of James Bond or Batman. What man hasn't daydreamed of indulging like Homer and failing upward? What man wouldn't want to foment unrest against spoiled movie stars ("And when it's time to do the dishes, where's Ray Bolger? I'll tell you where! *Ray Bolger* is looking out for *Ray Bolger!*"), become the voice of a focus-grouped addition to your kids' favorite cartoon show ("The Itchy & Scratchy & Poochie Show"), or (in 2007's *The Simpsons Movie*) adopt a pet pig and teach it to walk the ceiling like Spider-Man? Okay, maybe those aren't common fantasies, but Homer's imagination was the only dazzlingly uncommon thing about him. An early running gag saw Homer peevishly telling Marge that his latest scheme—such as managing a country-western singer in season 3's "Colonel Homer"—was his lifelong dream, only to be reminded that his lifelong dream was something far less grandiose, like eating the world's biggest hoagie. The character's idiocy, so perfectly captured by Castellaneta, could be heroically perverse—and never more so than in "King-Size Homer," where he gains more than a hundred pounds so that he can get on disability and work from home. (Lisa: "Ew! Mom, this whole thing is really creepy. Are you sure you won't talk to Dad?" Marge: "I'd like to, honey, but I'm not sure how. Your father can be surprisingly sensitive. Remember when I giggled at his Sherlock Holmes hat? He sulked for a week and then closed his detective agency.")

Homer himself has gone through as many changes as the show, from week to week as well as season to season; if you look at his actions in terms of a rap sheet, he's more monstrous than any of the characters on *Seinfeld*. Only his genuine (though often submerged) love for his wife and kids and town keeps him redeemable. His oafishness, selfishness, drunkenness, belligerence, and other unpalatable qualities were there from the start, but in the early seasons (the first two especially) he was a melancholy figure, for the most part more a danger to himself than others. Castellaneta's voice even sounded gentler, verging on a Walter Matthau sad sack. Until longtime writer-producer Al Jean began his current marathon stint as showrunner in season 13, the series went through many bosses, each with their own sense of where to draw the line on Homer's behavior.

The character's moral and emotional mood-ring quality creates yet another obstacle to defining what, at its best, *The Simpsons* is. Some writers (and fans) believe that the jerkier Homer is, the more memorable he is. Others prefer that kindness and/or self-awareness—or at the very least haplessness—dominate. The Rorschach test episode for this question tends to be "Homer's Enemy" from season 8, where new plant employee Frank Grimes is driven mad by the realization that Homer is an incompetent drowning in unearned privilege while Frank, a smarter, more hardworking, more ethical person, struggles and suffers. When Homer is too intentionally cruel, it can give the show a more tragic feeling and make it seem sadder when Marge or Lisa forgives him his latest sin; but when he stumbles into his worst behavior, the family feels more in balance. The impact of moral choice was never far from the show's mind. *The Sopranos*, *Seinfeld*, and *Mad Men* built a good part of their reputations on showing the dynamics of such decisions: how people can have the correct or right decision presented to them and still ignore it and do whatever gives them pleasure. But *The Simpsons* was more economical, often distilling the process down to a muttered aside by Homer about food. When the chronically unhealthy Simpsons patriarch suffers a heart attack from nervousness while asking Mr. Burns, his boss at the nuclear plant, for a raise, he falls dead on the floor, and Burns tells his assistant to send a ham to the widow; Homer's spirit murmurs, "Mmm...ham...," and climbs back into his body in hopes of eating some.

While the five core Simpsons remain the show's most valuable characters, *The Simpsons* owes its longevity as much to the ever-expanding, ever-stranger population of Springfield (state unknown) as it does to the writers' ability to keep cranking out variations on stories where Marge gets a job, Lisa makes a friend, or Homer offends a celebrity. In the ancient, malevolent, supremely self-centered Mr. Burns, the series was making fun of the one-percenters decades before it became de rigueur. Springfield's Kennedyesque mayor "Diamond Joe" Quimby offered a window on corrupt, self-interested politics and the complacent electorate that does nothing to change it. The elementary school, the nuclear plant, Grandpa Simpson's nursing home, Moe's Tavern, Comic Book Guy's shop, and many more Springfield locations gave the series an endless bounty of characters (incompetent police chief Clancy Wiggum, ambulance-chasing lawyer Lionel Hutz, slack-jawed yokel Cletus Spuckler) who could stumble in, get a laugh, then step aside to let the story continue on its merry way. You wouldn't want to move most, maybe any, of the Springfieldians into their own series (an idea the show mocked in season 8's "The Simpsons Spin-Off Showcase"). But their tonnage has given the series a richness that belies its animated format, as well as the one-note quality of local citizens like Disco Stu, mob boss Fat Tony, and Doris the Lunch Lady. After all this time, Springfield can feel disturbingly like a real city, complete with people you'd cross the street to avoid.

The Simpsons is similar in a way to a couple of other long-running TV series, 60 Minutes and Sesame Street, in that when a program remains a part of national life for more than two decades, it ceases to be a mere show and becomes something in between an institution and a utility: a thing that we have, use, and take for granted.

This is most apparent in the still-constant use of Simpsons quotes in daily life. The show has supplied a sentiment for every occasion, so many that it now gives the King James Bible a run for its money. Any stupid mistake can be acknowledged with a frustrated cry of "D'oh!" If you want to explain why you prefer a clearly inferior option, just say, "Barney's movie had heart, but Football in the Groin had a football in the groin." If you've just heard someone say something unrealistic or unhinged, you can dismiss them with "Your ideas are intriguing to me and I wish to subscribe to your newsletter." If you're bracing yourself to deal with a new boss, a new presidential administration, or any other sort of dreaded leader, channel Kent Brockman and announce, "I, for one, welcome our new insect overlords." If you need a bald-faced lie to explain where you were last night, say, "It's a pornography store! I was buying pornography!" If you're struggling to get across a basic concept, as Homer's brain once did when it tried to teach him why $20 can buy many peanuts, say, "Money can be exchanged for goods and services." If you're lost for words when making a toast, there is no better fallback option than "To alcohol! The cause of, and solution to, all of life's problems."

That *The Simpsons* has been on so long past its peak is really the only reason to suggest it shouldn't be considered the best series of all time. But the narrative that the current show is a ghost of its former self doesn't withstand scrutiny if you pay close attention to the second half of its run, which has had lackluster periods (over the course of almost three decades, what person, or nation, doesn't?) but has continued to produce episodes so imaginative and funny that if *The Simpsons* had started its run in 2004 instead of 1989, it still might've cracked this book's top 100. Whenever you're about to count *The Simpsons* out, it produces a magnificent segment like the 2008 "Treehouse of Horror" short "It's the Grand Pumpkin, Milhouse," in which a giant humanoid pumpkin wreaks havoc on the town after discovering the ritual butchery of jack-o'-lanterns and the cooking of their seeds (*"You roast the unborn?"*). Or it stages a crossover episode that amounts to a withering referendum on its would-be competitors (see the *Simpsons* half of a 2014 crossover with *Family Guy* that rebuked the upstart not by slagging it but by being more inventive, visually striking, and humanistic). The shift to high-definition animation and a more rectangular 16×9 frame (versus the original 4×3 format) has made the series more visually daring; even when the writing failed to match the depth of the show's first decade-plus, the compositions, editing, and production design equaled or bested them. Modern episodes like "Eternal Moonshine of the Simpson Mind" (Homer tries to re-create the forgotten events of the night before), "Holidays of Future Passed" (a flash-forward where Bart and Lisa grapple with the disappointment of their middle-aged lives), and "Halloween of Horror" (the show's first in-continuity Halloween episode, where Homer tries to protect a terrified Lisa from a trio of home invaders) demonstrate a level of formal and/or emotional complexity that make them worthy of consideration alongside the best made when Conan O'Brien and Greg Daniels were on the writing staff.

"Treehouse of Horror" has been a consistent bright spot, mainly because of its freestanding nature. Its segments treat the Simpsons and their fellow Springfieldians as players in a repertory company and cast them according to their most metaphoric qualities, as a fairy tale or a Rod Serling screenplay might. The ability to derange, mutate, mutilate, kill, and resurrect the main characters for shock effect without regard for continuity (or perhaps we should say *less* regard) seemed to energize the writers even during weak seasons. The tonal and visual variety displayed in a quarter century's worth of "Treehouse" shorts (seventy-three as of this writing) constitutes a triumphant achievement in itself. The show has attempted other anthology-styled episodes over the years—everything from the aforementioned "22 Short Films" to episodes based on Greek mythology and the Bible—and elsewhere you can find still more examples of shows-within-shows. These include the hyperviolent *Itchy & Scratchy* shorts played on Krusty's kiddie program—Tom and Jerry by way of Ralph Bakshi, minus the sex, thank Jeebus—which could be *The Simpsons'* way of critiquing audience bloodlust even as the goriest sight gags elsewhere on the show feed it ("I told that idiot to slice my sandwich!"). The fresh couch gag at the end of every opening credits sequence amounts to an anthology on the installment plan; the shift to HD has encouraged the show's writers and animators to experiment more boldly within it, and even to allow outside animators to try their hand at it. The twenty-sixth season opened with a couch gag from aggressively outré animator Don Hertzfeldt, who imagined *The Simpsons* continuing through the year 10,535, and pictured the family as black-and-white octopuses with tentacles and eyestalks, screeching gibberish catchphrases at one another.

Once upon a time, the notion of *The Simpsons'* continuing forever—past the life spans of Groening, Brooks, Simon (who died in 2015), Jean, Castellaneta, and everyone else who's contributed to its current incarnation—would have seemed horrifying. But the series has reinvented and rediscovered itself enough times over the decades that the idea of its pumping out new episodes in perpetuity can be oddly comforting. Arguably no show should last eight hundred seasons, but if any show can, it's *The Simpsons*.

The playwright Anne Washburn seems to agree. Her 2012 off-Broadway production, *Mr. Burns, a Post-Electric Play*, pushes the idea of *The Simpsons* as pop culture's lingua franca to science-fictional extremes. Act one, set immediately after an unspecified apocalypse, observes a group of terrified refugees wondering why humankind suddenly lost all electrical power and struggling to bond by trying to remember the plot of "Cape Feare." Act two is set a few years after that, with surviving members of the group forming a theatrical troupe that performs stage versions of *Simpsons* episodes; their story lines are bizarrely and somewhat poignantly garbled by virtue of being handed down via the oral tradition—not unlike the epic poems of, ahem, Homer. Their production-in-progress is interrupted by the appearance of a murderous rival troupe that aims to steal the first group's *Simpsons*-derived "plays" and add them to their own repertoire. Act three is set seventy-five years after that—a self-contained play within *Mr. Burns*. It takes place entirely on a storm-tossed boat, the same setting as the climax of "Cape Feare," which was inspired by the 1991 film *Cape Fear*, which was a remake of the 1962 film *Cape Fear*, which was adapted from the 1957 novel *The Executioners*. Here the Simpsons are tormented not by Sideshow Bob but by a demonic figure who seems to be a mix of Bob, *Cape Fear*'s maniacal redneck Max Cady, Mr. Burns, and Satan. The performers wear spiky masks that invoke the traditions of Greek tragedy and Noh. When blood is shed onstage, it's hideous—a hellish spectacle befitting a society that has lost hope along with law, order, and electricity. The closing section is sung-through, in the minor key of a lament: a grim homage to the moment in "Cape Feare" where Bart distracts Bob by getting him to sing all of the songs from *H.M.S. Pinafore*. When good triumphs and order reasserts itself, the audience feels not the warm reassurance of low-stakes weekly ritual (the feeling we get from watching *The Simpsons* today) but cathartic relief at being alive at all, as well as giddy incredulity at the idea that bug-eyed banana-yellow cartoon characters would survive the end of civilization. Wolfcastle's muttered aside in "Krusty Gets Kancelled" might have been the tagline for Washburn's play: *It's not a comedy.*

But then, neither is *The Simpsons*—not exclusively, anyway. It always had the culture and the species on its mind even when it was clowning around; in those infrequent moments when *The Simpsons* drops its grin and goes melancholy or lyrical, you can see it. Think of the lovely moment near the end of the season 6 episode "Bart's Comet," wherein the town of Springfield reacts to news that a comet (named after Bart, who discovered it) is fated to wipe them out. When panic spreads, Ned Flanders—as usual, the town's only unselfish citizen—opens the doors of his bomb shelter and lets his neighbors pile in. The comet peters out after striking Principal Skinner's weather balloon and all's well that ends well, but the episode is best remembered for a moment of existential terror that gives way to graceful resignation: The camera tracks slowly across the faces of Springfieldians packed into Flanders's bomb shelter as they sing "Que sera, sera / Whatever will be, will be / The future's not ours to see…"

Indeed, it's not. But if a modern-day Nostradamus predicted an apocalypse that would wipe out most of humanity but leave a resilient handful quoting *The Simpsons*, what TV fan would doubt him? We've come this far.

—MZS & AS

The Sopranos (HBO, 1999–2007) Total score: 112

The last words heard on *The Sopranos* are delivered not by New Jersey mob boss Tony Soprano (James Gandolfini), not by wife Carmela (Edie Falco), daughter Meadow (Jamie-Lynn Sigler), meathead son Anthony Jr. (Robert Iler), nor by Paulie Walnuts (Tony Sirico) or any of the other wiseguys who survived the HBO mob drama's bloody final season.

No, the last words we hear come from Journey front man Steve Perry, who belts out, "Don't stop…," right before everything does.

The series' place on TV's Mount Rushmore was secured long before that divisive final moment, when *Sopranos* creator David Chase denied his audience closure on everything, from Tony's fate to the last word of the Journey song's title. *The Sopranos* was the Big Bang of the cable drama explosion that led to TV's latest golden age. It was consistently excellent in every department: direction, performance, cinematography, editing, sound design, music, dialogue, and overall narrative architecture. At its peak, it produced moments so transcendently funny, sad, brutal, and mysterious that they make even the finest moments of other great series seem underachieving.

But even if *The Sopranos*' impact on the medium had been far milder, even if the rest of the series didn't so often scale such amazing heights and give us riveting scenes like Tony wailing in frustration at being denied the ability to murder his joyless sociopath of a mother, it might still have wound up in this Pantheon just because of the last four minutes of its finale, which in the past decade have come to be regarded as the Zapruder film of scripted TV. No ending in television history, and few in cinema, inspired as much debate about what happened, what it meant, and what an insistence on a particular interpretation revealed about the viewer. It's so famous, or infamous, that even those who've never seen a frame of the series know the gist: Tony, Carmela, A.J., and the late-arriving Meadow meet at a diner and share a communion-like meal of onion rings; Tony glances around the place with what could be anxiety or bored complacency, depending on how you read the moment, until the front door rings, the Journey song hits another chorus, and Tony looks up and…

The ellipse implied by the abrupt cut to black is everything here. Despite the way it seems to echo the deaths of so many *Sopranos* characters, from Big Pussy (Vincent Pastore) and Adriana La Cerva (Drea de Matteo) to Bobby Bacala (Steve Schirripa) through poor Christopher Moltisanti (Michael Imperioli), it remains resolutely unresolved; Chase even insisted on a long moment of silence after the cut, which convinced many viewers that their cable signal had gone out. Given the density of the "clues" (multiple possible assailants, none of whom actually move against Tony) and the vague but palpable aura of tension, the only definitive thing one can say about it is that it's ambiguous.

But that did not stop legions of viewers from insisting that they could "prove," like mathematicians solving for X, that Tony got murdered at the diner, perhaps by that sneaky-looking guy in the Members Only jacket, and that no other interpretation was possible—as if *The Sopranos* had ever been a "puzzle box" show like *The Prisoner* or *Lost*, rather than a half-satirical meditation on family, psychology, consumerism, suburban life, and the twilight of the American Empire, dolled up in the wide-lapelled sharkskin jackets and pinky rings of the Mafia potboiler.

Chase has repeatedly insisted over the years, in a series of increasingly forlorn-sounding public explanations, that it doesn't matter what happened next, much less whether Tony lived or died; that the point of the ending was never what came next but that life was fragile and could be ripped from us (though not necessarily Tony's life, and not necessarily at that moment) without warning. Admittedly, that is surely not all there was to the ending, or nonending; Chase, like most real artists, works close to his subconscious, so explanations of what the art means can often feel like oversimplications after the fact, intended to appease viewers who cannot just absorb a story but need to feel they've mastered it. There have been notes of sheepish apology in some of Chase's statements, as if he were gently reprimanding himself for failing to make things crystal clear. But it also seems possible that, intentionally or no, Chase devised a clever means of giving both gangster-movie traditionalists and art-film-minded contrarians the endings they craved: You could see Tony as being punished for his crimes (proving that there is justice in the universe, and absolving viewers of having spent six seasons watching vicious people do vicious things) or not punished (there is no God, there is no justice, morality is a social construct, etc.). And then you could argue about what that meant or didn't mean, even though *The Sopranos* never revealed what happened after that cut to black.

Years after the finale, and with more awareness of the kind of show that everyone had actually been watching for six seasons, the ending seems not merely in character but the apotheosis of everything *The Sopranos* is about. Characters are constantly drifting toward epiphanies but failing to seize them, and some of them regurgitate the language of therapy and self-help—including Tony's mother, Livia (Nancy Marchand), his grasping and manipulative sister Janice (Aida Turturro), mob captain Paulie Walnuts, and foot soldier and on-again, off-again drug addict Christopher; but very few of them actually cross over and make permanent, substantive changes for the better. One of the eeriest and most heartbreaking moments in the show comes in season 6's "Kennedy and Heidi," when Tony, who recently survived a shooting at the hands of his uncle Junior (Dominic Chianese) but soon reentered mob life with a vengeance, then murdered his own nephew and slept with his girlfriend in Las Vegas, takes peyote in the desert and stands on the top of a mesa screaming, "I get it!"

Like so many proclamations on this show, that turns out to be wishful thinking. It's questionable whether anyone on *The Sopranos* ever truly gets anything, and for those who plausibly do (such as mob soldiers Eugene Pontecorvo and Vito Spatafore, who realize how morally and emotionally suffocating their lives are, and violently fail to escape them), the knowledge can be more tragic than liberating. The problem, for the most part, isn't that the characters aren't capable of self-knowledge or criticism but that they're simply too lazy or easily distracted to implement the realizations they have. The prognosis for human change is so bleak here that the only things preventing *The*

Sopranos from seeming oppressively nihilistic, even glibly cynical, are the continual reminders of the mysterious beauty that exists beyond the bounds of most people's awareness, as indicated in the repeated shots of wind rustling through trees, and the references to history and theology, art and architecture, and the show's literally elemental sense of what it means to be alive. The show's North Jersey is at once prosaic and poetic, full of chain stores, tacky strip clubs, and tackier hairstyles, but also a place where nature is presented at its extremes, whether the crippling snow that strands Paulie and Christopher in the Pine Barrens or the oppressive sunlight that always seems to be shining down on the pork store whenever Tony has to make a big decision.

But none of the show's meditations on morality, philosophy, theology, consumerism, popular culture, deli meat, ziti, and espresso would have found a mass audience without compelling plotlines, complex and eccentrically written characters, and high and low humor. (Paulie Walnuts insists that his place is so clean you could "eat maple walnut ice cream off the toilet"—it's the "maple walnut" that makes it art.) *The Sopranos* was instantly notorious for the way it pushed pay-cable sex and violence far beyond the already minimal boundaries that had been established before, and the aura of continual disreputability helped sell it to people who might not otherwise have sat still long enough to savor Chase's other fascinations. Audiences saw characters strangled ("College"), graphically raped ("Employee of the Month"), cough themselves to death after murdering a man ("Another Toothpick"), sexually humiliated and then beaten to death ("University," "Cold Stones"), beaten to death and then beheaded and hacked into pieces ("Whoever Did This"), shot at close range (too many examples to list), and crushed or killed by cars ("Toodle-Fucking-Oo" and "Made in America"). But the totality of the series is not nearly as violent as its reputation suggests. The vast majority of any given episode consists of people talking to one another, or sitting by themselves thinking. Or in Tony's case, dreaming.

In some of its best seasons (particularly the first and last), *The Sopranos* had the structure of a long movie, or a televised novel, weaving mob plotlines (Uncle Junior wants to be boss, or the New York mob wants to wipe out its little brother across the river) in with more intimate personal crises for Tony (Livia's outrage over being moved into "a retirement community," a depressed A.J. attempting suicide in the family pool). In other seasons, though, like the third, *The Sopranos* was less novel than short-story collection, each week presenting fully realized, dark and amusing tales of both family and Family life that were connected by the presence of the same characters, rather than by the propulsive arcs that many post-*Sopranos* dramas would make their bread and butter.

The Sopranos was a show of great climaxes—most memorably involving Tony, having learned that his own mother talked his uncle into ordering his murder, barreling through the nursing home with a pillow in his hands—but also of divisive anticlimaxes. Before season 2 villain Richie Aprile (David Proval) can go to war with Tony, Janice shoots him in response to a punch in the face. Tony's enforcer Furio Giunta (Federico Castelluccio) begins a flirtation with Carmela that seems likely to end in his death, or maybe hers; instead, he flees back to Italy before much of anything has happened. Tony's therapist, Dr. Jennifer Melfi (Lorraine Bracco), is raped near her office but denies the audience's desire for vengeance, or closure, by refusing Tony's offer of help; similarly, the Russian whom Paulie and Christopher chased through the Pine Barrens never returns. Even some of the most powerful gratification was delayed, and presented ambiguously: Tony wants Joe Pantoliano's insufferable capo Ralphie Cifaretto dead from the moment Ralphie beats a stripper to death behind the Bada Bing! club, but the reckoning doesn't come until late the following season, and it's only implied in a roundabout way that her murder played any role in it.

E Street Band member turned Soprano crew member Steve Van Zandt (who plays Tony's pompadoured consigliere Silvio Dante) once described the show as "the gangster *Honeymooners*." There are long stretches of the series where this summary fits perfectly. Of TV contemporaries, its closest spiritual kin isn't another drama but *Seinfeld*, another vaguely purgatorial look at vain twits making an already miserable world more miserable through their selfishness. Tony was one of TV's most complex characters, with Gandolfini breathing as much life into him with simple shifts in body language as with his thunderous delivery of Chase's dialogue. (There is a moment in season 1 where he is really and truly acting with the back of his neck.) But he was surrounded by relatives, friends, and fellow wiseguys who shared his crippling inability to change his worst behavior. Every significant character moment feeds back into the show's fascination with what people are made of, and whether it's possible for them to control and change their destinies. Even the showiest moments of performance and character-ization enrich Chase's themes, but they have such humor and life force that they never feel merely demonstrative. The show and Edie Falco give Carmela moments of powerful self-realization, but inevitably have her choose the path of least resistance over the one she knows is right. She keeps calling out Tony for his betrayals and infidelities, only to return to his embrace when he offers her a bigger bribe: jewelry, a new car, a new house. Christopher's dreams of becoming a screenwriter give the show pathos ("Where's my arc?" he wonders, perhaps dimly recognizing that he is but a minor figure in Tony's story). But they also gave the writers an opportunity to satirize the most hackneyed conventions of the busi-ness Chase and company had chosen to work in. Their contempt for TV-as-usual is demonstrated most vividly in a moment from season 5's "In Camelot," where a gambling addict writer tries to pawn his Emmy only to be told that it's worthless.

Livia was modeled closely on Chase's own mother, and it showed in the detailed and darkly hilarious cataloging of her phobias and vendet-tas. Livia's stock dismissal of Tony's troubles—"Poor you!"—reappears in a coded way in season 6, when Tony, recuperating from gunshot wounds, encounters an old Ojibwe saying posted on a wall: "Sometimes I go about in pity for myself, and all the while, a great wind carries me across the sky." This is, not coincidentally, the season where Tony hal-lucinates encountering Livia again. Like *Twin Peaks*, a show that Chase adored, the series was attentive to dream logic, and it often seemed to deliberately blur the boundaries separating waking and sleeping life.

Tony's mind is the nexus point for this blur. In season 2, he realizes there's an informant in his crew after experiencing a series of night-mares brought on by food poisoning; the dream literally tells him the answer to a riddle that's been tormenting him. Season 5's "The Test Dream" is even more tantalizing, staging a twelve-minute sequence containing dream scenarios that also happened in life. Did they happen as Tony was dreaming them, and he somehow saw them in his dreams? Did his dreaming cause them to happen? Is Tony's dream, or are Tony's dreams, plural, or all dreams, merely extensions of, or windows into, what we call "reality"? On *The Sopranos*, life itself often seems like one long dream, not in the hack sense of "It was all a dream," but in the sense of the same-titled Lewis Carroll poem, which ends:

In a Wonderland they lie,
Dreaming as the days go by,
Dreaming as the summers die:

Ever drifting down the stream—
Lingering in the golden gleam—
Life, what is it but a dream?

Cut to black. The dream is over.

—MZS & AS

The Wire (HBO, 2002–2008) Total score: 112

The Wire is about a clever cop who doesn't play by his bosses' rules.

Or is it about how that cop pushes his bosses to create a task force to take down a dangerous inner-city drug crew?

Maybe it's about the charismatic leaders of that drug crew?

Could it be about dysfunction inside the police department?

Wait…now it's about the stevedores' union?

Only now the mayoral campaign is the most important thing?

How is the show suddenly about four boys in middle school?

And here at the end it's about the inner workings of the city's biggest newspaper?

What on earth is this show supposed to be about, people?

Actually, it *is* about people: not only the cops fighting a self-destructive War on Drugs, not only the criminals who view slinging dope as their only viable life choice, but everyone whose life is in some way affected by that war, and every person in power who through conscious action or blithe indifference makes things worse.

It's about one city in which that war is being fought, but by implication is about every city, and about the many great failings of the American experiment.

The Wire is about all those things, and so many more. It starts with one detective, Jimmy McNulty (Dominic West), and expands outward, introducing us to a kaleidoscope of cops, dealers, junkies, hookers, politicians, teachers, students, reporters, and more—a teeming mass of Baltimore citizenry, most of whom never meet even as their actions affect one another. McNulty and his partner, William "Bunk" Moreland (Wendell Pierce), lead us to D'Angelo Barksdale (Larry Gilliard Jr.), a glorified middle manager in the dope conglomerate of his uncle Avon (Wood Harris). Through D'Angelo and Avon we gradually get to meet other players in the Game: Avon's right-hand man, Stringer Bell (Idris Elba), who wants to apply economic theory from his community college business classes to the distribution of heroin; Lt. Cedric Daniels (Lance Reddick), a company man who will learn in time how badly his particular company is being run; Omar Little (Michael K. Williams), a stickup artist operating with a strict moral code; Baltimore PD superior Bill Rawls (John Doman), a profane master of vendetta against all who try to rock the boat; and D'Angelo's teenage deputies Bodie (J. D. Williams), Poot (Tray Chaney), and Wallace (Michael B. Jordan), each viewing the Game as the only career available to them. *The Wire* treats each character as worthy of being at the center of his or her own story rather than orbiting someone else's. As one of the show's more unabashedly heroic characters, wily detective Lester Freamon (Clarke Peters), puts it to a colleague, "All the pieces matter."

The Wire grants abundant humanity to all but the most minor characters, insisting that they were all connected, and that the only thing stopping them from walking in one another's shoes is a simple twist of fate. And it locates them in mundane reality. The world of *The Wire* is not a clichéd or stylized TV world. It strives to approximate this one. The first season's cops-and-robbers routine is a Trojan horse gambit. It upends our expectations about its detectives and drug dealers, as evidenced by how it lends its ultimate sympathy to Daniels the traditionalist rather than McNulty the wild card. And it poses questions about police tactics, and the drug war in general, that would resonate beyond the projects and precinct houses of season 1. Both sides of the conflict are shown to be prisoners of a system interested only in perpetuating itself, a grim farce in which idiocy becomes policy because that's how life works.

Such a grim and unrelenting worldview should have made the show unwatchable, but its message about the fundamentally broken system of America came intertwined with abundant humor, suspense, action, and revelatory human drama. It lectured, but it entertained, too. It was a show that could bring us to the edge of despair as D'Angelo repeatedly asked Stringer, "Where's Wallace?" in response to news that his young friend had been murdered, but also one that could put us in stitches watching Stringer run drug distribution meetings according to *Robert's Rules of Order* ("Chair recognize Slim Charles"), and watching Omar talk rings around Barksdale attorney Maury Levy (Michael Kostroff) in open court. "I got the shotgun; you got the briefcase," he says. "It's all in the Game, though, right?"

The characters were so sharply delineated and imaginatively acted that we came to care about the likes of beleaguered union leader Frank Sobotka (Chris Bauer), his aggressively stupid son Ziggy (James Ransone), parolee Dennis "Cutty" Wise (Chad L. Coleman), police district commander Howard "Bunny" Colvin (Robert Wisdom), and middle schooler Randy Wagstaff (Maestro Harrell) as deeply as we did about the core group. We could even understand, if not feel much sympathy for, people who seemed to have no soul, like the dead-eyed young kingpin Marlo Stanfield (Jamie Hector) and the egomaniacal politician Tommy Carcetti (Aidan Gillen).

Once you know that the show's cocreator, David Simon, was a crime reporter for the *Baltimore Sun*, this worldview makes sense. We're seeing things through the eyes of someone who simultaneously has the sensibilities of a journalist and a novelist (not for nothing is a season 5 episode titled "The Dickensian Aspect"), and whose age and life experience shaped his sense of what storytelling could and should do. Simon came of age in the post-Vietnam era, a transformational time for the Fourth Estate. Before the 1970s, journalism was a blue-collar profession inhabited by observers who tried to capture the human circus in terse but lyrical prose; afterward, it became a middle-class profession filled with university-educated baby boomers who thought of journalism not as a job but as a calling. Some of these younger writers, especially ones who covered city politics and policy, were equally concerned with describing how things were and envisioning what they could be if readers could only be made to care.

Simon shared that mind-set, but he tempered it with an old-school newspaperman's sensibility that prized hard-won emotion over pandering sentiment. He teamed up with Ed Burns, a Vietnam veteran and Baltimore police detective. Burns knew Simon from his work at the *Sun* and would eventually collaborate with him on *The Corner: A Year in the Life of an Inner-City Neighborhood*. Burns's knowledge of police work and the drug trade lent a grubby reality to the cat-and-mouse games between dealers and cops, and his exasperation with police bureaucracy mirrored Simon's frustrations with the *Sun*. Because both creators came into television through the side door, they had little patience for the simple black-and-white morality and hermetically sealed storytelling that typified TV crime shows.

The Wire's structure owed a bit to both journalism and police work. Throughout its run, it kept adding new characters, stories, and communities that were at once separate from and connected to the rest, like precinct maps or sections of a newspaper. Season 2 revisited the dope slingers of season 1, but mixed in stories set at the docks, where contraband (including sex workers) was shipped in from overseas. Season 3 moved up one layer in both the police department and the local drug trade, showing how ego battles and turf wars affected the rank and file on both sides of the law. There was also a prominent subplot about Bunny Colvin conducting an unauthorized drug legalization experiment by establishing a free-market zone called Hamsterdam. Season 4 focused on a group of children moving through Baltimore's understaffed, underfunded, crime-ridden public schools; watching it, you understand how the next generation of criminals was formed through economic deprivation and societal neglect. Season 5 pivoted into broad media satire, showing how the decline of daily newspapers (including Simon's old employer the *Sun*) inspired them to concentrate on tabloid-type stories rather than the social-policy-driven reporting that Simon championed. He and Burns weren't making episodic TV—watched in isolation, no episode (not even the show's very first) makes much sense. They were building a novel for television, shaped by the aesthetics of big-city journalism and down-and-dirty crime fiction by authors like George Pelecanos, Richard Price, and Dennis Lehane (all of whom ended up writing for *The Wire*).

The show's opening credits summed up its ever-more-elaborate ambitions. The season 1 opening was all images of cops and criminals and surveillance, but each successive credits sequence retained elements from earlier ones while adding new material, some of it playfully fore-shadowing future twists. The effect was a bit like watching *The Wire* itself, a series that piled layer upon layer upon layer while somehow managing to check in with major characters from earlier seasons and tie their progress and their fates to what was happening in the dramatic foreground. Fittingly, the theme music was Tom Waits's "Way Down in the Hole," performed in successive seasons by the Blind Boys of Alabama, Waits, the Neville Brothers, DoMaJe, and Steve Earle—the peppiest, catchiest way of telling people that when they watched *The Wire*, they were hearing the same song sung in different voices.

The Wire's great triumph is that for all of its detail, and all of its Cassandra-like prophecies of the moral damage done to society by institutionalized corruption and individual ambition, it is ultimately a restrained humanist work: a pointillist mural comprised of faces. It makes you care, often deeply, about what happens to every individual who passes before its lens—even long after it has become clear that the most sympathetic characters will suffer the worst. Conventional TV precepts about good and evil didn't apply here. Evil was done to many people, and good to a few, but the motivations were far more complex, and had far more to do with the immutable nature of the various machines (the police department, city hall, the school board, and, of course, the drug corners) than with decisions made by individuals. We're left to wonder if any of the four boys at the center of season 4's devastating middle school arc, all of them with lives at least adjacent to the drug world, will manage to avoid being touched by it. In the end, only one escapes that life: not the smartest, or bravest, or even most likable one, but simply the one who was in the right place at the right time. The scripts showed how one tiny action could trigger a chain of tragic, unintended consequences, then observed the unfolding tragedy with a numbed sorrow that left its audience in tears, wondering why on earth they kept watching this show. They watched because of the level of craft exhibited by Simon and Burns and their collaborators, and because the stories had the sting of truth. In *The Wire*, good things rarely happened to those who deserved it, and terrible things often happened to those least suited to handle them, yet the show was so entertaining that we were willing to accept the heartbreak as the cost of doing business with it.

—AS & MZS

Cheers (NBC, 1982–1993) Total score: 112

As a baseball player for the Red Sox, Sam Malone (Ted Danson) was never seriously considered for the Hall of Fame. To begin with, he was a relief pitcher, and only the most otherworldly of those have any business in Cooperstown. "Mayday" Malone, on the other hand, had a career derailed by a drinking problem, not to mention a pitch nicknamed the "Slider of Death," not because it was lethal to opposing hitters but because it tended to get hit back over the Green Monster. (Sam's teammates coined the phrase.)

As the main character on a sitcom, though, Sam was part of a phenomenon so astonishing and unprecedented that you could split the series into halves, and each would be a plausible contender for a TV Hall of Fame like this one. The first five seasons of *Cheers*, which focused on the recovering alcoholic's incendiary romance with the disdainful, Ivy League–educated, grammar-correcting waitress Diane Chambers (Shelley Long), are a guaranteed inner-circle member— a smashing ensemble comedy whose lead characters perfected the will-they-or-won't-they model that has become a foundational cliché of television. But seasons 6 through 11, which locked Sam into a fitfully adult relationship with the bar's new manager, Rebecca Howe (Kirstie Alley), then ruefully concluded that he was better off by himself, would be a lock for inclusion as well.

Rather than merely put Sam and his castmates through the usual paces over and over, the series dared to ask itself, and us, what might actually happen to such people were they to experience the situations devised by the show's writers, taking into account the effects of age and disillusionment, the painful recognition (or denial) of failure, and the way the inevitability of death makes some people double-down on their pathologies and makes others work harder to subdue them and create something like a contented life. To put it in terms Sam would understand, *Cheers* had Sandy Koufax's peak, but instead of retiring early, it kept going for the comedy equivalent of Nolan Ryan's career—and damned if it didn't achieve the impossible. No long-running series in TV history had a better idea of precisely what it was or articulated it so clearly over such a long span of time without any notable loss of inventiveness. And no long-running series has reinvented itself as vividly, much less as successfully.

As written by brothers Glen and Les Charles (who created the series and oversaw the first five seasons) and as directed by James Burrows (who helmed all but one episode of the show's first four seasons, and more than 200 out of 275 episodes), *Cheers* was always content to be an intimate, even small sitcom—practically a weekly repertory stage production, confined mainly to the bar, Sam's office, and the poolroom, with action on the street indicated by silhouettes, footfalls, and strategically overheard bits of dialogue. But there was nothing minor about *Cheers'* artistry. Week in and week out, the show's writers, directors, and cast pulled off tiny miracles of characterization and timing, and the scripts covered the spectrum of comedic possibilities in the space of a half hour minus commercials, moving from poignant barroom-loser melancholy (with nearly dramatic moments that evoked the lighter moments in *The Iceman Cometh* of all things) to literal bedroom-door-slamming farce to Abbott and Costello–style smart-dumb wordplay (often courtesy of Woody Harrelson's good-hearted but dim-witted bartender, Woody Boyd, and John Ratzenberger's know-it-all postal carrier, Cliff Clavin) to postgraduate cultural commentary (when Diane recuts Woody's home movies, Woody says his dad liked it but thought it was "derivative of Godard").

In its first incarnation, *Cheers* was a dazzling romantic comedy, pitting Danson's streetwise ladies' man Sam against Long's pretentious but indomitable Diane. Both are prideful, even arrogant people, with frequent delusions of grandeur, yet at the same time vulnerable. They boast and preen because they're not-so-secretly terrified by the possibility that their happiest years are behind them and they're doomed to live lives that make no impression on anyone other than those who know them personally. They are the biggest personalities in the bar—but when the main stage of your life is a bar, how big are you, really? And yet they complete each other, as Jerry Maguire would say, even as they pick at each other's scabs and drive each other batty. "Do you know what the difference is between you and a fat, braying ass?" Diane asks in the season 2 finale, where they break up for the first of many times. "No," says Sam. "The fat, braying ass would!" Diane says. She slaps him; he slaps her back. "You hit me," Diane says. "Well, not hard," Sam says. "What does that mean?" Diane asks. "Not as hard as I wanted to," he admits.

The volatility of their relationship would raise hackles today. They don't just insult each other, to an extent that many would consider emotional abuse, they manhandle and strike each other. In the first-season finale, Sam promises to bounce Diane off every wall in his office; not that he would actually do it—it's more of a *Honeymooners*' "Pow, right to the moon!" type of pledge, made at the last possible cultural moment before the threat of domestic violence ceased being acceptable comedic fodder—but it still expresses a level of desperate, angry frustration rarely seen in TV romances now. "You disgust me," Diane tells him, right before their first kiss. "Are you as turned on as I am?" Sam asks. "More!" she gasps. They are uniquely suited and unsuited to each other, natural enemies who can't keep their hands off each other. There are few better TV examples of sexual attraction as a chemical phenomenon than Sam and Diane. "You two should not only not get married," warns a marital expert played by John Cleese in season 5. "You should never see each other again…you have absolutely nothing in common…you have an appalling lack of communication." Diane asks about the idea that opposites attract, and Cleese responds, "Ah, the song of the truly desperate!" Those two thoughts aren't mutually exclusive. Sam and Diane keep proving this time and again, to the horror of their friends and colleagues, who want them to be happy but can't stand their simpering when they're enjoying each other or their corrosive rage when they're at odds.

When her contract was up after five seasons, Long decided she wanted to be a movie star. This wasn't a great choice for her, even if *Troop Beverly Hills* still has its nostalgic middle-aged fans, but it did wonders for *Cheers*. The show had gone through every iteration of the Sam-and-Diane relationship over five years, up to and including her being understandably afraid for her life whenever she was around him. There might have been another season or two's worth of stories out of having them get married (instead of her leaving Sam at the altar in her final appearance as a regular character) and perhaps even having a baby, but that also would have pulled the focus away from the bar.

Though Rebecca was introduced as a would-be romantic conquest for Sam—an icy professional immune to his charms—the series abandoned the idea (and that initial characterization of Rebecca, once everyone saw how much funnier Kirstie Alley was at playing a mess) quickly and devoted its energy to building a full-on ensemble. The show's back half took advantage of all the time it spent in early seasons turning Woody; the philosophical barfly Norm (George Wendt); Cliff; the sarcastic but fertile waitress Carla (Rhea Perlman); and Diane's bitter psychiatrist ex Frasier (Kelsey Grammer) into characters the audience had come to love just as much as (if not more than) the central couple.

Sam's relationship with Rebecca is less explosive, and therefore less superficially exciting, even though she's even more highly strung than Diane was and more prone to burst into tears, à la Lucy Ricardo, when things don't go her way. She enters his life when he's getting over Diane, doubling-down on his womanizing as a reaction against losing a woman he assumed was the great love of his life. Their struggle to negotiate a working relationship is as fascinating as Sam and Diane's almost entirely sexual bond, but thornier, because so much of it is about delaying gratification or finding middle ground in a dispute, rather than continuing to fight until one party either climbs into bed or storms out into the night.

The two phases, or ages, of *Cheers* (Diane and Rebecca) feel like childhood/adolescence and adulthood. Its binding narrative is the stop-and-start evolution of Sam Malone, who goes from arrogant peacock to grizzled old rooster, learning to stay in contact with his inner horny teenager without letting it rule his actions or his self-perceptions.

Shelley Long had worked miracles in making Diane lovable. And the sense of loneliness that underscored that relationship neatly fit the show's slightly darker earlier seasons, where there was room for an episode like "Endless Slumper," in which Sam candidly tells Diane about his fear of falling off the wagon again, or "Coach's Daughter," where the sweet but addled bartender Ernie "Coach" Pantusso (Nicholas Colasanto, who died midway through production of season 3) tries to convince his daughter not to settle for marrying a jerk out of a belief that she's not pretty enough to do better.

Once it was clear that Rebecca was, at most, going to be another conquest for Sam, *Cheers* became a more relentless joke-delivery system, trusting that its writers and cast could go punch line for punch line with any comedy in TV's past, present, and future without needing the narrative and emotional spine that Sam and Diane's relationship provided.

Whether it was Norm's one-liners upon entering the bar ("It's a dog-eat-dog world, and I'm wearing Milk-Bone underwear"); Frasier's constant struggle to fit in with the blue-collar crowd he was so desperate to impress (in one episode, he tries reading them *A Tale of Two Cities*, but has to incorporate attack helicopters and the evil clown from Stephen King's *It* to keep the gang entertained); Cliff's windbaggery (it's a little-known fact that Cliff was the original mansplainer), which eventually lands him on *Jeopardy!* (asked to recognize the real names of Cary Grant, Tony Curtis, and Joan Crawford, Cliff suggests, "Who are three people who have never been in my kitchen?"); or the annual "Bar Wars" episodes where Cheers faced off against the more successful crowd from Gary's Olde Towne Tavern, *Cheers'* comic reserves seemed everlasting.

The show and its characters got a bit broader and dumber as they got older, to the point where Sam realized the only thing in his life not calculated to attract women was his love of the Three Stooges. But even at an advanced age, *Cheers* could lean back and deliver, if not Mayday's patented Slider of Death, then a vintage fastball. The series' eleventh and final season opens with Rebecca accidentally setting fire to the bar. As workmen rebuilt the place, the show's writers found a way to restore the more down-to-earth, and at times outright melancholy, tone of the Diane years. The characters were older and a bit sadder now, none more than Sam, who realized he suffered from sex addiction and revealed to Carla that he had been wearing a hairpiece for years.

The Charles brothers returned to write the series finale, the first script with their names on it since Rebecca's introduction six years earlier. Rather than ignore all that had happened in their absence and focus on the vintage years, the finale turned into a survey of the series' bifurcated history, as well as the most satisfying sitcom end of all time.

Diane returns just long enough for her and Sam to rekindle their sexual flame before they again recognize that it's the only part of their relationship that ever worked. The supporting characters all move on with their lives in the manner of most series-enders—Woody and Norm get new jobs, Rebecca gets married (albeit to a plumber rather than the corporate baron of her dreams)—but first gather to support Sam after his latest failure with Diane.

In a simple, delightful scene, the gang sits around a Cheers table smoking cigars and contemplating the meaning of life. Some of the suggestions are silly (Cliff the mailman argues for comfortable footwear), some are profound (Carla the mom suggests that having kids is what matters most), and some are spare and poignant (struggling to tell the group what they've meant to him, Frasier the logorrheic therapist can't find the words). Finally, the bull session breaks up as each member of the group heads home to a life much fuller than what Sam believes he has. It's up to Norm to slip back in and explain that what matters most in life is what you love.

(Even in this quiet, bittersweet moment, the Charles brothers' instincts for when and how to insert a joke are as keen as ever: Norm asks if Sam knows what he loves, and when Sam replies, "Beer, Norm?," Norm bellies up to the bar, shrugs, and says, "Yeah, I'll have a quick one.")

Norm leaves, and as Sam looks around the place he bought at the lowest point of his drinking problem, but that somehow gave his post-baseball life order and meaning, he understands what his favorite customer was trying to tell him, running his hand along the bar as he mutters to himself, "Well, I'll tell ya: I'm the luckiest son of a bitch on earth."

When a lone customer knocks on the door, Sam turns to him and utters the series' elegant final words—really, the only last line that made sense for this magnificent show about a bar where everybody knows your name:

"Sorry. We're closed."

—AS & MZS

Breaking Bad (AMC, 2008–2013) Total score: 112

When he pitched *Breaking Bad* to executives at AMC, series creator Vince Gilligan promised, "We're gonna take Mr. Chips and turn him into Scarface." That sounds simplistic, even glib. But the result was so fiendishly intricate and altogether thrilling that TV drama's post-*Sopranos* antihero boom could have ended with it, for what could top the story of Walter White's transformation into the family-deceiving, drug-dealing, bomb-planting Heisenberg, the Mephistopheles of Albuquerque?

But watch *Breaking Bad* enough times (not a bad idea considering the complexity of its plot), and Gilligan's pitch feels reductive. For one thing, what little we see of Walter White, high school chemistry teacher, in seasons 1 and 2 implies that he was never entirely Mr. Chips. As presented by Gilligan and his writing staff, and as incarnated by star Bryan Cranston, Walt is clearly as bored by his chemistry class as it is by him. The mutual contempt displayed by Walt and his former student and future drug-cooking partner, Jesse Pinkman (Aaron Paul), is just a more extreme, comical version of Walt's relationships with nearly every other significant person in his life, including his put-upon and very pregnant wife, Skyler (Anna Gunn), her sister Marie (Betsy Brandt), and Marie's husband, Hank Schrader (Dean Norris), a barrel-chested DEA agent with the braying laugh of a jock who likes to stuff nerds into lockers. The only person Walt treats with undiluted affection is his teenage son, Walter White Jr., aka Flynn (R. J. Mitte), who has cerebral palsy. When Walt is diagnosed with lung cancer—the inspiration for his criminal career—it's unclear who outside of his immediate family would miss him.

In almost every early scene, Walt exudes the specific resentment of a man who thinks himself entitled to more than he already has and hates every instant spent in the company of those he deems intellectual or moral inferiors. His second job at a local car wash is so personally degrading to a man who thinks himself a genius (and perhaps is one) that as he runs the cash register and wipes down students' cars, his mortification seems to shade over into masochistic pleasure. It's as if Walt has become so detached from himself that he's observing his own suffering and cruelly laughing at it, just as *Breaking Bad* viewers will laugh at twists of fate in seasons to come.

The series observes a version of the *Godfather* or *Sopranos* template, building each season around a series of escalating rivalries between Walt and would-be competitors, employers, or doppelgängers, including Raymond Cruz's hot-tempered Tuco Salamanca in seasons 1 and 2; Giancarlo Esposito's fast-food magnate and secret drug lord Gus Fring in seasons 2 through 4; and Michael Bowen's neo-Nazi gang leader Jack Welker in season 5 (which was split into two mini-seasons, each with a rise-and-fall structure). Throughout, Walt contrives to keep his criminal alter ego a secret from Skyler, Flynn, Hank, Marie, and other law-abiding loved ones—a process that feels desperate, at times comically so, at first, but seems more knowing and playful once Walt starts getting away with bigger outrages. At one point, Hank is on the verge of accepting that Gus's murdered chemist Gale Boetticher (David Costabile) was Heisenberg, but Walt, unable to allow anyone else to take even posthumous credit for his work, no matter the benefit to himself, steers Hank away from that theory.

As a chemist, Walt has had a lifetime of training in how to use chemicals to achieve specific effects, from the creation of a superpotent string of "crystal blue" methamphetamine to the improvisation of bombs and poisons that he can use to terrorize or destroy anyone who dares stand between him and the fortune he's trying to amass. He says he's doing it for his family—to make sure they're taken care of should the cancer treatment fail—but though Walt's love of his wife and kids seems genuine even when he's at his most domineering and repugnant, there's never much doubt that his altruistic stance is entirely self-serving.

Much was written throughout the show's run about Walt as a wish-fulfillment fantasy for generations of middle-aged, married white men, and there is a sense in which it does feel like a fantasy/nightmare of the American patriarchy in decline—a strangely fitting companion to AMC's other great drama, the 1960s period piece *Mad Men*, which shows where, on the American time line, that decline began. But the whole thing gains a parablelike dimension, thanks to Gilligan's heightened sense of stylization, which draws on the funny-sentimental-grotesque sensibility of the Coen brothers (*Fargo, No Country for Old Men*), but ultimately owes much of its personality to its merger of the crime thriller and the science-fiction horror film. As *Breaking Bad* unfolds and Walt becomes increasingly bold, brutal, and self-regarding, we start to wonder if what we're seeing is the story of a man transforming into a monster who might not otherwise have existed or that of a monster nestled for decades very deep inside of a man, and waiting to be activated by the right combination of circumstances: say, a cancer diagnosis; a new baby; a financial crunch; the opportunity to learn about the drug trade from Hank; and access to a former student who is already cooking crystal meth.

Gilligan's last major series before *Breaking Bad* was *The X-Files*, on which he served as a writer, director, and producer, and there are points when this solo outing traffics in familiar imagery from science fiction. As the show itself reminds us, New Mexico is where the United States tested atomic bombs. Many sci-fi movies from the Cold War era concerned monsters created in the desert by atomic testing, or by secret government skulduggery that was ultimately a stand-in for atomic testing. Through the metaphorical prestidigitation of this genre, the monster birthed by radiation is the United States itself, a nation that had plenty of experience with genocide already by way of the Native Americans (some of whom were exterminated in New Mexico), and that remains the only nation ever to use the bomb against civilians. The sci-fi echoes are graphical, too: Walter and many other bald men in the show's main cast are often lit and framed so that they evoke the mutants of *Beneath the Planet of the Apes*, the steel-hearted drones of *THX 1138*, or the bug-eyed aliens of 1950s drive-in flicks. The numerous scenes of Walt and Jesse cooking in the Winnebago or in Gus's red-floored, high-ceilinged meth lab channel David Cronenberg's body-horror movies (*The Fly*, *Dead Ringers*), particularly when the bodies of enemies are dissolved in tubs or bathtubs filled with acid or when the duo spends a whole episode chasing a fly they believe is contaminating their cook.

In this respect and others, *Breaking Bad* is a treasure trove of sociological and pop culture signifiers. But nobody would care about that stuff (and the show would not have become a sensation) without Gilligan's determination to entertain at every second. You wouldn't think the series could top the season 2 image of the severed head of character actor Danny Trejo (cast as a cartel enforcer turned DEA informant) atop an exploding tortoise, but it did, again and again. As shot by series cinematographer Michael Slovis, and directed by such aggressively visual filmmakers as Michelle MacLaren, Rian Johnson, Adam Bernstein, John Dahl (*Rounders*), David Slade (who went on to design the look of NBC's *Hannibal*), and Gilligan (who is nearly as strong a director as he is a writer), no image was ever obvious. The show always looked for angles and camera moves that would make a scene or moment pop, like the high-angled shot of a poolside covered in corpses ("Salud"), the fleeting ghostlike images of civilians in Hank's rearview mirror before the parking-lot shoot-out that climaxes "One Minute," or the way the camera slowly moves toward and then *around* Gus Fring at the end of

"Face Off," revealing not only his fate but the fact that the episode's title is a groaner of a play on words.

The show's structure, too, is clever, at times to a fault: Starting in season 2, which interpolated flash-forwards of debris in Walt's pool before gradually revealing how he was responsible for the midair collision that deposited it there, *Breaking Bad* played around with time, often to create and resolve puzzlement. *What are we looking at? What does it mean? How will it all fit together?* (Strung end-to-end, the titles of the season 2 episodes with plane crash flash-forwards form the FAA's announcement of the collision.) This approach is at once intuitive (the *Breaking Bad* writing staff later admitted that they often wrote themselves into corners and then had to test their powers of invention by writing themselves out) and mathematical (the way some of the season 5 subplots are broken up, cliff-hanger style, feel like the result of scientific tests to determine how best to torment the audience).

In the end, it comes back to Walt and Heisenberg. Was the monster in there the whole time, or was he truly created from circumstance? The latter fits Gilligan's original pitch and helps viewers justify the time and emotional investment they gave to a character who turned out to be a shatterer of worlds. Cranston and Gilligan walked us down the path to monsterhood so delicately that some viewers didn't want to accept Walt's outrageous villainy long after it had become undeniable to everyone else. As a result, they turned on Skyler—who in any other version of the story would have been considered a sympathetic heroine—in an ugly confluence of the *Breaking Bad* fandom, unexpected empathy, and latent misogyny that had plagued cable TV's antihero drama boom from the earliest days of *The Sopranos*.

Upon repeat viewings, it seems clear that the show was warning us early on not to believe Walt's self-mythologizing and excuses. On those rare occasions when we saw flashbacks set prior to the events of the show, Cranston played Walt with the same steely arrogance that would become a Heisenberg trademark. (Objecting to a shabby starter home Skyler wants to buy—the very home they would wind up living in for twenty years—he asks her, "Why be cautious? We've got nowhere to go but up.") And too many of Walt's explosions of temper—at Skyler, at Jesse, at anyone foolish or unlucky enough to get in his way at the wrong moment (which was, in time, every moment)—were fueled by resentment that started building long before Walt saw his oncologist or went on a ride-along with Hank. Heisenberg might never have emerged—certainly not in such homicidal form—if not for the cancer. But he was there the whole time.

Gilligan doesn't like to explain his show too much, nor should he be required to, but it's telling that he considers the climax of the series to be not Walt going out in a blaze of glory against Uncle Jack and the neo-Nazis but a quiet moment from earlier in the finale, when a chastened Walt finally says out loud what he's known for a long time was his true motivation: "I did it for me. I liked it. I was good at it. And I was…really…I was alive."

—AS & MZS

Mad Men (AMC, 2007–2015) Total score: 110

"Whatever happened to Gary Cooper?" Tony Soprano once lamented. "The strong, silent type. *That* was an American! He wasn't in touch with his feelings. He just did what he had to do."

Tony's Gary Cooper fixation was part of a larger belief that he had been born at the wrong time—"I came in at the end," he also complained—and one that would be proved right in a way by *Mad Men*. Debuting a month after *The Sopranos* cut to black, it featured a main character who was very much like Tony's masculine ideal of Cooper (or Gregory Peck). Then again, Tony probably would have hated *Mad Men*, since the show treated advertising executive Don Draper's strong, silent qualities as something not to celebrate, but for him to grow beyond.

The Sopranos and *Mad Men* shared Matthew Weiner, who had been a writer and producer on the former, and creator of the latter. Despite the new show's 1960s production design and trapped-in-amber social attitudes, the sense of continuity was inescapable.

Weiner came late to *The Sopranos*, at a time when the show was amping up its already considerable fascination with the effect of social change and dreams on individual psychology, to the point where the series frustrated viewers who craved more whackin' and less yakkin'. *Mad Men* would feature the occasional death (plus a man's foot getting mutilated by a riding mower during a drunken office party), but it was even talkier and more introspective than its predecessor.

Don Draper (Jon Hamm), creative director of the mid-level ad agency Sterling Cooper, is a charismatic antihero, different from other TV bad boys in some details (he was an impostor who was born to a desperately poor farm family and stole a dead soldier's identity in Korea) but not in others (funny, hard-drinking, chain-smoking, self-destructive, domineering, intensely quotable, a natural leader, married with mistresses).

And, like *The Sopranos*, *Mad Men* put nature-versus-nurture questions at the center of many of its plots and subplots, and subjected them to scrutiny nearly as merciless. Just as Chase's mobsters were gangsters with animalistic appetites who posed as tediously ordinary suburbanites, so, too, do Don and his friends and coworkers—who are employed by the American '60s' most glamorous profession outside of Hollywood—chafe at the roles that they have either accepted since birth or consciously sought as grown-ups.

When the series begins, Don has a house in the suburbs, a beautiful and too-trusting wife, Betty (January Jones), and two (later three) cute kids, the eldest of which, Kiernan Shipka's Sally, is the apple of his otherwise jaundiced eye. But he keeps undermining, straying from, even actively destroying the Eden he's labored to create: running away from his family, his job, and himself; attempting to re-create the domestic ideal in a second (or is that third?) marriage to a secretary (Jessica Paré's Megan) who had proved to be good with his kids; plunging into alcoholic despair, pulling out of it, then diving into it again more deeply; often simultaneously acting like his "true" self (Dick Whitman, son of a sex worker who died giving birth to him) and his "invented" self.

Those quotation marks are necessary because on *Mad Men*, the very idea of authenticity is repeatedly, forcefully questioned. The characters are never less trustworthy than when they're announcing who they are and what they're about, and never more open to alternative possibilities than when their delusions have been smashed and their lives ruined and they're momentarily humbled enough to listen as others describe who they are, or could be. One fine example of this is the moment in season 2's "The Mountain King" when Don visits his first wife (technically the wife of the dead man he's impersonating), Anna Draper, played by Melinda Paige Hamilton. Anna delivers a tarot card reading that predicts a time when Don will accept love and be at peace with the universe (a scene that seems in retrospect to foretell the show's very last scene, down to the sunlight, ocean wave sounds, and chimes). The show is obsessed by the relationship between people's polished exteriors and roiling interiors. It loves to zoom in to catch moments when the mask slips and you can see how one face hides another (and another, and another). One of the most self-aware yet perfect acknowledgments of this tendency is in season 3's "The Gypsy and the Hobo," when Don finally admits his prolonged deception to Betty on Halloween, and then the couple has to take their children out for trick-or-treating. "Who are you supposed to be?" a neighbor asks them.

Most of the other major *Mad Men* characters go through some version of Don's quest, though few flame out in as spectacular a fashion, or demonstrate flashes of genius convincing enough that we believe other people would (mostly) put up with their bullshit. Agency senior partner Roger Sterling (John Slattery) was born into money (his father cofounded Sterling Cooper) and coasts on his privilege but seems to hate himself for it; like Don, he has maybe-unconscious sympathies for the counterculture types that he mocks. As the series unfolds, he cycles through three marriages, starts taking LSD and going to therapy (something Don never does), and briefly lives in a hotel room that looks like a miniature version of the commune he's horrified to learn that his daughter has moved into.

The arc of Peggy Olson (Elisabeth Moss), secretary turned copywriter, is likewise circuitous and tied to the character's attraction-repulsion to her roots. She's a working-class Catholic of Northern European lineage who at first seems doomed to either toil forever as a secretary or go the route outlined by the buxom, worldly-wise office manager Joan Holloway (Christina Hendricks) and escape to the suburbs by marrying an executive. The Peggy of later seasons is outwardly unlike the anxious, virginal secretary we met in the pilot. She smokes pot. She enjoys one-night stands and affairs with married men. She insists on being treated as a social equal by the men in her life. She demands to be properly compensated and awarded for her work. But she never entirely loses that model-grind quality or the sense that she's always detached from the world she inhabits—a quality that links her to Don, a merciless student of human nature who can translate other people's fears and longings, as well as his own, into resonant ads.

But if Weiner had apprenticed at *The Sopranos* and learned much from it—including an obsession with detail that made *Mad Men*'s 1960s feel more lived-in than any previous pop culture trip back to the decade of JFK, the Fab Four, and Richard Nixon—he wasn't bound by David Chase's rules. He found his own way immediately, a fact that's instantly apparent in *Mad Men*'s treatment of the human personality. Among the most enduring *Sopranos* themes was the enormous difficulty of personal growth and change: The Tony seen eating onion rings in the finale has spent years of self-examination in therapy but is largely indistinguishable from the Tony who first walked into Dr. Melfi's office years earlier. *Mad Men*, though, went in the opposite direction, telling and showing us that every person is in fact many selves, all in a constant state of flux, evolving and devolving from one year or month or week to the next, just like the national history unfolding all around them. The show took place during a decade of great social change, but it didn't limit the transformation to the world outside the ad agency's windows. The characters' meandering, semiconscious journeys toward change reflected the alterations occurring in America as a whole without one being forced to mirror the other in too direct or reductive a fashion. So Joan could begin the series scornful of a woman using her job as anything but a means to a lucrative and married end, and conclude it threatening to call the ACLU and Betty Friedan on her bosses for creating a hostile workplace. Pete Campbell (Vincent Kartheiser) could start out as a weasel with a bottomless appetite for acknowledgment and respect, and end up recognizing that the simple married life he'd thrown away was really all he ever needed.

And Don was in a near-constant state of metamorphosis, even if he often took three steps back for every two forward, and he never seemed to get the balance right between the traits belonging to Dick (cowardly, wounded, but also more sensitive and open) and those belonging to Don (master of all he surveyed, even if he had to push his loved ones out of the way to improve the view).

Even the series' final moment—the most abstract, instantly polarizing conclusion to a series since, well, *The Sopranos*—left things very much up in the air as to how far Don had or hadn't come from the day we met him. While doing yoga on a cliff overlooking the Pacific, he has an epiphany and translates his experience at a New Age retreat into the iconic ad with all the singers who'd like to buy the world a Coke. Does his serene smile signify great personal growth or is this one last instance of the ultimate adman looking at a genuine emotional experience and figuring out how to sell something with it? Given how much *Mad Men* loved to live in ambiguous moral spaces—inviting us to perpetually quote grand Don insults like "THAT'S WHAT THE MONEY IS FOR!" even as we were horrified by the effect the line had on Peggy—maybe it was both. Or perhaps we should say: *Of course it was.*

That *Mad Men* ends not on an image of any of its actors, but a forty-four-year-old Coca-Cola ad, spoke to the series' intimate understanding of our relationship with popular culture. Weiner liked to say that the series wasn't really about the big historical events of the '60s, though he presented many of them from his characters' perspectives. But if presidential assassinations, thwarted armageddons, and giant leaps for mankind were held at a remove from Don and Peggy's world, the films, music, and television of the era were tied into everything they did, and not just because their ads were meant to accompany episodes of *The Defenders* and *Green Acres*. Don does his best thinking at the movies. His least fraught moment with Peggy involves the two of them slow dancing to "My Way." The wife of flamboyant but closeted art director Sal Romano (Bryan Batt) doesn't begin to recognize the fundamental flaw in her marriage until she watches her husband act out the title song from *Bye Bye Birdie*. Weiner saw advertising as just as important and creative an art form as the works those ads sponsored (even as he allowed the writers and executives to mock their profession as glorified hucksterism, epitomized by Roger suggesting, "I'll tell you what brilliance in advertising is: ninety-nine cents"). But there was always another, subtle kind of mirroring going on here: While *Mad Men*'s characters advertised products, the characters, the firm, the city, and the nation advertised themselves.

Mad Men's attention to detail manifested not just in the attention paid to music or politics but in its memory for the tiny details that embodied the relationships between characters. In the first episode, Peggy, believing that sex with the boss is part of the job description, makes a clumsy pass by putting her hand on top of his. From that point forward, nearly every crucial turn in Don and Peggy's relationship—their brief reconciliation in one of the series' finest episodes, "The Suitcase," her quitting the agency to escape their codependent relationship, or them finally reaching equilibrium with their "My Way" dance in "The Strategy"—is signified by the joining of hands, in a way that added enormous emotional value to those moments even if viewers didn't consciously identify them as callbacks.

Nowhere is the show's dramatic architecture more impressive than in season 1, which introduces Don as a master of his little universe, then charts his systematic unraveling. The first of the show's many flashbacks to his childhood occurs in the fourth episode, "New Amsterdam," when a slip on the stairs inspires a flashback to his brother Adam's birth; this presages the adult Adam's reemergence in the following week's episode, "5G," and from then on, the flashbacks become more frequent. Episode 8, "The Hobo Code," includes Don's stepmother's memorable description of life as being like a horseshoe: "round on both ends, fat in the middle, and hard all the way through." Episode 12, "Nixon vs. Kennedy," which juxtaposes Pete's attempts to blackmail Don by threatening to expose his identity theft, gives us the longest flashback yet, an account of Don's stint in Korea as Dick Whitman that takes up one-third of the episode. This in turn sets up Don's psychological implosion, which alienates Betty and brings Don's Whitman-ish fear of failure and exposure to the forefront of his mind, driving him to demand that his mistress Rachel Menken (Maggie Siff) flee to California with him. (Wisely, she refuses, telling him prophetically, "You don't really want to run away with me; you just want to run away," a statement that nails Don's response to every dire predicament.) The season's emotional peak is the Carousel pitch in "The Wheel," in which Don describes Kodak's new slide projector as a "time machine" that "lets us travel the way a child travels—around and around, and back home again, to a place where we know that we are loved." It is only after repeat viewings that you notice which toy Don slips on in "New Amsterdam"—a Whee-Lo, which consists of a plastic wheel with magnetized tips that can move backward and forward, around and around, on a horseshoe-shaped track.

Like so many touches on *Mad Men*, this one bespeaks an attention to detail (not merely clever but narratively meaningful) that is breathtaking in its totality of vision. That word, "vision," has been cheapened by critical overuse, but when a show really, truly has it, we recognize it. *Mad Men* doesn't just have vision, it's about vision, and visions, and seeing, and seeing *through*. Don is at heart a copywriter, but even he recognizes the way imagery is beginning to overtake words as the currency of his business. As the series moves along, it becomes more and more visually adventurous, presenting stunning, haunting images like Don walking across a darkened soundstage where Megan is filming a commercial, the distance between husband and wife seeming geographically as well as emotionally insurmountable; Don staring down a distressingly empty elevator shaft in the Time-Life Building, literalizing the abyss over which every *Mad Men* character hovers, and into which Don's colleague Lane Pryce (Jared Harris) will plunge a few episodes later; Betty descending the steps of the Savoy Hotel in slow motion, looking every bit the movie-star vision Don wants rather than the emotional reality he can't find a way to honor and cherish; mirrored shots of Don grieving the suicides of Adam and Lane; Don, bored in a new job at McCann-Erickson, being mesmerized by the view of a jet plane flying behind the Empire State Building, its vapor trail stretched across the sky like a pen stroke. At the end of season 6, we even get a dark mirror of the Carousel pitch when Don becomes too candid about his childhood in a meeting with Hershey executives. It plays like the Carousel's booze-soaked, pathetic kid brother—or, if you prefer, Dick Whitman to the Carousel's Donald Draper, or Nixon to Kennedy.

The lie of closure has never been more completely articulated in any American series, nor has the myth of nonstop forward personal progress been so thoroughly (if compassionately) demolished. The characters move through history—and destiny, if indeed the word means anything here—not in a straight line but in a series of horseshoe movements or a zigzag pattern or spirals, and they can never be entirely sure if they make decisions or decisions make them. Their restless dissatisfaction feels true; they're happy only when they're working, and then only when they have maximum freedom and are demonstrating maximum creativity and control. In season 5's "Commissions and Fees," Don and Roger force a meeting with executives at Dow Chemical, who claim to be perfectly happy with their current ad agency. Don aggressively, if unsuccessfully, tries to shake that confidence, asking them, "What is happiness? It's a moment before you need more happiness." The show ends not with a bang or a whimper or a cut to black but with a cheerfully upbeat song promising a utopian convergence of humanity on a sunlit hilltop. Like every other campaign on the show, it's just another advertisement, but like every great ad, there is a part of it that feels sincere in spite of itself. This closing moment, too, like every *Mad Men* character, is more than one contradictory thing at the same time and should be embraced but not held too closely. If you've made it through seven seasons of *Mad Men*, you know more or less what to make of it: It's saying *trust the feeling* and *let the buyer beware*.

—MZS & AS

Seinfeld (NBC, 1989–1998) Total score: 110

"Well, what's the show about?" Jerry asks his friend George.

"It's about nothing," George tells him.

"No story?"

"No, forget the story."

"You gotta have a story," Jerry insists.

"Who says you gotta have a story?" George counters. "Remember when we were waiting for, for that table in that Chinese restaurant that time? That could be a TV show."

The actual origin of *Seinfeld* is far more complicated—and wildly improbable for any series, let alone one that would eventually become TV's most popular—than that exchange in *Seinfeld* season 4 that gives birth to *Jerry*, the terrible show-within-the-show created by the fictional Jerry Seinfeld and the spineless George Costanza (Jason Alexander). But because Seinfeld was playing himself, because George was famously a stand-in for misanthropic *Seinfeld* cocreator Larry David, and because lines constantly blurred between *Seinfeld* and *Jerry* that season, the notion that *Seinfeld* was the "show about nothing" stuck.

And in many ways, it fit. Here was a series that could build entire episodes around a barely visible red dot on a white sweater, or whether a local yogurt shop's product was actually nonfat, or even, as George noted, the wait to get a table at a Chinese restaurant. It was, like its characters, obsessed with what Jerry's ex-turned-friend Elaine Benes (Julia Louis-Dreyfus) once referred to as "the excruciating minutiae of every. Single. Daily. Event."

Yet saying *Seinfeld* was about nothing gets the point almost entirely backward. In its fascination with zooming in on life's most insignificant details, it actually wound up offering a broad view of life at the end of the twentieth century: the show about nothing that was really about everything.

Okay, maybe not *everything*. The show's world was very much New York—and a very white, affluent subsection of that. (On the rare occasions minority characters appeared, they tended to be even more caricatured than the show's other bit players, and even Michael Richards's glorified hobo, Cosmo Kramer, never had to worry about money.) But even viewed through that lens, the series continually managed to identify, classify, and find humor in everyday phenomena we all recognized yet had never given name to.

Think of how many *Seinfeld* social constructs set such deep root in our larger cultural lexicon that they felt like they had always been there and are known even to people who've never seen an episode: the bad manners of double-dipping a chip or regifting a present, or the male mortification of shrinkage after swimming in a cold pool, or the various unconventional manners of speaking (low-talkers, close-talkers, shushers), to name just a few.

But *Seinfeld* was so much more than its catchphrases and sociological dissections. It was a relentless joke machine with a black comic heart that ran against every decades-old tradition about sitcom sentimentality. Seinfeld and David's mantra for the show was "No hugging, no learning," and it featured a quartet of characters who were never in danger of doing either.

George was a desperate, pathetic ball of misery with a superhuman gift for deception, once explaining, "It's not a lie if you believe it." Kramer was a magical fool, forever stumbling upon money, women, trouble, and the entrance to Jerry's apartment, moving and speaking like a pilot who was still figuring out the controls of this particular vessel. Elaine and Jerry tended to look down their noses at the other two, but they were every bit as shallow and self-destructive, just wrapped up in more socially acceptable packages. But put her on the dance floor or ask him to lie (or anything else that stretched out Jerry Seinfeld's charmingly limited range as an actor), and they became part of the freak show.

Neither creator was exactly an outsider to the medium, but nor had they been entirely comfortable in it before. David wrote for *Saturday Night Live* for a season when Louis-Dreyfus was a cast member, though his ideas were so unconventional that only one of his sketches ever made it to air. Seinfeld had a recurring role on *Benson* but was fired after only a handful of episodes and went back to focusing on his stand-up career. NBC executives didn't know what to make of their pilot for an observational sitcom where Seinfeld played a fictionalized version of himself—NBC president Brandon Tartikoff feared it was "too Jewish"—and the show was nearly killed in development before the network's head of late-night programming, Rick Ludwin, stepped in and offered to fund a four-episode first season out of his own budget. The show had a rollout that suggested a complete lack of confidence from the network: The pilot episode aired on its own in the summer of 1989, the four Ludwin-backed episodes the following summer, then a half-season in the spring of 1991, before the first full season finally found its way onto the schedule that fall.

That long stretch in obscurity gave David, Seinfeld, and company the freedom to fine-tune their ideas: for Alexander to stop doing a Woody Allen impression and start doing a Larry David one, for the writers to figure out the show was best served by throwing the four leads in different directions before having their stories converge at the end of an episode, and to realize that something as low-concept as "The Chinese Restaurant" actually represented the show at its most creative.

By the time the rest of NBC began to realize *Seinfeld*'s value, and to groom it into the successor to *Cheers*, it had grown into its full, incredible potential. Its four regulars were surrounded by a cavalcade of ever-more-bizarre foils, some wholly fictional and some only semifictional: contemptuous mailman Newman (Wayne Knight), who served as both Kramer's sidekick and Jerry's nemesis; George's intolerable parents Frank (Jerry Stiller) and Estelle (Estelle Harris); long-winded globe-trotter J. Peterman (John O'Hurley); Yev "Soup Nazi" Kassem (Larry Thomas), who ruled his soup stand with an iron fist; and even irrational Yankees owner George Steinbrenner (a *Doonesbury*-style abstraction voiced by Larry David), who employed George for a few seasons. The show could attempt almost anything in terms of subject matter, mocking the JFK assassination (or, at least, Oliver Stone's *JFK*) with an expectoral assault involving Kramer, Newman, Keith Hernandez, and a "second spitter," or having Jerry and his latest girlfriend get caught making out while watching *Schindler's List*. It mixed comic anthropology with slapstick, vaudeville routines with sexual farce. An episode like season 6's "The Fusilli Jerry" could on one level use Jerry's special bedroom technique as a metaphor for his stand-up act—and the story of a man who appropriates the move as a commentary on comics who steal others' jokes—while also going lowbrow with a subplot where Kramer reaps the benefits of accidentally getting vanity license plates that read "ASSMAN."

Though David would later take pleasure in the lack of content restrictions as the creator and star of HBO's very *Seinfeld*-esque *Curb Your Enthusiasm*, *Seinfeld* itself frequently demonstrated the power generated by being forced to work within limitations. The series' most famous episode, season 4's "The Contest," has the gang of four wagering on who can go the longest without masturbating. However, because it was 1992 and NBC wasn't yet relaxing its broadcast standards in an attempt to compete with cable, the word "masturbate" was never used. Instead, the phrase used to describe their abstention—to the raucous response of a studio audience that (a) couldn't believe a sitcom was doing an episode about this, and (b) was impressed by how cleverly the show got the idea across—was "master of your domain." The series pushed the outer edge of the envelope without ever ripping it outright, allowing Elaine (who hoarded her preferred method of birth control after it was discontinued) to judge sexual partners on who was "sponge-worthy," or asking Jerry to guess his girlfriend's name only with the knowledge that it rhymed with a part of the female anatomy ("Mulva?").

If there were limits on what David, Seinfeld, and the show's other writers could allow their four leads to say, there were precious few on what they could allow the quartet to do. Their crimes, sometimes on purpose (Jerry mugs an old woman to steal her loaf of marble rye bread), sometimes by accident (Jerry ruins a man's business and later gets him deported), were so frequent, so tasteless, and so horrifying that David devoted the bulk of the divisive series finale to putting the four of them on trial just so we could be reminded of what swine they always were.

David, who stepped back from showrunner duty for most of the series' final two seasons, perhaps felt that the audience needed one last reminder that they'd spent close to a decade in the company of despicable human beings. As a result, the finale played more like a lecture—and, by that point, a redundant one. In David's final episode as hands-on producer, he not only killed off George's long-suffering fiancée Susan Ross (Heidi Swedberg) by having her die of a toxic overdose from the glue on the cheap wedding invitations that George insisted on buying, but also had George (who had been so desperate to get out of the wedding that he tried asking Susan for a prenup in hopes she'd be too offended to marry him; instead, she laughed in his face, knowing she was rich) react to the news more with relief than anything else. Meanwhile, Jerry, Elaine, and Kramer shrugged off Susan's death as a curious development, less worthy of comment than the time Kramer accidentally hit a golf ball into a whale's blowhole.

What David didn't seem to fully grasp until he'd moved on to *Curb* was that the audience already knew, on some level, that they were watching the adventures of four awful people but had decided that their awfulness was outweighed by how well-drawn they were, how sharp their dialogue was, and how cleverly their stories came together, and said, after each despicable act, much like Jerry and George's reflexive apology each time they denied being a gay couple, "Not that there's anything wrong with that!" The phrase might as well have been the mantra of all four friends no matter the people they deceived, mistreated, or stepped on.

The playwright's adage "Drama is about people changing; comedy is about how people never change" was demonstrated more vividly on *Seinfeld* than on any other network sitcom. To the bitter end, nobody hugged and nobody really learned anything. The finale ends with the core quartet behind bars, bantering and repeating dialogue from the very first episode. Jerry, George, Elaine, and Kramer were locked inside a cage of their own narcissism from the start, but because it never occurred to them to think there was anything wrong with that, they carried themselves like the freest people on earth. The final shot is of Jerry in a prison jumpsuit doing stand-up for his fellow inmates. He's the center of attention. Life is good.

—AS & MZS

I Love Lucy (CBS, 1951–1957) Total score: 109

Think of *I Love Lucy*, and you likely think of Lucy and Ethel in the candy factory, with good reason: Not only is it one of the great slapstick set pieces—a vaudeville riff on Charlie Chaplin's factory mishaps in *Modern Times* that's still hilarious after sixty-plus years—it's also emblematic of everything that made *Lucy* the most enduring sitcom of TV's first few decades and an innovatively produced series.

The routine starts innocuously enough—but then every *Lucy* routine does. Lucy Ricardo (Lucille Ball) and her best friend, Ethel Mertz (Vivian Vance), are in the midst of their rocky first day of working in a candy factory. Their supervisor parks them in front of a conveyer belt in the wrapping station and warns them, "If one piece of candy gets past you and into the packing room unwrapped, you're fired!" We know things will go wrong—public embarrassment, after all, is Lucy's specialty—but things start out rather smoothly, with candy coming across the belt slowly enough that Lucy can boast, "Oh, this is easy."

Then the belt moves a little faster, and they begin to notice that unwrapped candies are making it past them. "I think we're fighting a losing game," says Lucy, normally a blind optimist who takes much longer to admit she's failed. Then the belt speeds up even more, and they start shoveling excess candy into their hats, their blouses, even their mouths, just to keep them from going into the packing room unwrapped.

The supervisor wanders in, mistakenly assumes they're doing a great job, and screams for the machinist to "speed it up a little!" And at that point, the defeat turns into a candy massacre, with the women not even bothering to wrap candy anymore, but simply hiding it anywhere and everywhere on their persons that a TV sitcom could comfortably depict in 1952.

Lucy versus the conveyer belt is a dazzling bit of comic construction, building and building until things can't seem to get any more ridiculous, at which point they do. It was a viral video before such a term existed, appearing in every retrospective of *Lucy*, TV's first golden age, the evolution of the sitcom, and of course documentaries about Lucille Ball and Desi Arnaz, married costars whose success with *Lucy* made them the most powerful couple both on and in television. It's so well-known that it has effectively obliterated the rest of the episode, "Job Switching," which finds Lucy and Ethel leaving the house to work while their husbands, Ricky (Desi Arnaz) and Fred (William Frawley), stay home to do the cooking and cleaning.

But here's the thing: Go back and watch the entire episode, and you'll realize just what a mother lode of comic wealth *Lucy* was, week in and week out. "Job Switching" features several other dazzling comic sketches, including one of Ricky and Fred fighting a losing battle of their own in the kitchen after foolishly trying to cook four pounds of rice at once, Lucy struggling to match the technique of a veteran candy dipper, and Ricky getting into a wrestling match with the ironing board. Any one of those scenes would have been enough for the *I Love Lucy* creative team to justifiably call it a day, dump some exposition into the rest of the episode, and move on to next week's big idea. Instead, they kept layering big joke onto big joke, sending them in nearly as fast as the conveyer belt kept taunting Lucy and Ethel with its fathomless candy supply.

But that was *I Love Lucy*, a show nobody quite believed in, starring an actress Hollywood had never quite figured out how to use and the husband CBS wasn't crazy about hiring as part of a package deal, and using a format that was both expensive and untried. The show kept pushing and pushing and finding new ways to exploit the previously untapped comic potential of its leading lady until it not only had become an enormous hit but had invented a new stylistic language for TV comedy. It's not only one of TV's very best sitcoms ever, but its most influential.

Lucille Ball was already forty when *I Love Lucy* debuted, having spent years in the movies never quite achieving stardom, nor having established a niche, and not making enough of an impression in dramatic roles. And as a physical type, she was in an impossible position, not hubba-hubba enough to play bombshells or femme fatales or innocuous enough to play bland hearth-keeper types (the easy-pop eyes and braying laugh made that tough even when she was younger), but she was paradoxically considered too pretty to play goofballs and freaks. She finally got a great role in that last category courtesy of *My Favorite Husband*, a popular radio comedy that CBS wanted to turn into a TV series. Ball wanted her real-life husband, a bandleader, to play her onscreen spouse. CBS worried that the audience wouldn't accept a curvy redhead marrying a Cuban man, and Arnaz wanted to produce the show out of Los Angeles, which, in an era when most TV was produced in New York, made *Lucy* a time-zone nightmare.

Astonishingly, Lucy and Desi got everything they wanted from CBS, including the right to shoot their series on location on a Los Angeles soundstage before a live studio audience, their way. This turned out to be the couple's masterstroke—a decision that revolutionized not just the visual and structural grammar of the sitcom but the business of TV itself. It helped make *Lucy* the number one show during four of its six seasons, and built Lucy and Desi's company, Desilu Productions, into the medium's first independently owned and operated mini-empire.

Prior to *Lucy*, most TV sitcoms (most TV, period) were shot and broadcast live with grainy black-and-white video cameras, and it was understood that all that work would vanish into the ether unless the network pointed 16mm- or 35mm-film cameras at the monitors to produce a permanent record, known as a "kinescope." (The first broadcast-standard videotape system wasn't unveiled until 1956, five years after *Lucy*'s debut.) The kinescope method resulted in a record that was even more crude than what people saw on their then-tiny TV screens: a soupy, smeary image that captured phosphorescent-looking light trails when the camera or an actor moved too quickly. Ball and Arnaz eliminated these problems by inverting the usual production process. Rather than produce the series as a TV program and record a rough impression of it on celluloid, they shot *Lucy* as if it were a series of twenty-six-minute feature films, on 35mm black-and-white, then cut it on film and shipped finished prints to the network. The network then projected each new *Lucy* episode at New York headquarters and beamed it to the public, just as it would a feature film or cartoon short shot on celluloid.

Besides eliminating a step and producing a more pleasing image, this method had a number of other benefits, all of which accrued to Desilu.

First, the Ball-Arnaz production model let the show's directors design musical numbers and comedy routines for the camera, as a feature film-maker might, rather than treating them as stage-bound events that happened to have cameras pointed at them. If you look at old blueprints and photos of Desilu's soundstages, you'll see that a number of permanent sets were built so that the performers and crew could move about (and move their cameras about) with maximum freedom. The 35mm-film cameras blocked the sight lines of most visitors; when scenes took place at the Tropicana nightclub, the audience was anywhere from thirty to forty feet back from Ricky, and there was plenty of space between the four "front" tables so that cameras could be pushed between them to follow dancers or push in for a close-up of the bandleader or the kooky redhead who'd somehow managed to sneak in as a waitress or chorus girl.

Second, the Desilu model captured every moment with three film cameras and then pieced together the best takes later to create a complete scene. This resulted in a more consistent comedic product than shooting things live and filming whatever happened to be captured on the monitor (including blown lines, botched camera moves, and moments where the studio director switched from camera A to camera B too late to catch an important moment). Directors could, and did, reposition the cameras between takes and get alternate angles on the same action, or reaction shots from peripheral characters. All of this cumulatively made *I Love Lucy* seem somehow bigger and more intense than other sitcoms of its time—more like a "little movie" than a televised play. When people use the phrase "multi-camera sitcom" to describe the format of a TV show, they are naming a type of production that *I Love Lucy* perfected.

Third, the Desilu model let Ball and Arnaz control their show in ways that prior sitcom makers could not have imagined. They weren't creating half-hour episodes that were then broadcast by the studio on the studio's terms, and recorded as kinescopes if the studio felt like it at whatever quality they deemed suitable, then filed away on a shelf at network headquarters; they were creating *properties*, entries in an ongoing library. And they were doing it on their own terms: insisting upon a certain kind of film stock, a certain way of lighting, a certain way of moving the camera. Finally they were letting CBS broadcast the result, and keeping properly stored copies for themselves on 35mm film. Forward-thinking as Ball and Arnaz were, they had no way of knowing how important a good image would become. High-quality celluloid didn't just produce a more attractive picture than anything coming through TV sets in 1951, it produced an image that would remain viable even as TVs got better over the course of many decades, while kinescopes of shows like *The Honeymooners*, *The Ernie Kovacs Show*, and *Playhouse 90* started to look as if they'd been filmed through a fish tank. Any TV production company known for putting out great-looking shows should have a shrine to Lucy and Desi in their lobby and meditate in front of it each morning.

Ditto any production company, network, or media conglomerate that refers to its "library of titles," a notion that Desilu made real. When CBS balked at the high cost of shooting on 35mm film, Arnaz worked out what is now considered one of the most producer-favorable deals in the history of TV: Desilu would cover all costs associated with making the program their way, and in return they would retain rights to all film prints and negatives. This meant that when *Lucy* was sold into syndication, in the first so-called ancillary rights deal ever worked out by an independent TV producer, CBS did not receive a penny. The network made money from ads during its first broadcast and repeats. And that was it.

Meanwhile, as Desi Arnaz acted as a combination Orson Welles and

David O. Selznick of sitcom production, Lucille Ball kept busy on the creative side, looking for additional projects for Desilu to oversee. Her judgment was superb. Desilu was founded in 1951, sold to Paramount Television in 1967, and discontinued as a "brand" in 1975. During that time, it produced thirty-one series, including such long-running hits as *The Untouchables*; *Star Trek*; *Mission: Impossible*; *I Spy*; *The Dick Van Dyke Show*; *The Lucy Show*; *My Favorite Martian*; *Gomer Pyle, U.S.M.C.*; *Family Affair*; *Hogan's Heroes*; *That Girl*; and *Mannix*.

Given all this behind-the-scenes technical and financial innovation, the show would be a shoo-in for the Pantheon even if it were artistically hit-and-miss. But it was never that. *Lucy* could be formidable even during its unsteady later years—which found Lucy and Ricky struggling to recapture that old spark after having a baby, Ricky Jr., in what was the highest-rated single episode of a TV show aired up to that point in time. And during its comic peak, roughly seasons 2 through 5, *I Love Lucy* was sidesplittingly funny in the manner of early sound comedies by Laurel and Hardy, the Marx Brothers, Abbott and Costello, W. C. Fields, and Mae West.

Ball pushed for Arnaz to play Ricky as a last-ditch attempt to save a relationship that had nearly ended in divorce once before—and that would end permanently in 1960, shortly after the end of *The Lucy-Desi Comedy Hour*, a series of specials that continued *I Love Lucy*'s story and characters. If the Ricardo marriage didn't reflect the problems Lucy and Desi were going through, it was nonetheless fraught with tension. Lucy Ricardo wanted the fame, the glamour, or at least the opportunity to express herself that Lucille Ball had, but her quest to escape the drudgeries of housewifedom inevitably ended in embarrassment for her, and exasperation for Ricky. Later seasons were set predominantly in Hollywood, and then in Europe—serialized comedy, sort of, decades before it was enshrined on shows like *Soap* and *Mary Hartman, Mary Hartman*—with Ricky's career pressures wreaking havoc on the marriage. Most episodes hewed to the same farcical template, with Lucy failing at whatever scheme she'd tried to engineer and being chastised or punished by Ricky. Her fate would be purely humiliating if the love between them weren't self-evident. Warmth notwithstanding, this aspect of the series has dated badly, to put it mildly—it was raising the hackles of feminists as early as the 1970s, when the series was still a big earner in syndication—and it will prove a deal-breaker for some. Ditto Lucy's and Ethel's gibes about men and Ricky's and Fred's grousing about women, which encapsulate the hidebound attitude toward gender roles that made life unbearable for women (and men) who couldn't fit into 1950s America's rigidly defined slots.

But if so many of Lucy's escapades ended in misery for her, they gave joy to the audience by demonstrating Ball's command of verbal and physical comedy. If Lucy Ricardo was often a clown or a victim, the actress who created her remained in control of both the character and the series built to showcase her dazzling gifts. You want verbal comedy? Ask Ball to play progressively drunk as Lucy tries to extol the virtues of 46-proof health tonic Vitameatavegamin while filming a commercial. You need comedy even more physical than the conveyer belt? Put Lucy in a vat of grapes for a knockdown brawl with an Italian vineyard worker. You want to know what the absence of vanity looks like? Slap a putty nose on her face to disguise her from William Holden (one of many guests playing themselves in the Hollywood season), then light the thing on fire. Want to make clear she's as great a comic performer as Groucho Marx? Have her re-create the mirror scene from *Duck Soup*, opposite Harpo.

Even more so than the candy factory, the mirror scene might be Ball's greatest moment as a performer. It equals its inspiration in physical assurance, but it also serves as a comment on Ball's influences and the traditions that her sitcom deepened and expanded. And it shows how, by moving to television, Ball achieved a dream that had eluded her in movies: to be acknowledged as the equal of the men who preceded her.

—MZS & AS

Deadwood (HBO, 2004–2006) Total score: 107

Whenever arguments are held about the best TV dramas of all time, and particularly of this modern golden age, *Deadwood*—like Deadwood's craven mayor, E. B. Farnum (William Sanderson), whenever there's important scheming to do—gets left out. It's not that people can't recognize the brilliant performances, particularly by Ian McShane as the show's cutthroat antihero, bartending crime lord Al Swearengen, or the poetry of the dialogue by the show's creator, David Milch. It's that

Deadwood ran only three seasons when Milch had been very publicly angling for at least four, and that HBO's promise of two sequel movies was never fulfilled. How can a show that finished so abruptly, and in such a messy fashion, possibly compete with a *Sopranos* or a *Wire*, whose creators got to end their creations on their own terms?

Easy. Because messiness and an aversion to closure were parts of the deal with *Deadwood* from the start—and because the real-world furor over the cancellation obscures the fact that the actual ending Milch wrote under tough circumstances was as appropriate and true to the spirit of the thing as anything he might have devised if he'd had a couple of more years to think about it.

Not that Milch—a devout believer in the notion that when men plan, God laughs—was ever much for long-range preparation. The series is not only TV's great unfinished masterpiece, but its greatest improvised masterpiece, with many of those incredible lines of dialogue—"What a type you must consort with, that you not fear beating for such an insult"—dreamed up only days, or even hours, before the actors spoke them before HBO's cameras.

Deadwood tried to retell the story of the founding of civilization (American and otherwise) by reimagining Deadwood, a Dakota gold-mining camp that went from a chaotic hellhole in an unincorporated territory to an incorporated town within an incorporated US state in the space of a few post–Civil War years. The show was, in no particular order, a Western, a gangster picture, a political drama, a lewd farce, and a comedy of manners; an operatic potboiler chock-full of sex, violence, and profanity; a sustained long-form narrative that interweaves parallel plots tighter than a hangman's rope; a satire on American hypocrisy and greed; a portrait of needy, ambitious people who see through other people's illusions but cleave tight to their own; a revisionist look at frontier life; a case study of a civilization struggling to create itself; and a weekly showcase for characters and dialogue so rich in complexity and contradiction that they deserve to be called Shakespearean.

Milch was uniquely suited to this quixotic task. A Yale-educated recovering drug addict and onetime pupil of Robert Penn Warren, he had written and produced for *Hill Street Blues* and *NYPD Blue*, so he understood the project from a literary and philosophical as well as populist standpoint, and even when he was writing theatrically complex, ostentatiously profane monologues for his characters, he always kept his finger on the show's humanist pulse. Like Robert Altman's town-based Western *McCabe & Mrs. Miller*, which Milch cited as a primary influence, *Deadwood* took a sardonic yet compassionate God's-eye view of its setting, observing powerful and helpless individuals as they tried (and often failed) to better themselves.

There are no pure heroes in *Deadwood*, but two characters dominate: Swearengen and newly appointed sheriff Seth Bullock (Timothy Olyphant). On first glance, Swearengen resembles a nineteenth-century mob boss—a mustachioed godfather in a stinky suit, making a fortune dealing dope, liquor, gambling, and sex in his saloon, the Gem. Bullock is a terse, tightly wound man of action in the Gary Cooper–Clint Eastwood mode. (His ramrod posture and machinelike stride suggest he really does have steel in his spine.) Yet both men are more complex, at times confounding, than this summary suggests.

Swearengen is a vicious sociopath who lectures employees on the right way to clean up a bloodstain and delivers ornately profane monologues while being serviced by prostitutes. But he has a weird tender streak. He claims to employ a handicapped cleaning woman, Jewel (Geri Jewell), to give penniless johns a hooker they can afford, but that seems to be a macho lie. Al dominates and abuses another of his prostitutes, Trixie (Paula Malcomson), but seems incomplete and dissatisfied after Trixie takes up with Bullock's business partner, the Jewish frontiersman Sol Star (John Hawkes). In the first-season finale, when the Reverend H. W. Smith (Ray McKinnon) lies dying in dementia from a brain tumor, Al—recalling the similar struggle his late brother went through—strangles him to end his suffering, tenderly whispering, "You can go now, brother," as he holds a rag over the man's mouth and nose.

If Swearengen is an evil man with good in him, Bullock is his opposite—a straitlaced, married businessman who intervenes in other people's troubles yet seems incapable of controlling his own volcanic rage. These flaws combine to devastating effect in the first-season finale, when Bullock's lover, widow Alma Garret (Molly Parker), receives an unexpected visit from her ne'er-do-well father. When Alma's dad tries to blackmail her by threatening to spread rumors that she killed her husband and took over his gold claim, Bullock goes berserk and beats the man to a pulp in the middle of a crowded casino, then asks a visiting

Army colonel to protect the man against various enemies, Bullock included. "We all have bloody thoughts," the colonel tells Bullock, a half-statement that completes itself in the mind.

Bullock and Swearengen's psychological-poetic connection forms the core of *Deadwood*. They're surrounded by characters every bit as tangled, from Swearengen's murderous right hand, Dan Dority (W. Earl Brown), who clings to Al the way a toddler clings to Daddy, to Swearengen's chief competitor, saloon maven Cyrus Tolliver (Powers Boothe), who treats his onetime employee, prostitute-turned-madam Joanie Stubbs (Kim Dickens), like an ex-wife, a surrogate daughter, and a business rival all at once. The show's complexities are embodied in Milch's dialogue, which weds profanity to poetry, encloses thoughts inside thoughts, and back-loads its sentences in the manner of pre-twentieth-century verse, unpacking its components in order of importance and withholding the most potent image or idea until the end. Tending a wounded Sol Star, Trixie says, "I pray to God your shoulder pains like some sharp-toothed creature's inside you and at it and gnawing." Swearengen chides smart-mouthed henchman Silas Adams (Titus Welliver), "Over time, your quickness with a cocky rejoinder must have gotten you many punches in the face," and heals a dispute with Dan by promising, "Whatever looks ahead of grievous abominations and disorder, you and me walk into it together like always."

All Milch's characters are this rich and slippery. With her doe-eyed "respectability," flirting skill, and secret drug habit, Garret is part sturdy frontier widow, part femme fatale. Farnum, Swearengen's emissary and foil, is a scheming little weasel, but he's got an agile mind, a poetic tongue, and grand ambitions. Doc Cochran (Brad Dourif) is a one-man board of health and an angry hermit drowning his Civil War nightmares in whiskey. Trixie's gutter mouth and matter-of-fact carnality contrast with her devotion to Sol, Swearengen, and an orphaned girl, while the romanticized toughness of Calamity Jane (Robin Weigert)— who in another era had been played in a movie by Doris Day—was revealed to be a defense mechanism of a profoundly damaged woman.

Deadwood pairs the characters' private struggles with larger events. In the fourth episode of the first season, famous gunslinger and dying alcoholic Wild Bill Hickok (Keith Carradine) is shot dead by Jack McCall (Garret Dillahunt). McCall's flight, capture, and subsequent trial are public events, the outcomes of which affect every citizen. Milch presented the shooting not just as a random act of murder but as a celebrity assassination and a signpost marking the end of the Old West as both fact and legend. The first-season finale mirrored Bullock's accepting his destiny as sheriff with a cavalry garrison's arrival in town—complementary images of order confronting chaos.

The second season deals with the arrival of Francis Wolcott, chief geologist for mining mogul George Hearst. (He was played by Dillahunt, with Milch not caring if viewers recognized him as Jack McCall sporting a beard and a more cultured accent.) On the one hand, Wolcott represents the encroachment of both capitalism and civilization—that a man as powerful as Hearst sees value in the camp only makes the place more appealing to the political swells in the territory's capital, Yankton. On the other hand, Wolcott is a serial killer of women, and the techniques he and his lackeys use to gain a monopoly on the camp's gold claims suggest that the optimism so many of Deadwood's citizens arrived with should be severely tempered.

Hearst himself (TV veteran Gerald McRaney, giving—like so many of the show's actors—the best performance of his career) arrives at the end of the second season and dominates the third. He is a revolting depiction of pure capitalism, uninterested in any issue beyond acquiring more gold (or, as he puts it, "the color"), and with the physical and political might to run roughshod over Swearengen, Bullock, and the rest of the camp. Though Al would gain the occasional victory—like Dan beating Hearst's chief goon to death in the thoroughfare at the end of the most savage fight scene in TV history—Hearst's ultimate victory would be absolute. At the same time, we also meet Jack Langrishe (Brian Cox), head of an acting troupe whose members aim to bring some culture to this remote community. Years later, Milch would say that the stories of Hearst and Langrishe were linked: "It's seemed to me that when the bosses seem to be in charge, there's always room for art as a compensatory dynamic. I think that what we do in our society, the best of us as storytellers, present an alternative to the story the bosses are telling."

At the time of its cancellation, *Deadwood* was the most expensive regular series on TV, costing $6 million per episode. This was partly due to the difficulty of creating a full-scale replica of an Old West town, with period clothes, horses, and carriages, in which many of the interiors and exteriors were fully functioning, stage-play-like sets, with catwalks covered in fixed lights that could instantly mimic the position of the sun at particular times of day. But Milch's methods were a much bigger problem. Actors spoke of having just a few minutes to rehearse fiendishly complex dialogue that had been written or rewritten minutes earlier by Milch. There were stories of whole sequences, sometimes whole episodes, being junked and then recast or reshot because Milch wasn't happy with them for whatever reason. During a set visit in early 2006, Milch admitted to one of the cowriters of this book that much of the third season had been completely reshot. These stories make one wonder if *Deadwood* wasn't an example of a great artist going from "worth the trouble" to "not worth the trouble" in his patron's eyes based on the perusal of a balance sheet.

Between the expense (not helped by HBO having to share ownership of the series with Paramount) and the way Milch's creative process made outside input impossible, there had always been tension between the show and HBO's executives, and Milch suspected the end was coming faster than he wanted. The finale is a triumph of bloody-toothed capitalism: Bullock and Swearengen spend the season amassing an army to battle Hearst's hired thugs, but after Hearst arranges the murder of Alma's devoted prospector husband, Whitney Ellsworth (Jim Beaver), and Trixie botches an impromptu assassination attempt on Hearst, the camp loses its will to fight. Alma sells Hearst her claim, Bullock loses a rigged election to remain sheriff, and Al murders innocent young prostitute Jen as a sacrificial stand-in for Trixie, whose death Hearst has demanded. The camp is saved, and still on deck to be absorbed into the American experiment, but at a horrible cost. As Hearst smugly rides out of the camp, we end the show with Al on his knees in his office, scrubbing Jen's blood from the floorboards. Junior henchman Johnny Burns (Sean Bridgers), who was sweet on Jen, awkwardly steps in and asks if she suffered. "I was as gentle as I was able, and that's the last we'll fuckin' speak of it, Johnny," Al replies, then returns to the bloodstain, muttering, "Wants me to tell him somethin' pretty."

Was there more story to tell? Sure. Hearst's victory proved less absolute in the long term, and there are a lot of other fascinating historical details to work in, including Sol's political career, Bullock's friendship with the young Teddy Roosevelt, and the 1879 fire that burned down the Gem and a large swath of the town, forcing Swearengen and others to rebuild bigger and fancier than ever. But it's hard to imagine a final moment better representing the totality of Deadwood than Al Swearengen up to his arms in blood, covering up one of the violent truths of building a civilization with one last lie agreed upon by all involved.

—AS & MZS

All in the Family (CBS, 1971–1979) Total score: 106

> *Boy, the way Glenn Miller played*
> *Songs that made "The Hit Parade"*
> *Guys like us, we had it made*
> *Those were the days!*

That's the opening theme to *All in the Family*, which premiered January 12, 1971, and ran eight years, spawning multiple spin-offs (including the continuation series *Archie Bunker's Place*) and making its executive producer, Norman Lear, into a TV powerhouse.

Lear's sitcom revolved around a working-class Queens family: Archie Bunker (Carroll O'Connor); his "dingbat" wife, Edith (Jean Stapleton); his daughter, Gloria (Sally Struthers); and his liberal son-in-law, Mike "Meathead" Stivic (Rob Reiner). The plots contained some of the expected sitcom fodder: misunderstandings, silly deceptions, crises that turned out to be no big deal. But the heart of the show was topical humor. The Bunkers and their friends and neighbors debated war, religion, drugs, gun control, sex, sexism, gay rights, race relations, immigration, taxation, the environmental movement, and everything else under the sun. The series wasn't just a situation comedy, it was an ongoing national conversation rooted in multifaceted characters.

"If your spics and your spades want their rightful share of the American dream, let 'em get out there and hustle for it like I done," Archie groused to Mike, who was agitating about civil rights yet again. "So now you're going to tell me the black man has just as much chance as the white man to get a job?" Mike demands. "More," Archie says. "He has more. I didn't have no million people marchin' and protestin' to get me my job." "No," Edith interrupts. "His uncle got it for him."

"Racial balance is important in everything," Mike declares in another episode. "Take education: Why do you think it's so tough for a black student to become a doctor?" Archie: "Because nobody wants to see a black guy coming at them with a knife."

It's hard to imagine the shock audiences felt the first time they saw this series on commercial TV, in prime time. Prior to the late '60s and early '70s, pop culture either made an ostentatiously big show of grappling with hot-button topics (usually in Oscar-baiting message films or dour live TV dramas) or plugged its ears and whistled a happy tune. There was a deep schism between how people talked in private (and what they talked about) and what you saw on TV and on movie screens and heard on the radio. When Norman Lear got approval from CBS to create an American version of the popular British sitcom *Till Death Us Do Part*—which had the same concept as *All in the Family* but was less elegantly directed and tonally adventurous—the boundaries that once separated socially aware popular art from mainstream entertainment became more porous. In the aftermath of the '60s, pop culture started to let the world in, and not in dribs and drabs. The floodgates opened. *All in the Family*'s 1971 debut helped knock them down. Three seasons of Lear's surprise hit helped prepare audiences for Mel Brooks's 1974 smash *Blazing Saddles*, a racial burlesque on horseback that you could imagine Archie's African American neighbor George Jefferson (Sherman Hemsley)—a pioneering small businessman whose language was nearly as racist as Archie's—recommending to everyone he knew.

Some of the show's nonwhite supporting characters were Sidney Poitier–style credit-to-his-race types to whom Archie could have no rational objection (George's son, Lionel, for example, was a handsome, unflappable cipher), but a surprisingly high percentage were as flawed and raucous as Archie. Their talk was sometimes smart, sometimes dumb, always blunt. It was scalding but necessary, like steam from a teakettle. The show's core sensibility was basically liberal; that's why Archie got stuck with all the malapropisms. But it would be wrong to claim that Archie was just a rhetorical punching bag, or that Mike was intended as a righteous truth-telling character. O'Connor was such an appealing performer—never more so than when Archie dropped the bluster and spoke from the heart—that the character became an emblem of working-class grit and Depression-era resilience. (In one of President

Richard Nixon's secret White House tapes, Nixon and his staff decry the show's ribbing of Archie and affectionately label him a "hard hat.") And it wasn't lost on the writers—or the audience—that Mike and Gloria sponged off Edith and Archie even as they lectured them on the right way to live. Archie ridiculed Mike's mooching in almost every episode; it was the knockout punch he threw after Mike zinged him with college-boy jabs.

The program switched from broad comedy to kitchen-sink drama and back so subtly that the shift rarely felt forced, even in the harrowing season 8 episode in which Edith narrowly escaped being raped, or in the quietly devastating second season premiere for *Archie Bunker's Place*, when we gradually realize that Edith has died by watching Archie putter around the house without her. Throughout, the blocking owed more to live televised theater than to *I Love Lucy*–style three-camera sitcoms. When characters turned introspective, the camera crept in slowly from a medium shot to a tight close-up, creating a protected space where delicate monologues could flower. The finest example might be the 1978 episode "Two's a Crowd," in which Archie and Mike accidentally get locked in the storeroom of Archie's bar and pass the time by boozing and talking. Archie casually states that his father taught him everything he knows, and when Mike gently suggests that Archie's father was wrong to pass on his bigotry to his son, episode director Paul Bogart zooms in on O'Connor, watching Archie's face soften. Wading into memories, he turns into a boy who lives in terror and awe of his old man. "Your father?" Archie says, to Mike and to himself. "The breadwinner of the house, there? The man who goes out and busts his butt to put a roof over your head and clothes on your back? You call your father *wrong*?"

The success of Lear's show inspired good spin-offs (*The Jeffersons*, *Maude*), bad spin-offs (*Gloria*, *Archie Bunker's Place*), and one half-great, half-terrible spin-off of a spin-off (*Good Times*, starring Esther Rolle as Florida Evans, Maude's former housekeeper). None equaled their inspiration in comic force. For a long time after its run ended, broadcast TV was inhospitable to shows like *All in the Family*. This was partly due to TV's splintering from a handful of channels into hundreds. But an equal or larger part of the blame can be laid at the feet of broadcast network executives and their marketers, who figured out (sometime in the '80s) that they could make more ad money by junking the "Big Tent" model and appealing to white college graduates with loads of disposable income—a description that rules out anyone who looks or sounds like a character from *All in the Family* (even Mike or Gloria). In the '80s and '90s, networks gentrified prime time, banishing demographically déclassé minority characters to "netlets" like UPN and the WB, and all but banning straightforwardly political topics while retaining harsh language and cutting remarks (a trend that reached its apotheosis on Fox's casually ugly *Married... with Children*). Except for certain corners of cable, you didn't hear people talking about race, class, religion, or politics, unless their talk was treated as the centerpiece of a special episode (like the episode of *NYPD Blue* where Sipowicz uses the n-word) or treated as jocular and sarcastic and "just kidding" (like the banter on *Glee* and *Community*, which enclosed inflammatory terms inside facetious air quotes).

Thankfully, recent series like *Black-ish*, *Fresh Off the Boat*, *Master of None*, *The Carmichael Show*, and *Modern Family* have picked up Lear's torch—perhaps a delayed reaction to a two-term presidency by a chief executive of color as well as social advances like the battle for marriage equality and a growing awareness that straight white people weren't going to be the dominant demographic group for much longer, and pop culture would have no choice but to acknowledge it. These are the days.

—MZS

No-Doubt-About-It Classics

M*A*S*H (CBS, 1972–1983) Total score: 105

Nearly 106 million people watched "Goodbye, Farewell and Amen," the series finale of *M*A*S*H*. At the time, that was the biggest audience ever for a TV broadcast in America, shattering the previous record of 78 million for *The Fugitive* finale, and holding on to the title for nearly thirty years until the Super Bowl started averaging a bigger audience beginning in 2010. And if you treat sports as a separate thing, then *M*A*S*H* not only still has the record for an episode of television but will always have the record. More people than ever are watching TV, but their eyeballs are split among so many different shows, at so many different times, that there's just no way a modern series will generate the same kind of mass audience that was available in 1983, when there were essentially only three channels to choose from (four if PBS counts).

But why does *M*A*S*H*, of all shows, have the record? It's one of the greatest shows of all time, sure, and it aired during the height of the Big Three network era, but a lot of other classics did as well; *All in the Family*'s run largely overlapped with *M*A*S*H*'s, and was often the more popular and acclaimed show, but its finale (before it transitioned into *Archie Bunker's Place*) averaged a little over a third of the audience that came for "Goodbye, Farewell and Amen."

M*A*S*H had a few built-in advantages. First, it ended at a time when grand TV series finales were still the exception rather than the norm. For most of the medium's history to that point, TV shows didn't so much end as stop. Last episodes told stories very much like the ones from the week before: Gilligan and the Skipper would have to wait for a reunion movie or three to get rescued from the island because in the last regular episode, Gilligan was dressing up as a woman to trick the native king of a nearby island out of throwing Ginger, Mary Ann, or Mrs. Howell into a nearby volcano. (You can look it up.) Television narratives were designed to be open-ended, and many executives believed the syndication value would be hurt if the story ever concluded and Wednesday's rerun of the definitive ending was followed by Thursday's repeat of the pilot episode. But if the business didn't like final chapters, the audience did: One of the reasons that the *Fugitive* audience was so huge was because the finale avoided tradition and (spoiler) let Richard Kimble catch the one-armed man and clear his name.

Second, *M*A*S*H* was Important with a capital *I* in a way that even *All in the Family* or *The Mary Tyler Moore Show* (another '70s sitcom with an atypically final finale) could not be. It debuted in 1972, two years after the release of the beloved, Oscar-winning film (both of them based on the novel by Richard Hooker). Like the movie, it was technically set in the time of the Korean War but was really telling stories about Vietnam, and at a time when all but the most blinkered of hawks had accepted that we had lost that conflict. It provided not only laughter as a tonic for the horrors

on the network news but at times an incredibly thoughtful examination of what it was like over there, all with the comforting filter of the Korea references. And though it kept running for seven years after the last US chopper left Saigon (and outlasted America's involvement in Korea by almost nine years), the later seasons coincided with a time when the country was finally ready to more directly confront the subject on film, through the likes of *Apocalypse Now*, *The Deer Hunter*, and *Coming Home*.

Beyond its value as a coded, cathartic narrative about an ongoing national trauma, *M*A*S*H* was a great TV show almost all the way around, and it shared a quality with many other beloved series: It was not ultimately about any individual character but a place (the 4077th Mobile Army Surgical Hospital unit), which in turn represented a particular institution (the United States military) and a certain way of dealing with the world (bureaucracy, God forbid). This might have been the real secret of its popular success: Even though most of us aren't in a life-and-death business, we've all chafed under rules that seemed nonsensical or self-defeating, or tried to do good work without proper funding or moral support, or resolved to grin and bear it while an incompetent or cruel superior made our lives difficult.

The style and structure did a lot to make an experience that was thankfully foreign to most viewers feel welcoming. The consistent storytelling ensured that no matter where you joined the narrative, you could find your footing within a couple of scenes. Every episode included one or more familiar story beats: the arrival of choppers bearing fresh wounded; gory surgeries leavened by snide or silly jokes; corpse disposal; pranks and group activities (such as dances or parties or Alan Alda's Hawkeye trying to see how many people he could cram into a Volkswagen); griping about bad food; the reading and writing of letters. This all drove home the grinding repetitive nature of life in the camp and anchored all the silliness in the blood and muck of reality and showed how the former made the latter more bearable, at least some of the time. Care of the wounded was shown to be an assembly-line process that was meant to heal the sick, or at least make their deaths as painless as possible, but was hampered by a lack of funding and proper equipment (the doctors and nurses were constantly having to improvise with materials that weren't designed for

medicine) as well as by the indifference of the military brass or their paper-pushing underlings and acts of sabotage by someone that a major character had offended. Colonel Blake (McLean Stevenson) and especially Colonel Potter (Harry Morgan) were constantly angling to get rest and recreation (R&R) for their men and women, or horse-trade for much-needed supplies (the Holy Grail was always a jeep), and there were times when Hawkeye or B.J. (Mike Farrell) or some other character would fudge paperwork or pull a switcheroo that would make life bearable for someone else, if only for a while.

The series' original producers, Larry Gelbart and Gene Reynolds, resisted CBS's orders to add a laugh track. They wanted the show to have real stakes, so that the jokes would feel like welcome relief from the horrors beyond the camp. As a compromise, they were allowed to mute the laughter during surgical scenes. Even in the first season, M*A*S*H wasn't shy about going for the tears with an episode like "Sometimes You Hear the Bullet," where a childhood friend of Hawkeye's dies in the 4077th operating room; afterward, Colonel Blake tries to snap Hawkeye out of his grief by reminding him of the first two rules of war he learned: "Rule

Number One is young men die and Rule Number Two is, doctors can't change Rule Number One."

The series kept experimenting and shifting the line between comedy and tragedy. The characters drank hard and there were many subplots about soldiers, doctors, and nurses self-medicating to numb the pain of facing horror every day; season 3's "The Consultant" introduces Hawkeye and his original sidekick Trapper John (Wayne Rogers) to a sort of Ghost of Boozing Future in the form of a veteran Army doctor who didn't drink during World War I, drank only after the end of the workday during World War II, and now drinks all the time in Korea. "I'm suffering from one of the three sure signs of age," he tells Hawkeye, who judges him harshly. "Bit of a spread, gray hair, feet of clay. I wish you better luck on your third war." Blake was eventually replaced by Morgan as Sherman T. Potter, a World War I cavalry veteran and regular Army man, who, unlike Henry, was no pushover, but who also came to appreciate the need for Hawkeye's pranks and quips amid the theater of war. Morgan's innate, unflappable dignity in the role would come to define the show as much as Hawkeye's shift from womanizing cad to liberal crusader. There were

many stories in which the loss of physical ability became a metaphor for the realization that dreams can't always come true and you unfortunately have to accept it: Among the better examples are season 4's "Smilin' Jack," about a hotshot chopper pilot who's on track to set a service record when he's grounded by a diabetes diagnosis, and season 5's "End Run," which finds Radar comforting a college football star whose leg has to be amputated.

Psychology, and the value of psychotherapy, became increasingly important as the show wore on, especially in stories that involved Major Sidney Freedman (Allan Arbus). In season 6's "War of Nerves," he stays at the 4077th to heal physical wounds and ends up setting up a makeshift practice in a tent and offering all of the major characters a chance to talk about their problems; nearly everyone initially resists but almost immediately gives in. Among other things, he helps chief nurse Margaret Houlihan (Loretta Swit) and recently arrived surgeon Charles Emerson Winchester III (David Ogden Stiers) realize that they bicker all the time because they have feelings for each other. Sidney is at the heart of the series finale's most heart-wrenching subplot, helping Hawkeye push past denial and realize that a chicken a woman strangled so as not to reveal a busload of refugees' position to the enemy was not a chicken after all but her own baby.

The show took risks with form as well as content, growing bolder by the season. You could see harbingers of this restlessness in the season 1 finale, "Showtime," which crosscuts a performance by a visiting USO show with Henry Blake's waiting for word on whether his wife has given birth back home; the staccato editing (hard-cutting between cornball USO comedy and musical performances and the mundane daily life of the camp) evokes Bob Fosse's innovative *Cabaret*, which had come out eighteen months earlier. The show did many episodes with de facto voice-overs (in the form of letters being written or read; season 4's "Dear Ma," from Radar's point of view, is the sweetest), as well as stories told from the perspectives of minor characters or visitors to the camp (the peak was season 7's "Point of View," where the camera becomes the first-person representation of what a wounded soldier sees). Season 4 ended with "The Interview," an oft-imitated episode presented as a black-and-white news documentary.

The only aspect of *M*A*S*H* that hasn't aged well is its portrait of women. It was openly if benignly sexist in its early years, though not as brutally as Altman's film (where Trapper John, played by Elliott Gould, pleads with Henry to "give me at least one nurse who knows how to work in close without getting her tits in my way"). But there were never any major recurring female characters except for Margaret, who spent the series' early years as a cartoonish foil besotted with Larry Linville's craven Major Frank Burns; she would mature over time and become Hawkeye's ally (and occasionally more than that), though their accord took away most of the humor associated with a character once known as "Hot Lips." For the most part, the other nurses were depicted as a Greek chorus for the men in the foreground, as emblems of domesticity or motherly/big sisterly nurturing during off-hours, and sexual prizes for Hawkeye. They were so neglected that whenever they appeared, the show worked their names into the dialogue so that we could tell them apart. The series doesn't deserve to be called misogynistic, as the nurses were treated with affection; it was homosocial (meaning it was concerned with male values in a male world). There's truth to the perception that in later years it became one of the most aggressively feminist series on network TV, thanks mainly to Alda's influence behind the scenes. His name became a synonym for "sensitive New Age man," but Hawkeye's nonstop sexual remarks around women undercut this perception. In terms of representation, M*A*S*H never quite put its money where its feminist mouth was.

But, judged purely as an extended piece of comic storytelling, the show was truly bold, and it grew more audacious by the season. As executive producer, Alda transformed M*A*S*H from a comedy with serious moments to a drama that paused for wisecracks. The more anarchic early years of Gelbart and Reynolds, or even the middle seasons with head writers Ken Levine and David Isaacs, were better and more well-rounded versions of the show—and ones that had no problem going very grim when the occasion called for it. But despite fans' gripes about the more virtuous, late-'70s incarnations of Hawkeye, B.J., and Hot Lips, those later seasons gave M*A*S*H an added weight that made "Goodbye, Farewell and Amen" feel less like a sitcom finale than a wake for a revered institution.

The finale's size—the length of five episodes spliced together—reinforced that feeling, as did the somber tone. Hawkeye has landed in an Army mental hospital after a nervous breakdown, and over the course of the first hour or so, Sidney Freedman helps him come to grips with what that chicken really was. The snobbish Winchester (a more impressive foil for Hawkeye and B.J. than Burns had been) befriends a surrendering unit of Chinese musicians, whom he teaches to play his beloved Mozart, only to be devastated when they're killed after leaving his care. Even perennially upbeat Father Mulcahy (William Christopher) doesn't seem likely to leave the war unscathed: An injury suffered during an act of heroism slowly robs him of his hearing.

The final moments present Hawkeye and B.J. as the paragons of tender '70s masculinity that they had become. "I want you to know how much you meant to me," Hawkeye tells B.J. "I can't imagine what this place would have been like if I hadn't found you here," B.J. replies, fighting back tears. B.J.'s refusal to admit that this would be the last time he and Hawkeye would see each other also functioned as a commentary on how hard it can be for fans to let go of their favorite shows, and vice versa, and of course the final image would be the message B.J. spelled out in rocks for his best friend to read as his chopper left the 4077th forever:

"GOODBYE."

—AS & MZS

Hill Street Blues (NBC, 1981–1987) Total score: 104

For a show that's one of the most groundbreaking and influential in TV history, there actually aren't a lot of elements of *Hill Street Blues* that, on their own, were all that original. The serialized structure was borrowed from daytime soaps. The black comedy and sense of urban decay were straight out of '70s cop movies. The chaotic look of the project (with desaturated colors, handheld photography, and abrupt cuts from scene to scene) came from documentaries. The roving camera that pushed in and out of crowds of characters owed a lot to the ensemble-driven films of Robert Altman (*MASH, Nashville*). Daniel J. Travanti's precinct captain Frank Furillo was a blend of righteous but sensitive '70s heroes like Frank Serpico and Hawkeye Pierce. And so on.

Then again, you could say the same thing about *Citizen Kane*, whose impact on what movies could aspire to look and sound like was as far-reaching as *Hill Street*'s impact has been on TV drama. In both cases, the pieces were old, but put together in a way that no one had thought to try before. Not all cop shows before *Hill Street* were pablum. You might have expected sophisticated characters or plotting or even a rich visual palette from many of them, including the ones written in the '70s by *Hill Street* creators Steven Bochco (*Columbo, Delvecchio*) and Michael Kozoll (*Kojak, Quincy, M.E.*), or directed in the '60s by the series' first director, Robert Butler (*The Untouchables, The Fugitive*). But a police drama that was adventurous morally, visually, *and* narratively, all at the same time, was unheard of. The rest of the business raced to follow in the show's footsteps.

Hill Street Blues plunged the audience into the poorest, filthiest, most crime-ridden precinct of an unnamed Midwestern city, not even bothering to differentiate the major players from the extras at first. The first episode opens with the soon-to-be-customary roll call by philosophical Sergeant Phil Esterhaus (Michael Conrad), which orients the viewer less to upcoming plots than to the general sense of chaos and decay. At one point, he reads a department memo "concerning the alleged carrying of bizarre and unauthorized weapons by the officers of this precinct," which leads to every actor onscreen producing an astonishing collection of pistols, switchblades, nunchakus, and other deadly instruments per Esterhaus's request, then immediately retrieving them all as they head out to deal with the junkies, perverts, and gang members who consume so much of their beat. They are the police force as unruly mob, barely kept in control by Esterhaus, who has to yell at them at the end of each roll call, "Hey! Let's be *careful* out there." And as we see the streets they have to patrol, we come to understand how they got this way, or why undercover cop Mick Belker (Bruce Weitz) has gone feral to the point where Furillo has to admonish him not to bite a detainee who has gone wild and beaten up a half dozen uniformed officers. ("Two years ago, I bit off a nose," Belker laments. "One lousy nose! I'm branded for life here: Belker the Biter!")

Bochco and Kozoll had begun referring to the series as "Cop Soap," but this was a dark, challenging sort of soap opera, and one that took a while for audiences to get used to. NBC at the time was run by Fred Silverman, who had presided over CBS during the early '70s golden age of *All in the Family* and *M*A*S*H*, then turned ABC into a powerhouse with *Happy Days*, *Charlie's Angels*, and *The Love Boat*. His NBC tenure was for the most part an utter catastrophe in which he green-lit several contenders for

the title of Worst TV Show Ever Made, including *Supertrain* (which attempted to translate the *Love Boat* formula to a luxury...train?) and *Pink Lady and Jeff* (a variety show whose two main stars spoke virtually no English). But Silverman hadn't completely lost his CBS sensibilities, and one of his last acts before leaving NBC was to renew the dismally rated *Hill Street*, sending Bochco a note that read, "Dear Steve, You're going to sweep the Emmys and go on to be a big hit. Fred." (He was mostly right: *Hill Street* got a record twenty-one Emmy nominations that first year, winning eight of them, and ran seven seasons, but only grew into a midsized success.)

Though it was breaking from previous formula, *Hill Street* quickly developed a formula of its own: a couple of stories to be resolved in the space of each episode, one or two others that might be spaced out over three or four, and some concluding thoughts after Furillo goes home to his clandestine love affair with public defender Joyce Davenport (Veronica Hamel). But the formula was elastic enough to allow ridiculously big characters like fascistic SWAT commander Howard Hunter (James B. Sikking) to interact with more human-scaled ones like Furillo or liberal detective Henry Goldblume (Joe Spano), and jump from the farce of uniformed patrolmen Bobby Hill and Andy Renko (Michael Warren and Charles Haid) trying to get a live bull out of a fifth-floor tenement apartment to the drama of Furillo inadvertently driving a corrupt precinct captain to suicide by ruling against him in a Board of Rights hearing.

Though many of its creative descendants—including other shows created by Bochco and/or *Hill Street* writers David Milch (*NYPD Blue, Deadwood*), Dick Wolf (*Law & Order*), and Anthony Yerkovich (*Miami Vice*)—inspire debates among their fans about the best episode, that rarely happens with *Hill Street*. That's partly because there's an obvious answer: the third-season premiere, "Trial by Fury," Milch's debut screenplay, in which the rape and murder of a nun pushes the virtuous Furillo to a breaking point where he's willing to use the threat of mob justice to coerce a confession from one of the perpetrators, then sends him to confession afterward to deal with the guilt. But it's also because the show had such a sprawling narrative, with wild shifts in tone and focus, that few installments stand out as appreciably better than the rest. *Hill Street Blues* was bigger than any one episode, one character, one stylistic device. It put all those familiar puzzle pieces together to form something so much greater than the sum of its individual parts that it forever changed the way TV dramas were built.

—AS

The Shield (FX, 2002–2008) Total score: 102

Television shows are living, breathing organisms that quickly evolve past whatever designs their creators originally had for them. One actor might leave abruptly, or another might turn out to be more talented (and more in need of screen time) than anyone expected, or a story designed to last two seasons might exhaust itself in a quarter of that time.

Because of that, endings in TV are much harder than beginnings. A show can be propped up for commercial reasons long after it's creatively finished, and thus give you something like Dexter Morgan: Lumberjack at the end for lack of any good remaining ideas. Or a conclusion hatched in season 1 or 2 may no longer apply to where the characters are in season 8 (see *How I Met Your Mother* later in this book). Or a creator may simply have something very different in mind from what the fans were expecting, which leads to Tony Soprano eating onion rings, or the explanation for the *Lost* sideways universe, or Larry David lecturing his audience on what terrible people the *Seinfeld* gang of four were.

So it's rare to find a completely satisfying end to a truly great show. Even in this new golden age of television, the most common feeling at a series' end is simply relief that the people in charge didn't screw it up.

But then there is *The Shield*, whose ending was so powerful, so unflinching, and so very much a culmination of the entire series that it retroactively made everything that came before it better. Without that finale, *The Shield* is still a great show. With it, it's one for the ages.

Born of FX's desire to position itself as a basic-cable version of HBO, and creator Shawn Ryan's fondness to apply the lessons of the LAPD Rampart scandal to the formula of gritty '90s cop dramas like *NYPD Blue* and *Homicide*, *The Shield* took place in one of LA's worst police districts, where the only men apparently preventing full-scale gang anarchy are Detective Vic Mackey (Michael Chiklis) and the members of his strike team. Some colleagues viewed him as a hero, while his new boss David

Aceveda (Benito Martinez) saw him as "Al Capone with a badge." Mackey shrugged off all labels, telling a pedophile kidnapper, "Good cop and bad cop left for the day. I'm a different kind of cop."

Aceveda has assigned Terry Crowley (Reed Diamond from *Homicide*) to go undercover in the strike team and get the goods on Vic. And just as the series seemed to be setting itself up for a classic battle of wits between a corrupt cop and an honest one, Vic shot Terry in the face during a raid on a drug dealer's house, leaving himself untouchable, given that his only potential opponents were a calculating politician in Aceveda, precinct joke Dutch Wagenbach (Jay Karnes), and Claudette Wyms (C. C. H. Pounder), a veteran cop wise enough to know what Vic was really about and wiser still to know she'd get nowhere fast chasing him.

Instead, Vic's greatest enemy over the life of the series turned out to be himself, as he was so caught up in trying to amass a retirement fund, and cover up the many crimes required to do that, that he was perpetually digging himself out of quicksand, temporarily freeing himself while ultimately finding himself in even deeper than before.

Yet even from that starting point with Vic and Terry, *The Shield* managed to exist in morally gray territory for much of its run. Vic was an unrepentant cop-killer and all-around criminal, but he also had his uses as a cop, and the series was able to function as a high-end police procedural—sometimes involving Dutch and Claudette investigating the city's most disgusting murders, sometimes with the strike team trying to shut down gang wars—even as it was chronicling Vic and his protégé Shane Vendrell's (Walton Goggins) descent into lawlessness. Shot guerrilla-style on LA's east side, by an impressive group of directors including Clark Johnson, Paris Barclay, Scott Brazil, and David Mamet, it looked and felt like no cop show before it.

And it ended like none had. By the final seasons, the need for colorful external villains, like Anthony Anderson as local drug kingpin Antwon Mitchell or Forest Whitaker as unstable Internal Affairs investigator Jon Kavanaugh, vanished as the strike team rotted from within, particularly after Shane murdered fugitive strike teamer Lem (Kenny Johnson) to eliminate any chance of his testifying against the rest of them.

The final season is less a collection of stories than an agonizing endurance test, designed to keep the audience guessing about who would live, who would die, and who might possibly emerge unscathed. In the end, it's a mix of triumph and tragedy, sometimes for the same character.

Claudette and Dutch are on the verge of busting a new serial killer, but Claudette reveals that she's close to losing her series-long fight against lupus. Shane goes on the run from the law and murders himself, his young son, and his pregnant wife in a horrifyingly misguided bid to protect his family's innocence. Vic somehow cons his future employers in the federal government into giving him immunity for *every* crime we've seen him commit, but loses his family, friends, and reputation in the process. He winds up a prisoner of an untraditional form of jail, where he has to report to a tiny cubicle every day to do paperwork assigned by bosses who rightly despise him.

It's a finale that builds on every single thing that happened over the previous eighty-eight episodes, that shows that Ryan and his team were paying attention to all of Vic's and Shane's past sins, and that reveals all that came before not as another aggressive celebration of a swaggering male antihero but an intricate, inescapable tragedy involving a man who thought he was a different kind of cop, when really he was just a different kind of crook.

—AS

TV'S MOST MEMORABLE DEATHS

1. **Henry Blake, *M*A*S*H*:** Sent home from war, shot down over Sea of Japan.
2. **Joyce Summers, *Buffy the Vampire Slayer*:** A natural death in a supernatural world.
3. **Ned Stark, *Game of Thrones*:** Beheaded as an example to his supporters.
4. **Rosalind Shays, *L.A. Law*:** She really thought there would be an elevator.
5. **Gus Fring, *Breaking Bad*:** Lost half his face, but not his sense of style.
6. **Chuckles the Clown, *The Mary Tyler Moore Show*:** While wearing a peanut costume, shelled to death by elephant.
7. **Susan Ross, *Seinfeld*:** Died from licking toxic envelope glue from off-brand envelopes her fiancé picked out.
8. **Rocket Romano, *ER*:** Eventually, the helicopter's gonna get you.
9. **Mags Bennett, *Justified*:** It was already in the glass, not in the jar.
10. **Shane Vendrell, *The Shield*:** Killed entire family to ensure their innocence.
11. **Ralphie Cifaretto, *The Sopranos*:** Lost his head.
12. **Lori Grimes, *The Walking Dead*:** Gave birth to one child, stabbed in head by other.
13. **Kenny McCormick, *South Park*:** Impaled on flagpole, eviscerated and decapitated by football players, cooked in microwave oven, crushed by Mir space station,

---

The Twilight Zone (CBS, 1959–1964 and 1985–1989; UPN, 2002–2003) Total score: 101

Imagine, if you will, an innovative writer and producer who feared two things almost equally: death and irrelevance. Death claimed him in 1975. Irrelevance: never.

The writer-producer is Rod Serling. He was best known to the public as the dapper, grimly ironic host of his great half-hour anthology series *The Twilight Zone* (1959–1964). But he was more than a TV personality. Throughout his brief heyday—which lasted from the live TV era of the 1950s through the late '60s—he fought hard, often losing the battle to put meaningful drama on television. He was one of its earliest and greatest auteurs, an artist of integrity and vision.

Raised in Binghamton, New York, and scarred by his experience

pierced by Iraqi sword, tied to tetherball pole and asphyxiated, gored by bull, expired from chicken pox, drowned by goldfish, squashed by derailed mining cart full of underpants, struck by lightning, pulled into giant fan by magnet, mauled by bear while impersonating deer, frozen in carbonite by CIA as gift to Sally Struthers, voids self to death after playing "The Brown Note" in concert, dies of boredom riding a boat going five mph, stabbed through heart by member of Cthulhu cult, perishes of autoerotic asphyxiation after choking self with belt while dressed as Batman, jumps from headquarters of Sony Japan while dressed as "Princess Kenny," head bitten off by Iguana Entertainment logo, and others.

14. **Flock of turkeys, *WKRP in Cincinnati*:** As God was his witness, Mr. Carlson thought they could fly.

15. **Charlie Pace, *Lost*:** Drowned, but not before warning Desmond it was "NOT PENNY'S BOAT."

16. **Wild Bill Hickok, *Deadwood*:** Inadvertently created the dead man's hand.

17. **Omar Little, *The Wire*:** Died an old gunfighter's death, but in West Baltimore.

18. **Bobby Simone, *NYPD Blue*:** Literally died of a broken heart.

19. **Lane Pryce, *Mad Men*:** Jaguar engineering proved unreliable, but a necktie did not.

20. **Nate Fisher Sr., *Six Feet Under*:** Died as he lived; gone but not forgotten.

as an infantryman in World War II, Serling was a walking paradox: a Jew who converted to Unitarianism; a bookish intellectual drawn to the most popular medium yet devised; an alienated, profoundly lonely man who became one of the most recognizable and widely imitated celebrities of the twentieth century.

He broke through to national success with *Patterns*, a ninety-minute teleplay about a young corporate climber who learns he was hired as the final element in a cold-blooded corporate plot. The public, the critics, and the industry embraced Serling when he wrote prosaic "little" dramas for live theater, such as *Patterns* and his more successful follow-up, *Requiem for a Heavyweight*. But he wanted to write more pointedly about politics and social issues— much to his employers' chagrin. In

1958, he and director John Franken-heimer tried to produce a live drama about the fate of Emmett Till, a cocky black Chicago teen who went to visit relatives in small-town Missis-sippi and got lynched for whistling at a white woman. Network execu-tives and censors "chopped it up like a roomful of butchers at work on a steer," Serling later said. When the play finally aired, the cocky black teen had become a Mexican folk musician, and the story had been transplanted to the American South-west circa 1870. Throughout the late '50s, Serling got in trouble with net-work bosses and advertisers for writ-ing plays drawn from modern events (including the civil rights move-ment, the Cold War, and the threat of nuclear annihilation) and recent his-tory (including World War II and the Holocaust). He angered them further by giving newspaper interviews that painted network TV as being hostile to drama that dared challenge, pro-voke, or enrage viewers.

Luckily for Serling (and for view-ers), the next stop was *The Twilight Zone*. The irony was exquisite. CBS, the same network that routinely neutered Serling's social dramas, let him write, host, and oversee a weekly anthology series that fea-tured such unrespectable elements as time travel, robots, monsters, space creatures, and cameos by the Grim Reaper and Satan. The for-mat disguised social commentary so pointed that if the series had been conceived in a more straightforward way, Serling's scripts never would have seen the light of day. Season 5's "I Am the Night—Color Me Black," in which the sky turns black over a small town on the morning of a man's execution, is one of many *Zone* episodes to grapple with the moral implications of capital pun-ishment, mob violence, and the generalized desire for retribution. At the end, when the sky turns black over Vietnam, the Berlin Wall, a political prison in Budapest, a rough neighborhood in Chicago, and several cities in the segregated US South, Serling tells us that the black-ness represents "a sickness known as hate. Not a virus, not a microbe, not a germ...Highly contagious. Deadly in its effects. Don't look for it in the Twilight Zone. Look for it in the mirror. Look for it before the light goes out altogether."

The best *Zone* episodes are simul-taneously of their time and timeless. Consider (if you will) "The Monsters Are Due on Maple Street," about a small town destroying itself during a blackout over fear of an unspecified invasion. The episode was Serling's condemnation of McCarthy-era paranoia over Communism, which encouraged Americans to inform on one another for the greater good of the society. Substitute "terrorism" or "drug dealing" or "pedophilia" for "Communism," and you have a drama as fresh as this morning's headlines. "Eye of the Beholder," about an "ugly" woman undergoing an operation to make her look "normal," is often described as a parable about moral and aesthetic relativism. (The "ugly" woman turns out to be beautiful by our standards, but everyone else in her society—the "beautiful" people—are hideous pig creatures.) But pay close attention during the climax, which shows the young woman rushing down a corridor. The TV on the hospital wall shows a Big Brother–type pig creature in a military uniform, hollering about how there is "a single virtue, a single morality!" The episode is a dark fairy tale about how society and its leaders pressure individuals to conform—a tendency that, unchecked by law, leads to dictatorship. The apocalyptic ending of "Time Enough at Last"—which ends with bibliomaniac Henry Bemis (Burgess Meredith) left alone in the rubble of a freshly nuked city with a trove of books, only to break his glasses—is one of the show's many effective riffs on the end of "The Monkey's Paw" episode from The Alfred Hitchcock Hour; but the sight of a great city in ruins is also redolent of 9/11, Hurricane Katrina, and other modern catastrophes. Serling narrates, "Henry Bemis, now just a part of a smashed landscape, just a piece of the rubble, just a fragment of what man has deeded to himself." An episode about an astronaut-in-training who hallucinates he's alone in a small town while being hounded by unseen forces now plays like a prophecy of our modern age of total surveillance. "Somebody's looking at me!" the astronaut screams. "Please help me!"

Some motifs recurred so regularly that they became in-show clichés. Characters kept selling their souls to the devil, belatedly realizing that they were dead, and figuring out, long after the audience, that the place they were stranded in was heaven, hell, or purgatory. "This is what is meant by 'paying the fiddler,'" Serling tells us at the end of season 1's "Judgment Night," about a German U-boat commander condemned to endlessly relive his own sinking of a Scottish civilian ship. "This is the comeuppance awaiting every man when the ledger of his life is opened and examined, the tally made, and then the reward or the penalty paid." Twilight Zone characters heard voices and saw things and wondered if they were crazy and ultimately found out that they weren't, too late to defend their sanity. (The most striking of the latter was "Nightmare at 20,000 Feet," starring William Shatner as an airplane passenger who thinks he sees a gremlin tearing apart the engine.) As the series wore on, a repetitiveness set in, epitomized by Serling's narration, which could sound slapped-together. "There are many bromides applicable here," Serling explains at the end of season 5's "The Brain Center at Whipple's," about a man who creates laborsaving machines that render most human labor unnecessary. "'Too much of a good thing,' 'tiger by the tail,' 'as you sow, so shall you reap.'" You could almost hear him sighing as he read it.

But even at its least inspired, there were always flashes of poetry and tenderness in *The Twilight Zone*; moments of eeriness, menace, and joy; fragments of narration by Serling that turned such a lovely phrase you almost didn't care if the episode was working or not, or that felt like glimpses of a creator's mind ruminating en route to a breakdown. "A man can think a lot of thoughts and walk a lot of pavements between afternoon and night," he says in season 1's "Walking Distance," about a man so consumed by nostalgia for his childhood and adolescence that he can't enjoy the present.

Sadly, Serling spent his final years thinking of himself as a second-rater and a sellout. It's true that the medium accustomed him to a lifestyle that he didn't dare give up; by the late '60s, he was hosting a series over which he had no creative control (*Night Gallery*) and appearing as a pitchman in ads (a *Zone*-worthy fate for a man who despised commercialism). He had joined a certain system (network TV), done what he could to change it from within, and failed—or so he thought. Later in life, Serling disparaged his best writing. "My stuff has been momentarily adequate," he told an interviewer.

Try permanently influential.

The Twilight Zone inspired two official TV remakes (CBS, 1985–1989, narrated by Cliff Robertson; UPN, 2002–2003, hosted by Forest Whitaker) and a 1983 feature film produced by Steven Spielberg, with segments by Spielberg, John Landis, Joe Dante, and George Miller and narration by none other than Burgess Meredith, who appeared in four episodes of the original *Zone*. (The film's playful artistry was overshadowed by the preventable deaths of Vic Morrow and two child actors, Myca Dinh Le and Renee Shin-Yi Chen, in a helicopter accident.) The show's post-Serling TV incarnations had their merits. The finest was the '80s version, which debuted in a one-hour time slot. Although its production values were dwarfed by those of NBC's competing anthology *Amazing Stories* (a Spielberg project), it admirably reimagined Serling's format, and lured heavy-hitting pop artists to write or direct episodes ranging in length from twelve to thirty-eight minutes. Highlights included Harlan Ellison's "Shatterday," starring Bruce Willis as a man tormented by a mirror version of himself; "Opening Day," a John Milius–directed, neo-noir-styled nightmare about a man working up the nerve to murder his girlfriend's husband during a hunting trip; and the unrelenting "Nightcrawlers," directed by William Friedkin, in which a Vietnam veteran exposed to an Agent Orange–type chemical is pursued by the zombie-ghosts of soldiers he betrayed.

Aside from the official reboots and Serling's own 1969–1973 ABC horror series, *Night Gallery* (which gave a young Spielberg his first professional directorial credit, in an episode starring Joan Crawford as a blind woman), *Zone* inspired countless homages and rip-offs. The short list includes *Thriller* (ABC, 1960–1962, hosted by Boris Karloff); *The Outer Limits* (ABC, 1963–1965); *Darkroom* (ABC, 1981–1982, hosted by James Coburn); George Romero's *Tales from the Darkside* (syndicated, 1984–1988,

inspired by 1982's *Creepshow*, Romero's *Zone*-styled anthology film with Stephen King); *The Ray Bradbury Theater* (HBO and USA, 1985–1992); *Tales from the Crypt* (HBO, 1989–1996); *Dead Man's Gun* (Showtime, 1997–1999, hosted by Kris Kristofferson); England's *Black Mirror* (2011–); *Deadtime Stories* (Nickelodeon, 2012–); and *From Dusk till Dawn: The Series* (El Rey, 2014–). Its influence could also be felt in such allegorically minded science-fiction and horror programs as *Star Trek* (NBC, 1966–1969); *Fantasy Island* (ABC, 1977–1984 and 1988–1989); the rebooted *Battlestar Galactica* (Syfy, 2003–2009); and Ryan Murphy and Brad Falchuk's *American Horror Story* (FX, 2010–) and *Scream Queens* (Fox, 2015–). The Rod Serling homage tree branches off via the cult favorite *Kolchak: The Night Stalker* (1974–1975), a monster-of-the-week series starring Darren McGavin that drew on *The Twilight Zone*, *The Outer Limits*, and *Night Gallery*, and that looked forward to the morality-play genre tales of *The X-Files* (Fox, 1993–2002); *Buffy the Vampire Slayer* (WB and UPN, 1997–2003); and *Supernatural* (CW, 2005–).

It's too bad Serling couldn't have lived to see the modern version of TV, which filled hundreds of channels with dozens of shows, all of which learned from Serling that it was possible to make magic in a system that seemed designed to extinguish it, and create stories so clever that the powers that be didn't know they had messages as well. "Someplace between apathy and anarchy is the stance of the thinking human being," Serling said. The name of that someplace: *The Twilight Zone.*

—MZS

Arrested Development (Fox, 2003–2006; Netflix, 2013)
Total score: 100

At least half the members of *Arrested Development*'s Bluth family have their own personal chicken dance, which they deploy when they think another family member— usually sensible middle son Michael (Jason Bateman) or freakish youngest son Buster (Tony Hale)—is acting cowardly. Yet none of these impressions remotely resemble how a chicken might move or sound: Eldest son GOB (Will Arnett) claps aggressively while doing the Running Man, sister Lindsay (Portia de Rossi) waggles her fingers atop her forehead while doing a spastic hoedown, mother Lucille (Jessica Walter) flutters her arms like an entirely different kind of bird and

recites baby talk, and father George (Jeffrey Tambor) simply stretches out his arms and utters a singsong "Coo-coo-ka-chah!" (Michael's son George Michael, played by Michael Cera, apparently also has his own chicken dance, but the Netflix season of *Arrested Development* cruelly taunted fans with the possibility only to interrupt George Michael before he had a chance to do it.)

Michael, at one point presented with the spectacle of three Bluth chicken dances at the same time, mutters, "Has anyone in this family ever seen a chicken?" This accomplishes nothing. His relatives, as usual, not only are ignoring the one relatively sane adult in the family, but they would be incapable of processing the idea that they're doing anything incorrectly. (At one point, even the cowardly Buster has had enough of GOB's taunts and screams at him, "Chickens don't clap!" GOB pays him no mind.)

As the show's wonderfully deadpan narrator (and, along with Brian Grazer, its executive producer guardian angel) Ron Howard puts it simply at the top of each episode: It's *Arrested Development*, which more or less turns into Michael Bluth's version of *Chinatown*. He should forget all these defiant ignoramuses, grab George Michael, and move far, far away, but he can't—because, as this great, underwatched comedy slowly reveals over time, he's just as vain and stubborn and foolish as the rest of them, and takes far too much satisfaction from being there to point out their many mistakes.

Created by Mitchell Hurwitz, *Arrested Development* was an incredible Rube Goldberg contraption of a sitcom, elaborately setting up most of its jokes in a way that seemed like far too much effort, until the punch lines started rolling at the audience with devastating speed.

Take Buster's unhealthy relationship with Lucille, who still infantilizes him in his thirties and takes him annually to a creepy dinner dance event known as Motherboy. Over time, he rebels against her the only way he can: by starting a relationship with her next-door neighbor and oldest frenemy, who is conveniently also named Lucille. ("Lucille 2" is played by Liza Minnelli, just one member of an army of odd guest stars used to their fullest and most unexpected comic potential: Henry Winkler as perverted Bluth family attorney Barry Zuckerkorn, who in one episode literally jumped over a shark; Julia Louis-Dreyfus as a lawyer pretending to be blind; Carl Weathers as a cheapskate version of himself; and Amy Poehler as GOB's drunken soldier bride, whose name he never

learns, and thus is known only as "Wife of GOB.") Later, Lucille Bluth has Buster enlist in the Army after being ambushed by a Michael Moore impersonator, only for Buster to be spared from combat because his hand is bitten off by a loose seal, the warnings of which he ignores because he assumes he's being told about his mother.

The series debuted only a few months after the invasion of Iraq, and though silliness was the first order of business—when Barry is temporarily unavailable, the family retains Bob Loblaw (say that three times fast), played by Winkler's former *Happy Days* costar Scott Baio, who notes he can do anything Barry can do, "Plus, I skew younger"—*Arrested Development* was also a vicious satire of the head-in-the-sand thinking that got America into that mess overseas. George goes to jail in the first episode for embezzling from the family business, and is later accused of building houses for Saddam Hussein. He becomes a fugitive for a while and is later found by George Michael in a scene choreographed to resemble the footage of Saddam being examined after he was discovered in his spider hole.

More than any comedy before it (and almost every one after), the series demanded complete viewer attention and loyalty for most of its jokes to work properly. Fold a piece of laundry, and you might miss the blue handprints—a reminder that Lindsay's transparently closeted husband Tobias Fünke (David Cross) was constantly covering himself in blue body paint in the hopes of becoming an understudy for the Blue Man Group—dotting the wall of the model home where most of the Bluths were living. Miss a week, and you might not understand that George's business rival Stan Sitwell (Ed Begley Jr.) suffers from alopecia, and thus has to wear a series of absurd wigs and false eyebrows.

This was more work than most viewers were willing to do, and thus *Arrested* struggled in the ratings for all of its three seasons. But the rewards for those who wanted to pay attention were enormous, like interlocking running jokes about Michael's contempt for George Michael's boring girlfriend Ann Veal (Mae Whitman), whose existence he kept forgetting ("Her?"), and George Michael's own uncomfortable feelings for first cousin Maeby (Alia Shawkat).

Sometimes, Hurwitz and company got too clever for their own good, like a story arc in the third season where guest star Charlize Theron played Michael's new girlfriend, who was revealed near the end to have the mental age of a preschooler; it's the rare sitcom plot that plays much better the second time you watch it (and thus know what to look for) than the first. And when Netflix revived the series years later for a disappointing sequel season, tweaks to the formula—most episodes featured only one or two main characters, due to the difficulty of coordinating the actors' busy schedules, and episodes could run anywhere from seven to sixteen minutes longer than they did in the Fox days—revealed how fragile the comic alchemy had been in the first place. (*Coauthor's note: Matt vehemently disagrees with every complaint Alan has about the Netflix season, and also thinks he smells like a loose seal.*)

But the cast was so devoted to bringing their ridiculous alter egos to life, and the writers so prepared to go anywhere for a joke, no matter how dumb and/or filthy (Tobias, noting that he's worked as both an analyst and a therapist, decides to combine the two job titles, not realizing that his new business cards read "analrapist"), that you can understand why the show's creators, stars, and fans keep returning to it. Like Michael with his relatives, it's just too hard to walk away, no matter how much sense it makes at this point.

—AS

The Larry Sanders Show (HBO, 1992–1998) Total score: 100

If one were to make a list of the most influential TV series that almost nobody watched, HBO's *The Larry Sanders Show* would be at the top. During its run, it never got the industry accolades fans felt it deserved, and although it routinely ended up on critics' year-end Top 10 lists, it got a meager handful of Emmy nominations and just three awards. It also rarely drew more than a couple of million viewers per episode, puny by broadcast standards. But history has rendered a glowing verdict. Created by actor-writer Garry Shandling and Dennis Klein, *The Larry Sanders Show* changed the look and feel of TV comedy. Its influence was felt almost immediately, and its impact continues to resonate. Although it wasn't the first half-hour series to strip-mine the comedy of embarrassment, assume a laid-back, naturalistic style, or do without a score or a laugh track (except in the talk show sequences), the program's combination of these elements was so distinctive that they amounted to a new template— one that subsequent programs borrowed and customized, from actor-writer-producer Ken Finkleman's seriocomic Canadian series *The Newsroom* through the British and American versions of *The Office* and NBC's *30 Rock*.

Larry's warning to viewers before cutting to a commercial, "No flipping," could double as praise for Shandling's series. Once those white-on-black credits appeared, backed by the offscreen sound of sidekick Hank Kingsley (Jeffrey Tambor) warming up the crowd, the viewer was in a comic universe that was immaculately detailed and hermetically sealed: a snow globe full of bile. From its pitiless portrait of showbiz narcissism to its on-a-dime switching between videotape and film (establishing an art/life boundary that the characters willfully breached) to its then-innovative use of the Steadicam to transform long dialogue scenes into kinetic "walk and talks" (a technique pushed to the breaking point on *Sports Night*, *ER*, *The West Wing*, and other programs), *The Larry Sanders Show* infused sitcom conventions with cinematic flair and refused to sugarcoat its corrosive wit. (It also made the greatest use of the final-kicker freeze-frame since *Police Squad!*)

The title character—brilliantly underplayed by Shandling—is a vain, pampered jackass whose insecurity and self-regard destroy his relationships with women and lead

him to off-load rejection and failure onto his employees. He's late
night's Narcissus, holding court
during afternoon tapings and then
going home to watch himself. (He
sometimes invites his dates to join
him; what a turn-on.) Larry throws
himself into the show because he
can't function outside of it. "You're
like one of those goddamn creatures out of Greek mythology," Artie
(Rip Torn) tells him. "Half-man,
half-desk." At the end of season 2,
Larry quits the program in a fit of
pique and moves to a remote cabin
in rural Montana, where he watches
old tapes of himself over and over.
(To get back on the air in season
3, Larry lies to the network's new
owner, telling him that he's addicted
to prescription painkillers; by the
end of that season, Larry's addiction is genuine—and the metaphor
is impossible to miss.) His sign-off
prior to this short-lived retirement is, "You may now flip," and
he delivers it dry-eyed, perhaps
subconsciously realizing (as we
do) that he doesn't mean it. Larry
says something similar near the
end of the show's multiple-Emmy-
winning 1998 finale, "Flip"—a
stunning reimagining of Johnny
Carson's farewell that replaces
Bette Midler's farewell torch song
to Johnny with Jim Carrey belting

out the *Dreamgirls* anthem "And
I Am Telling You I'm Not Going."
But this time there's no backing
out; that's why Larry's tears are real.
Separate a man from his desk—or a
junkie from his drug—and you get
waterworks.

Larry's second banana, Hank
Kingsley, is one of the most venal
and pathetic characters in TV history. A former cruise ship enter-
tainer elevated to minor stardom
by Sanders, he's sadly lacking in
the charisma necessary to take
the spotlight and plagued by fears
of irrelevance and worthless-
ness. He works out his insecuri-
ties by throwing drama-queen
tantrums and casually insulting
those lower on the production's
totem pole. Larry's producer,
Artie, is a showbiz veteran of near-
mythological awesomeness—a
four-times-divorced Korean War
veteran who seems to have made a
friend, enemy, or lover of everyone
in Hollywood (he once dated Kim
Novak). He has a knack for delivering kiss-off lines with a raised eye-
brow and a grin, so that the person
on the receiving end doesn't quite
know how to respond. ("Don't take
this as a threat," Artie tells an interfering female executive from the
network, "but I killed a man like
you in Korea. Hand-to-hand." He

smiles as he says it.) But beneath his assured facade, Artie is as damaged as Larry or Hank. In the season 4 episode "Arthur After Hours," Artie gets soused with the show's Russian janitor late at night on a deserted soundstage and belts "I Wanna Be Around," a song about rejection that's plainly directed at his boss and a long-running show that doesn't appreciate his devotion.

The tertiary characters are no less troubled. The show's first head writer, Jerry (Jeremy Piven), is a lazy, horny, substance-abusing screwup who eventually gets axed for incompetence. (When Jerry tries to save himself with a self-pitying three-hankie monologue, Artie cups a hand to his ear and crows, "Do you hear that, my boy? I believe that's the sound of the needle breaking on the Bullshit-O-Meter!") Jerry's replacement, Phil (Wallace Langham), is a wheedling suck-up who undermines his colleagues at every turn. The program's hip, cynical talent booker, Paula (Janeane Garofalo), tries and often fails to focus her energy on a job, and a medium, that she secretly feels is beneath her. The series' closest equivalent to functioning people are Larry's loyal, tough right-hand woman, Beverly (Penny Johnson Jerald), and Hank's two assistants,

the kindhearted Darlene (Linda Doucett) and the quick-witted, openly gay Brian (Scott Thompson). But their willingness to subject themselves to discomfort, even abuse, makes you wonder what demons *they're* wrestling with. (Brian's list of unpleasant tasks assigned by Hank includes "digging through Great Dane poop looking for a ring.")

The Larry Sanders Show also presents what other industries would call "inappropriate behavior" as the show business norm. Larry has little patience for any woman as strong or accomplished as he is. He dates and sometimes beds the female guests but rarely views their attention as anything but a referendum on his power. He has a one-night stand with Beverly following his divorce; briefly reunites with his first ex-wife, a journalist named Francine (Kathryn Harrold); and gets sued by a fan who claims Larry impregnated her (after denying that he knows her, Larry sheepishly admits that she gave him a hand job in the parking lot of a Denny's). His colleagues are just as sexually dysfunctional. The place is a fetid pit of hormonal distress. During Hank's own postdivorce crisis, he numbs his loneliness with booze and hookers, lamely flirts with female guests, and puts the moves on a horrified Darlene. Late in the show's run, Brian gets fed up with the constant stream of homophobic jokes—mostly from Hank—and sues the program for sexual harassment. "Goddamn it, what has happened to courtesy and respect in this world?" bellows Hank, a prime suspect in their disappearance.

Shandling and his team (including head writer Peter Tolan and regular director Todd Holland) regard Larry and company with wry detachment. But they also leaven the characters' misbehavior, cruelty, and pain with wry banter, elaborate profanity, rude slapstick, and empathy that wells up subtly, naturally, often when you least expect it. In the season 3 episode "Hank's Divorce," for example, Hank is in such pain—and projects so much of his agony onto others—that he's nearly unwatchable. Artie, who is to divorce what Clint Eastwood's *Heartbreak Ridge* character was to war, visits Hank at the hotel where he's holed up to marinate in despair, and witnesses a breakdown that's too raw to be amusing. The moment pushes further into darkness when Artie produces a pistol and dares Hank to kill himself. It's a gamble that no therapist would endorse, but in the straight-male-dominated culture of '90s talk shows, it's just

what Hank needs—and the episode's final scene reveals that Artie's macho veneer was just that. He ambles into Larry's office to tell the boss that Hank will be returning to work, then produces the pistol. Larry grins as if reuniting with a long-lost friend. "Is that the divorce gun?" He beams, then lights Artie's cigar with it. Freeze-frame; roll credits.

—MZS

The Honeymooners (CBS, 1955–1956) Total score: 99

The Honeymooners was written by, produced by, and starred Jackie Gleason. He even wrote and conducted the theme music; then he made extra certain that everyone knew he was in charge by adding an "Entire Production Supervised by" credit. He wanted to leave no doubt about who ran the show, even though, since the beginning of his career, there had never been any. Gleason, a late-period vaudeville and radio star who made the jump to TV in the '40s, was one of TV's earliest auteurs, an Orson Welles of the small screen. Even though his finest creation ran just thirty-nine episodes during its regular presentation (after appearing for four years as part of the DuMont network's *Cavalcade of Stars*, episodes of which were added to syndication decades after the fact), it expressed his sense of life in every conceivable way: raucous, grotesque, sentimental, and ultimately life-affirming.

The Honeymooners was one of the most influential of all series. Its influence can be felt not just in every three-camera sitcom built around a blustering, scheming doofus of a husband and his poised and improbably patient wife (see Everybody Loves Raymond and King of Queens, to name two obvious examples), but also on All in the Family and The Sopranos, which learned a lot from Gleason's staging of domestic arguments in tight spaces and his willingness to drop the comic bluster for a moment, zoom in for a close-up, and observe a character's face as it got lost in a reverie, or a realization of a grave but not irrevocable mistake.

Gleason played Ralph Kramden, a bus driver who fantasized about escaping his Brooklyn tenement and living the life of a swell. His wife, Alice, played by Audrey Meadows, is a sardonic mate who casts a side-eye on his idiocy, weathers his explosions of distress and anger, and punctures his bluster by needling him about his temper, his long record of idiotic schemes, and his weight. (Ralph: "We got any lard laying around here?"

Alice: "Yeah, about three hundred pounds." Ralph: "Oh, you're gonna get *yours!*") Nearly every week, Ralph gets the bright idea to take a shortcut to fortune and draws his best pal, the sewer worker Ed Norton (Art Carney), into his scheme, which always ends in disaster, capped by Ralph begging Alice for forgiveness and Ed doing the same with his own wife, Trixie (Joyce Randolph), who's more chipper than Alice but equally unwilling to suffer a fool gladly.

Much of The Honeymooners is shtick-based, setting up comic situations and letting them play out at length, the better to showcase Meadows's laser-beam focus, Randolph's ebullient timing, Gleason's improbable grace and mercurial energy, and the physicality of Carney, a porkpie-hatted string bean with the posture of a shrimp. (When Ralph tries to teach his friend to play golf—a ridiculous notion in itself—he tells him to begin by addressing the ball, and Norton salutes it and exclaims, "*Helloooooo*, ball!") The show has become, as they say, problematic, thanks to Ralph's oft-repeated promise to send Alice "to the moon…bang, *zoom!*" But viewers knew he would never raise a hand to her—not just because he was a kind soul deep-down, but because Alice would knock him right out. ("I'll go fix my lipstick," she tells him. "I won't be gone long, Killer. I call you 'Killer' 'cause you slay me.")

Beneath this veneer of tomfoolery was a melancholy strain. The settings were unapologetically urban and dire—the sorts of places where you might expect to see a private detective rooting through trash or a lout in a tank top yelling up at his wife in a window. Economic distress and depression over the impossibility of leaving one's social class drove Ralph's schemes. He always felt like a failure for not being rich enough to support Alice in the manner to which he believed she should become accustomed, even though he was a hardworking stiff who was doing the best he could. Ralph was a product of his conditioning, even though it's doubtful that Gleason or his costars would describe the character's predicament in those terms.

"No wife of mine is gonna work," he tells Alice. "I got my pride. You know, no Kramden woman has ever supported her husband. The Kramden men are the workers in the family." "Wait a minute, Ralph," she says. "What about your father? For a long time there he didn't work at all." "But neither did my mother. At least he kept his pride, Alice. He went on relief."

Few contemporaneous series even spoke about such things—not in the postwar United States, where everyone was supposedly happy and prosperous—and fewer wove them into every story line. While other popular sitcoms set in 1950s America, like *Leave It to Beaver* and *Father Knows Best*, reassured viewers that patriarchal wisdom was always comforting and that the relative opulence of suburban life was "normal," *The Honeymooners* showed a life of struggle by those left behind in the cities to drive buses and work in sewers, and to live vertical rather than horizontal lives. Ralph and Alice may live near the top of their tenement apartment building, but socioeconomically they're closer to the bottom of what their leaders and their media told them was each American's birthright.

The show's low-tech visuals enhance its sneaky power. *The Honeymooners* in all of its incarnations was videotaped before a studio audience, like a theater production. The only records of the earliest episodes come from black-and-white film cameras pointed at monitors. The alchemy of video-into-film, known as kinescope, crushes blacks and blows out white spaces and creates what could be ectoplasm trails behind characters as they move across the screen. *The*

Honeymooners is a dream of itself without having aspired to be any such thing. The aesthetic is haunting: We are aware that we're seeing a memory of a time and place long gone and that was fading away even as it appeared on TV screens.

—MZS

Louie (FX, 2010–2015) Total score: 99

What makes *Louie*, focused on the surreal misadventures of a divorced New York comedian, so remarkable? It isn't the content, which is alternately funny, sweet, and mortifying. Nor is it the form, which was close to revolutionary. Sometimes Louis C.K., a stand-up comic and skilled filmmaker who played the title character, would spend his allotted twenty-two minutes telling one story. Other times he'd deliver the TV equivalent of a couple of short stories, or (as in the divisive fourth season) serve up what amounted to feature-length films in twenty-two-minute chunks (two of which cast other actors as younger versions of Louie). Within any given sequence, C.K. might stick with the show's dominant mode— melancholy sitcom, no laugh track— or shift into a dream sequence, a bit of stand-up, a flashback, even a sort-of documentary.

Nor is the show's uniqueness simply the result of C.K. asserting creative control. Television history is filled with sitcoms driven by stand-up comics who had a vision (or thought they did); without exception, they all chose a format and tone and more or less stuck with them for the duration. *The Bob Newhart Show, The Cosby Show,* and *Everybody Loves Raymond,* to name three influential sitcoms fronted by stand-ups, were pretty much the same at the end of their runs as they were at the start. Others, such as *Roseanne* and *Seinfeld,* evolved but never lost touch with their essence. *Louie* morphed from week to week, episode to episode, sometimes minute to minute. In doing so, it translated the thought processes of stand-up comedy into cinematic terms, and in a way that that was new to commercial television.

Most episodes would start with Louie performing onstage (just like most episodes of *Seinfeld*) and then segue into the narrative, with fictional characters speaking scripted lines. But if you go back and rewatch any episode through the lens of cinematic stand-up, you realize that even when Louie moves out of the nightclub, you're still watching stand-up. The segmented nature of the series evokes the stop-and-start rhythms of a stand-up routine, an art form in which it's acceptable to lurch from one subject to the next with a blunt transition: "Women." "Football fans are the worst." "Now I'm gonna talk about things that you can do to keep people on their toes." C.K. was always talking to you directly, in the way that a stand-up comic would address the audience from the stage, but he was doing it through the language of film.

The results were hit-and-miss, just as stand-up routines are hit-and-miss, because at heart, the whole show was an extended riff. Sometimes he was reflecting on ethics or politics or teaching a moral lesson. Sometimes he was telling you about a dream or fantasy he had, or an encounter that became fodder for a fantasy: see season 2's "Subway," a short piece that starts with Louie encountering a homeless man washing himself on a subway platform and ends with Louie fantasizing about becoming a hero to fellow riders by doffing his shirt to mop up a spill on a seat. Other times C.K. was mining experiences from his life (or experiences that happened to his friends—especially his occasional cowriter, Pamela Adlon). An example is season 2's "Pamela," wherein Louie made a heartrending confession of love to his female friend Pamela (Adlon) and was gently rebuffed. "Pamela" was contained in the same half hour as "Subway," and it worked, because stand-up routines pivot from descriptions of dreams to accounts of romantic disaster all the time without inducing imaginative whiplash.

Similarly extreme juxtapositions happened over the course of seasons. Season 3 began with a series of personal, professional, and sexual humiliations for Louie—some ridiculous, as when Louie's car gets gratuitously destroyed, and others wry and "realistic," as in the episode where Louis develops a man crush on a hotel employee in Miami—and then built to a surprisingly intense dramatic peak in episodes 4 and 5, which starred Parker Posey as a dark free spirit who forced Louie to confront his depression and suicidal urges. Soon after, *Louie* aired a segment in which the hero babysat a brat who ate only raw meat, pushed baby carriages into traffic, tossed rugs through apartment windows, and voided his bowels in Louie's bathtub. Neither the boy nor his loathsome mother were "realistic"; they were the sorts of absurd caricatures who might appear in a routine by a comic who had just been through a rotten experience and was using hyperbole to vent.

Yet this segment—as well as the subsequent "Dad," which climaxed with Louie racing through Boston on foot and on a stolen motorcycle and speedboat—existed within the same fictional framework, one in which anything was possible. The show's most daring episode, the season 3 finale, "New Year's Eve," unreeled like a dream that might or might not have become another dream that might or might not have included the death of Posey's character. It ended with Louie impulsively getting on a plane to China, meandering through a city and a village, and being taken in by a rural family, who seemed to have a lively conversation with him over dinner even though he was speaking English and they were speaking Mandarin. ("New Year's Eve" owes so much to late-period David Lynch films like *Mulholland Drive* and *Inland Empire* that when Lynch appeared in season 3 as a TV executive mentoring Louie in his bid to take over for David Letterman, his presence felt redundant.)

To find an equivalent to what *Louie* did with the sitcom format, you have look at what another former stand-up turned auteur, Woody Allen, did in theatrical cinema between 1969's *Take the Money and Run* and 1984's *Broadway Danny Rose*. These films mixed straightforward comedy and drama, voice-over, direct address, documentary devices, fantasies and nightmares with relaxed precision. C.K. clearly learned a lot from watching Allen's films, and seemed to acknowledge the lineage by using jazz in his sound tracks and hiring Allen's regular editor, Susan E. Morse, to work on season 3. (He cut her loose immediately, though, and went back to editing the series himself.) Allen seemed to recognize C.K. as a kindred spirit when he cast him as a supporting player in 2013's *Blue Jasmine*. Despite all this, *Louie* never feels purely imitative of Allen or anyone else, because its tone, style, and emotional temperature swing as widely from week to week as Allen's did from year to year.

The freedom of which C.K. avails himself could be construed as a cop-out. If a series has no set mode and no established baseline of "reality," it becomes harder to complain that, say, Louis C.K. is painting himself as too much of a sad sack to gain sympathy, or that some of the portrayals of female sexuality have a touch of bitter-white-guy misogyny (an episode near the end of season 4 made it seem as if *Louie* were on the verge of raping Pamela, then had her fall in love with him—but did either thing actually "happen"?). The easiest response to these concerns would be to say that every moment of every segment is happening inside Louie's mind. But that would raise the question of whether *Louie* would be a greater achievement if it weren't such a grab bag—if the creator decided to stick with one mode or tone for a bit longer, and develop his character and other characters more meticulously, instead of jumping to another thing as a stand-up comic might, or introducing biographical touches that don't make a lot of real-world sense (such as giving his alter ego two blond, Nordic-pale daughters, but an African American mother).

But C.K. never seemed interested in giving audiences the show they wanted, only in making the show that he wanted. More often than not, his show came off confident rather than arrogant, perhaps because the lead character was so often humbled, even humiliated, by life. This, ironically, could be the only area in which the issue of believability might apply to *Louie*: No one brash enough to make a show like this could be entirely credible as a man who's muddling through life.

—MZS

The Mary Tyler Moore Show (CBS, 1970–1977) Total score: 98

In the early 1970s, Ethel Winant, CBS's vice president of talent and casting, had to place her high heels outside the restroom to alert men that the room was occupied, because there was no ladies' room and no lock on the door. Winant was in exactly the right environment for *The Mary Tyler Moore Show*, a series about a single woman trying to make it in the male-dominated TV industry, and maybe find love in the process, on her own terms, and on her own timetable. She protected *The Mary Tyler Moore Show*, a gentle sitcom from executive producer James L. Brooks that became one of the most culturally important series of the 1970s.

Mary Richards (Mary Tyler Moore, still beloved for her success on *The Dick Van Dyke Show*) and her sidekick, Rhoda Morgenstern (Valerie Harper), stood in for all the changes affecting US women in the Me Decade, but what was happening behind the scenes was just as important. Under Brooks, *The Mary Tyler Moore Show* became the first major network series to hire women writers and directors and entrust them with ongoing responsibilities. Their perspective was reflected in the weekly stories about Mary, an office drone at a TV station who worked her way up to producer under station manager Lou Grant (Ed Asner) while dating and breaking up with various men, some fascinating and others rather trivial, without ever having to tacitly apologize to viewers for not having gotten married and squeezed out children before her thirtieth birthday.

The show's opening credits summed up the show's laid-back sense of empowerment: a series of images showing Mary going about the streets of Minneapolis, the show's hometown, while a man sang about how she could turn the world on with her smile and was gonna make it after all, capped by a triumphant freeze-frame of Mary tossing her knit winter cap into the air. There were no hostage episodes, no sudden pregnancies, nothing too dark; everything that happened in the workplace felt real, right down to the battles over propriety in said workplace. (Blustering newsman Ted Baxter, played by Ted Knight, pinched a woman's backside in an elevator, only to discover to his horror that it belonged to his newly hired station manager.) When the series did go "big," it was in the service of comedy, first and foremost—never more so than in the beloved episode about the death of children's performer Chuckles the Clown, who was crushed to death by an elephant at the circus while wearing a peanut costume. A bit of the minister's eulogy inadvertently describes the magic of The

Mary Tyler Moore Show: "Chuckles the Clown brought pleasure to millions. The characters he created will be remembered by children and adults alike: Peter Peanut, Mr. Fee-Fi-Fo, Billy Banana, and my particular favorite, Aunt Yoo Hoo. And not just for the laughter that they provided—there was always some deeper meaning to whatever Chuckles did."

The show fought an uphill battle against its own network. Brooks and Allan Burns originally pitched Mary as a divorcée, but the network's research department insisted that would be an instant show-killer. So Brooks and Burns had audiences meet Mary as she was getting out of a long relationship with a man she'd supported through medical school. The show's other characters were not so conciliatory toward TV's milquetoast norms: Lou Grant is a hard drinker who gets divorced; Rhoda Morgenstern is an abrasive New Yorker, and exuberantly Jewish. As the show wore on, other taboos fell, often so casually that nobody seemed to notice, much less get worked up about them. Mary had lived with her former boyfriend, in the same apartment (i.e., "in sin"), and in the later years of the show it was revealed (in a casual bit of dialogue) that she was on birth control. *The Mary Tyler*

Moore Show was one of the first network series to refer to a gay character as gay, and to insist, week in and week out, that one's real family consists of the people you choose to be around, not necessarily the ones related by blood.

"I just wanted you to know, that sometimes I get concerned about being a career woman," Mary says in the 1977 finale. "I get to thinking my job is too important to me. And I tell myself that the people I work with are just the people I work with, and not my family. And last night I thought, 'What is a family anyway?' They're just people who make you feel less alone and *really loved*. And that's what you've done for me. Thank you for being my family."

—MZS

The X-Files (Fox, 1993–2002)
Total score: 97

"We work in the dark," narrates FBI agent Fox Mulder, the questing hero of *The X-Files*, in a season 3 episode about a man who claims to be possessed by the spirit of a gargoyle. "We do what we can to battle the evil that would otherwise destroy us. But if a man's character is fate, this fight is not a choice but a calling. And sometimes the weight of this burden causes us to falter, breaching the fragile fortress of our mind, allowing the monsters without to turn within, and we are left alone staring into the abyss. Into the laughing face of madness."

The reverent momentousness of Mulder's words, perched as always on the edge of parody, is the essence of *The X-Files*. Part paranoid thriller, part *The Twilight Zone*– or *The Outer Limits*–style anthology, part platonic romance (between Mulder, played by David Duchovny, and his partner, Gillian Anderson's agent Dana Scully), Chris Carter's series was kidding and serious, manipulative and naive, touchingly straightforward and hopelessly overstuffed, often in the same week. It split the difference between serialized and anthologized storytelling, alternating grim and despairing chapters in an ongoing "mythology" and so-called Monster of the Week episodes. But its most significant achievement is historical. *The X-Files'* versatile format bridged the gap between the conservatism of broadcast TV and the creative restlessness of cable in the 1990s, at the same time that its subject matter channeled the political and cultural chaos of the '90s, putting the darkest undercurrents in US life under the show's warped microscope and scrutinizing it.

The X-Files debuted on Fox in the fall of 1993, less than two years after

Oliver Stone's hit potboiler *JFK*, which collected major conspiracy theories in a single narrative, and six months after the first World Trade Center bombing; it ended its run in May 2002, eight months after the second World Trade Center attack, which spawned more conspiracy narratives than any catastrophe since Kennedy. Its nine-season run overlapped all manner of paranoia-inducing events, including the 1995 bombing of the Alfred P. Murrah Federal Building in Oklahoma City (an event that was knowingly referenced in the 1998 film *The X-Files: Fight the Future*, in the bombing of a federal building in—of all places—Dallas). Throughout, there were moments when Carter's series felt like a conduit for fringe fantasies and nightmares of the culture that surrounded it—a culture that was increasingly intertwined with the Internet. By the late '90s, it was plausible for computer users to spend a few hours in an *X-Files*-centric chat room and then hop over to another one dedicated to arguing how many shots were fired at Dealey Plaza and whether this bombing or that terrorist attack was "really" carried out by the parties who'd been blamed for them, or if they were "false flag" operations that served the interests of a government or business cabal whose tentacles reached across the globe and back through time, and that might've included the Illuminati or the Masons.

Fox "Spooky" Mulder, who worked in a marginalized (and in the real world, nonexistent) department of the FBI, became the patron saint of conspiracy theorists, not just because he was played by a handsome but self-deprecatingly funny actor but because nearly every hunch Mulder played while unraveling the show's fantastically complex, borderline nonsensical conspiracy—the "mythology"—about Roswell and alien invasions and DNA and black oil and bees seemed right, even though Mulder and his allies couldn't prove it. The audience knew, or felt, that he was on to something, even when the powers that be buried incriminating details, or contrived to prevent him from seeing the bigger picture. Mulder's science-minded, proof-demanding partner, Scully, was initially presented as a foil, and a lot of early episodes ended on a tantalizingly inconclusive note. But after a few seasons even Scully had no choice but to get on board with Mulder's theorizing, and her insistence on evidence and explanations became a means of strengthening Mulder's claims rather than shooting them down. Mulder and Scully were sometimes aided by the Lone Gunmen (Bruce Harwood's John Fitzgerald Byers, Tom Braidwood's Melvin Frohike, and Dean Haglund's Richard "Ringo" Langly), Internet-savvy characters who played like fantasy identification figures aimed at fans who dreamed of helping the heroes.

If *The X-Files* had concentrated on Scully and Mulder's attempts to unravel the conspiracy, the series wouldn't have become the longest continuously running science-fiction drama in the history of US broadcast TV. Instead, the über-plot grew more tangled by the season, and the conspiracy episodes were brutal and despairing—the '90s fantasy version of '70s downer thrillers like *The Conversation*, *Chinatown*, and *The Parallax View*, tales in which it was never possible to know the whole story. Over nine seasons, Mulder's famous poster "The Truth Is Out There" seemed less hopeful than fatalistic.

But Carter and his fellow writer-producers alternated these episodes with self-contained "Monster of the Week" stories. These owed more to *The Twilight Zone*, *The Outer Limits*, and *Tales from the Crypt*, and were showcases for gruesome makeup, puppetry, and now-crude-looking digital effects,

and for Mulder and Scully's banter, which encompassed aspects of a sibling rivalry, platonic friendship, and will-they-or-won't-they flirtation. Over the years, the agents investigated a murderous computer ("Ghost in the Machine"), an arctic worm ("Ice"), a set of genetically identical girls developed as super-soldiers by the military ("Eve"), a pyrokinetic who made British politicians catch on fire ("Fire"), were-creatures ("Shapes," "Alpha," "Chimera"), vampires ("3"), a jaguar spirit ("Teso Dos Bichos"), a giant alligator called Big Blue ("Quagmire"), a sewer-dwelling "Flukeman" played by regular *X-Files* writer Darin Morgan ("The Host"), a car mechanic who could control lightning ("D.P.O."), a mutant emergency medical technician who could regenerate his body parts ("Leonard Betts"), an assassin who could will people into killing themselves ("Pusher," "Kitsunegari"), a shape-shifter—played by Morgan again—who fathered several children with vestigial tails ("Small Potatoes"), a soul-eater ("The Gift"), and an extraterrestrial who became an exceptional Negro League ballplayer ("The Unnatural"), to name just a few. There were also encounters with what could be described as human monsters: serial killers, mostly, but also people victimized by ways of life. The most notorious of these is the family from "Home," a clan of inbred, deformed hillbillies so revolting that the episode was shown only once during its regular run and yanked from syndication after viewer complaints.

The X-Files was arguably at its best in these one-offs, which tended to be light in tone and cleanly plotted. They were often slyly sexy, too, thanks to Duchovny and Anderson's charged banter, and laugh-out-loud funny. The episodes written by Darin Morgan often had a satirical and self-aware vibe; the best was season 3's "Clyde Bruckman's Final Repose," starring Peter Boyle as a man cursed to foretell the time and place of people's deaths. "You know, there are worse ways to go, but I can't think of a more undignified way than autoerotic asphyxiation," he blurts out during a car ride with the agents. "Why are you telling me that?" Mulder asks.

Science fiction has a spotty commercial track record on TV, but *The X-Files* was able to build a big and broad fan base because it was sci-fi in cop show drag, attracting viewers who would never have watched a version told from the point of view of the aliens, or even of William B. Davis's conspirator-in-chief, the Cigarette Smoking Man (who claimed the spotlight in one of the show's most mordantly funny episodes, "Musings of a Cigarette Smoking Man"; basically, "Evil Forrest Gump"). That audience cross-pollination was apparent in fans' fascination with the unresolved sexual tension between Mulder and Scully. *The X-Files* wasn't the first show to play that game, but it was the first with a collection of fans used to obsessing over everything about their favorite shows each week online. It popularized the concept of 'shipping (short for "relationshipping"), where some fans' desire to see their favorite characters get together overwhelms their interest in any other aspect of the series. Carter played a longer game with this than many other creators would, not letting Scully and Mulder have their first proper kiss until season 7, and not turning them into an actual couple until season 8. Fans still aren't entirely sure when the two officially became an item or whether their baby was produced the old-fashioned way. That Carter would leave the circumstances mysterious seems, in retrospect, like a bolder storytelling stroke than anything in his conspiracy episodes.

The first five seasons were shot in Vancouver, lending the proceedings a gloom and geographical vagueness that fit the show as snugly as

Mulder's red Speedo. An unhappy Duchovny pushed for production to shift to Los Angeles, which moved Mulder and Scully's adventures out of the shadows and into harsh sunlight. Foggy forests were replaced by deserts and highways, most successfully in season 6's "Drive," which introduced writer Vince Gilligan to actor Bryan Cranston (as a man with a deadly implant in his head who carjacks Mulder), paving the way for Cranston and Gilligan's reunion (in similarly sun-bleached terrain) on *Breaking Bad*. *The X-Files* became more technically ambitious, which helped compensate for the increasingly convoluted storytelling. Season 5 staged a black-and-white homage to the 1930s Universal Frankenstein pictures titled "The Post-Modern Prometheus." The sixth season featured the Carter-directed "Triangle," an episode where each act was presented as a continuous take on board a German-occupied British ocean liner during World War II and in FBI headquarters in the present. Its aesthetic peak found the 1940s version of Scully and the latter-day version passing each other across the frame-line of a split-screen composition; both Scullys pause and shiver as if each has been passed through by a ghost.

The X-Files was the first major show since the original *Batman* to release a theatrical film while the mother-ship series was actively on the air and producing new episodes. A more remarkable, related milestone: The tie-in movie, titled *The X-Files: Fight the Future*, was integrated into the series' ongoing story line, amounting to a two-hour, big-budget episode that fans had to pay to see. It hit theaters the summer after the conclusion of season 5 and set up events in season 6.

In addition to branching into film, Carter built out his personal brand with the bleak, exceptionally violent *Millennium* (1996–1999), starring craggy-faced character actor Lance Henriksen (*Aliens*, *Near Dark*) as a criminal profiler who works for the shadowy Millennium group; the dystopian action series *Harsh Realm* (1999–2000), set mainly inside of a virtual-reality combat simulator used to train US soldiers; and the one-season *The Lone Gunmen* spin-off (2001). The latter is remembered mainly for its pilot, which found its titular trio foiling a scheme to crash a remote-piloted commercial jetliner into the World Trade Center; it aired March 4, 2001, six months and seven days before the attacks of 9/11. *The X-Files*, *Millennium*, and

The Lone Gunmen were all part of a shared universe; when *Millennium* was canceled, its story lines were concluded in an *X-Files* episode.

If Carter had a coherent plan for the mythology at the start, *The X-Files'* popularity—and, therefore, the need to elongate the mysteries, save certain big reveals for the movie, et cetera—began to turn what had once been the biggest narrative hook into a stone around the series' neck. Even then, there was still the Mulder-Scully partnership to keep things interesting, but Duchovny stepped back his involvement with the show, appearing in only half of season 8's episodes, and only twice in the final season, and replacement characters John Doggett (Robert Patrick) and Monica Reyes (Annabeth Gish) didn't hold the same appeal. That the series ended with so many questions unanswered felt appropriate, even if it wasn't reassuring. A second film, *The X-Files: I Want to Believe*, was released in 2008, four years after the end of the series; while a box-office disappointment, it proved that there was still a loyal fan base for Scully and Mulder's adventures, and helped jump-start talk of a third feature, which morphed into a six-episode miniseries that aired on Fox in 2016.

Carter's attempts to build a multilayered franchise across two media never quite gelled, but he showed that such a thing could be done, and the executives at Marvel and DC Comics took notice, intertwining theatrical films and TV series that were part of a shared universe, every part embellishing and hyping every other. The comic book universes' triumphs are mainly financial and logistical rather than artistic, though; Carter's characters have more wit and soul, and feel like true adults rather than action figures trapped in an eternal twilight between adolescence and adulthood. The six-episode 2016 series was hit-and-miss, awkward in many ways and overly dependent on Easter eggs and fan service (to the point of repeating catchphrases). But it inspired affection anyway, mainly for how it acknowledged the burden of the show's long-running popularity on Carter, his fellow writers and filmmakers, and on the core trio of Duchovny, Anderson, and Mitch Pileggi (as FBI assistant director Walter Skinner), who were wiser, sadder, and visibly older than during the last go-round, but still game to whip their flashlights out and wade into the gloom in search of the truth.

—MZS & AS

Curb Your Enthusiasm (HBO, 2000–2011) Total score: 96

Imagine George Costanza from *Seinfeld*, but with a little bit of fame, a lot of money, a beautiful (if often irritated) wife, and almost zero accountability. That's the starting point for *Curb Your Enthusiasm*, an inventively plotted, scathingly funny, joyously foulmouthed comedy series created by *Seinfeld* cocreator (and Costanza inspiration) Larry David.

David played himself opposite a floating repertory company of regular costars, recurring cast members, and cameo players. Some played versions of themselves: Richard Lewis, Ted Danson, Wanda Sykes, all four *Seinfeld* alums at different times. Others played fictionalized characters: Cheryl Hines as Larry's frustrated wife, Cheryl; Jeff Garlin as his business manager; Susie Essman as Garlin's spectacularly profane wife; and, in later seasons, Bob Einstein as Larry's frenemy Marty Funkhouser and J. B. Smoove as Larry's gregarious sidekick Leon Black, who had even less of an internal censor than Larry.

As on *Seinfeld*, each episode would feature a mixture of plots that tended to converge at the end, usually in a way that righted the cosmic scales by severely punishing or humiliating Larry for having been a horrendous asshole for the preceding twenty-five minutes. As on *Seinfeld*, characters were defined by their pathologies, misconceptions, tics, prejudices, grudges, and so on; they were often defined by one or two traits (Larry's arrogant certainty of his own rightness, for instance, or Richard Lewis's insecurity and manic behavior, which fueled his comedy offscreen as well), and the show rarely asked us to sympathize with any one character (even the long-suffering Cheryl could be annoyingly passive-aggressive at times).

Social anthropology was the main order of business. Like *Seinfeld*, but with a more desperate, at times furious edge, the series did a brilliant job of identifying phenomena we vaguely recognized but had never put a name to before—for instance, "pig parking," the practice of parking in a way that takes up more than one space and screws things up for people who park after you. The tightly interwoven subplots emboldened Larry to flout, subvert, reinvent, or game every social nicety, rule, and law. The show wasn't shy about pointing out the ways in which Larry's social prominence, wealth, and white skin emboldened him to condescend to people who didn't have one or more of those traits in common with him. His rudeness and cruelty led to shenanigans, still more shenanigans, and sometimes to wholesale destruction, occasionally capped with a fleeting moment of enlightenment or a freeze-frame of Larry being hoisted on his own petard. David's skill at manipulating audience sympathies came through as strongly here as it did in the later, darker years of *Seinfeld*.

The first half of any given episode might style Larry as half id-beast, half anti-political-correctness crusader. His ire was often so hilarious (never more so than when he was teeing off on some puny annoyance, such as the pretentiousness of the Starbucks menu) that viewers' rational objections disappeared for a while until they had to emerge again because Larry's horrendous behavior made them feel vaguely ashamed for identifying with him. You rooted for him to tear through Los Angeles like a balding, stooped-over tornado (in one episode, Larry is outraged that he can't drive in a high-occupancy vehicle lane with just one passenger, so he picks up a prostitute), but then he'd go too far, then way too far, and right when Larry threatened to become entirely monstrous, he'd receive his comeuppance (the punch line of the HOV-lane gag finds Larry getting photographed by a traffic camera in a compromising position with his passenger, who wasn't even doing anything compromising with him). There was an O. Henry–like ironic purity to how things turned out. After years of race-baiting by Larry, the now-divorced antihero dates a black woman whose last name is actually Black. In season 5, Larry, who had previously used his Jewish identity as an excuse to duck obligations and act on impulse (he once ate the baby Jesus out of a nativity cookie plate, then claimed he'd mistaken it for a monkey), learned that his birth parents were devout Christians from Bisbee, Arizona, and (before finding out that this was all a mistake and his parents were his parents) threw himself into learning to hunt, sing hymns, and chug cheap beer.

HBO gave David more creative freedom than he'd ever had on NBC, starting with the ability to play himself rather than filling the role with Jason Alexander (whose *Curb* appearances displayed contempt for qualities associated with his alter ego—and thus the man on whom George was based). David was also able to use profanity and ethnic, racial, homophobic, and sexist slurs (a third-season episode revolves around an obituary typo that mistakenly refers to Cheryl's beloved aunt as a "beloved cunt"), improvise most of the dialogue in any given scene (while sticking to strict plot outlines), and root many of the subplots in fine points of culture, politics, and religion. The latter was especially striking because David and his *Seinfeld* collaborators had to fudge particulars to avoid antagonizing censors and sponsors. Jerry, for instance, was a Jew who never explicitly identified as one until a late-series episode, whereas *Curb* did stories that treated specific and dire material irreverently (a Holocaust survivor and a former *Survivor* cast member wind up at the same dinner due to a misunderstanding) or trafficked in Jewish esoterica (such as the special section in some Hebrew cemeteries set aside for suicides and people with tattoos).

Even more than the series that provided its structural template—not to mention many similar plotlines, like the main character befriending a figure from the 1986 World Series (again being generous, David provides Red Sox goat Bill Buckner the chance to redeem himself for letting the ball go through his legs)—*Curb* was a meticulously constructed comic contraption, not only within each episode but over the course of

seasons, most of which ended on notes that would've constituted a pretty, pretty, prêt-tay good series finale had he decided to quit there (Larry dies but gets kicked out of heaven for being annoying; Larry triumphs in a Broadway production of *The Producers*, not knowing that Mel Brooks cast him hoping that he'd kill the show). The finality of each season's end made sense when you understood David's sweet deal with HBO, which put him under no obligation to ever make another season but gave him the freedom to do another the minute he had a good idea for one.

David even managed to defend, interrogate, and stealth-remake the *Seinfeld* finale, building a whole season around TV Larry assembling the old show's core cast for a reunion special. This ruse let David tie a more satisfying bow around his earlier hit without having to give viewers more than a taste of what Jerry, George, Elaine, and Kramer had been up to since we last saw them in jail. (The season also made clear that Jerry Seinfeld—or, at least, this version of him—was indistinguishable from Larry David aside from sporting a lush head of hair and a willingness to at least fake being interested in other people.)

One of the subtexts of *Curb* was

a craving to prove that *Seinfeld* was no fluke. The stories mock this obsession even as the scripts validate its usefulness as a wellspring of comic ambition. The show you're watching is the show that "Larry David" could never create, and its mercurial energy comes from watching David dismantle and rebuild the perfect comic engine he created with Jerry Seinfeld back in the day—the better to reflect his own wilder, nastier vision of life, which at times feels like a Jerry Lewis movie with splashes of Federico Fellini's magical-grotesque, circus-of-life sensibility. (The sound track repeatedly quotes passages from Fellini's favorite score composer, Nino Rota.) *Curb*'s "Larry" is as rich, famous, and relatively untouchable as the genuine article, but he's clearly bothered by the idea that his best work is behind him. All the money and perks he's accumulated can't quell his fear that his cultural footprint is fading, that his achievements mean nothing beyond this circle-jerking corner of Hollywood, and that he's at risk of morphing, Cinderella-like, back into George Costanza. And so he lashes out at everyone and everything, with a mad-eyed force that would be devastating if the character had better aim and wiser taste in targets.

If the show itself weren't such a masterpiece of scabrous wit, it would come off as unseemly and pathetic: the ranting of a sore winner. Much of *Curb*'s nearly horrifying humor comes from the sight of Larry trying to bend the world to his will in the way that the ineffectual and cowardly George Costanza never could. Relief arrives when you step back and admire the show's comic architecture and keen sense of when to pull back from the brink and when to dive headfirst into the abyss. While TV Larry fumes and schemes and makes an ass of himself, the real Larry David bends TV comedy into spikier shapes than NBC would ever allow.

Perhaps the quintessential *Curb* moment comes at the end of season 3, when the opening of a restaurant Larry, Danson, and others have invested in threatens to go awry due to a profane outburst by the head chef, who's afflicted with Tourette's. Larry, who often means well but is usually too lazy, selfish, and/or clumsy to make his intentions into reality, tries to help out the chef and normalize his behavior by shouting curses, and soon Jeff, Cheryl, and everyone else in the restaurant has joined in, until the place is a cacophony of four-letter words, all in the service of a good deed performed by a delighted Larry David, who has reshaped his environment into something more reflecting of who he is inside.

—MZS & AS

SpongeBob SquarePants
(Nickelodeon, 1999–present)
Total score: 96

The Rocky and Bullwinkle Show
(ABC, 1959–1961; NBC, 1961–
1964) Total score: 78

Who lives in a pineapple under the sea? Why, one of the stars of the most brilliantly imagined and sustained display of surreal humor in pop culture, that's who. SpongeBob SquarePants: bug-eyed, buck-toothed exponent of the phylum Porifera, and the most indestructibly innocent ninny since Candide—an ebullient, yammering, shrieking dolt, playing nautical melodies on his slide-whistle nose; disassembling and reassembling and exploding and imploding from shock and joy; singing songs about the best day ever and the best time to wear a striped sweater (*"All the time!"*); frolicking through the best of all possible undersea worlds with his dear friends Patrick the starfish and Sandra "Sandy" Cheeks the squirrel; doting on his pet snail Gary; inadvertently tormenting his anal-retentive cephalopod neighbor Squidward and his penny-pinching boss, Mr. Krabs; improving and destroying and rebuilding and improving and destroying his underwater hometown, Bikini Bottom; and bringing joy to children and Dadaesque humor to adults both straight and stoned.

SpongeBob: Patrick, you're a genius!
Patrick: Yeah, I get called that a lot.
SpongeBob: What? A genius?
Patrick: No. *Patrick.*

Created by animator and biologist Stephen Hillenburg, *SpongeBob SquarePants* is in every way a classic work of family entertainment, hitting the same conceptual sweet spot as the Marxes, Laurel and Hardy, *Looney Tunes*, *The Simpsons*, and *The Muppet Show*: silly creatures and voices and wild slapstick for little kids, outrageous puns and non sequiturs for slightly older kids, pop culture parody and thinly veiled social commentary for grown-ups, and brazen inventiveness for all. The universe that contains Bikini Bottom maintains rigorous internal consistency by doing whatever the heck the writers and animators feel like doing; as in *Duck Soup*, or certain defiantly patched-together films from W. C. Fields, the show favors situations over stories and comic effects over messages, and given the choice between doing something expected yet clever and something that seems to have been released from the reincarnated id of Marcel Duchamp or Salvador Dalí, it goes with option B.

> **Squidward:** Could you not stand so close? You're making me claustrophobic!
> **Patrick:** What does "claustrophobic" mean?
> **SpongeBob:** It means he's afraid of Santa Claus.
> **Patrick:** Ho ho ho!
> **SpongeBob:** Stop it, Patrick! You're scaring him!

The show is set mostly underwater, but not so you'd notice—when characters get excited or scared or unduly exert themselves, you might or might not see bubble trails, depending on whether the artists feel like drawing them, perhaps—and for the most part, "under the sea" amounts to a Yellow Submarine–styled fantasy of life above the waterline. There are houses and office buildings, fast-food restaurants and schools, highways and railways, cars and trucks and bikes, swimming pools and beaches (!), and boats (!!). Sometimes it rains (!!!) or snows (!!!!). There are moments when humans or mammals somehow

find their way down to the ocean floor; when they do, they're usually played by human actors in ridiculous outfits or very cheap animal costumes. (A gorilla in a diving helmet that terrorizes our heroes seems to have been inspired by the titular beast from *Robot Monster*.) The passage of time is indicated by the monotonous mutterings of a French-accented narrator modeled on Gallic explorer Jacques Cousteau: "Three hours later." "Four days later." "So much later that the old narrator got tired of waiting and they had to hire a new one." The hero is a good-natured, wandering peanut-brain, a perforated Gomer Pyle. "Well it's no secret that the best thing about a secret is secretly telling someone your secret, thereby secretly adding another secret to their secret collection of secrets," he peals. "Secretly!" His laugh could curl your hair, even if your hair is already curly, and his fearful shriek could strip the barnacles from the deck of Mr. Krabs's pirate ship, the *Krusty Krab*, which supposedly was reformatted into the Krusty Krab restaurant, but which might actually have once been a retirement home called the Rusty Krab, according to the *Krusty Krab Training Video*, which may or may not be a reliable source of information.

[Squidward asks if anyone can play an instrument.]

Patrick: Is mayonnaise an instrument?

Squidward: No, Patrick, mayonnaise is not an instrument.

[Patrick raises his fin.]

Squidward: Horseradish is not an instrument, either.

Bikini Bottom has its own fables and legends and myths and bedtime stories and detailed mythologies. In an episode that sends up campfire stories, Mr. Krabs decides he can make more money by staying open twenty-four hours, which traps the eager-to-please Sponge-Bob and the dour Squidward in the restaurant all night and causes Squidward to devise the bloodcurdling tale of the Hash-Slinging Slasher ("The Slash-Bringing Hasher?" SpongeBob asks), a one-time fry cook who accidentally sliced off his hand and replaced it with a spatula. In another episode, Patrick and SpongeBob decide to go camping (which entails pitching a tent between SpongeBob's pineapple and Squidward's house, which looks like a tiki idol and has the exact address 122 Conch Street) and warn him not to do anything that might summon the dreaded Sea Bear. The list of summoning behaviors includes playing the clarinet badly, waving your flashlight back and forth really fast, stomping the ground, eating cubed cheese (sliced is safe), wearing a sombrero in a goofy fashion, wearing clown shoes or a hoop skirt, running, limping, crawling, and screeching like a chimpanzee. Of course Squidward insists on doing all of those things (and it's impressive how he can rush offscreen and reappear moments later with clown shoes, a hoop skirt, and a sombrero—but hey, Bugs Bunny could produce a mallet out of thin air and bonk Elmer Fudd on the head with it, so give the squid a break), and lo and behold, a Sea Bear appears and subjects Squidward to a Scorsese-level beatdown (off-camera, thankfully). SpongeBob and Patrick are safe because they've drawn a circle around themselves, but unfortunately this can't insulate them from a follow-up attack by the Sea Bear's dreaded enemy, the Sea Rhinoceros, who is drawn by the sound of a Sea Bear attack and can be repelled only by Anti–Sea Rhinoceros Undergarments.

It all makes perfect non-sense. The more demented the visuals become, the more sublime *Sponge-Bob* is.

The highlight of the aforementioned Hash-Slinging Slasher episode is SpongeBob's fearful reaction to Squidward's patched-together story: First he chews his nails, then he eats his arms over and over (they make a buzz-saw sound as they arc into his gullet), and finally he pops an endless series of disembodied SpongeBob arms into his maw from a popcorn bucket. In the Fry Cook Games, a fast-food version of the Olympics, Patrick and Sponge-Bob compete in a chocolate high dive and grapple in a wrestling ring atop a giant sandwich bun. "The inner machinations of my mind are an enigma," intones Patrick in one of the many moments when he becomes lost in thought or insists on being recognized for his intellect, whereupon we see a thought balloon of a carton of milk tipping over. In another episode, filled with dreams of material success by *Fancy Living* magazine, SpongeBob and Patrick envision owning a house with a swimming pool inside of another swimming pool and decide that the best way to get rich is by selling chocolate door-to-door, but get bamboozled by a con-fish who sells them individual zippered bags for every chocolate bar and still more bags to hold the bags, and then takes what's left of their money by pretending that he's in constant pain because he has glass bones and paper skin and injures himself whenever he moves.

And then there's the Iron Butt. Look it up.

At the core of all this situational and verbal absurdity lies very, very silly and very, very stupid humor, of a type that parents know is sure to delight a child who has been verbal for only two or three years and therefore hasn't yet been conditioned by authority figures to demand that stories be consistent or scenarios "believable." ("That smell...A kind of smelly smell... The smelly smell that smells smelly," says Mr. Krabs, a mini-monologue equally likely to slay a five-year-old or Salman Rushdie.) The same indestructible faith in the transformative power of imagination that can turn a refrigerator box into a spaceship or a bath towel into a Superman cape powers the imaginations of the show's creative team. The apotheosis of *Sponge-Bob*'s methodical madness could be "Frankendoodle," a segment in the spirit of Chuck Jones's classic *Duck Amuck*, wherein SpongeBob and Patrick acquire a magic pencil accidentally dropped from a rowboat by an artistically inclined pirate and draw a black-and-white golemesque doppelgänger of SpongeBob who takes possession of the pencil and embarks on a campaign of eraser-driven terror, rubbing out portions of the animated landscape and—in a moment that distills the show's aesthetic to a single gesture—SpongeBob's crack. Always hold on to your magic pencil, kids, and remember that mayonnaise is not an instrument.

That last "moral" would not be out of place on *The Rocky and Bullwinkle Show* (sometimes known as *Rocky and Bullwinkle and Friends* or *The Bullwinkle Show*), a groundbreaking cartoon series whose excellence resonated far beyond its Saturday morning time slot. Created by Jay Ward, Alex Anderson, and Bill Scott as a means to sell sugary cereal to children (to this day, the characters remain wholly owned properties of General Mills), the show was the most radical thing to appear on children's TV until that point: arguably much more of an "adult" cartoon series than the prime-time hits *The Flintstones* and *The Jetsons* (both of which essentially ripped off *The Honeymooners* but added prehistoric anachronisms and Eisenhower-vintage sci-fi jokes, respectively), *Rocky and Bullwinkle* owed more to the unself-conscious deconstructions of *The Jack Benny Program* and the quasi-experimental formalism of Ernie Kovacs than to anything that was genuinely aimed at tots. Little kids laughed at the goofy-looking animals and humans with their silly voices and accents and perhaps at the broader slapstick bits, but the excited archness of the storytelling and the plethora of puns, double entendres, and fourth wall–breaking asides were aimed at parents and adult caregivers, as well as college students who'd been up all Friday night and wanted a splash of absurdism with the hair of the dog that bit them.

Each episode was a grab bag of recurring bits, most self-contained (the sardonic spoofs "Fractured Fairy Tales" and "Aesop and Son"), others serialized in the manner of theatrical cliff-hangers, albeit without a trace of suspense about how things would resolve. The wanderings of Bullwinkle J. Moose (Bill Scott) and Rocket "Rocky" J. Squirrel (June Foray), previously the favorite sons of Frostbite Falls, Minnesota, were interspersed with other ongoing shows-within-shows. In "The Adventures of Dudley Do-Right," Scott stars as the voice of a square and square-jawed Canadian Mountie battling a literally mustache-twirling villain named Snidely Whiplash (Hans Conried). In "Peabody's Improbable History," a genius dog (Scott) and his adopted human son, Sherman (Foray), travel through time and get involved with Napoleon, Pancho Villa, and the like. "The

World of Commander McBragg" chronicles the exaggerated exploits of an elderly veteran of every war of the preceding century. Some of the wordplay is skull-smackingly obvious (Bullwinkle and Rocky's alma mater is Wossamotta U). The rest is so brainy that it takes a moment to register the nature of the joke (when Mr. Peabody and Sherman try to capture a dreaded bandit known as Zero, who brands things à la Zorro, there's a pan across a wall of "Wanted" posters that includes a sketch of an outlaw named Joaquin Behindu). The dumber the joke, the bigger the belly laugh, generally—and the responsibility for earning it often lies with Bullwinkle, who misperceives situations that a toddler would grasp. (When the moose and squirrel's nemeses, Russian spies Boris Badenov and Natasha Fatale, fail to kill them by dropping a safe from a window, Bullwinkle stares at the crater in the sidewalk, then yells, "Hey, up there! *Ya dropped yer safe!*")

The eye-popping yet crude animation added to the sense of wonder. The gap between the sophistication of the writing and the sight of characters practically sliding across the screen, their feet moving out of sync with the ground beneath their feet while background elements, including blank-faced and often immobile "extras," reappeared ad nauseam (as they would on *South Park* generations later), multiplied the aura of benevolent madness. Even the interstitial materials, which existed to segue in and out of ad blocks, displayed a level of imagination and beauty that was unnecessary given their function, yet marvelous for that very reason: Rocky helping Bullwinkle try and fail to pull off the "rabbit in a hat trick" (he kept producing ravenous lions, tigers, bears, and the like); "Bullwinkle's Corner," featuring illustrated renditions of poems read aloud by the moose; a repeated sequence showing the silhouetted Rocky and Bullwinkle flying down past a jagged mountain peak during a thunderstorm, getting buried in the earth, and then erupting into the sunlight amid a crop of flowers.

Like its direct spiritual descendant, *SpongeBob*, this show found the sublime in the ridiculous and vice versa. It's easy to dismiss comedies as being innately inferior to dramas because their main purpose is to make people laugh and brighten their moods, and because dramas tend to be sticklers about structure, whereas in comedy it's all about the moment, the pun, the punch line, the sight gag. That mandate can make noncomic minds think there's no art to winning a laugh—that you just keep saying and doing and drawing things until someone guffaws. That's true, insofar as it goes. But there the best slapstick comedy can achieve an expressive richness that rivals that of the most meticulous entertainment that calls itself drama. Image and sound, dialogue and composition, color and texture come together in shows like *SpongeBob Squarepants* and *The Rocky and Bullwinkle Show* to create a hallucination of life, a snapshot of chaos and joy.

—MZS

Twin Peaks (ABC, 1990–1991)
Total score: 96

Five minutes and fifty-nine seconds. That's how long it takes for the pilot episode of *Twin Peaks* to unwrap the plastic sheeting on the corpse of Laura Palmer (Sheryl Lee) and reveal her masklike face. Her hair is plastered back against her scalp and there are gritty flecks of soil on her forehead and cheeks.

Who killed Laura Palmer? That was the question in the minds of the thirty-four million people who watched the premiere of David Lynch and Mark Frost's indescribably original drama, and as the series unfolded over the next two seasons (one and a half, really; the first contained just eight episodes), they grew increasingly frustrated by Lynch and Frost's refusal to solve it, as well as by the playfully sadistic way the show prolonged the suspense until it began to dissipate. Some viewers started to get annoyed as early as the end of the third episode, when FBI special agent Dale Cooper (Kyle MacLachlan) had a dream about a plush red room containing a Laura Palmer look-alike and a dancing dwarf whose cryptic dialogue ("Where we're from, the birds sing a pretty song, and there is always music in the air") was recorded backward and then played forward; Cooper woke up and called to tell his partner, local sheriff Harry S. Truman (Michael Ontkean), that he'd figured out who killed Laura Palmer, then added, "And yes, it can wait till morning," but when the morning arrived at the start of the next episode, he said he'd forgotten that part of the dream and that they'd have to recapture it through an intuitive process involving meditation, target shooting, and word association.

Lynch, Frost, and their fellow writers and filmmakers—a formidable bunch that included the brilliant cinematographer Caleb Deschanel (*The Black Stallion*), *River's Edge* director Tim Hunter, and future Hall of Fame series TV director Lesli Linka Glatter (*Homeland, Mad Men*)—continued to test the audience's patience ever more brazenly. The season 1 finale showed Cooper getting shot in his hotel room by an unseen assailant, then season 2 opened with a protracted comic bit of business between the wounded Cooper and a shuffling elderly bellhop. When the murderer was finally revealed to be Laura Palmer's own father, Leland (Ray Wise), under control of a savage woodland demon known as BOB (Frank Silva, a set dresser on the pilot who was cast after Lynch saw his face reflected in a mirror), he committed another killing (of Laura's look-alike cousin Maddy Ferguson, also played by Lee), and the show spent an entire episode following him as he drove around town with Maddy's corpse in the trunk of his car.

After that, the ratings plunged, and in the spring of 1991, ABC pulled the plug; by that point the series had moved on to other, less compelling plotlines, delving into the paranormal aspects of the show's mythology (including a puzzle box, a possible UFO, and the Black Lodge, where evil doppelgängers of all the main characters dwelled) and tying up loose ends. A good case could be made for the idea that *Twin Peaks* should have been a self-contained miniseries rather than an ongoing series. (Years later, Frost acknowledged that he and Lynch never expected the show to succeed, and that they'd therefore have to resolve those story lines.)

But if you go back and watch that pilot again—or other Lynch films, notably his 1986 thriller *Blue Velvet*—you can see that Laura's murder was merely the clothesline along which the show's writers and directors could string a story that was more perverse, frightening, sensual, and self-aware than most, but that still owed much to the daytime and nighttime soaps that it mocked in its show-within-a-show, *Invitation to Love*.

Like most Lynch, *Twin Peaks* was at once a deconstruction and parody of the genres it invoked (the police procedural, the horror movie, the gothic-inflected small-town potboiler) and a satisfying example of same. The show could be silly in one moment (Lynch gave himself a recurring role as Cooper's hearing-impaired supervisor, who would shout things like "COOPER, YOU REMIND ME TODAY OF A SMALL MEXICAN CHIHUAHUA!") and shockingly violent in the next. The casual portrayal of teen sex with multiple partners, cocaine use, incest, rape, corpse mutilation, and other cable-ready material was shocking by 1990 broadcast TV standards (though no big deal in the post–*Law & Order: Special Victims Unit* era); Lynch and Frost's goofy humor etched the darker elements in even sharper relief. Cooper was both a sincere, square-jawed hero and a Lynchian weirdo, a smile plastered across his face as he extolled the virtues of the local food and drink ("Damn good coffee! And hot!") and dictated his thoughts into a tape recorder for transcription by an unseen assistant ("Diane, I'm holding in my hand a box of chocolate bunnies"). Half the town's population seems borrowed from a swoony '50s melodrama, the other half from a mental hospital. Nadine Hurley (Wendy Robie), wife of gas station owner Big Ed (Everett McGill), is obsessed with inventing silent drape runners, then falls into a coma, only to wake up acting like her teenage self. Leland Palmer's overwhelming grief was contrasted with the hammy scheming of his business partners Ben Horne (Richard Beymer) and Ben's brother Jerry (David Patrick Kelly). (The two acting styles cross paths when Leland seemingly overcomes his pain and bursts into Ben's office singing "Mairzy Doats," inspiring the brothers to start break-dancing;

it's possibly the pinnacle of Western television.) Truman wouldn't seem out of place as a sheriff in a John Ford Western, even as he takes the community's eccentricity at face value; when Cooper wonders about the woman (Catherine Coulson) who carries a small log around town, Truman deadpans, "We call her the Log Lady."

None of these elements—not to mention the slow and mournful score by Angelo Badalamenti and the fusion of hard-boiled crime fiction and talk of demons and parallel dimensions—had any business working in concert; but in the show's first half, with the Laura Palmer investigation as a unifying element, it did. Lynch and Frost constantly went for big moments, knowing that the feelings they evoked would make complaints about consistency seem petty: teen siren Audrey Horne (Sherilyn Fenn) dancing provocatively around the jukebox or tying a cherry stem into a knot with her tongue; Sarah Palmer (Grace Zabriskie) screaming at the sight of BOB lurking behind Laura's bedpost; or sensitive, dim-witted Deputy Andy Brennan (Harry Goaz) crying at the sight of corpses.

It's not only the strangest show to ever air on US network television, but the strangest one to (briefly) become a hit. The larger audience lost interest when they figured out that solving Laura's murder wasn't high on Lynch and Frost's to-do list. But the show's commitment to its passions and eccentricities left a mark, becoming a clear influence on more mainstream-oriented series like *The X-Files*, *The Sopranos*, and *Lost*, and inspiring such a devoted cult that Showtime belatedly commissioned a follow-up miniseries, with Lynch set to direct every episode. Originally the resurrection was scheduled for 2016, a quarter-century after the finale, which saw the spirit of Laura Palmer promising Agent Cooper, "I'll see you in twenty-five years."

—MZS & AS

Lost (ABC, 2004–2010) Total score: 95

The first season of *Lost* ended on a profoundly aggravating note. After spending months teasing viewers about what was inside a mysterious hatch that Locke (Terry O'Quinn) had found on the island where he and his fellow plane-crash survivors were trapped, the finale concluded with Locke using dynamite to blow the hatch open, followed by a swooping camera shot down past a broken ladder, followed by . . .

Nothing. See you in the fall, everybody!

When the show returned four months later, it didn't waste additional time showing us who and what were in the hatch: a futuristic research station, manned by an unhinged Scotsman—who in time would be revealed to have the ability to project his consciousness across time, space, and even the veil of death—listening to Mama Cass Elliot's "Make Your Own Kind of Music" as he exercised, did laundry, and entered numbers into a computer every 108 minutes in an attempt to stave off the end of the world.

That, right there, is everything that was maddening but delightful about *Lost*. What other show would not only dare to frustrate its audience to that degree with the cliff-hanger but follow it up with such a bizarre yet riveting payoff? What other show could have its viewers cursing its very existence in one breath and then cheering at the top of their lungs the next?

For six seasons, *Lost* aimed higher, wider, and further than anyone could have expected from a show born out of the chairman of ABC's desire for a scripted version of *Survivor*. In the process, it demonstrated how thin the line in television can be between inspiration and insanity, and for fandom, between love and hate. Only a show capable of moving us so deeply could make us so enraged when it screwed up.

Created in a rush by Damon Lindelof and J. J. Abrams, and eventually run by Lindelof and Carlton Cuse, *Lost* mashed up different genres like they were unlikely smoothie ingredients, turned the island itself into as dense, complex, and physically impressive a fictional world as any TV has ever had, bounced backward and forward in time, and raised five new questions for every old one it answered.

It went big all the time, which meant sometimes it failed big, like the period when chief heroes Jack (Matthew Fox), Kate (Evangeline Lilly), and Sawyer (Josh Holloway) were locked in polar bear cages for several episodes while we found out where Jack got his tattoos. But it also meant that it often succeeded enormously. Before the fake-out with the hatch, first-season finale "Exodus" is a marvel, packed with suspense, action, black comedy, and every last tear the show could wring out of Michael Giacchino's gorgeous score. The moment at the end of the fourth episode, "Walkabout," which revealed that Locke was wheelchair-bound before he came to the island, is a spine-tingler in every sense. All throughout the series, up to and including the divisive final episode, there were soaring emotional moments that were possible only because Lindelof, Cuse, and company were attempting something that common sense and conventional TV wisdom would call risky at best, mind-bogglingly stupid at worst. I mean, they did a whole episode where Sawyer helped Hurley (Jorge Garcia) fix up an abandoned VW van they found on the island—not because there was any value to it at the time (though Hurley did later use it to run over a bad guy and save his friends), but because it would help Hurley get over his fear of being a jinx—and it's among the ones I'm most eager to rewatch when the opportunity arises.

Look, did *Lost* do a satisfying job of resolving many of its mysteries? Not particularly. Sometimes, it was a victim of being the first show crowd-sourced by the Internet, as viewers teamed up on message boards to try to solve the mysteries—an option not available in the days of "Who shot J.R.?"—so that they figured out that Claire (Emilie de Ravin) was Jack's half sister, or that Locke's con artist father was the man responsible for the deaths of Sawyer's parents, years before the characters on the show found out. But other times, the answers were just underwhelming, whether learning that the six castaways who briefly got off the island just happened to be the ones nearest a helicopter as it was flying away from an explosion, or, more glaringly, discovering that all the island's weird properties and conflict could be traced back to a mysterious golden pool of light.

But if the business with the hatch at the end of "Exodus" hadn't already conditioned the viewer to be underwhelmed by answers on the show (or at least to be incredibly patient about waiting for them), then dozens of moments since should have. *Lost* was always better with questions than answers. Yet, despite that, its finales tended to be its most potent, beloved installments, because in addition to explanations, they offered payoffs to spare in terms of action, plot, and character arcs.

However angry it still makes some fans to talk about the series finale all these years later, and however flawed the final season's conception was of a "sideways" universe (revealed at the end to be a corner of the afterlife where all the island's residents could reunite before going on to their final rewards), that last episode still offers ample thrills and tears and laughs. It doesn't necessarily forgive some of the mistakes and odd choices made earlier that season, or in previous ones, but the great *Lost* moments and the baffling ones all came from the same genuine place, and the same messy process. The sideways universe may have not been the best use of time in the last season, but it gave us Sawyer's awestruck reunion with his Juliet (Elizabeth Mitchell), and Kate, Claire, and Charlie (Dominic Monaghan) reexperiencing the birth of Claire's baby, and the finale as a whole concluded Jack's transformation from lovably flawed hero to petulant story obstacle and back again in a way that had to choke up even the most devout of Jack deniers. It all came together, even when it didn't.

In some other sideways universe, there's a more consistent, more logical, less puzzling version of *Lost*.

It's probably also a lot less fun.

—AS

Buffy the Vampire Slayer (WB, 1997–2001; UPN, 2001–2003)
Total score: 94

TV show titles rarely bring viewers into the tent, but they can keep them away. If you want to give your charming blended-family comedy an ironic name like *Trophy Wife*, don't be surprised if your target demographic takes it literally and stays far away. (See also *Terriers, Selfie, Crazy Ex-Girlfriend . . .*)

Now, *Buffy the Vampire Slayer* ran seven seasons, was never in danger of cancellation at any point (it jumped networks after season 5 only because UPN was looking to steal a hit from its rival the WB), launched a long-running (and, eventually, very good) spin-off in *Angel*, was beloved by its fans, and helped define the identity of an entire TV network for the short but memorable existence of the WB. By any standard you want to measure, *Buffy* was a success.

Except maybe this one: If you tell someone who's never watched it that a show called *Buffy the Vampire Slayer* is among the best TV dramas of all time, they will roll their eyes at you and change the subject to something less divisive, like immigration policy.

Would a *Buffy the Vampire Slayer* by any other name have been a crossover hit rather than a cult classic, or won more awards, or simply have been an easier sell to nonfans? Certainly, you can imagine WB executives thinking that, which is why they briefly tried to get Joss Whedon to shorten the title to just *Slayer*.

Whedon held firm, and not just because it might have created confusion between the show and the thrash band that brought the world songs like "Reign in Blood" and "Mandatory Suicide." He knew that *Buffy the Vampire Slayer* was the perfect title for his series, because it captured the exact spirit of what he was planning to make.

You could give it a more serious or distinguished title, but no matter the packaging, the show inside would be about a vapid teenage girl, Buffy Summers (Sarah Michelle Gellar), who discovered that her destiny was to protect humankind from vampires, demons, and other creatures of the underworld, and a show whose tone shifted rapidly between horror, melodrama, action, and pure comedy. The name tells you all of that, and suggests that if you're turned off by it, you're probably not going to like the series to which it's applied.

It was a tonal balance that director Fran Rubel Kuzui didn't even bother attempting with the campy *Buffy* movie adapted from Whedon's first script. The show, though, would have room for many different emotions, all juggled expertly by Gellar, Anthony Stewart Head, Alyson Hannigan, and the rest of the cast. It was a series made cheaply even by the standards of TV's fifth-place network, but it almost never seemed ridiculous despite the primitive effects and awkward stunt-doubling for Gellar. If it wanted to make you laugh at a bit of witty banter ("I laugh in the face of danger. Then I hide until it goes away."), it could. If it wanted its latest monster to creep you out, it found the most disturbing context possible. And if it wanted to make you cry, it was pointless to try fighting it.

If anything, the exaggerated nature of the various undead villains only made the high school setting more effective, because what is adolescence if not a time when every problem gets blown wildly out of proportion?

In the real world, a girl whose boyfriend started treating her badly after they finally have sex wouldn't need to worry that he had turned pure evil, as happened with Buffy and her vampire love interest Angel (David Boreanaz), but it might feel that way for a while. And a real teen boy going through the changes of puberty might occasionally imagine himself a monster, but laconic guitar player Oz (Seth Green) actually transformed into a werewolf every time the moon was full.

Turning monsters into metaphors for teenage emotional turmoil was a clever gambit, and one that played particularly well during the show's three seasons set in high school. *Buffy* is (by our rankings, anyway) one of the best TV shows ever set in high school, but it wasn't

entirely immune to the same problems that eventually beset all such shows when their characters head to college. Even so, those later seasons still had a knack for landing on the right parallel between the supernatural and the universal, like Buffy's little sister Dawn (Michelle Trachtenberg) literally being put on earth to cause her problems (which in this case involved the literal end of the world).

(Those later years also offered some thrilling formal experiments, including "Hush," an homage to silent horror movies, involving demons who rob people of the ability to speak or scream; "The Body," a stripped-down outing where Buffy confronts the mundane reality of her mother's death from natural causes; and the musical episode "Once More, with Feeling," where a curse forces everyone to express their feelings through song.)

Back to that title. Whedon once suggested to the *New York Times*, "If I made *Buffy the Lesbian Separatist*, a series of lectures on PBS on why there should be feminism, no one would be coming to the party, and it would be boring. The idea of changing culture is important to me, and it can only be done in a popular medium."

Whedon didn't invent feminism in TV storytelling, or even the idea of cross-pollinating it with fantasy and sci-fi tropes. (For much of its run, *Buffy* overlapped with *Xena: Warrior Princess*.) But he created one of the finest examples of it, and wrapped it up in a wildly entertaining package that included a name that may have made some potential viewers roll their eyes, but that made enough of them smile and think this might just be a show for them.

And it was.

—AS

Freaks and Geeks (NBC, 1999–2000) Total score: 94

On New Year's Day, 1962, a group of four young musicians arrived at the London office of Decca Records to audition for a recording contract. They played fifteen songs, but Decca rejected them because "guitar groups are on the way out," and because the other band that day was local and would allow the label to save on travel expenses.

The band Decca signed? Brian Poole and the Tremeloes.

The band Decca passed on? The Beatles.

And for the rest of his life, some executive from Decca probably had to answer questions about rejecting the Beatles at every job interview, and likely had to lose every

argument when his opponent started humming the opening bars to "She Loves You."

Obviously, NBC's decision to cancel *Freaks and Geeks* after eighteen episodes were produced (three of which never aired on NBC) wasn't a financial calamity on the scale of Decca's with the Fab Four. *Freaks and Geeks* was critically adored, but its ratings were terrible, even after NBC moved it from a Saturday night death slot to a more hospitable home on Mondays.

And yet... NBC at one time had under contract actors Seth Rogen, James Franco, and Jason Segel, not to mention *Freaks* creator Paul Feig, and executive producer Judd Apatow. Just counting those five men (and leaving out other contributors—say, writer Mike White, who would go on to pen *School of Rock*), their combined domestic box-office gross at the time of this writing is more than SIX BILLION DOLLARS. With a *B*. Oh, and Franco's been nominated for two Oscars (and hosted the ceremony once), while Franco and Rogen made a movie that somehow nearly started a war with North Korea.

That level of success obviously wasn't attainable for *Freaks and Geeks*, a small and uncomfortable-by-design story about teen outcasts in a suburban Michigan high school in 1980. But the DNA of that show is visible in some way in virtually everything those five have done since in defining the voice of twenty-first-century film comedy. And NBC had all of them—not to mention Linda Cardellini, John Francis Daley (now working on a Spider-Man movie script), Martin Starr, Busy Philipps, Samm Levine, and others—on one show! And a show that was at times just as gut-bustingly funny as the best moments of *The 40-Year-Old Virgin* or *Superbad*, and which had a level of poignance to which all those films aspire, even if they don't get there as often as the gang did when they were all together here.

It feels appropriate that so many people involved in this unloved, unwatched show have gone on to such enormous commercial success—often by doing work very similar in style, tone, and/or theme to the show that NBC was so eager to be rid of. The series was about the transformational power of adolescence—how a stereotypical good girl like Cardellini's Lindsay could one day decide to ditch the Mathletes and hang with the freaks, how Lindsay's little brother, Sam (Daley), could briefly have a relationship with the most popular girl in his grade, how Daniel (Franco)

wanted so desperately to be something other than the unofficial king of the burnouts—and the adults on the show were constantly telling the kids that who they were then wasn't at all who they would become in the future. The head of the AV club promises geeks Sam, Bill (Starr), and Neal (Levine) that they'll be much more successful as adults than the jocks and bullies who torment them now; the popularity of *Knocked Up* and *The Heat* and all these other projects feels like that prophecy coming true.

On a pure comedy level, Feig, Apatow, and company understood how to wring laughs out of adolescence's most mortifying situations better than anyone has before or since. The show was both uncomfortable and hilarious in moments like Sam's being laughed at as he tries to strut through school in his new baby blue "Parisian night suit," or Segel's Nick serenading an unhappy Lindsay (who joined the freaks because of a crush on Daniel but somehow ended up dating Nick) with an awful love song he's written for her called "Lady L," or a gym class dodgeball game being presented as an exercise in carnage akin to soldiers storming the beaches at Normandy. (Rogen, Franco, and Segel have become bigger draws, but it was Starr who was the show's not-so-secret comic weapon, delivering every line in the most off-kilter yet sincere fashion and exhibiting a gangly abandon for scenes where Bill struggles to be a baseball star or tries to dance like Rerun from *What's Happening!!*)

But the pain beneath those comic moments was never far from the surface, and it was in the intimate, knowing dramatic moments when *Freaks and Geeks* went from great comedy to all-time classic series. The writers were drawing on their own adolescent experiences, and it showed in the details, like latch-key kid Bill sadly making himself a grilled cheese sandwich but then cracking up as he watches Garry Shandling do stand-up on TV, or Lindsay and Kim (Philipps) cowering in terror inside Kim's car as her angry, resentful stepfather threatens them both, or Daniel sitting on the floor of his bedroom, trying to experience the catharsis of listening to Black Flag's punk anthem "Rise Above" on headphones while being as quiet and still as possible so as not to wake his ailing father.

Later in that episode, Daniel dresses up in full punk regalia, and we would see nearly all the kids adopt different guises and costumes over the series' short life. Lindsay briefly returns to the Mathletes, and later lies to her parents so she can spend a few weeks of her summer following the Grateful Dead with Kim. Neal dabbles in ventriloquism as a way to cope with his parents' impending divorce. Rogen's sarcastic, apathetic Ken falls hard for a girl who plays tuba in the school marching band (whom he later learns has ambiguous genitalia, in a story that made a bull's-eye on the tiny overlapping target between sensitivity and comedy). Nick fails at becoming a drummer like his idol Neil Peart from Rush, and later discovers—to the dismay of both his friends and, on some level, himself—that he's a great disco dancer. And the happiest we ever see Daniel is when he befriends Sam and the other geeks and joins them for a night of Dungeons & Dragons, where he gets to play a role within a role, dubbing himself Carlos the Dwarf.

That desire to transform wasn't specific to suburban Michigan high school kids in 1980, but *Freaks and Geeks* found a way for the stories of these particular, beautifully drawn characters to speak to larger truths about growing up and wanting to be and feel anything other than miserable and alone. Sometimes the transformations worked out, like Lindsay and Kim improbably becoming best friends; other times it didn't, like Sam dating his long-time crush, only to discover that she's boring, conceited, and, worst of all, hates *The Jerk.*

The heads of NBC at the time reportedly hated the show because it was much more serious, dark, and uncomfortable than they had expected. They complained that the freaks and the geeks needed to win more often.

They didn't get the point. At all. Growing up is a struggle. It can be hilarious (especially from the perspective of someone not living the Sam and Bill moments anymore), and it can at times be rewarding, but it's tough.

The good news: It ends for all of us, even if *Freaks and Geeks* itself ended much too soon, and long before anyone at the network understood what an absurd collection of talent they had on hand.

—AS

My So-Called Life (ABC, 1994–1995) Total score: 94

It's wonderful and awful being a teenager. It's old news to the world, but it's all new to you. You have to go through all this crap—hormones, sexual anxiety, psychological separation from one's parents, fear for one's future—knowing full well you're not the first person to go through it, but maybe sometimes wishing you were, so that you could just deal with it on its own terms, in your own way, without adults diminishing the gravity of your emotions by reminding you that you're not a special snowflake, that everybody goes through this, and that someday it'll be over and you'll be nostalgic for your lost innocence, blah blah blah, just shut up, Mom and Dad, *gah! (Door slam.)*

My So-Called Life got all this. It got it better, in fact, than any network series about teens since *James at 15*, which aired almost twenty years earlier on the same network, ABC, and caught flak for dealing with many of the same issues (including adolescent drinking and premarital sex) that were woven so matter-of-factly into *Life*'s story lines.

"What's amazing is when you can feel your life going somewhere... Like, your life just figured out how to get good," said the show's heroine, Angela Chase (Claire Danes). "Like, that *second.*" That's just one piece of the show's intermittent narration, in which Angela obsesses on her middle-class teenage problems. But rather than let Angela's musings sit there unexamined, writer-producers Winnie Holzman, Marshall Herskovitz, and Ed Zwick put a knowing yet compassionate frame around them. Her roiling emotions (and those of her friends, and her parents, and their friends) were respected and understood, even as the show signaled to older viewers that it knew full well that Angela's problems weren't really at the center of the universe, and that the notion that they were was but one small part of the condition of being a teenager, which can be treated and even managed through experience and maturity but never quite goes into remission. *This life has been a test,* Angela thinks to herself. *If this had been an actual life, you would have received instructions on where to go and what to do.*

This unusually supple and complex point of view—let's call it what it was: a *voice*—anchored the show's pilot and manifested itself in the eighteen episodes that followed. The result, though sadly truncated, stands as one of the great one-season wonders in TV history, and one of the finest depictions of American adolescence since Holden Caulfield donned his hunting cap with earflaps and took a train to New York City.

The characterizations of Angela's mother, Patty (Bess Armstrong); father, Graham (Tom Irwin); and little sister, Danielle (Lisa Wilhoit), had as much warmth and intelligence as the heroine's, and Angela's classmates (and her relationships with them) were so rich that they could have supported series of their own. Angela's relationships with her onetime best friend, Sharon Cherski (Devon Odesssa), and her new best pal, Rayanne Graff (A. J. Langer), were great explorations of the notion that friendships have life spans that can end suddenly for all sorts of reasons. (The episode where Angela declines to participate in a traditional mother-daughter fashion show demonstrates that the same is true of stages in a parent-child relationship.) Rayanne and Angela's bond was also a reminder of why "good" girls are so often drawn to troubled ones: They're frustrated by their own respectability and need to feel at once dangerous-by-proxy (Rayanne was a burgeoning alcoholic with bad sexual judgment and often encouraged Angela to push limits) and more "mature" than someone else their age. Angela is often put in the position of worrying about a teenager who's gone off-radar, just as her own mother and father worry about her—proof that Angela herself has good parents who had already passed down their values. And we didn't have to take the show's word for that because it was very conscientious about showing Graham and Patty engaged in the nitty-gritty of parenting. They talked and sometimes fought about how to raise their daughters, how to balance child-rearing against the need to tend their own romantic/sexual spark, and whether or not to sit in judgment of other parents (such as Rayanne's mother, who sometimes acted more like her big sister or roommate). "Nobody wants to hear they may have made a mistake with their kids," Graham says. "Nobody wants to be accused of not being a decent parent."

Then there was Brian Krakow (Devon Gummersall), the prototypical "nice guy" nerd pining after Angela; and Angela's crush object Jordan Catalano (Jared Leto), who perfectly captured the discombobulated entitlement of the long-haired dreamboat stoner ("I like the way he leans," Angela said); and, of course, Rickie Vasquez (Wilson Cruz), the stealthy conscience of the show. Rickie was a revolutionary character, as real and affecting as Angela and Rayanne but more surprising and original. At that time, it was rare to see Hispanic or openly gay characters on TV, period, much less on a teen show, and he was both. The show was unstinting in its willingness to look at what it meant to be Rickie, a double outsider who had to deal with all of the same pressures as the heterosexual white kids, plus identity issues that, in 1994, the white suburban educational mainstream was only beginning to understand and care about.

The series impressed at the level of sheer craft as well: Everybody who makes a TV series claims at some point that they're making a series of little films, and usually they're kidding themselves, but in this case it felt true. The novella-like scripts by Holzman and the writing staff, complete with Salingeresque unreliable narration (the opening of the New Year's–themed episode, "Resolutions," offered snippets of narration by seven characters); the moments of connection between characters you wouldn't have expected to have any (such as Brian pulling a Cyrano de Bergerac and writing Angela a love letter on behalf of the nearly illiterate Jordan); the sometimes dreamlike visuals, with white-gold sunlight blasting through schoolroom windows, reddish brown shadows that seemed fogged-up as in a hormone-addled daydream, and scene transitions featuring vertical "wipe" transitions created by walls and doorframes; W. G. "Snuffy" Walden's sprightly score, which had a "life goes on" feel even when Angela was so depressed she wanted to die; the astute deployment of pop tunes (including Brian circling Angela on his bike to R.E.M.'s "Everybody Hurts" in the pilot, and Angela dancing away her infatuation with Jordan to the Violent Femmes' "Blister in the Sun"): These touches and others might have seemed too on-the-nose were the series not so disarmingly sincere. They were the products of discernment and empathy, and they have ensured that the show retains its power to illuminate and move even as the fashions, music, and cultural references (Rayanne wants CDs for her birthday!) became "period." *My So-Called Life* reproduces the commingling of wonder, anxiety, and bitterness that defines adolescence, so faithfully that teens not born when Angela first appeared on ABC can watch it and say, "Yes, thank God, finally, someone got it right." Grown-ups, to their amazement, can say the same.

—MZS

Oz (HBO, 1997–2003) Total score: 93

Among the *many* ways characters died on *Oz*:

- Burned to death
- Throat slit with long, sharpened fingernails
- Internal organs ruptured after being fed meals laced with ground-up glass
- Executed by lethal injection
- Buried alive when an escape tunnel collapsed
- Electrocuted in a bathtub
- Injected with an HIV-infected needle, then smothered to death in the infirmary
- Executed by a firing squad
- Fatally allergic reaction to eggs hidden in food
- Shot with a staple gun
- Executed by electric chair
- Face melted off with hot steam
- Buried alive behind a wall, then rescued after suffering horrific burns, then buried alive behind *another* wall

So, yeah, Tom Fontana and company got creative with the way they doled out death among the inmates of Oswald State Penitentiary, the men who guarded them, and at times the loved ones who got mixed up in their blood feuds. Seeing how the show was going to bump off yet another character could be thrilling and revolting at the same time. Cumulatively, it was a lot for the viewer to endure, and is likely one of many reasons that *Oz*—HBO's very first original drama series, and thus the great-granddaddy of this new golden age of television we have before us—hasn't had the afterlife of immediate descendants like *The Sopranos*, *Six Feet Under*, and *The Wire*.

But the sheer amount of thought, and daring, that went into figuring out the most macabre way to kill off characters on *Oz* was emblematic of the amount of creativity that went into every single element of the show itself. Week after week, season after season, *Oz* functioned very much like one of its outlaw protagonists (most likely Dean Winters as perpetual schemer Ryan O'Reily), awe-inspiring in everything it kept getting away with.

It featured acts of unspeakable violence, along with the men (and, occasionally, women) who committed them. But it also dealt with matters of sexuality, aging, health care, and organized religion with a candor (particularly among its many male couplings) made possible by HBO's near-complete lack of content restrictions.

Sometimes, great breakthroughs in TV storytelling happen because someone relatively new to the medium doesn't know or care about all the unofficial narrative rules. (Fontana's protégé David Simon, who went from newspapers to *Homicide* to creating a run of unconventional HBO dramas like *The Wire*, qualifies.) Often, though, the best rule-breakers are the ones who have spent so long working inside the system that they know exactly how to tear it apart from within.

Fontana had a list of things he had always wanted to do, but had never been allowed to, during his time on network shows like *St. Elsewhere* and *Homicide*. With *Oz*, he got to do them all.

Wait, so I can't kill off my main character in the first episode? Watch me. Oh, on an ensemble drama you're supposed to go back and forth between your stories across the whole hour, rather than telling them one at a time? Who said that was the only way to do it? You can't mix gritty violence with magical realism? Why the hell not?

Along the way, he made *Oz* into a show that could be enjoyed simply as a never-ending revenge thriller—particularly in the sick central love triangle between well-heeled lawyer Tobias Beecher (Lee Tergesen), white supremacist leader Vern Schillinger (J. K. Simmons), and omnisexual predator Chris Keller (Christopher Meloni)—but also as a profound meditation on so many aspects of American life, not least of which was our penal system and the conflicting agendas of retribution versus rehabilitation.

It was even more experimental than the shows that followed it on HBO and elsewhere, and more uneven as a result. If *The Sopranos* was a heavyweight Broadway drama, *Oz* was an avant-garde theater production in the West Village. Some of its experiments worked, like bringing back a series of dead characters from past seasons to join recently deceased narrator Augustus Hill (Harold Perrineau) to link together the stories of the final season. Some didn't, like a bizarre story line where inmates were offered a drug that would unnaturally age them in exchange for a reduced sentence. But it kept trying, kept striving to do more, to be different, and to be memorable.

—AS

MOST IMPORTANT ARTICLES OF CLOTHING

1. Fonzie's leather jacket, *Happy Days*
2. The red shirt, *Star Trek* (What other item of clothing describes the plot function of an entire group of characters?)
3. Maxwell Smart's shoe phone, *Get Smart*
4. Pastel suits with T-shirt and no socks, *Miami Vice*
5. Carrie's entire shoe collection, *Sex and the City*
6. Raylan's hat, *Justified*
7. Wonder Woman's costume, *Wonder Woman*
8. The embroidered L on Laverne's blouses, *Laverne & Shirley*
9. Gilligan's hat, *Gilligan's Island*
10. Magnum's Hawaiian shirts, *Magnum, P.I.*
11. Captain Stubing's white socks, *The Love Boat*
12. Xena's leather bustier, *Xena: Warrior Princess*
13. B. A. Baracus's gold chains, *The A-Team*

The Dick Van Dyke Show (CBS, 1961–1966) Total score: 92

When you hear the words *The Dick Van Dyke Show*, imagine the gears of a Swiss watch ticking. Created by and eventually costarring *Your Show of Shows* writer Carl Reiner, and based partly on his own experiences working for that variety series' star, Sid Caesar, this sitcom is a lovingly crafted object that has only one purpose, to entertain, which it executes flawlessly.

There are slight variations from season to season and episode to episode, of course. In the opening credits, sometimes the hero, Rob Petrie (Van Dyke), a comedy writer for

The Alan Brady Show, trips over an ottoman after his wife, Laura (Mary Tyler Moore), opens the door for him, and other times he hops over it and laughs defiantly. Sometimes the show focuses on Rob, a slim, stylish, witty, dashingly goofy fellow who's about as nice as a person can be and not be dull; other times it focuses on Laura, a slim, stylish, witty, glamorously goofy knockout ("Raaah-h-h-h-h-b!!" she quavers when the pressure gets to be too much). Still other episodes shift focus to Rob's Manhattan TV writing job, where he and his fellow comedy writers and banter buddies, Buddy Sorrell (Morey Amsterdam) and Sally Rogers (Rose Marie), work up sketches for Alan and submit them to their humor-impaired, chrome-domed supervisor, Richard Deacon's Mel Cooley. (Mel: "I have a feeling someone's pulling my leg." Buddy: "Maybe your garter belt's too tight.") For the first few seasons, Alan Brady is talked about but never fully seen—just slivers of his face or the back of his head, with Reiner providing the voice; later, Reiner played the role on-camera and became a series regular, frequently making sport of the character's vanity. (In a precursor of the *Seinfeld* arc where George and Jerry pitch a *Seinfeld*-like show to NBC, Alan options Rob's memoir about working on the show and says

he plans to play Rob, but that Rob "doesn't need to shave his head—I'll wear a toupee." Like Reiner in real life, Alan is as bald as Mel.)

There were several episodes with Laura worrying that Rob had grown tired of her and taking drastic steps to spice things up, beginning with season 1's "My Blonde-Haired Brunette," where she botches a dye job and turns her head into a yin-yang symbol. There were plenty of jealousy plotlines, starting with season 2's "The Two Faces of Rob," where Rob pretends to be somebody else while flirting with Laura on the phone to gather material for a sketch and becomes jealous of himself. And of course the series did its own variations on primordial sitcom plots, such as the unexpected spiral into paranoia: The best of these is season 3's "That's My Boy??" where Rob becomes convinced that he brought the wrong baby home from the hospital and that his son, Ritchie (Larry Mathews), is not his son; runner-up is season 2's "The Secret Life of Buddy and Sally," where Rob becomes convinced that the duo is having an affair. (Of course they aren't; Buddy adores his wife, Pickles, even though he gripes about her constantly. "Did you ever see my wife in the morning? I keep yelling at her, 'Take off that ridiculous cask of brandy!'")

Despite its very-showbiz commitment to keep doing stuff that worked, the show was quietly groundbreaking. At a time when most sitcom couples either stuck to the *I Love Lucy* / *The Honeymooners* model (pairing a scheming, impulsive buffoon with somebody more obviously adult) or made both parties likable but quite dull (*Leave It to Beaver, Father Knows Best*), *The Dick Van Dyke Show* showcased a mutually respectful, fully functioning marriage between good-looking, witty adults who managed to be sexy as hell even though CBS made them sleep in separate beds. Many TV historians have argued that the popularity of John and Jackie Kennedy rubbed off on Rob (who was supposed to be played by Reiner until CBS made him cast a WASP) and Laura; they looked as if they could be the first couple's goofy cousins. They were also the earliest TV prototype of what would later be known as the Yuppie, though less whiny than versions that would show up on *thirtysomething* and *Mad About You*. Without making a big deal of it, or maybe even meaning to, the show legitimized the spread of a certain kind of college-educated urban liberalism, just by beaming into suburban and rural homes each week. (Sally: "Ooh, suburbs! Yeah, I'd like to look out my window and see a little green." Buddy: "Why don't you get an apartment in front of a stoplight?")

The Dick Van Dyke Show was also one of the first to be set mainly inside the TV industry itself (more so than *Lucy*, which was more interested in shenanigans than process). Every week it took the audience deep inside the factory. We got to see Rob, Sally, and Buddy work through a concept for a sketch or musical number (Buddy: "Hey, play *The Minute Waltz*." Sally: "I only know half of it." Buddy: "Play it twice."), brainstorming and writing and revising until they hit on something they felt sure would work, then starting all over when Alan rejected the result.

Besides the postmodern pretzel logic of having Dick Van Dyke play Carl Reiner working for a Sid Caesar character played by Reiner (and then pitching him the very show they were on!), the series gave us generous glimpses of the sketches and numbers themselves. This let the cast show off their sketch comedy and musical chops, which were dazzling. Rob and Sally and Buddy often broke into song while working on material for Alan, and Rob and Laura danced so well together that the writers kept contriving reasons for them to do it again; one of the most memorable numbers found Van Dyke and Moore hoofing it while dressed as Santa and Mrs. Claus. The rubber band–flexible Van Dyke did dandy impressions of Red Skelton, Emmett Kelly, and Charlie Chaplin, among other comedy legends. The show's writing staff (headed by Reiner) routinely went the extra conceptual mile. They livened up standard sitcom plots with odd framing devices (season 2's "The Night the Roof Fell In," which recounts a fight from Laura's and Rob's points of view, starts with a conversation between two goldfish); aspects of satire and parody (season 2's *Twilight Zone* parody, "It May Look Like a Walnut," is filled with surreal imagery, including Laura bodysurfing a wave of walnuts); even quasi-mystery plotlines (the crown jewel is season 5's "The Great Petrie Fortune," which weaves together a haunting photograph and the song "Me and My Shadow").

The Dick Van Dyke Show ended its run just when broadcast TV switched over to color. It kept smoothly ticking along for five glorious seasons, and has dated better than many sitcoms of its era, not just because Rob and Laura were ahead of their time, but because excellence never gets old.

—MZS

Friday Night Lights (NBC, 2006–2008; DirecTV/NBC, 2008–2011)
Total score: 92

There's a great episode of *Lost* called "The Constant," named after the idea that a time traveler needs some kind of emotional anchor that exists in multiple eras, or else becomes completely unmoored when traveling to one where the constant doesn't exist. We see the notion of the constant in action when Desmond in the past gets the phone number of his lost love Penny so that Desmond in the present can call her up and stay alive.

Friday Night Lights obviously didn't involve time travel (though it did cross the network/satellite barrier midway through its run when DirecTV and NBC came to a content-sharing arrangement to keep it alive). But it very much had its own constant in the marriage of Coach and Mrs. Coach, aka Eric and Tami Taylor, played by Kyle Chandler and Connie Britton. When all else was going awry for the high schoolers of Dillon, Texas—whether they were players on the local football team or not—they could turn to the Taylors for some semblance of order and stability. And when anything else was going wrong on *Friday Night Lights* creatively, the show could always find itself by looking back to the marriage at its heart.

Peter Berg, who developed the series after writing and directing the *FNL* movie (itself adapted from the nonfiction best seller by H. G. Bissinger), has a deliberately chaotic narrative and visual style, favoring naturalistic performances, jump cuts, and handheld camerawork, complete with wild sports-documentary-style zooms. The style, which the show maintained long after Berg had gone back to his film career, was messy but entirely by design, and in a way that brought out the spontaneous, natural best from its actors, most of them young unknowns under their first real spotlight. The show's visual language both embodied and intensified its substance. More so than any network series since *My So-Called Life* (where *FNL* showrunner Jason Katims broke into television), *Friday Night Lights* insisted that teenagers were as multifaceted, self-contradictory, and deep as adults, and that there was no easy explanation for why they did or didn't do things.

Sometimes, though, the messiness of *Friday Night Lights* could be unintentional. The football action, while always well-shot, tended to be crafted in a way that undercut attempts to paint Eric Taylor as a master offensive tactician. (At a minimum, he was horrible at clock management.) The age of the kids fluctuated wildly depending on the needs of the plot (Scott Porter's Jason Street and Taylor Kitsch's Tim Riggins are initially written as best friends since their preschool days, but in time it turns out that Riggins was a sophomore when Street was a senior), as did the status and history of East Dillon High (where Eric moved after being fired from football powerhouse Dillon High at the end of the third season). And in the second season, pretty much every storytelling choice Katims and company made was wrong, none worse than the decision to take two kids from what had been an incredibly grounded show and involve them in a murder plot.

But despite that, all *FNL* needed to do was give us one scene of Coach and Mrs. Coach together—Chandler's brow furrowed, Britton's eyes wide—to make everything feel normal and right again.

Across five seasons, *FNL* was about many things: football and the absurd pressure-cooker atmosphere in which Texas high school players and coaches resided; race, class, and the way so many of the disadvantaged in the area looked to football as a way to be seen or to get out; teen sexuality; religion (it's one of the most sincerely spiritual TV shows ever made); drug and alcohol abuse; and so much more. Through quarterback/cosmic punching bag Matt Saracen (Zach Gilford) alone, the show dealt with issues as disparate as eldercare and the war in Iraq.

(That it managed to place so many of these topics within the context of Texas high school football was both blessing and curse. The stakes of everything felt higher for those who watched, but the subject matter proved alienating to a mass audience in the same way it has for most TV sports dramas: Sports fans didn't want to try what they perceived to be a soap opera, and drama fans didn't want to try a show about football.)

The show handled all those subjects with remarkable nuance and sensitivity, especially given some of the demands and restrictions of being a broadcast network family drama. But the subject on which *FNL* was without peer wasn't football, but marriage. The union of Coach and Mrs. Coach was, simply put, the best, richest, most complex and satisfying portrait of a marriage TV has ever seen. In the process, it shamed every single TV writer who has ever argued that happy couples are boring.

Now, the two weren't happy every minute of every episode. He was incredibly stubborn, she could be staggeringly naive, and they often had conflicting philosophies about work and family. But that's a relationship. Disagreements and compromises and plenty of eye-rolling come with even the healthiest of marriages, and that is exactly what the Taylors had. They fought, they busted each other's chops, and they could annoy the hell out of each other, but there was also never any doubt that they were together for the long haul. (When Eric loses the Dillon High job, Tami promises him, "You know what? No matter what happens, no matter where you go, no matter what you do, I'm always going to be behind you. Always and always and always.")

Nearly all of the kids on the show were being raised by single parents—some just raising themselves—which made the admirable nature of the Taylor marriage so important for everyone. Saracen's mother had run out, his father was deployed overseas (season 4's "The Son," where Matt deals with the complicated feelings of learning his father was killed in an IED explosion, is among the most powerful hours of television ever made), and his grandmother was sliding deeper into senility, so when he had problems (and he, like everyone else on *FNL*, had many), he and the show could turn to Coach and Mrs. Coach for guidance and reassurance that things would eventually be okay.

A lot went wrong in that second season. It wasn't just the murder plot. Almost everything that happened that year was happily ignored in later seasons. Among the many misguided creative decisions (albeit one introduced the season before) was having Eric accept a college position hundreds of miles away from Dillon, even as Tami and the kids stayed in town. There was never a suggestion that the job would break up the Taylors, but it's also no coincidence that the show's universally least-liked period occurred while Coach and Mrs. Coach were living separately and arguing much more than usual on the rare occasions when they were together. They were the constant for the team, the town, and the show.

Texas forever? Sure. But more important, Taylors forever.

—AS

NYPD Blue (ABC, 1993–2005)
Total score: 91

Reckless, drunken, bigoted cop Andy Sipowicz asks assistant district attorney Sylvia Costas if she's accusing him of planting evidence in a case where he very obviously did.

"I'd say 'Res ipsa loquitur' if I thought you knew what it meant," she tells him, using the Latin phrase for "The thing speaks for itself."

Not a Latin speaker, Sipowicz prefers to respond in his own distinctive language, grabbing his crotch and telling her, "Hey, ipsa *this*, you pissy little bitch!"

And here was *NYPD Blue*, the breathtaking, groundbreaking balance of lowbrow and high, of profanity and poetry, of bare asses and bared hearts.

The series' two sides roughly represented the interests of its creators: Former *Hill Street Blues* collaborators Steven Bochco and David Milch. Bochco, fearing that network television was losing grounds to the R-rated content readily available on cable, wanted to push the outer edge of the envelope of what broadcast censors would allow in terms of language and nudity. (The series was in development for an extra year as Bochco and ABC boss Robert Iger figured out exactly where the limits were; reportedly, the two men made crude drawings of naked men and women to identify what could and couldn't be shown, and at what angle.) Milch, frustrated with what he felt were *Hill Street*'s compromises in form and content, saw Bochco's crusade as license to be far franker about the harsh realities of modern police work, whether the horrible nature of the crimes being investigated or the extralegal methods its cops would use to secure confessions.

The end result represented the alchemy of the two partners at their Lennon-and-McCartney best: Bochco's commercial instincts and strong command of narrative making Milch's challenging dialogue and raw emotionality more palatable, and Milch in turn giving soul to the relationships so that the frequent sex scenes felt profound rather than naked grabs for attention.

The show's heroes mirrored the passions of the two creators: Sipowicz (played by Milch's *Hill Street* muse Dennis Franz) the Milchian noble savage, struggling to rein in his many flaws and vices; John Kelly (David Caruso, a great actor before his ego turned him into a sunglasses-wielding self-parody on *CSI: Miami*), a sensitive and self-righteous firebrand in the vein of Frank Furillo from *Hill Street* or Michael Kuzak from Bochco's *L.A. Law*. Bochco took a step back after the complex initial thirteen-episode arc, where Kelly fell for beat cop Janice Licalsi (Amy Brenneman)

before discovering she was working for the mob; the storytelling not only became more episodic as a result, but otherwise more focused on Milch's interests. Caruso was difficult to work with (Milch would blame his first-season heart attack on having to work with his rising star), and Franz a legendary nice guy; between the leads' respective temperaments, the audience's growing love for Sipowicz (who would, in time, fall for and marry the pissy little bitch herself, played by Sharon Lawrence), and Milch's creative instincts, the focus shifted more and more to to the fat, crude sidekick than to the more conventional hero, and Caruso left early in the second season. (He was succeeded, with varying degrees of success, by Jimmy Smits as soulful widower Bobby Simone, Ricky Schroder as anxious Danny Sorenson, and Mark-Paul Gosselaar as confident rookie detective John Clark. Kelly was the most complex character of the four, but Smits's chemistry with Franz made Andy and Bobby the strongest pairing.)

The show was an unabashed love letter to law enforcement—"This is a good job for people like us," Andy tells son Andy Jr. (Michael DeLuise) as the younger Sipowicz studies to become a cop himself (before becoming the first of many Sipowicz loved ones to die over the series' run). "We don't have a lot of education, but we can read and write, and we're honest. Don't ever embarrass this job"—but also acknowledged the moral complexities of it. At times, it could play like an elaborate defense of police brutality, as Andy was as apt to use his fists as his wits to secure confessions. ("I'm gonna have such a migraine tonight because I didn't beat you," he laments to one perp.) But it also featured crooked cops and lazy ones, and constantly reminded its audience of how detectives like Sipowicz and Simone were exposed to the very worst that humanity had to offer. (In season 1's "NYPD Lou," Andy patiently elicits, and endures, the confession of a child molester who murdered his latest victim, then steps out of the interview room and shatters a door with his fists.)

The show didn't shy away from the ugliness of Andy's language, nor his attitudes about minorities. At one point, his African American commanding officer Arthur Fancy (James McDaniel) teaches him a lesson by taking him for dinner to a rib joint with a predominantly black clientele; noting Andy's clear discomfort, Fancy asks, "Now what if they had badges and guns?" In a later episode, Andy runs into trouble for using the n-word in front of a black activist, and even though he's throwing the man's words back at him, his behavior throughout the story suggests the activist is wise to distrust this cop.

In time, Sipowicz's rough edges would be sanded off. He married two beautiful women, had an adorable new son, became a mentor to the younger detectives in the squad as well as, in the series finale, their new commanding officer. At one point, he even encountered God himself (depicted as a surly trucker), albeit in the midst of a dream about reuniting with the late Andy Jr. at a crowded diner.

But the Sipowicz whom the audience fell for was the wounded animal, doing and saying things that had never previously been allowed on network television. (Andy to an irritating TV reporter: "All's we know so far, Norman, is we heard some reporter called a low-life asshole turd pimp with the brains of a flea and the balls of a moth. But we haven't nailed down yet who was being referred to.") Viewers loved Andy not because they wanted to see him have sex (though he did once show his ass while getting into the shower), nor even really because he had a way with four- and five-letter words, but because there was a depth and sadness to him that had rarely been glimpsed in TV characters before, and because we trusted him to be our guide into this cruel and crude world.

Broadcast dramas grew more formulaic post-*Blue* as cable became the place to experiment with form and content. And the Janet Jackson / Justin Timberlake wardrobe malfunction during the 2004 Super Bowl halftime show instantly rolled back most of the progress *Blue* had made in expanding the boundaries of what you could say and show in network prime time.

But Sipowicz and the show around him had proved that there was an audience hungry for not only more adult content but more difficult characters. Bochco and Milch had inadvertently blazed a trail that would be followed, mainly on cable, by characters with more than a touch of Sipowicz in them, such as Tony Soprano, Vic Mackey, Walter White, and (also from the mind of Milch) Al Swearengen.

Andy was a dinosaur who notoriously hated change—after new partner Simone introduces himself by genially asking how he's doing, Sipowicz charges into Fancy's office and announces, "It's not gonna work out"—but he did as much to transform the way people on TV spoke and acted as any character in the history of the medium. If you told him that, he'd probably grumble and go looking for some skell to intimidate.

—AS

Frasier (NBC, 1993–2004) Total score: 90

Between *Cheers*, *Frasier*, and a guest spot on *Wings*, Kelsey Grammer played Frasier Crane for twenty years, tying the record for the most seasons playing the same character in prime time with James Arness as Marshal Dillon on *Gunsmoke*. Of course, Arness did it in an era where TV shows made more episodes per season, and on a show that did hour-long episodes for most of its run, so his record for number of minutes onscreen in the same role is likely safe for all time.

Still, it was an amazing run for Grammer, who was supposed to play the role for only a handful of episodes in *Cheers* season 3 before the creators recognized that their newest obstacle to Sam and Diane's couplehood added a great flavor to the bar in his own right. Other supporting characters were perhaps more popular, and thus easier choices for a spin-off, but it was Frasier's very outsiderness as an erudite man brought low by his association with the bar that made him the perfect choice for *Frasier* creators David Angell, Peter Casey, and David Lee to remove from that setting and start over elsewhere.

The Frasier who returned to his Seattle home was in some ways more like Sam Malone in his confidence and success with women, while young Grammer look-alike David Hyde Pierce was cast as Frasier's brother, Niles, who occupied much of the same comic space that Grammer had on *Cheers*. But a Frasier who was no longer a regular at a sports bar was also fussier and more apt to put his high-culture fixations on display without fear of being mocked by Norm and Carla. (Though the earthier trio of father Martin, radio producer Roz, and physical therapist Daphne—played, respectively, by John Mahoney, Peri Gilpin, and Jane Leeves—still did plenty of that.)

The series followed Frasier's lead: clearly descended from *Cheers*, but with different stylistic touchstones. Where *Cheers* had been a Howard Hawks romantic comedy, *Frasier* leaned more on Noël Coward and the world of slamming-door farce. Many of its best episodes involve characters having to support outrageous lies—in "The Two Mrs. Cranes," Niles and Daphne pose as a married couple, Frasier as married to Niles's chilly wife, Maris, and Martin as an astronaut—or conceal embarrassing secrets. It was unapologetically highbrow in its references—in "Look Before You Leap," Frasier backs out of singing an aria from Verdi's *Rigoletto* on a PBS pledge drive, and instead bombs when he forgets the words to "Buttons and Bows" from *The Paleface* (stumped, he improvises lyrics like, "Let's all go to a taco show!")—yet was as comfortable with slapstick as wordplay.

Holding it all together was Grammer: a preening peacock one moment, a desperate buffoon the next, and a sensitive son and brother the moment after that. He and his costars had a knack for wringing every drop of humor out of every line. At one point, Frasier finds himself in a feud with some morning-zoo types, and Martin is tickled, asking, "How often do you get to hear your son on the radio?" Frasier replies, with thunderous indignation, "I'M ON THE RADIO EVERY DAY!" A good line on the page, it's a great one out of the mouth of the star.

When *Cheers* ended, it was *Seinfeld*, not *Frasier*, that moved into its old time slot. But it was Frasier that won five straight comedy-series

Emmys—one more than *Cheers* got in its entire run. I'll take the parent show, but *Frasier* is the rare spin-off of a classic that's immortal in its own right.

—AS

Homicide: Life on the Street (NBC, 1993–1999) Total score: 90

"What you will be privileged to witness," Frank Pembleton explains to his new partner, "will not be an interrogation, but an act of salesmanship—as silver-tongued and thieving as ever moved used cars, Florida swampland, or Bibles. But what I am selling is a long prison term to a client who has no genuine use for the product."

In the world of the police procedural, there are action shows and there are talking shows. *Homicide*, particularly in its first, best few years, was as great a talking show as the genre has ever seen, and one that posited that cops like Pembleton (Andre Braugher), Meldrick Lewis (Clark Johnson), John Munch (Richard Belzer), and Kay Howard (Melissa Leo) would be just as good at talking outside the interrogation room as inside it.

So, yes, they were sensational at coercing confessions out of killers who had foolishly wandered into what they referred to as "the Box." They were so exciting in this area, in fact, that the show could be even more satisfying on those occasions when they failed—like the episode-length interrogation of "Three Men and Adena," which offered a frustrating end to the first murder investigated by Pembleton's young partner Tim Bayliss (Kyle Secor)—as when they closed the deal.

But they could also hold the viewer spellbound talking about almost nothing at all, whether it was Steve Crosetti (Jon Polito) and his Lincoln assassination conspiracy theories, or Munch suffering the withering disdain of his revered partner Stan Bolander (Ned Beatty), or the entire squad uniting in their dislike of the haughty Pembleton.

Pembleton had reason to be haughty. In an ensemble show filled with more recognizable actors, it was Braugher's face, and voice, that quickly became the most important. Half of the abbreviated second season is devoted to the murder of a drug dealer, in which Pembleton suspects a police-involved shooting, while shift commander Alphonse "Gee" Giardello (Yaphet Kotto) pushes him to look for a civilian suspect to protect the shield.

Indignant and deeply hurt at his mentor for letting him down, Pembleton decides to prove a point by hauling one of the victim's innocent friends into the Box and verbally twisting him up like a pretzel until the weeping man is grateful for the opportunity to confess to a crime he didn't commit. It's a virtuoso performance and one the creative team rewarded by opening the following season with a three-parter where Pembleton's Catholic education proved instrumental in catching a serial killer. The character became so important to the show, and so powerful, that the writers eventually had to give Frank a mild stroke just to humble him and keep Braugher interested.

That *Homicide* always had at least three African American cast members at any one time, plus several other recurring actors of color playing cops up and down the ranks, meant the series could casually do something unheard of at the time: put multiple black characters together in scenes, featuring no white characters, that had nothing to do with race. The show certainly dealt with racial issues—even prejudice within the black community, like a story where the dark-complected Gee laments being rejected by a lighter-skinned woman—but its characters didn't have to be defined by them.

The show's depiction of police work as work was equally sophisticated. Better than any cop drama before it, *Homicide* captured the world-weariness and emotional armor that come with the job. The characters and many of the early stories were drawn from *Homicide: A Year on the Killing Streets*, a non-fiction book by *Baltimore Sun* crime reporter David Simon. Simon made his entree into television by co-writing (with David Mills) season 2's "Bop Gun," in which a grieving husband and father (guest star Robin Williams) is disgusted to hear the detectives investigating his wife's murder cracking jokes and boasting of the overtime they'll earn on it; Gee explains to him that this is how they all have to think in order to function, and some are just better at hiding it than others.

That attitude, the deliberately jarring filming style (early episodes were shot under harsh light with frequent jump cuts), and a cast full of craggy middle-aged men made *Homicide* perhaps the most uncommercial show to ever debut after the Super Bowl. Viewers who had just watched the Cowboys rout the Bills were treated to a weirdly philosophical cop drama that opened with Crosetti and Lewis in a dark alley searching for a shell casing, with Crosetti musing, "You never really find what you're looking for, because the whole point is looking for it. So if you find it, it defeats its own purpose."

NBC executives would spend the next six years chasing a wider audience for *Homicide*, never quite understanding that looking for it defeated the show's own purpose. Though the series ran a healthy seven seasons, it lived on the cancellation bubble for most of them, and grew flashier and less realistic with each passing year. The filming style got prettier, and so did the cast: Lewis began the series partnered with the stocky, bald Crosetti, and ended it teamed with Michael Michele as beauty queen–turned–cop Rene Sheppard. The mundane murders and murderers of the early seasons never entirely went away, but now they had to compete for screen time with charismatic drug lords, precinct shoot-outs, even a helicopter chase. In its later years, *Homicide* was a talking show that kept trying to convince itself it could be an action show even though the best moments were still the small ones. Erik Todd Dellums was certainly charismatic as local kingpin

Luther Mahoney, but *Miami Vice* and other more visceral cop shows had already covered this territory far better than *Homicide* could hope to, whereas few shows could pull off a scene as darkly comic as Munch and Bolander convincing a dumb witness that their copy machine is a lie detector emitting so much radiation that prolonged exposure leads to "an 11 percent chance of penile stustification."

Meldrick Lewis once laid out the challenges of the job by explaining, "Murderers lie cuz they got to, witnesses lie cuz they think they got to, and everyone else lies for the sheer joy of it."

There was a lot of joy to be found in watching these clever cops talk liars into telling the truth, even if things rarely ended as neatly as they wanted them to.

—AS

Battlestar Galactica (Sci Fi, 2003–2009) Total score: 89

Developed by Ronald D. Moore (who worked on three *Star Trek* spin-offs), this reboot of the 1978 Glen A. Larson *Star Wars* rip-off was initially greeted with suspicion by fans of the original. But it used its derivative and silly source as a jumping-off point for a dark-and-gritty reboot, and reconceived almost everything about it, except for its basic story and settings: Humans in a distant galaxy are almost wiped out in a sneak attack by the Cylons, a race of intelligent machines, and the handful of survivors are forced to flee across the cosmos in search of a new homeworld. The titular military vessel's commander, William Adama, formerly played by *Bonanza*'s silver-haired patrician Anglo, Lorne Greene, was incarnated by pockmarked Mexican American character actor Edward James Olmos, while the hotshot fighter pilot Starbuck, portrayed by Dirk Benedict in the original series, was now played by actress Katee Sackhoff. Fanboy pushback went away when viewers saw the breadth and depth of this reimagined space opera, which treated the first line of the original's opening narration—"What if life here began out there?"—as the beginning of a deliriously ambitious TV epic that owed as much to Homer, the Talmud, the Bible, and the Bhagavad Gita as it did to George Lucas or Gene Roddenberry.

The revised *Galactica*'s somberness was well-suited to the political debates of the early aughts. The show burst onto the airwaves in 2003 as a miniseries, two years and three months after the 9/11 attacks, while the US military was fighting a global war against terrorism, taking over Afghanistan and Iraq, rolling back domestic privacy rights in the name of security, valorizing the military to an extent not seen since World War II, and advocating torture as a valid intelligence-gathering tool. *BSG* dealt with all of these issues and more, starting with the miniseries, which showed human homeworlds scorched by nuclear sneak attacks. The crew and passengers of the *Galactica* and its fleet (including Mary McDonnell's cancer-stricken President Laura Roslin, formerly the secretary of education) make brutally expedient choices about whom to save and whom to abandon, and debate whether to devote their remaining resources to fighting the Cylons or traveling across space to find a prophesied home.

The show never stints on scenes of brutal close-quarters combat and outer-space dogfights, which, like the show's conversations, sex scenes, and official pageantry, are captured with handheld (or handheld-seeming) cameras. *BSG* has a knack for following large numbers of overlapping, ongoing story lines, including Adama's thorny relationship with his fighter pilot son, Lee "Apollo" Adama

(Jamie Bamber), and the twisted sexual relationship between the traitorous scientist and future political leader Gaius Baltar (James Callis) and his Cylon handler, Number Six (Tricia Helfer), a curvy blond apparition who slinks through his mind like a femme fatale version of Harvey the rabbit.

BSG is less interested in plot-driven serialized storytelling than in making audiences see themselves in more than one mirror at once, and challenging them to ask who they're rooting for, and why. In some ways, Moore's *Galactica*'s biggest screen influence was *The Twilight Zone*, which likewise plays tricks with perception, revealing that what we assumed was Mars was actually Nevada, that what we describe as "beautiful" could be "ugly" when seen through different eyes, or that the real monsters are on Maple Street. The show's humans are polytheists, like the "pagans" despised by previous generations of Westerners, while the ruthless machines worship one god that seems to have Christian characteristics. The memorable New Caprica arc from *Galactica*'s midpoint, which placed members of the show's core cast on a planet occupied by Cylons, put viewers in the position of rooting for insurgents who were at that very

moment waging guerrilla warfare against US troops in Afghanistan and Iraq. The series finale, a brain twister that caused more consternation than any finale since the end of *Lost*, folded aspects of the Old and New Testaments, the Koran, and *Chariots of the Gods* into a cosmic finale partially scored to a cover of Bob Dylan's "All Along the Watchtower." *What the hell?*

Yes—what the hell; as in, *why not.* Even when the show seemed on the verge of vanishing into its own navel, it was hard not to admire its commitment to its peculiar vision, and its seeming disinterest in doing what fans wanted or expected. The chintzy original *Galactica* was a heroic melody played on a rusty squeeze-box; Moore's was an alternately mournful and dissonant symphony performed by an orchestra, chock-full of narrative, structural, and thematic flourishes that subverted sci-fi clichés, upended viewer sympathies, and endlessly revisited fundamental questions: What does it mean to be human? Is it a biological condition or a moral one? Can intelligent machines lay claim to the status and moral rights of biological humans? If humans created the Cylons, Frankenstein-style, does it follow that wiping them out, even in self-defense, is tantamount to parents murdering their children? Can a democratically elected civilian authority be trusted to guide a society that's endangered by a ruthless enemy bent on extermination, or should citizens place their trust in the military? Is torture a necessary part of war, or sadism indulged under the guise of survival? Is one form of religion more valid than another? Is there a God? An afterlife? A world beyond what we can sense? Can prophecies come true? Did life here begin out there?

—MZS

In Treatment (HBO, 2008–2010)
Total score: 89

In one of the final episodes of *In Treatment*, psychiatrist hero Paul Weston (Gabriel Byrne) gets exasperated with Sunil (Irrfan Khan), a patient who has taken advantage of their working relationship, particularly after Sunil refers to Paul as his good friend.

"I meant to be your therapist, not your good friend!" Paul insists.

"Is it not possible to be both at once?" Sunil suggests. "Because you, you have certainly given me that impression."

This is why Paul Weston is both a wonderful therapist and a terrible one, and perhaps the only kind of man who could have been placed at the center of *In Treatment*, a narratively audacious, emotionally riveting TV experiment.

Based on the Israeli series *Be'Tipul*, the show was formatted unlike any American TV drama before or since: five half-hour episodes a week (reduced to four for the third and final season), each one more or less covering the entirety of a therapy session between Paul and one of his patients, followed at the end of the week by Paul visiting his own shrink (Dianne Wiest's Gina for the first two years, Amy Ryan's Adele for the third) to discuss both how he feels about his patients and the many problems he's enduring in his own life.

(The show's format, and HBO's attempt to allow the audience to access episodes as many ways as possible—making episodes available On Demand even before they'd aired, scheduling it differently across multiple channels—presaged today's binge-viewing culture, though *In Treatment*'s audience was tiny no matter how you measured it.)

Most fiction has to heighten the dramatic realities of a profession for narrative and dramatic convenience. Viewers wouldn't want to see a show about young lawyers in a big firm who spent all their time writing briefs, and a show where an ordinary therapist sat and calmly listened to patients go on about their familiar problems would have been even more audience-repelling than the show's actual format. Those who tuned in did so because it was a show featuring an extraordinary doctor, in ways both good and bad, helping patients in extreme situations: a naval aviator (Blair Underwood's Alex) who inadvertently bombed a school, a college student (Alison Pill's April) refusing to get her cancer treated, a CEO (John Mahoney's Walter) in the midst of a career-ending scandal, a teen gymnast (Mia Wasikowska's Sophie) insisting she didn't recently attempt suicide, and so on.

And they tuned in because Paul's approach was so confrontational, so active, and—perhaps because his personal life was an ongoing wreck throughout the series—so very much blurring the line between therapist and friend, as Sunil noted in their final meeting. The very first patient the show presents is Laura (Melissa George), who becomes sexually attracted to Paul, and vice versa, even as he insists that their feelings are emotional transference gone awry. But we see that Paul puts too much of himself into relationships with all his patients, unwittingly playing would-be lover, or father (the one constant of the series is how good he is with younger patients), or buddy. At times, this has enormous value, like his willingness to personally take April to chemo when all other attempts at persuasion have failed. At others, he gets so close that the therapeutic relationship just can't continue, or so that someone like Sunil—a Bengali widower desperate to be exiled back to his homeland rather than live in misery with his assimilated son and white daughter-in-law—can take advantage of him.

But Paul could also challenge them, and be challenged in turn by his own therapists, whether his emotionally thorny weekly dance with former mentor Gina or his fumbling in the darkness with total stranger Adele. TV loves what critic Daniel Fienberg calls a Vocational Irony Narrative, and rarely was a physician's difficulty in healing, or even diagnosing, himself as acute or poignant as here.

"It's not about you, Paul," Gina tries to warn him at one point. "They're human beings. They're struggling with profound problems. If only you could find courage to sit with the fact that what we do is hard, and sometimes it makes you feel like an idiot. It's a humbling profession, and if you lack anything as a therapist, it's humility."

None of this would have worked without a performer as committed, as tireless, and as good at reacting to his costars as Gabriel Byrne. He and lead director Paris Barclay turned each episode into a tight two-character play, where the silences—say, Paul trying to contain his anguish at hearing the tragic details of Walter's childhood—were often as powerful as the speeches being delivered by his amazing scene partners. The second year in particular is one of the greatest TV drama seasons ever, with nary a weak link in casting, character, or episode.

Even with *Be'Tipul* stories and characters to adapt for the first two seasons, making the show proved so exhausting that its head writer changed each year: Rodrigo Garcia in the first (he also directed many of the early episodes), Warren Leight (who put so much of himself into it that he hasn't watched a minute of it since leaving) in the second, and Dan Futterman and Anya Epstein in the third. By that last year, the show was running on fumes a bit, with the patients' problems, and Paul's reactions to them, inevitably echoing therapeutic relationships from seasons past. Paul had threatened to quit therapy (both the giving and the taking of it) at the end of each of the previous seasons, but it felt more final this time, even though HBO didn't officially cancel the show for several months after the last episode aired.

"I need to stop," he told Adele, plainly and simply, before disappearing into a busy crowd of New York pedestrians. By then, we could understand why. A more stable, less emotionally raw and invested therapist might have been able to keep going, but he wouldn't have been nearly as fascinating to watch.

—AS

South Park (Comedy Central, 1997–present) Total score: 89

Are *South Park* creators Trey Parker and Matt Stone America's greatest and most consistently inventive humorists, or only in the top 5? We'll see, but the smart money is on the duo's receiving a Kennedy Center honor before their show turns twenty-five and then pantomime jamming the trophies into each other's asses before the director can cut to a commercial. In longevity as well as consistency of vision, they have few equals. Their closest rivals might be *The Simpsons*, a landmark show that started to flag halfway into its (similarly) endless run, and Seth MacFarlane of *Family Guy*, whose series has its moments but has never risen to the heights of conceptually driven insanity that Parker and Stone reach without breaking a sweat. At its best, this show about the continuing misadventures of Stan Marsh, Kyle Broflovski, Eric Cartman, the repeatedly killed and resurrected Kenny McCormick, and the kids' parents, teachers, and classmates can stand tall beside some of the giants of chaotic absurdism: Zucker-Abrahams-Zucker (*Airplane!*), Mel Brooks, Richard Pryor, the Marx Brothers, George Carlin, and W. C. Fields.

Parker and Stone's success is all the more remarkable when you consider that they started with no showbiz connections to speak of. Back in 1992 they were students at the University of Colorado who'd produced a goofy short film titled *The Spirit of Christmas*, which climaxed with a kung fu fight between Jesus and Santa. Within five years—thanks to help from Fox executive Brian Graden, who gave them $2,000 to turn the short into a "video Christmas card" that he could send to friends and birthed the very first viral video sensation—they'd landed a Comedy Central series, *South Park*. Not only have the duo lasted,

they've continued to plausibly maintain outsider status (despite being entrenched at a cable channel owned by Viacom) by being more provocative than even their most jaded viewers expect. (They've been repeatedly censored or preempted by their own venue, most famously in 2011, when they flouted Muslim taboo by depicting the prophet Muhammad.) Some episodes have been sharper and more coherent than others; Parker and Stone practice a type of humor that is by nature hit-and-miss, and their accelerated production schedule, which allows them to riff on current events, guarantees that the show's writing is at times as rough-edged as its crude animation. But if you comb through the series' online archive, you might be shocked by how few total duds there are, and by how well much of their rapid-response humor holds up. And some of *South Park*'s most gleefully outrageous situations and images (Mecha-Streisand; the token black character named Token; Mr. Hankey the Christmas Poo; Chef's "Salty Balls" song; class pet gerbil Lemmiwinks going on a Tolkienesque odyssey when inserted up the rear end of Mr. Slave; Tom Cruise trapped in a closet; Jesus urging mortals to cut out the middleman and communicate with God directly, only to be killed again) have detached from their cultural context, becoming as timeless as "Who's on first?"

Stuff that seemed vital at the time still does, and stuff that felt like mere adolescent provocation—such as the season 1 episode with the Ethiopian, and the season 2 episode with the "Joozians"—has nuggets of warmth or vitality that mitigate the shock factor. And just when you start to get burned out, an A+ episode—such as season 10's "Hell on Earth 2006," wherein Satan decides to rent out the W Hotel in downtown South Park and throw himself a Sweet 16 party—reminds you of what the series is capable of. The Satan scenes in that installment (a continuation of the hell sequences in their 1999 animated feature *South Park: Bigger, Longer & Uncut*) are a skewering of reality show participants' narcissism and their audience's rubbernecking smugness, so sharp they might have been enough to sustain a half-hour episode by themselves. But Parker and Stone always go much further than you expect, to overwhelm viewers with irreverence, bad taste, and excess. Here they add a subplot with the boys summoning the spirit of murdered rapper Biggie Smalls by repeating his name into a mirror (à la *Candyman*), and another subplot that finds mass murderers Ted Bundy, Jeffrey Dahmer, and John Wayne Gacy

being dispatched from the underworld to pick up a giant cake shaped like a Ferrari and deliver it to Satan's bash. The "Three Murderers" become the supernatural version of the Three Stooges, squabbling among themselves, getting into wacky hijinks, and beating, stabbing, and disemboweling themselves and innocent bystanders. These bits explore the connection between comedy and cruelty incisively, but without becoming dry or self-regarding. This level of conceptual sophistication, improbably wedded to humor so low that mitochondria might sneer at it, is as rare a sight as Eric Cartman eating salad. It can only exist because Parker and Stone have as much respect for how things are supposed to be done as their big-boned avatar, who once proclaimed, "I don't make the rules, Kyle; I simply think them up and write them down."

—MZS

BEST MUSTACHES

(With apologies to the mostly nonfictional Alex Trebek, Gene Shalit, Geraldo Rivera, et al.)

1. Thomas Magnum, *Magnum, P.I.*
2. Andy Sipowicz, *NYPD Blue*
3. Ron Swanson, *Parks and Recreation*

4. Gomez Addams, *The Addams Family*
5. Gus Witherspoon, *Our House*
6. Isaac Washington, *The Love Boat*
7. Doc Cochran, *Deadwood* (not all the Deadwood mustaches were real, but that glorious horseshoe was)
8. Bob Belcher, *Bob's Burgers*
9. Captain Kangaroo, *Captain Kangaroo*
10. Ned Flanders, *The Simpsons*
11. Jim Dangle, *Reno 911!*

MOST IMPORTANT HAIRSTYLES

1. The Rachel, *Friends*
2. Jill's feathered shag, *Charlie's Angels*
3. Felicity's curls, *Felicity* (the only show in TV history where a ratings decline was blamed on the leading lady cutting her hair)
4. (tie) Julie's flat-ironed hair and Linc's afro, *The Mod Squad*
5. Doug Ross's Caesar cut, *ER*
6. Jesse's mullet, *Full House*
7. Denise's braids, *The Cosby Show*
8. Angela's cinnamon hair, *My So-Called Life*
9. Julia's bouffant, *Julia*
10. Thelma's natural, *Good Times*
11. Kojak's bald dome, *Kojak*
12. Claire Underwood's pixie undercut, *House of Cards*

The West Wing (NBC, 1999–2006) Total score: 89

History tends to take a global view of presidential administrations, when in fact most of them tend to be broken down into smaller and more complicated eras, and the same is true of the seven seasons of *The West Wing*, which chronicled the majority of Josiah Bartlet's two fictional terms as president of the United States (or, in an acronym the show helped popularize, POTUS). The first two seasons were shiny and full of possibility, in many ways the apex of what traditional network TV drama could achieve; then, as so often happens in politics, the new bosses got a bit too full of themselves, cratered due to infighting and scandals, flirted with irrelevancy, then mounted an unexpected comeback. What a long, strange trip it was.

The West Wing started out in 1999 as an unabashed celebration of center-left political values, which had dimmed in the aftermath of President Bill Clinton's impeachment by House Republicans for lying about an affair with an intern. Writer Aaron Sorkin and director Thomas Schlamme, who had gotten used to each other's rhythms on ABC's *Sports Night* (located elsewhere in the Pantheon), hit the ground running with a Capraesque political fantasy stocked with passionate, charismatic policy wonks. The top-notch cast was headed by Martin Sheen as Bartlet, whom you could view as Bill Clinton without the scandals or Jimmy Carter without the political naïveté or perhaps a delibidinized John F. Kennedy who was socially liberal but a hawk on defense. John Spencer played Bartlet's wise chief of staff, Leo McGarry, a recovering alcoholic; Bradley Whitford, Richard Schiff, Allison Janney, and Rob Lowe played inner-circle members of the senior staff, flitting around Bartlet and Leo like screwball gnats, spitballing proposals and correcting one another's grammar and citing factoids about military history, constitutional law, astronomy, US currency, the postal service, even Gilbert and Sullivan operettas (one of Sorkin's passions). They bantered at top speed while gliding Steadicams tracked their progress through the White House, their bodies moving in and out of bustling frames like fish in an overstocked tank. The whole production had the gloss of a prestige studio blockbuster like the Sorkin-scripted 1996 drama *The American President*, which costarred Sheen as that POTUS's chief of staff.

Conventional wisdom said that viewers had little interest in watching fictional politics, much less on a program with an explicit ideological bent. Sorkin and Schlamme proved them wrong, hatching engaging stories out of wonky topics like the census and arguments in favor of discontinuing the penny, and drawing a large audience (particularly in the early seasons) to a show that was unabashedly liberal, even though Sorkin threw in token sympathetic Republicans like junior legal adviser Ainsley Hayes (Emily Procter). People came because the characters and actors were smart, passionate, and essentially lovable, even when they succumbed to arrogance or made mortifying tactical blunders. In three consecutive seasons, the show got Emmy-winning performances out of Schiff, Whitford, and Spencer in each year's Christmas episode; Janney won four Emmys for playing by far the most nuanced and capable female character of Sorkin's TV career (even if C. J. was often kidded for her height—her Secret Service code name was "Flamingo"—and used as a viewer proxy to whom the other characters could mansplain complex issues). Sheen's series-long shutout remains a historic Emmy black mark.

There's not a lot of subtext to Sorkin's writing (it's one of the reasons he made a bumpy transition into cable drama with *The Newsroom*, a show whose dialogue served up pre-chewed food for thought). And the sheer speed and density of the banter could be overwhelming: Scripts routinely came in at nearly twice the standard length, and rather than cut them, Sorkin and Schlamme ordered the actors to talk as fast as they could. But *The West Wing* text was so deft, confident, and sometimes genuinely lyrical that even viewers who made fun of Sorkin's tics adored the show. The banter was sparkling. The rhetoric soared.

Consider Bartlet's introduction, late in the pilot, where he's been oft-discussed but unseen, until he barges into the middle of a meeting where Whitford's Josh and Schiff's Toby are having a shouting match with Christian fundamentalists, one of whom admits to being confused about what's actually said in the First Commandment. "I am the Lord your God; thou shalt worship no other God before me," intones Jed Bartlet as he barges into the room, before flashing a delighted grin and saying, "Boy, those were the days, huh?" The complicated relationship between the president and his deity would lead, in the season 2 finale, to the show's grandest moment: Bartlet, furious and grief-stricken over his secretary Mrs. Landingham's death in a random traffic accident, commandeers National Cathedral, curses out God in both English (calling Him a "feckless thug" and a "son of a bitch") and Latin, then stubs out a cigarette on the marble floor.

That episode, "Two Cathedrals," was the series' peak. The second half of Sorkin's tenure on the show (he was muscled out after four seasons over escalating issues with budget and scheduling, owing in part to his insistence on writing all but one out of close to ninety episodes) felt like a presidency moving past giddy optimism and into the grotty reality of governance: the internal squabbles, the overreaching, the solutions that only worsened the problems. In an earlier episode, for example, Sorkin had wanted an excuse to write a scene where President Bartlet is watching a daytime soap; the only way he could justify it to himself was to give the POTUS a case of secret, relapsing, remitting multiple sclerosis—only later recognizing that a president who kept a serious illness from the public would get into big trouble over it. Season 3 bogged down in congressional hearings over the cover-up, while also introducing the show's ultimate conservative straw man in Robert Ritchie (played by James Brolin), Bartlet's dim-witted, George W. Bush caricature of an opponent for reelection. The transparent lameness of Ritchie was emblematic of a cockiness that crept into the show in Sorkin's later years, which also included season 3's "Isaac and Ishmael," a hastily conceived, preachy, awkward attempt to use the fictional Bartlet administration to talk about the recent horrific events of 9/11. (In general, the show foundered whenever Sorkin tried to create overlap between what Bartlet's gang was doing in *West Wing* land and what Bush's administration was up to in reality.)

On his way out the door, Sorkin dug a deep hole for his replacement— longtime *ER* showrunner John Wells, who had been a largely hands-off producer for *The West Wing*'s early seasons—by having Bartlet temporarily resign the presidency when his daughter was kidnapped, leaving Glenallen Walken (John Goodman), the Republican Speaker of the House, to take over. Once Wells figured out a way to unring that bell, he overcompensated for the show's reputation as a liberal fantasy by miring the Bartlet administration in gridlock from a Republican-controlled Congress, then ratcheting up tension between the senior staff to a degree that felt contrived. Without Sorkin's voice or the original spirit of optimism, it seemed pointless for the show to continue.

But late in the fifth season, Wells hit on a new kind of fantasy: a bipartisan one, where people with wildly different ideologies could come together and disagree in ways that only increased their respect for one another. It started with an episode called "The Supremes," where Josh, realizing the only Supreme Court justice Congress will approve is a milquetoast moderate, hatches a scheme to replace two justices at once with a revered liberal and a brilliant conservative who take genuine pleasure in debating each other. The following season, the series pivoted away from the lame-duck days of the Bartlet administration and onto the race to succeed him, eventually spotlighting two bold candidates played by familiar actors: Jimmy Smits as Matt Santos, a hawkish congressman with a military background and devout Catholic (read: pro-life) beliefs; and Alan Alda as Arnold Vinick, a pro-choice, agnostic senior senator. The twist was that Santos was the Democrat, Vinick the Republican. Even though neither man (particularly the fiscally conservative but socially moderate Vinick) would have a prayer of getting his party's nomination in the real world, both characters were so vividly drawn and their new prominence so fundamentally altering to the balance of the show that the final years felt like a well-crafted *West Wing* spin-off embedded within the original framework.

And even when the show's power began to ebb in season 3, after 9/11 violently shut the book on the Clinton era that had defined those magnificent early scripts, *The West Wing* never lost faith in language's power to stir the mind and heart. "Words when spoken out loud for the sake of performance are music," Bartlet says in the Sorkin-penned "War Crimes." "They have rhythm and pitch and timbre and volume. These are the properties of music, and music has the ability to find us and move us and lift us up in ways that literal meaning can't."

—AS & MZS

Mary Hartman, Mary Hartman (Syndication, 1976–1977) Total score: 88

It's Garry Shandling's Show (Showtime, 1986–1990) Total score: 78

The Jack Benny Program (CBS and NBC, 1950–1965) Total score: 78

Soap (ABC, 1977–1981) Total score: 70

Television has long had a reputation as an oblivious medium, comfortably middlebrow and not prone to introspection. This is mainly the product of a smugness encouraged by devotees of media that had more time to develop: theater, literature, and most recently cinema, which was considered a mostly escapist or vulgar art in the United States until young French critics patiently explained to Americans, in the middle of the twentieth century, that Westerns, musicals, gangster films, and the like could be art, too, even when they weren't based on a Tony Award–winning play or a Pulitzer Prize–winning novel or some other pedigreed source. The truth is, TV began contemplating its own properties immediately. It aired shows that put a great deal of thought into what made TV different from radio or movies, and integrated those observations into their stories and situations. For some reason, this was more starkly apparent in comedies than in dramas. Where half-hour and hour-long dramatic series tended to embrace the so-called invisible storytelling of the Hollywood feature, sitcoms were much more anarchic in their aesthetic, inviting audiences to enjoy their awareness of the show being put on before their eyes.

By no means is this entry suggesting that *The Jack Benny Program*; *Mary Hartman, Mary Hartman*; *Soap*; and *It's Garry Shandling's Show* are the only programs to attempt the sorts of effects described here; self-awareness, self-criticism, fourth wall–breaking asides and other distinguishing features can be found in many other series that are discussed in this book (including *Moonlighting* and *Seinfeld*) and many more that are not. The four programs, which qualify as Pantheon shows on their own, have been grouped here for purposes of illustration. If you think about what they did and represented, you recognize an artistic through-line that carries a certain self-aware brand of TV comedy from 1950 (the medium's bronze age, probably) through the 1990s. The culmination of this tendency, for now, anyway, is *Community* (NBC and Yahoo!, 2009–2015), a work of such richness and ambition that it has been dealt with in a separate entry elsewhere in the Pantheon; but there are many more.

Jack Benny went there first. His CBS and NBC TV series *The Jack Benny Program*, descended from his 1932–1955 radio show, was continuously and delightfully aware of itself as a show. Benny played "himself"—the only version of Benny that anyone ever saw— as a vain, neurotic skinflint who inflicted his rotten violin playing on everyone in earshot; insisted that he was thirty-nine no matter how old he got; griped about women and how little money he made; bantered with his chauffeur, Rochester Van Jones (Eddie Anderson); and alternated situation comedy–type story lines with fourth wall–breaking asides, monologues, and musical numbers. Some actors played characters, others were simply performers appearing under their own names, and still others (Benny first and foremost) blurred such distinctions. At the end of each broadcast, Benny summed up what the audience had just seen and what, if anything, they should take away from it. The italicized artificiality of *The Jack Benny Program*'s format bound the various types of performances together, and became a shared joke between Benny and his audience.

The syndicated daytime series *Mary Hartman, Mary Hartman* ran just one season, but it built on Benny's innovations and served as a bridge between TV's early developmental years and its somewhat more sophisticated middle period. Created by writers Gail Parent and Ann Marcus and producers Jerry Adelman and Daniel Gregory Browne, and set in the town of Fernwood, it was yet another pet project by sitcom innovator Norman Lear (*All in the Family*, *Maude*). Lear executive-produced two episodes only to see them rejected by all three broadcast networks as too intellectual and off-putting. Sold to a syndicator, the show became the first high-profile example of a TV series that spoofed the soap opera and needled the audiences that craved soaps while simultaneously providing many of the genre's satisfactions. (Even the title was self-conscious: a goof on the idea that soap opera characters always said things twice.)

Louise Lasser's Mary was a send-up not of the typical soap opera heroine (not even the most outwardly unremarkable "housewife" character was as life-sized as she) but of the hypothetical ideal viewer of daytime soaps: a female homemaker who was housebound for most of the day, caring for young children or running errands and cleaning house while waiting for the house to fill up with life again. The plotlines were as knowingly ludicrous as anything on *General Hospital* or *One Life to Live*; the first episode focused on Mary; her husband, Tom (Greg Mullavey); her mother, Martha Shumway (Dody Goodman); her best friend, Loretta Haggers (Mary Kay Place); and her neighbors as they reacted to a spectacular crime: the mass murder by Davey Jessup (Will Seltzer) of an entire family, including their goats and chickens. The series ran five days a week, like the thing it parodied, and aired 325 episodes that didn't stint on soap opera–style melodrama and borderline Grand Guignol flourishes. Mary's husband had an affair with a bisexual. Mary's grandpa Raymond Larkin (Victor Kilian) turned out to be a flasher. An abusive husband played by Martin Mull (of the fake talk show *Fernwood 2-Night*, a show in this vein that perhaps inhabited the same fictional universe) was impaled by the star atop an aluminum Christmas tree. A child evangelist was electrocuted in a bathtub. There were political protests and extramarital affairs and even a hostage situation.

Running beneath the show's outrageous surface was a depressing account of the deadening effects of suburbanized, advertising-saturated American consumerist life. One episode found Mary obsessing over her failure to scour the "Waxy Yellow Buildup" (the phrase that gave the episode its title) from her kitchen floor, then hearing sirens that might or might not be real—a predicament that wouldn't have been out of place in a film by John Waters (*Pink Flamingos*) or Todd Haynes (*Safe*). The show's core creatives weren't baby boomers, but the overall sensibility was counterculture-friendly: knowing and mocking and sometimes sinister. Mary and many of the other characters were grown-ups who had been infantilized by modern life; her Pippi Longstocking pigtails and schoolgirlish dresses made this official. The show was in quiet rebellion against a venal and fatuous society that made pop culture intoxicants like soap operas (and TV commercials) seem as necessary as oxygen. The characters were constantly striving to get outside of their consciousness and their society and discover something authentic, but no matter what avenue they chose, they still seemed unreal to themselves, to others, and to the audience—as plasticized and packaged as characters in a soap opera. They could not simply exist and be happy. "The art of being, of knowingness, of knowing how to be," the social worker Roberta Wolashek (Samantha Harper) intones in a mid-season episode, trying to sell Mary on a faddish 1970s New Age belief system called Survival Training Existence Therapy (STET). "I say 'I am' because I know how to be. Here, now, completely." "That's wonderful," Mary says. "What does it mean?" "Mary, it means that when I'm here, that's the only place I am. I'm complete, I'm whole, no pieces of me are anywhere else. I'm together." Samantha urges her to do some STET exercises and Mary

can't handle it and begins freaking out; by the end of the episode she's in full retreat from Samantha, who shouts at her, "There is only *now!*" "When I get there, I'll call you," Mary says, spooked and exhausted, "and we'll work this whole thing out."

Soap, a saga about the wealthy and troubled Tate and Campbell families, arrived on ABC a year later, mainstreamed *Hartman*'s innovations, and repackaged them for prime time, creating one of the first hit sitcoms that was simultaneously kidding and not kidding. Katherine Helmond and Robert Mandan played Jessica and Chester Tate, opposite Cathryn Damon and Richard Mulligan as Mary and Burt Campbell; they all had affairs, the earliest of which inadvertently led to the murder of Mary's stepson Peter (future *Spenser: For Hire* star Robert Urich). The Campbells had mob ties and a tragic past and attracted death the way a magnet attracts iron filings. The huge supporting and recurring cast included Robert Guillaume as the Tates' sardonic butler, Benson (later spun off into his own self-named prime-time sitcom), and Billy Crystal as prime time's first openly gay character, Jodie Dallas, who impregnates a lawyer he meets at his aunt's murder trial, gets embroiled in a custody battle after his wife flees to join the rodeo, and enters hypnotherapy to forget the past and ends up believing he's an old Jewish man named Julius Kassendorf (which let Crystal do one of his favorite bits of shtick, impersonating his own grandfather). The series was nowhere near as unnerving as *Mary Hartman*; the humor was more broad and accessible, more obviously campy, with fewer moments that audiences weren't sure how to take. Jessica's daughter Corinne (Diana Canova) falls in love with a priest (Sal Viscuso), convinces him to leave the priesthood and marry her, then gives birth to his son, who is possessed by Satan. Burt comes to believe that he can become invisible by snapping his fingers, gets abducted by aliens and replaced with a double (also played by Mulligan), and is eventually elected the town's sheriff.

Both *Mary Hartman, Mary Hartman* and *Soap* were part of a wave of post–World War II humor that built audiences' awareness of showbiz clichés into the DNA of the stories it told; Showtime's *It's Garry Shandling's Show*, the most Brechtian sitcom of the '80s, took the tradition further, even as aspects of it felt as though the sitcom had come full circle. It was a cable-saucy *Jack Benny Program* for the Reagan era,

cocreated, written, and fronted by a performer whose mortified cringes, pregnant pauses, and narcissistic lies were Bennyesque. Shandling played, well, Garry Shandling, a stand-up comic who's starring in a sitcom and is hyperaware of what that means. The opening theme by Bill Lynch consists solely of assertions of what the song is doing at any given moment:

This is the theme to Garry's show,
The theme to Garry's show.
Garry called me up and asked if I
*   would write his theme song.*
I'm almost halfway finished,
How do you like it so far,
How do you like the theme to
*   Garry's show?*

Nearly every aspect of the series was drawn from Shandling's life, including the character's hometown (Sherman Oaks, California), the design of his condo, and the life milestones of friends who stopped by as guest stars. Garry addressed the audience directly, like a stand-up comic hired to warm up a studio audience, and revised the show's plots when they didn't reflect favorably on him or seemed like they might not turn out the way he wanted. Recurring characters were often described by Garry in terms that you might encounter in a production casting notice or a TV critic's review (Molly Cheek's Nancy Bancroft was described in dialogue as his "attractive but nonthreatening platonic neighbor"). When former *Saturday Night Live* cast member Gilda Radner appeared as herself, Shandling asked her why she hadn't been acting much lately, and she replied, "Oh, I had cancer, what did you have?" She died of cancer seven months later. Shandling elaborated on all these conceits—actually inverted them, in a way—on the aforementioned *The Larry Sanders Show*, which feigned "realism" but also included distancing devices.

Today the *Benny/Hartman/Soap/Shandling* tradition has been carried on by such a dazzling array of programs—everything from *Twin Peaks* and *The Simpsons* and *30 Rock* to *Futurama* and *Louie* and *BoJack Horseman* and *Rick and Morty*—that it has ceased to be noteworthy. The sophistication, even jadedness, of modern audiences, who start watching (or "consuming") TV from an early age and absorb all the genres and variants that the medium can devise, practically demands self-awareness—a frame around the frame that borders the TV set (or computer screen, or mobile device) on which stories or "stories" play out. The most radical thing a television series can do today is be *unaware* of itself as entertainment, as story, as product: to simply be, or pretend to simply be, and ask us to embrace the illusion and intellectually and emotionally commit—as one should commit to life, whatever channel that's on.

—MZS

The Andy Griffith Show (CBS, 1960–1968) Total score: 87

The Andy Griffith Show came into existence because CBS wanted to make a buck off people they thought of as country bumpkins. When TV sets became sought-after consumer items in the early '50s, big-city and suburban residents were the earliest adopters; it wasn't until the late '50s and early '60s that rural Americans started to buy them in droves, and once they did, networks rushed to give them entertainment they thought they'd like: Drawling small-town sitcoms like *Green Acres*, *The Beverly Hillbillies*, and *Petticoat Junction* were all a part of this cynical marketplace maneuver. Their characters spoke with exaggerated drawls and fished and hee-hawed and smacked their knees and played banjo and smoked corncob pipes and skinny-dipped in swimming holes. Their universe seemed more 1930s than 1960s. Even the characters in the comic strip *L'il Abner* might find them stereotypical.

Andy Griffith was several cuts above the competition. Its fictional small town, Mayberry, felt like a real place, although it was considerably whiter than a lot of small towns in North Carolina, where it supposedly was set. Its story lines were believable, sometimes believably uneventful. And the filmmaking was thoughtful and expressive, tracking the characters' movements through intricately detailed interiors, making time and space for quiet conversations and wordless moments of interaction and sometimes musical numbers.

More important was the show's aura of quiet dignity. These characters weren't dumb rednecks, they weren't cartoons, they weren't clichés. They were people. They weren't funny merely because they didn't live in the city. They were as full of life as Mark Twain characters, and as rooted in the real. Andy Taylor, a widower raising his young son, Opie (future *Happy Days* star and Oscar-winning director Ron Howard), was a good and complicated man, nice to his friends and dedicated to his job and always good for a quick-witted joke or a philosophical aside. He spent a lot of his time gossiping (while admonishing those who gossiped), eating Aunt Bee's cooking, and going out with schoolteacher Helen Crump (Aneta Corsaut) or spirited single gal Ellie Walker (Elinor Donahue). (You could tell they both wanted to marry Andy, but he didn't seem terribly interested in making that move; he didn't want to upset the apple cart, you know.)

The townspeople, and the ensemble of actors who portrayed them, were a constant source of delight. They were support for Andy, Opie, and Aunt Bee (Frances Bavier), but they had a life force; you could imagine them brewing moonshine in the woods or making pie in their kitchens when the camera wasn't looking. Town barber Floyd Lawson (Howard McNear) was a one-name CNN of bad information. Otis Campbell (Hal Smith), the town drunk, checked into the jail on Saturday night and checked out Sunday morning; he was such a regular that sometimes Andy would barely look up as he helped himself to the key to the cell. Gomer Pyle (Jim Nabors) and his cousin Goober (George Lindsey) were smiling goofballs who might have been played as one-joke comic relief on a lesser show, but the writing embellished them so lovingly and the actors imbued them with such decency that you wanted them to succeed at whatever harebrained scheme they were smitten with that week. More so than any sitcom of the '60s, *The Andy Griffith Show* blurred the line between the domestic and the workplace sitcoms. Andy was the nexus point between the two, treating everyone in town and everyone who drifted through town (including a lazy hobo played by Buddy Ebsen and assorted con artists and reprobates) as human beings worthy of being heard and understood, if not necessarily indulged. A longing for connection animates every scene on the show, even ones that seem frivolous or corny. Sometimes the filmmaking draws out this theme in faintly Expressionist ways, as in season 1's "Christmas Story," when the camera pivots away from Yuletide revelers and slowly pushes in on the window of a doorway where a Scrooge-like character, Ben Weaver (Will Wright), looks on others' happiness with paralyzed longing.

Andy's shrimpy string bean of a deputy, Barney Fife (Don Knotts), was the series' breakout supporting character, a sidekick with the sputtering self-importance, insecurity, and disarming romantic streak of a Preston Sturges dreamer-hick. His comic impetuousness was the earliest critique of masculinity on network TV. Andy knew full well how incompetent Barney was but was respectful of his fragile ego; he let Barney carry a gun but insisted on issuing him a single bullet, which he had to keep in his shirt pocket, effectively creating a "waiting period" that gave Barney just enough time to realize that it was better not to draw. Knotts incarnated the character so vividly that he became a comic legend in his own right. He left the show in 1965, hoping to become a movie star (he succeeded, kind of, in kid-friendly films like *The Reluctant Astronaut* and *The Incredible Mr. Limpet*); Jack Burns stepped in, playing Deputy Warren Ferguson.

The Andy Griffith Show spawned two spin-offs, the Jim Nabors vehicle *Gomer Pyle, U.S.M.C.*, and *Mayberry R.F.D.*, a reboot of *The Andy Griffith Show* that tried to continue the story of Mayberry without Griffith, who'd left by that point. Both series evoked some of the gentleness and decency of their predecessor, but neither had the same magic, because they didn't have Andy Griffith. The show wasn't named for Griffith just because he was the star. It seemed to take its artistic cues from his affable brand of cool. Griffith's performance hinted at a persistent sadness in Andy that could be managed only through service to his town, his friends, his family, and, most of all, his son.

Opie and Andy's relationship is the most important one on the series. The father is always teaching moral lessons to his son—often ones that reflect on his life experiences and his desire to make his town a peaceful, sensible, decent place to live, so that his son can believe that the world is a good place despite having lost his mother before he had a chance to know her. The series' aesthetic and dramatic high point is the first episode of season 4, "Opie the Birdman," in which Opie kills a mother bird in his front yard with a slingshot, then runs away in shame and tries to hide the deed from his father. When Andy stands in Opie's room and lectures him on the irrevocable impact of his actions, the episode literally darkens. The father seems to loom over the son like a specter whose outrage is held in check by grief. Without hitting the point too hard, the episode makes it clear that Opie's killing of the bird has awakened the trauma of a primal loss. He names the motherless birds Winkin', Blinkin', and Nod, and resolves to raise them himself, then

realizes he's not up to the task and releases them into the wild. He tells his father that the cage seems empty now. "Yes, son, it sure does," Andy says. "But don't the trees seem nice and full?"

—MZS

The Cosby Show (NBC, 1984– 1992) Total score: 87

My son looks at me hopefully and asks, "Dad, when are we going to watch another Cosby Show?"

My daughter grimaces and tells him we won't be watching it anymore. Unlike him, she's old enough to understand why our marathon viewing of The Cosby Show has come to an end, even if, thankfully, she's not yet old enough to fully comprehend the sheer horror of the acts in question.

And I shake my head and wish I'd never introduced them to the show in the first place.

If you want to avoid the work of an artist whose personal activities and views you find questionable, that's your prerogative, and everyone draws that line in a different place. You might view Mel Gibson as an anti-Semite, racist, and misogynist and still have to stop channel surfing whenever you land on the torture scene from Lethal

Weapon; or you might hold your nose about the various scandals and accusations in Woody Allen's past when you watch his latest film; or shrug off memories of Alec Baldwin's last six public tantrums because you really want to see the *30 Rock* where Jack role-plays as Tracy's dad. Saints are rare in any profession, let alone the entertainment industry, and chances are you adore the work of someone whose presence you wouldn't tolerate if you spent an hour getting to know them as a person.

With Bill Cosby, though, there's no easy way to separate the art from the artist. The preponderance of testimony against him is horrifying, painting him as a serial predator of women on a level that can't be rationalized away. And Cosby and Cliff Huxtable are as intertwined as any actor and character in TV history—including the ones like Ozzie Nelson and Jerry Seinfeld, who, like Cosby, more or less played themselves.

Cosby and his alter ego had different names, professions, and levels of income and fame, but in all ways that mattered to the audience, Cosby was Cliff and vice versa. They had the same number of kids with the same gender breakdown. Theo in particular behaved exactly like how Cosby had described his son, Ennis, in his comedy act, and in many episodes, *The Cosby Show* simply felt like a dramatization of the *Bill Cosby: Himself* stand-up concert. They had the same cultural interests, the same attitudes about parenting, and the same desire to lecture others about both. This was a sitcom-as-lifestyle-manual, and the only difference at times between the show and some of Cosby's own jeremiads against the state of black America was that the show had a lot of great jokes surrounding the harangues.

Because Bill and Cliff were one and the same, and because the show was so clearly bent on educating as well as entertaining, there's no way to watch a second of it now without flinching at thoughts of what Cosby allegedly did to all those women, and at the unmitigated hypocrisy of the whole enterprise.

My kids and I had started watching episodes on Hulu a few months before the Hannibal Buress stand-up routine that finally turned the public against the Cos. I was looking to get them watching higher-quality sitcoms than what they were watching on Disney and Nick, and there was even a part of me feeling smug that the experience might wind up like the tagline to another Cosby series, where they'd enjoy some music and fun, and if they weren't careful, they might learn something before it was done.

I shouldn't have been smug. I'd heard the rumors, had been at press conferences where BuzzFeed's Kate Aurthur had pressed NBC executives about their plans to do a new series with Cosby given the long string of accusations against him, even as they dismissed her questions as needless pot-stirring. Buress emboldened many other alleged victims to come forward—but with a sour reminder that, even in 2016, women's voices needed male amplification to be heard.

Once that happened, I knew this nostalgic experiment was over. My wife had to have a very difficult conversation with our daughter as she stared at a tabloid headline in the supermarket checkout aisle. My son's too young to understand any of this, and still occasionally asks to watch the slumber party episode again, but we'll have to talk with him about it eventually.

So what's it doing in this book, and ranked this highly? If you can somehow, even for only a moment, consider it independently from the real man at its center, you can still see that *The Cosby Show* was a masterpiece of the form: a simple, smart, elegant, and (especially in the early years, before the kids started to age past their respective plot utilities) hilarious family comedy. Cosby's interplay with Phylicia Rashad as Clair, Malcolm-Jamal Warner as Theo (whose growth from impulsive kid to thoughtful young adult gave the series its narrative spine even as other actors and producers came and went), Keshia Knight Pulliam as Rudy, and all the rest of his fictional family was inspired, and the series continually found novel ways to turn its sermons into sitcom plots.

Season 2's "Theo's Holiday" is a wonder in this regard, as Cliff and Clair teach Theo about the specific responsibilities and financial costs that come with being an adult by turning the whole Huxtable brownstone into a role-playing exercise, with Cliff as the gruff landlord, Clair as a fast-talking saleswoman with a lilting Caribbean accent, and little Rudy as a bank president not inclined to give would-be male model Theo a loan. It's fun to watch the whole cast try on these other roles, even as the episode's slipping in basic real-world knowledge, and also illustrating what a good job the Huxtables have done in raising Theo, such that he would go along with the stunt.

Cliff and Clair's firm but benevolent parenting style weighed on their kids, who felt pressured to equal their parents' achievements—an impossible ambition, considering that Mom and Dad came up during the civil rights era and had to fight much harder for everything they had. "Because of what you two have accomplished, the world expects a lot more from us than from other kids," Theo tells his father in season 6's "I'm 'In' with the 'In' Crowd." "And that's our fault?" Cliff says, exasperated. "Think about it," Theo says. "You're a doctor, Mom's a lawyer, that's a lot of pressure." "Theo, we never said, 'Become a doctor, become a lawyer.' We say, 'Go to school,' we say, 'Study,' we say, 'Become something,'" Cliff says. He means it, but Theo seems unconvinced, and considering the comfortable life he and his sisters have been given—a life that includes guest shots by entertainment and political heroes like Lena Horne, Roscoe Lee Browne, Rita Moreno, Pam Grier, Stevie Wonder, and NBA-star-turned-senator Bill Bradley—who could blame him? The show was criticized, by liberals of all colors, as being somehow "unrealistic" or unrepresentative of African American life in the 1980s, a time of resurgent racism and the unraveling of the social safety net. There were fears that by showcasing such wealth and success each week

on one of TV's most popular shows, Cosby and company were inadvertently devaluing the struggle for equality that was still going on, and contributing to the lie that discrimination was somehow "over." These complaints were amplified by Cosby's cranky, up-by-my-bootstraps remarks in interviews, sentiments that sometimes bled into the scripts of episodes. (In season 2's "Halloween," Cliff says of trick-or-treating, "Why don't we just call it what it is: begging!")

In the end, though, the show was more aspirational than fantastic, and entertaining enough to deflect any editorials that criticized it. It took an image of domestic life that network TV had long presented as "normal" for white Americans—a mutually supportive nuclear family with charming and basically happy kids, headed by loving, educated parents who owned their own handsomely furnished house—and put a black family at the center, without any indication that the sight was odd, or even worthy of comment. *The Cosby Show*, like Bill Cosby's long career before the show's debut, was a testament to artistry and willpower, forces that fused to shatter every barrier placed in front of Cosby and other black entertainers throughout the twentieth century. Cosby was the first

African American stand-up performer to cross over without doing any material related to race (his first performance on *The Tonight Show* was about karate); the first to create a recurring fictional universe of comic characters in his stand-up act (inner-city Philadelphia teens who appeared on multiple long-playing albums, and who later populated the hit cartoon series *Fat Albert and the Cosby Kids*); the first black actor to simultaneously pitch products and services for major corporations, including Jell-O, Coke, and Kodak; the first black actor to get equal billing with a white lead on a hit network drama (*I Spy*, opposite Robert Culp—the forerunner of *Miami Vice*, the *Lethal Weapon* and *48 Hrs.* movies, and other properties built around tough-sexy, salt-and-pepper teams); and the first to costar with another black lead actor in a series of hit action comedy films (opposite Sidney Poitier in 1974's *Uptown Saturday Night*, 1975's *Let's Do it Again*, and 1977's *A Piece of the Action*—without which the *Bad Boys* and *Ride Along* movies would be unthinkable).

Sadly, it is impossible to revisit these milestones without imagining the horror happening behind the scenes of their creation. As this book went to press, Bill Cosby stood accused of drugging and raping more than fifty women in incidents spanning decades. The details are so sickening that it seems blasphemous to point out the cultural collateral damage caused by his crimes; but that damage is real, too, and germane to this book: More than fifty years' worth of innovative popular culture has been soiled in the public imagination by a crime spree spanning half a century. It is now impossible to thrill to *I Spy*, imitate Fat Albert, swap lines from classic Cosby records like *Sports*, *Revenge*, or *200 M.P.H.*, or joke about Cliff Huxtable's sweaters or the family's dance moves in the show's opening credits, without shuddering with revulsion. Cosby's entire career has become a minefield of accidental reminders of the crimes he's accused of committing. His album titles *It's True! It's True!*, *For Adults Only*, *Bill Cosby Is Not Himself These Days*, *Inside the Mind of Bill Cosby*, and *Bill Cosby Talks to Kids About Drugs* now seem like accidental confessions or sick jokes. Worse still is the season 7 *Cosby Show* episode "The Last Barbecue," in which guests at a cookout become more amenable to sex when they sample Cliff's special sauce. "Haven't you ever noticed after people have some of my barbecue sauce, after a while, when it kicks in, they get all huggy-buggy?" he asks Clair, leering. "Haven't you ever noticed that after one of my barbecues, and they have the sauce, people want to get right home?"

Everything that was once funny, sexy, or inspiring about Cosby is unsettling now. Every value he claimed to stand for has been revealed as a lie. Everything he said or did, achieved or touched, has an asterisk, including his most significant achievement, *The Cosby Show*. The series was credited with single-handedly reviving the family sitcom at a time when the TV business had just about given up on it, and with changing national attitudes about race with its depiction of an admirable, relatable, upper-middle-class black family. It did all these things and more. Its legacy shouldn't be forgotten. It was a great show, but one that nobody will want to watch again for a very long time.

—AS (with MZS)

Moonlighting (ABC, 1985–1989)
Total score: 87

Maddie Hayes: David, get serious.

David Addison: Get serious? Maddie, I just touched your rear end. If I get any more serious they're gonna move us to cable!

How meta was *Moonlighting*? So meta that it didn't just toy with the structure, tone, pace, and style of the detective drama every single week, it toyed with network business practices and audience patience as well. Created by Glenn Gordon Caron—previously a writer-producer on NBC's *Remington Steele*, a show so similar to *Moonlighting* that Caron wrote *Steele* star Pierce Brosnan into a season 3 cameo—the scripts ran twice as long as the one-hour drama's usual, because there was so much overlapping dialogue, delivered at machine-gun pace. The show's commitment to Old Hollywood visuals (shot by series cinematographer Gerald Finnerman, who photographed *My Fair Lady*) doubled each episode's production time, and drove the budget up to almost a million dollars per hour. Sometimes fans had to wait weeks for a fresh installment; the delays became so commonplace that ABC recorded a promo showing executives waiting on the next episode. On a few occasions viewers tuned in to find that ABC had replaced a scheduled installment with a rerun because the producers had blown their deadline.

Despite this, *Moonlighting* was so original and beloved that both ABC and its viewers put up with all the mishegoss. It continued to be regarded with affection even in its last two seasons, when it seemed to be disintegrating onscreen. Cybill Shepherd revived her flagging acting career in the role of Maddie Hayes, owner of Los Angeles's Blue Moon Detective Agency. A then-obscure character actor named Bruce Willis got cast as Maddie's new partner, the horny, fast-talking smart aleck David Addison, when the only female ABC executive in the room during *Moonlighting*'s final round of casting told her male colleagues that Willis struck her as "one dangerous fuck." Caron built the show around Shepherd and Willis's palpable sexual chemistry (which was amplified by offscreen loathing) and had them bombard each other with innuendo, the better to tease viewers who wanted the couple to act out one of David's most memorable rhetorical questions: "Do bears bear? Do bees bee?"

The show's many formal experiments included "The Dream Sequence Always Rings Twice," a mostly black-and-white tribute to film noir introduced by Orson Welles, and airing just two days after Welles's death; "Big Man on Mulberry Street," an episode built around fantasy song-and-dance numbers; and "Atomic Shakespeare,"

a *Taming of the Shrew* spoof with nonsensical dialogue in iambic pentameter. ("Yea, I say, but why do you bray? Do not gainsay what I say that we may make headway! I foray this way that I may be home ere midday.")

And then...the phenomenon fell apart. In a classic case of "When the legend becomes fact, print the legend," *Moonlighting*'s postmortem reputation became a story about how the audience lost interest after David and Maddie slept together near the end of season 3—in an episode watched by more than sixty million people—thus proving why all ensuing TV comedies are wise to keep potential couples apart as long as possible.

It's a great story. Too bad it's not true. Here's what actually happened:

- Though the characters had sex again in the next episode, the show returned for season 4 with Maddie deciding to run away from David.
- Shepherd was pregnant, Willis was filming the first *Die Hard*, and the costars hadn't gotten along for quite some time, so it became easier for the show to keep the characters completely separate for the next eight episodes.

- As Maddie traveled by train back to Los Angeles, she met and impulsively married a nice nebbish named Walter Bishop (Dennis Dugan), which added yet another obstacle to the central characters' getting together in the long term, and one that made both of them look bad in the process.
- Caron's perfectionism had become especially problematic by this point. The delays were so bad that a month passed between the fourth-season premiere and the next episode.
- David and Maddie never actually became a couple after that, other than a meta scene in the series finale where they decide to get married before their show is canceled.

So you had a show where the characters got together and almost immediately split, didn't actually appear together on-camera for months after that, erected additional barriers that made the separation even more uncomfortable, and had abnormally long gaps between episodes. The audience didn't flee because they got bored after David and Maddie hooked up; they fled because the final seasons went out of their way to keep them apart and everyone got frustrated waiting.

Good luck telling this to many modern TV comedy writers, who've taken it as gospel that *Moonlighting* went from phenomenon to fiasco overnight because audiences prefer their romantic gratification to be perpetually delayed, and who thus put their characters through all manner of stupid, contrived delays to coupledom out of fear that happiness equals ratings death.

But damn, was it fun for a while.

"Did I happen to mention, did I bother to disclose, that this man that we're seeking has a mole on his nose?" said David in an early episode, talking his way past a security guard. "I'm not sure of his clothes or anything else, except he's Chinese, a big clue by itself."

"How do you do that?" Maddie asks afterward.

"Gotta read a lotta Dr. Seuss," he replies.

—MZS & AS

Taxi (ABC, 1978–1982; NBC, 1982–1983) Total score: 87

Midway through the first episode of *Taxi*, new cabbie Elaine Nardo (Marilu Henner) tells veteran Alex Rieger (Judd Hirsch) that she'll be working at the Sunshine Cab Company only part-time while she focuses on her real career in the art world.

"Oh yeah, I know," Alex tells her.

"We're all part-time here. You see that guy over there? Now, he's an actor. The guy on the phone, he's a prizefighter. This lady over here, she's a beautician. The man behind her, he's a writer. Me? I'm a cab-driver. I'm the only cabdriver in this place."

This is at once a funny mono-logue and a dark existential state-ment. Alex is comfortable with his station in life, and possibly so is cruel dispatcher Louie De Palma (Danny DeVito), but everyone else at Sunshine dreams of some-thing bigger—something that the very nature of a situation com-edy set at the cab company garage makes impossible. If a character on *Taxi* were to ever achieve his or her dream, they'd be off the show. Aspiring actor Bobby Wheeler (Jeff Conaway) is written off in exactly this manner after the third season, and when he returns in the fourth, we learn that his big break turned out to be less than he'd hoped. They come to the garage each day, hoping for something better, but make do with a life behind the wheel of a big yellow cab.

Most sitcoms have static situations—if Gilligan and the castaways were ever rescued, there would be no show—but rarely has a comedy been as acutely aware of the futility of its characters' dreams, or been tinged with so much sadness.

Taxi debuted near the end of a decade where shows like *M*A*S*H* and *All in the Family* had proved that audiences would accept seri-ous moments and episodes from their sitcoms, and *Taxi* fit perfectly into this new tradition. It features two of the great comic creations the small screen has ever shown us in the Napoleonic, bitter Louie, and the blissful '60s burnout "Rev-erend" Jim Ignatowski (Christo-pher Lloyd). The scene where a frustrated Bobby tries to help the addled Jim pass his driving test ("What does a yellow light mean?" "Slow down!" "What…does… a…yellow…light…mean?") is on the short list of the funniest sitcom sequences ever.

And yet the show could seam-lessly shift from broad hilarity to dark, moving drama. The first epi-sode climaxes with the bittersweet reunion between Alex and the teen-age daughter he hasn't seen since she was a toddler—a scene that acknowledges all the messy emo-tions of the situation, and one that a network development executive told me would never be allowed in a comedy pilot today. It set the tone for all that followed.

When I think of Reverend Jim, the first image isn't the driving test, but him addressing the empty suit of his late father, trying to make peace in death with a man he could never relate to in life, on the verge of tears as Stevie Wonder's "You Are the Sunshine of My Life" plays. When I think of Louie, my mind first goes to his confession to Elaine about his humiliating annual trip to buy clothes from the husky boys section of the department store. Even an unabashedly cartoonish character like immigrant mechanic Latka Gravas (performance artist Andy Kaufman at his most commercial) comes to suffer from multiple personality disorder, and though the condition is often played for laughs—as in an episode where he turns into an uncanny duplicate of Alex—there's always an underlying sadness to those stories because it's a problem that none of Latka's friends can help him with.

The show's run echoed the cabbies' own deferred dreams. It was a success at first, but only because it aired after the much broader Three's Company, then scuffled through two more seasons before ABC gave up. There was brief talk of its blazing a trail to cable by going to HBO—along with jokes that the first shot of such a fifth season would be of Henner's bare breasts—but instead it wound up on NBC, where it was paired for its final season with a new show from former Taxi writers Glen and Les Charles called Cheers. Cheers would eclipse its predecessor in commercial success and prestige, leaving Taxi behind like the Sunshine Cab drivers watching a colleague finally hit it big in their dream job while the rest of them had to keep hanging around that big, dark room where they spent every night together.

—AS

East Side/West Side (CBS, 1963–1964) Total score: 86

"As far as trivial, meaningless dramatic series are concerned, we've had it," East Side/West Side star George C. Scott told TV Guide in November 1963. "We have got to come to grips with controversial themes. We've got to try to say something about the way we live."

And they did. Shot in New York City, this series from Fred Coe, Herbert Brodkin, and TV producer and talk show host David Susskind followed employees of the Community Welfare Service (CWS), a private agency of social workers tasked with helping residents of a tough New York neighborhood. George C. Scott played Neil Brock, a gruff, mercurial fellow whose close-cropped hair, cheap shirts, and ugly ties testified to his lack of interest in dazzling with first impressions (he was later revealed to be a Polish immigrant's son who had changed his last name). Elizabeth Wilson played his coworker, Frieda Hechlinger; Cicely Tyson, the first African American actress to land a recurring dramatic role on TV, played the office's secretary, Jane Foster, who soon began working in the field.

Episodes dealt with juvenile delinquency ("I Before E, Except After C"); the struggle to raise an adult son with Down syndrome ("No Wings at All"); housing discrimination in the suburbs ("No Hiding Place"); the role of child abuse in creating runaways ("The Street"); discrimination against sex workers ("The Sinner"); and the contradictions in statutory rape laws from state to state ("Age of Consent"). Carroll O'Connor, aka Archie Bunker, starred in that last episode as a widowed police officer who accuses his teenage daughter's boyfriend of rape to stop her from marrying the boy and leaving him all by his lonesome. A subplot in that same hour saw Brock going on a public affairs show (hosted by none other than David Susskind) to speak about liberal versus conservative values and the obstacles to true social reform.

In "Who Do You Kill?" an African American couple's baby suffers a rat bite after months of their complaining to their white landlord about the building's conditions. (Michael Mann's *Crime Story* would pay homage to it with an episode a few decades later.) The episode asks whether racism is best met with nonviolent or violent resistance: civil rights marches, Martin Luther King Jr., and Malcolm X were all constantly in the news at that point. James Earl Jones plays the father, an unemployed man so fed up with the conditions that trapped his family in poverty that he finds phony white liberal expressions of sympathy nearly as noxious as racism itself. "The white man stick a knife in my back," he tells Brock and Cynthia, who have tried to find work for him. "Another white pull it out and stick on a bandage! You think I'm gonna kiss his hand?" The line anticipates a statement made by Malcolm X in a TV interview four months later: "If you stick a knife in my back nine inches and pull it out six inches, there's no progress. If you pull it all the way out, that's not progress. Progress is healing the wound that the blow made. And they haven't even pulled the knife out, much less healed the wound. They won't even admit the knife is there."

Network notes urged the show's producers to stir in more humor, avoid an "over-grim documentary feel," and resist the urge to blame characters' problems on the failure of institutions. Susskind orchestrated a letter-writing campaign to try to save the show, to no avail. The last episode, "Here Today," is one of the bitterest finales in TV history: Brock writes a series of articles about urban problems but no paper will publish it; he finally finds one that will run it, then learns that the paper is about to be absorbed by a rival publication that doesn't run those kinds of pieces.

—MZS

MOST AWESOME AND/OR RIDICULOUS NAMES

1. (tie) Bob Loblaw, Tobias Fünke, Maeby Fünke, GOB (George Oscar Bluth), George Michael Bluth, Ann Veal, Barry Zuckerkorn, J. Walter Weatherman, Gene Parmesan, Stan Sitwell, Larry Middleman, Cindi Lightballoon, Hel-Loh Bluth, *Arrested Development*
2. Truxton Spangler, *Rubicon*
3. Dr. Leo Spaceman, *30 Rock*
4. Mike Ehrmantraut, *Breaking Bad/Better Call Saul*
5. Julia Sugarbaker, *Designing Women*
6. Furio Giunta, *The Sopranos*
7. Dr. Beardface (pronounced "Beard-FUH-say"), *Scrubs*
8. Luanne Platter, *King of the Hill* (certainly the only regular sitcom character named for a menu item at Luby's Cafeteria)
9. Chandler Bing, *Friends*
10. Sonny Crockett, *Miami Vice*
11. Vic Hitler (the narcoleptic comic), *Hill Street Blues*
12. Bailey Quarters, *WKRP in Cincinnati*
13. Daenerys Targaryen, *Game of Thrones*
14. Ronald Ulysses Swanson, *Parks and Recreation*
15. Snidely Whiplash, *The Rocky and Bullwinkle Show*
16. Thurston Howell III and Lovey Howell, *Gilligan's Island*
17. Emma Pillsbury, *Glee*
18. Maynard G. Krebs, *The Many Loves of Dobie Gillis*
19. Festus Haggen, *Gunsmoke*
20. Mr. Eko, *Lost*
21. Rustin Cohle, *True Detective*
22. Jordan Catalano, *My So-Called Life*
23. Krystle Carrington, *Dynasty*
24. Mr. Peanutbutter, *BoJack Horseman*
25. Veronica Mars, *Veronica Mars*

Hannibal (NBC, 2013–2015) Total score: 86

Bryan Fuller's riff on the world of novelist Thomas Harris, the father of Hannibal Lecter, was one of the great TV shows of the twenty-first century, and one of the least likely candidates for greatness. By the time the creator of *Wonderfalls* and *Pushing Daisies* offered his take on the patient-devouring psychiatrist and all ancillary characters in his bloody universe, the good doctor had been the subject of four novels and five films, not to mention innumerable imitative books, movies, and shows built around puppet masters who killed bushels of people and inspired others to kill, all while staying a step ahead of FBI profilers who were all modeled on Harris's other innovative pulp archetype, Will Graham. On top of all that, Lecter had previously been portrayed by two actors whose work was so strong that partisans still argue over whose interpretation is greater: Brian Cox's ice-cold Lecter in *Manhunter*, or Anthony Hopkins's wicked hambone in *The Silence of the Lambs, Hannibal*, and *Red Dragon.*

As Lecter, Mads Mikkelsen offered a new interpretation of the character. He was even more brazenly a fantasy-identification figure than his predecessors—as much the hero of this sprawling nightmare as Satan was the hero of *Paradise Lost* or Tom Ripley the hero of Patricia Highsmith's fiction. Mikkelsen was

arguably the first performer to successfully incarnate every preposterous assertion made about Lecter in Harris's books. He was believable as a therapist with superior listening skills and a strategic capacity for warmth, capable of fooling the world into thinking he was treating patients rather than grooming them as victims or apprentice killers, and helping the FBI solve a seemingly unending parade of murders without tipping them off to the fact that he was the mastermind. Mikkelsen was also credible as an elegant lover who unwound by shampooing his lover's hair, an action hero who could go toe-to-toe with Jack Crawford (Laurence Fishburne), and a polymath aesthete who could play Carnegie Hall–quality sonatas on piano or harpsichord, cook five-star meals from meats of questionable origin, and (in the season 3 premiere) land a professorship at a university in Florence by revealing a heretofore unknown capacity for speaking fluent Italian. (The chair was open, of course, because Lecter had created the vacancy.)

By all rights, *Hannibal* should have been both too silly and too violent to sustain itself for more than a few weeks. But it got richer, more assured, and more audacious as it went along, always taking the most surprising, at times circuitous route toward a destination. The show ran just three seasons but took such great strides that by the end of season 3, viewers might have felt as if they'd been watching the serial-killer equivalent of one of those evolutionary charts that starts with a razor-toothed fish and ends with a man in a suit carrying a briefcase. Fuller's tour of Harris land jettisoned the occasionally dreamlike approach of earlier features in favor of a full-on nightmare, unbound by real-world logic or plausibility, that got weirder, more ostentatiously sensual, and more impenetrable as it went along.

The first season has an anthology or "case of the week" feel: Lecter manipulates patients into killing or allowing themselves to be killed (or mutilated) while simultaneously advising the FBI on how to catch those same killers. Woven through all the freak-show excursions is an ongoing story about Lecter's seduction of Will Graham. The profiler is played by Hugh Dancy as a tortured empath—a dog-loving sweetheart so sensitive that while visiting crime scenes, he appears to be struck by waves of horror until he quivers like a tuning fork. The show might have continued in this vein, but instead it changed and kept changing, not unlike a Thomas Harris serial killer

obsessed by the act of becoming. Near the end of season 1, Lecter frames Will for murdering Abigail Hobbs (Kacey Rohl), daughter and apprentice of serial killer Garret Jacob Hobbs (Vladimir Jon Cubrt), and gets him locked away in prison. Season 2 starts with a brutal fight between Lecter and Jack but withholds its outcome until the finale, a rain-drenched massacre in a house that spills almost as much blood as the prom scene in *Carrie*. Sandwiched in between is an increasingly baroque narrative mixing case-of-the-week elements; an extended subplot about the drawling, born-again billionaire Mason Verger, played by *Boardwalk Empire*'s Michael Pitt; a sexual relationship between Lecter and former student turned FBI behavioral researcher Alana Bloom (Caroline Dhavernas), who ends up bearing Verger's child; and a physically unconsummated love story between Lecter and Will so intense and psychologically rich (albeit twisted) that it inspired some of the most heartfelt slash fiction and artwork in the history of fandom. Season 3 feels almost like two mini-seasons. The first half follows the fugitive Lecter to Florence and watches Graham, Crawford, and local Italian cops try to catch him. The back half replays the plot of *Manhunter*, with its villain, Francis Dolarhyde, aka the Tooth Fairy, portrayed by Richard Armitage; it also features a return engagement by Mason Verger (Joe Anderson this time), who was horribly disfigured in season 2 after Lecter mesmerized him into slicing off pieces of his face and feeding them to Will's dogs. The final three episodes of *Hannibal*'s last season rank with the most extravagantly visceral storytelling ever seen on network television. The last ten minutes of the finale—a two-on-one battle royale at a house perched on a cliff overlooking a Byronic sea—is such an orgiastic display of sensory overload that it should have ended with Fuller's hands reaching through the screen and personally handing every viewer a cigarette and a towel.

Throughout, there are few grounding signifiers of "realism," just a series of set pieces, scenes, and moments, linked more by images, sounds, sensations, and tonal commonalities than by prosaic plot or character elements. You don't so much watch season 3 of *Hannibal* as allow yourself to be absorbed by it, like water filling every available air pocket in a sponge. Fuller and his formidable roster of directors (including David Slade, Michael Rymer, Guillermo S. Navarro, and Vincenzo Natali) cribbed bits from some of the most aggressively visual filmmakers in film history, starting with German Expressionists (such as the original dream-filmmaker, F. W. Murnau, whose *The Cabinet of Dr. Caligari* and *Nosferatu* are recurring touchstones) and continuing through Luis Buñuel, Jean Cocteau, Stanley Kubrick, Brian De Palma, Dario Argento, and the three Davids (Lynch, Cronenberg, and Fincher). The cinematography and production design prize emotional truth over common sense. Lecter's sessions with his patients (and with his own therapist and future lover, Bedelia Du Maurier, played by *X-Files* costar Gillian Anderson—a casting masterstroke) occur in rooms as murky-dark as an aquarium.

More so than any previous serial-killer tale, *Hannibal* presents the relationship between the FBI, Lecter, and his patients/pupils in terms of artistic metaphor, with the G-men as critics or art history students scrutinizing the handiwork of lesser "artists" striving to imitate, please, or outdo their idol or teacher. Bodies are hacked, torn, re-formed, or fused to make collages, multimedia presentations, gallery installations, and outdoor sculptures. Hannibal is pictured in dreams as a buck-demon with glowing eyes and antlers. Sex scenes give way to abstraction, with faces and torsos and limbs seeming to merge, and literal two-way trysts becoming (via fantasy) three-ways, then finally kaleidoscopes. Fuller gets around the visual tedium of epistolary or phone relationships by letting characters who've been geographically separated from Hannibal meet him in his "palace of dreams," and sit for a therapy session or light candles in a Florence church even when one party is languishing in a prison cell and the other wandering the Eastern Seaboard.

The whole series is a palace of dreams. Many are so peculiar, revolting, perverse, and altogether bizarre that the very notion of *Hannibal*'s airing on a traditional broadcast network (even with major funding from the French studio Gaumont) seems laughable in retrospect. How could something like this happen? How was it allowed to continue for three lurid, gorgeous years? And how soon can it happen again?

—MZS

ER (NBC, 1994–2009) Total score: 85

The doctors at *ER*'s County General faced blizzards, plane crashes, and shoot-outs. One was stabbed to death by a patient. Another died when the Turkish mob blew up his ambulance only a few years after he was nearly killed by a road rage–fueled motorist. Still another was killed by a falling helicopter, but only after a *different* helicopter was responsible for the loss of his arm the year before.

Through fifteen seasons, they weren't so much doctors as they were action heroes. Which made sense, because *ER* was less a hospital drama than an action show.

Before *ER*, all medical dramas— all TV dramas, period—had the leisurely pace of a routine visit to your general practitioner's office, and they were often more concerned with the stories of the patients than they were with the doctors. *ER* put the formula on fast-forward, borrowing its pace and production values from summer blockbusters. (Steven Spielberg had at one point intended to make a movie out of the Michael Crichton script that became the series' pilot episode.) Though the show in later years would occasionally employ very special guest stars as patients, in the early going, the bodies that came into and out of the ER may as well have been played by mannequins; they were there to demonstrate the heroic skills of the doctors and then be transferred to another part of the hospital (including, at times, the morgue) while we moved rapidly to a new case. The show rarely stopped to explain any of the medical jargon or procedures we were witnessing because the show trusted the audience to keep up, and to recognize the urgency of a given situation even if they didn't know what a peritoneal lavage was.

To pull that off, you need first-rate direction and production, which *ER* had throughout its run; even the most ridiculous disasters (like poor Rocket Romano's repeat bad luck with helicopters) looked and sounded sensational. (One of the more ill-advised experiments the show ever tried was a live episode that stripped away the quick editing, the pulse-pounding score, and the other effects; it was like watching the *ER* cast perform a community theater version of an episode.)

You also need doctors and nurses the audience will invest in so that they'll want to keep watching long after the novelty of the pacing wears off. Again, *ER* had those in abundance. It was the series that turned former show-killer George Clooney into a giant star with his role as maverick pediatrician Doug Ross. It had Anthony Edwards as the sane, wise *ER* chief Mark Greene, even if it prolonged Mark's death from brain cancer far too long; had Noah Wyle growing compellingly from boy to man (with a lot of help from Eriq La Salle's gruff Peter Benton) as point-of-view character John Carter; and passed the baton neatly from Julianna Margulies to Maura Tierney to Linda Cardellini as the lead nurse and unofficial heart of the ER.

In time, other dramas began moving even faster, and other hospital shows like *Grey's Anatomy* grew even more indiscriminate about killing off their characters. But even in the final years of *ER*, when the show was on its third-generation cast, the framework and craftsmanship remained so sturdy that when I would stumble onto an episode featuring the kind of disaster they'd done five times already, I'd laugh at first, and then quickly feel my pulse quickening in that same way it had back in the days of Carter, Benton, and company.

—AS

Parks and Recreation (NBC, 2009–2015) Total score: 85

Say hello to Leslie Knope. She is bright, enthusiastic, and completely delusional about the merits and power of her position as deputy director of the parks department of Pawnee, Indiana. Her coworkers mock her behind her back, she has no friends, and when she compares herself to Hillary Clinton and Nancy Pelosi, it sounds pathetic.

Now say good-bye to Leslie Knope. She has run her own office of the National Park Service, been governor of Indiana, married a future congressman, wound up (depending on how you interpret a scene in the finale) either president of the United States or First Lady, raised triplets, has an army of devoted friends (many of them national political powerhouses), and accomplished almost everything she wanted in life.

How does the first Leslie become the second? She does it in the same way that *Parks and Recreation* grew from an uneven, quickly dismissed first season into one of TV's all-time-best, and most underrated, comedies.

Conceived very early on as an *Office* spin-off, it had evolved into something else by the time Amy Poehler came on board to play Leslie. But the DNA was somehow still there, with Leslie's can-do spirit in the face of constant adversity and humiliation meant to seem admirable but instead coming across as second cousin to Michael Scott's mortifying, pitiable lack of self-awareness.

But just as *Parks* cocreator Greg Daniels had figured out how to write better for Steve Carell between the first two *Office* seasons, he and Mike Schur quickly tweaked how other characters reacted to Leslie—now intimidated rather than scornful—and also allowed Leslie to seem vulnerable and recognizably human from time to time when she wasn't amped up on sugar and waffles and making seventeen scrapbooks to commemorate adventures with her new best friend Ann Perkins (Rashida Jones). And to further help viewers appreciate Leslie's relentless positivity, they turned the city of Pawnee into a live-action version of Springfield on *The Simpsons* (where Daniels once worked), where the locals were all crazy and backward-thinking and anything could plausibly happen, like a city council election being covered with the intensity of a presidential race.

At the start, the show inadvertently mocked Leslie's fundamental goodness and belief in government's ability to help, but *Parks* rapidly became a celebration of both her and the dazzling collection of supporting characters around her. Leslie saw the best in people, and *Parks* brought it out of them.

Leslie's boss, Ron Swanson (Nick Offerman), was a mustachioed Libertarian misanthrope who took a civil service job to prevent the government from accomplishing anything, but rather than a caricature, he became an exemplar: Leslie's ideological antithesis, but also her most trusted ally, and someone whose love of strong women and supreme competence at woodworking, hunting, and the consumption of bacon proved far more bountiful a source of humor than if he'd been the butt of the joke. As Andy Dwyer, Ann's dumb musician ex-boyfriend, future action hero Chris Pratt was playing a familiar type, but he invested him with so much goofy energy, and improvised so many brilliant jokes—trying to diagnose an ill Leslie, he tells her, "I typed your symptoms into the thing up here, and it says you could have 'network connectivity problems'"—that it felt like the archetype needed to be retired for all future shows.

But the same could be said about the entire ensemble, whether it's Aubrey Plaza matching Offerman minimalist beat for beat as Ron's gloomy assistant, April Ludgate; Aziz Ansari's irrepressible hustle as the swag-obsessed Tom Haverford; Rob Lowe as *literally* the most positive character in TV history as Chris Traeger; Adam Scott's deadpan befuddlement as Leslie's adoring love interest, Ben Wyatt; Jim O'Heir's wounded dignity as schlemiel/schlemazel Garry Gergich; or the no-bullshit spirit of Retta as parks department veteran Donna Meagle. For that matter, the large recurring cast of Pawnee became so indelible that TV doesn't necessarily need another clueless news anchor to follow Jay Jackson's overly expository Perd Hapley ("The statement that this reporter has is a question"); and it's hard to imagine anyone topping Ben Schwartz's Jean-Ralphio in the area of hilariously oblivious bro-dom.

Because the cast was so versatile, *Parks* could shift from slapstick to sincerity without missing a beat. It always rose to big occasions, whether Leslie was saving the town economy—with some help from beloved tiny horse Li'l Sebastian— by organizing a harvest festival, or throwing one of the show's many strange, sweet, uproarious impromptu weddings. In an era when comedy was growing ever more cynical, the unabashed joyousness of *Parks* stood out as the tougher and more satisfying accomplishment.

Ultimately, it was a far more consistent comedy than *The Office* had been, not that many people noticed. Its highest-rated episode was its very first, back when it was a very faint sketch of the series it would become. So it had to work comic and romantic miracles in relative anonymity, not unlike all the things Leslie was accomplishing as a mid-level bureaucrat in a small city whose residents didn't appreciate or deserve her.

In the series' funniest episode (which belongs in the sitcom time capsule alongside Lucy at the chocolate factory, "Chuckles Bites the Dust," et al.), "Flu Season," a sick Leslie consumes an inadvisable amount of flu medicine to give an important presentation about the harvest festival. Incoherent and barely ambulatory only moments before, she somehow pulls her faculties together long enough to give the speech, then reverts to gibberish as soon as it's over.

Ben, awestruck by this woman he's just beginning to fall for, tries to find the appropriate sports metaphor for what he just saw: "That was amazing. That was a flu-ridden Michael Jordan at the '97 NBA Finals. That was Kirk Gibson hobbling up to the plate and hitting a homer off of Dennis Eckersley. That was..."

He pauses, thinks about it some more, and realizes there's only one framework that applies:

"That was Leslie Knope."

—AS

Roseanne (ABC, 1988–1997)
Total score: 85

Some of the greatest shows of all time were made by people who worked together with a smile, sat around the campfire, and sang "Kumbaya." Others were born of chaos, and at times brilliantly reflected all the difficulties behind the scenes.

Take *Roseanne*, where rancor and tension were the status quo practically from the first day to the last in a way that must have been deeply unpleasant for many of the people who worked there, but that resulted in a classic of the "kitchen sink" sitcom subgenre that started all the way back with *The Honeymooners*.

There was strife backstage, as star Roseanne Barr (then Arnold) feuded with the show's creator (Matt Williams, who was forced out midway through the first season because she resented him getting all the credit for adapting her stand-up act and life), with the show's revolving door of writers (including future show creators Joss Whedon, Chuck Lorre, Amy Sherman-Palladino, and Danny Jacobson), with second husband, Tom Arnold (who became an executive producer and recurring cast member, then got bounced after their divorce), the network, the studio, and even the notes of our national anthem.

But the end result of all that fighting was not only an enormous hit but a trailblazer (Roseanne's leap from the comedy clubs to her own show made it possible for the likes of Jerry Seinfeld, Ray Romano, and Drew Carey to do the same over the next decade) and a versatile, wonderful family sitcom. Whatever fighting took place off-camera only fueled the sense that Roseanne Conner and her husband, Dan (John Goodman), were living life under siege, struggling in many weeks simply to keep the lights on and put food on the table, let alone figure out how to prepare their three kids for the harsh realities of adulthood.

And if Roseanne treated her writers in demeaning ways (at one point assigning them numbers so she wouldn't have to be bothered to learn their names), they still produced work that was raw, honest, and at times shockingly funny, given the blunt financial and emotional realities of the Conner family members' lives. The show dealt with touchy issues (teen sex, PMS, mental illness) with unapologetic candor, but also wit and grace.

As Roseanne, Dan, and Roseanne's sister, Jackie (Laurie Metcalf), bounced from job to job, there was an inviting sense of looseness to the way the different members of the family interacted. Sitcoms are often reluctant to let characters laugh at someone else's punch line, but Roseanne and Dan were always cracking each other up, and there was a genuine sense of intimacy—along with all the aggravations that come with it—to their relationships with the kids, and the way sisters Darlene (Sara Gilbert) and Becky (Lecy Goranson and, later, Sarah Chalke) got along together, or didn't.

Roseanne ran one season too long, with a shark-jumping story arc where Roseanne won the lottery, Dan cheated on her, and everything that had been good and true about the series got turned upside down. But even that led to a fascinating final episode, which revealed that not only had the final season actually been part of a novel written by Roseanne Conner, but that much of the series we had seen previously wasn't "real." (Darlene and Becky had, for instance, married each other's husbands from the show.)

It felt like the show's star trying to seize control of her story one last time, even if the end result wasn't nearly as effective as the show had been in its tumultuous early years.

—AS

30 Rock (NBC, 2006–2013) Total score: 84

In the fall of 2005, NBC made an extraordinary commitment to a new prime-time series set backstage at an *SNL*-like sketch comedy series, agreeing to pay a near-record licensing fee for a first-year show (along with an enormous financial penalty if the network hated the pilot and decided to give up), on top of a promise of complete executive non-interference. The show, everyone believed, would help pull the network out of its millennial doldrums, and win many awards in the process.

The show? Aaron Sorkin's *Studio 60 on the Sunset Strip*, which instead turned out to be one of TV's more high-profile creative disasters in recent memory, brought down by Sorkin's struggle to write both convincing romantic relationships and convincing comedy sketches to illustrate the brilliance of his main characters. By the end of its one and only season, Sorkin more or less gave up on the faux-*SNL* idea and did a glorified *West Wing* arc about a medical crisis at home and a hostage crisis in Iraq.

In hindsight, it's remarkable that no one—not NBC's development executives, nor the entertainment press who follow their process—seemed nearly as excited about the Peacock's *other* new show that year set backstage at a fictional *Saturday Night Live*, even though it was created by and starred an actual *SNL* alum in Tina Fey. It was never a hit—accepting a critics award in 2008, Fey referred to the series as "the highest-rated cable show on broadcast TV"—but it did all the other things (including winning many Emmys) NBC was hoping for from *Studio 60*. Hell, it even had a more entertaining fake NBC executive named Jack, brought to terrifying deadpan life by Alec Baldwin.

Though Fey had the sketch-writing background Sorkin lacked, she never bothered putting it to much use here. Show-within-a-show *TGS with Tracy Jordan* was only occasionally glimpsed, and all indications were that it was terrible. (Sketches mentioned or seen included "Pam, the Overly Confident Morbidly Obese Woman," "Fart Doctor," and "Gaybraham Lincoln.") Instead of creating the pretense that we were watching fictional comic genius at work, *30 Rock* gave us the genuine article, lovingly but relentlessly satirizing television, politics, corporate greed, and much more, with jokes all presented at a machine-gun pace as Fey's Liz Lemon struggled to keep control of the lunatics around her.

30 Rock would do nearly anything

for a laugh: funny names (Tracy's deranged internist was Dr. Leo Spaceman, pronounced "Spuh-CHEH-men") and titles (*Honky Grandma Be Trippin'* or *Fresh-Ass: Based on the Novel "Tush" by Assfire*), unexpected punch lines ("I finally understand the end of *The Sixth Sense*: Those names are the people who worked on the movie!"), subversive use of guest stars (everything from Carrie Fisher telling Liz, "You're my only hope!" to a very game Jon Hamm appearing in blackface during a live episode), and once did a story revealing that chipper, ageless NBC page Kenneth (Jack McBrayer) saw all of his coworkers as Muppets.

The awkward dance between art and commerce, represented by Liz and Jack, was the series' most frequent topic, but *30 Rock* was also razor-sharp when it came to gender and race relations. Because Tracy (played by fellow *SNL*er Tracy Morgan) was simultaneously unstable and far smarter than he looked (in one episode, he took great advantage of Liz's assumption that he was illiterate), the show had license to go to ridiculous places, like a therapy scene where Jack broadly impersonates Tracy's father, mother, and Latina upstairs neighbor. (Faking Mr. Jordan's death, he moans, "Dey got me! Da honkies shot me!")

In the first episode, Kenneth confesses, "I just love television so much." This would be *30 Rock*'s ethos as well, even if that love came with no illusions about the many ridiculous aspects of the medium and the people who work in it.

NBC was on the brink of extinction for most of the series' run, which helped keep the show on the air for seven seasons. (The best thing about NBC being such a train wreck for a decade was that it allowed for healthy runs of fun but commercially marginal shows like this one, *Friday Night Lights*, *Parks and Recreation*, and *Chuck* when they'd have been canceled in a year or two on a network with actual expectations of success.) The fictionalized Peacock run by Jack and others was doing no better, cycling through bad ideas like *MILF Island* and *Bitch Hunter*, and while the show had great fun at the expense of the network suits, it had equal skepticism about the creative types, whether the hackiness of *TGS*'s writers or the way stars Tracy and Jenna (Jane Krakowski) were revealed to be erratic, emotionally needy sociopaths.

Yet, despite all that, the deep affection Fey and company felt for the business they had chosen was palpable through all seven seasons. It did so in gimmicks like the live episodes or the ones presented as a Bravo reality show about Tracy's wife, but also in the series' canny deployment of guest stars in ways that paid homage to TV history (Alan Alda, as the sensitive, liberal biological father Jack wished he never knew he had, once popped up to complain about someone on a comedy show crying about a chicken and a baby), and its frequent acknowledgment that television was the only place that weirdos like Liz (and, by extension, Fey herself) could belong and feel fulfilled.

30 Rock at its best was a live-action cartoon, but one with a pair of recognizable, if exaggerated, humans at the center of it in Liz and Jack. The show ran into creative trouble from time to time when it didn't keep at least a couple of toes planted in reality, even as Tracy and Jenna were getting into cross-racial drag to win an argument or Dr. Spaceman was describing what it's like to date Squeaky Fromme ("She is…difficult").

The *30 Rock* finale, of course, included the *TGS* finale, where Tracy summed up the whole experience for both series neatly: "That's our show. Not a lot of people watched it, but the joke's on you, because we got paid anyway."

—AS

The Bob Newhart Show (CBS, 1972–1978) Total score: 84

The show that made Mary Tyler Moore's production company into a TV powerhouse wasn't the star's beloved, self-titled sitcom but its time-slot follow-up, which starred stand-up comic and frequent guest actor Bob Newhart as Dr. Robert Hartley, a psychiatrist in Chicago. It made a TV superstar of Newhart and his onscreen spouse, Suzanne Pleshette (who played his loving but tart-tongued wife, Emily), and proved beyond a doubt that Moore and her fellow MTM executives had a knack for building shows around very particular comic talents in ways that made them as accessible as possible without tamping down their specialness.

The style and tone of the show came out of Newhart's stand-up career, which jump-started in 1960 when the onetime accountant released a solo album, *The Button-Down Mind of Bob Newhart*, featuring a series of one-way conversations between Newhart and people you never actually heard. Essentially, it was a series of comic duets where the straight man did all the work, and it was such a smash that Newhart recorded several follow-ups, deploying his expressive deadpan and mastery of the pregnant pause to suggest the subdued madness of the reasonable man living in an unreasonable world. *The Bob Newhart Show* cleverly expanded on this idea, deducing that psychiatry and therapy were basically one-way conversations, and pairing Bob with an endlessly amusing and fascinating array of patients, including Lillian Bakerman (Florida Friebus), a laid-back eccentric grandma and compulsive knitter; Jack Riley's cranky neurotic, Elliot Carlin; and John Fiedler's meek-seeming former Marine Emil Peterson. When Bob wasn't seeing patients, he was dealing with office and interoffice intrigue, featuring his secretary, Carol Kester (Marcia Wallace), the dentist Jerry Robinson (Peter Bonerz), and assorted other doctors on the floor. Bob's home life was generally a refuge from all the subdued chaos of work, though he and Emily did have to deal with their inept and thickheaded neighbor, airline navigator Howard Borden (Bill Daily).

Newhart paid tribute to his stand-up roots by doing phone sessions where you couldn't hear the person on the other end of the line, and the first couple of seasons' worth of episodes began with Bob picking up a receiver and saying hello, as if to remind viewers of the star's previous claim to fame. But very soon, *The Bob Newhart Show* settled into a comfortable groove as a low-stakes ensemble comedy par excellence, filled with lovable eccentrics who would've been at home in a Preston Sturges movie. Beneath it all was a soulfulness that might have caught viewers by surprise if they'd somehow missed the funky-jazzy opening theme by series cocreator Lorenzo Music and his wife, Henrietta, which captured the hustle and bustle of upper-middle-class suburban life but also the oasis provided by a loving, stable relationship.

—MZS

Malcolm in the Middle (Fox, 2000–2006) Total score: 84

Anyone who grew up in a house with too many people and not enough money will testify to the truth of *Malcolm in the Middle*, Linwood Boomer's stylish, relentlessly amusing sitcom. The family (whose last name, Wilkerson, is mentioned only twice in the show's seven seasons) lives in a California suburb in a small bungalow with cluttered rooms and a brown front lawn. Malcolm (Frankie Muniz), a brilliant child whose inclusion in his school's gifted program makes him a pariah, is the show's main character and narrator, often addressing the viewer in asides reminiscent of Albert Finney as Tom Jones or Matthew Broderick as Ferris Bueller. He fights for scraps of attention against his younger brother, Dewey (Erik Per Sullivan), and his older brother Reese (Justin Berfield). Malcolm's eldest brother, Francis (Christopher Masterson), spends much of the series in his own self-contained show-within-a-show (first at a military academy, then becoming an emancipated minor, getting married, and wandering around Alaska the western states), but he still manages to create drama for his relatives. Malcolm's mother, Lois (Jane Kaczmarek), is hot-tempered and a control freak. She's burned out from having to raise four boys while toiling at a spirit-crushing job at the Lucky Aide drugstore. Malcolm's father, Hal (Bryan Cranston), comes from money, but because his family rejected Lois, he rarely speaks of them; he's goofy and kindhearted but often chafes at his wife for insisting that he and the boys act mature every once in awhile. Their marriage is a contest of wills, with Lois representing a stifling, rules-oriented life and Hal an improvisational joie de vivre that could easily lead to chaos.

Boomer's sitcom was old-fashioned in concept but innovative in execution, always marrying form to content and pushing the boundaries of both. It was shot on 35mm film, sans studio audience or laugh track, and employed the cartoonish angles and dynamic camera moves of an early Coen brothers picture. Early on, while airing after *The Simpsons*, *Malcolm* was a big hit; its success helped break down the networks' prejudice against single-camera sitcoms. Within a few years, *Malcolm's* template would be used in *30 Rock*, *The Office*, *Modern Family*, and other popular comedies. Its structure was just as restlessly inventive. The season 2 opener, "Bowling," crosscut between parallel timelines, one where Lois took the boys out bowling, the other where Hal did it.

But the show never got too full of itself, because its plots were always driven by shenanigans and highlighted the feral wildness of the family. They would be unbearable if they lived next door to you, but they won your sympathy because the characters were lively and the actors committed. The episodes often revolved around one or more characters stealing or lying or breaking house rules or state laws or flat-out destroying something, then trying unsuccessfully to keep their relatives or local authorities from finding out, or else making a promise or threat and having to carry it out, in the process realizing its folly. Even their victories tended to be Pyrrhic: When Hal's scandal-ridden employer tries to make him a scapegoat for their worst sins, Malcolm bails him out by noting that all the misdeeds took place on Fridays, and provides incontrovertible proof that Hal had been skipping work on Fridays for years. (Lois, rather than act relieved that her husband avoided a lengthy jail sentence, yells at Hal for lying to her all that time while he was playing hooky.)

Right out of the gate, one of the show's most distinctive traits was its acknowledgment of what it's like to live paycheck to paycheck without a safety net. The family barely scrapes by after Lois gets temporarily fired from the drugstore ("Lois vs. Evil"). In "Malcolm Babysits," the family lives in a trailer while their house is fumigated; meanwhile, Malcolm fantasizes about an easier life while babysitting for a family with money. There are story lines that see Lois tearing the house apart to find a misplaced paycheck ("Stock Car Races") and suddenly using too much makeup after getting a negative customer review at work ("Lois' Makeover"). But a far greater percentage of story lines are gloriously madcap,

bordering on surreal, especially in later seasons. Lois ends up making like Henry Fonda in *Twelve Angry Men* while serving as a juror in a trial ("Jury Duty"), while her husband tries to solve the murder that he mistakenly thinks his wife is helping adjudicate. At various points, Francis becomes the roommate of a mad bomber in a woodland cabin, works as a rat catcher, and partners with a German-accented rancher (Kenneth Mars). In season 3's "Monkey," Lois's boss Craig's new helper monkey terrorizes the house while Reese thwarts a prowler, goes mad with power, and plots to control the neighborhood.

Where sitcoms about kids can struggle creatively as their young actors age, Malcolm never really had that trouble—and not just because Dewey's serene, knowing response to the house's chaos only became creepier and funnier the older Erik Per Sullivan got. The focus began shifting toward Lois and Hal almost immediately, and the strengths of the show's adult stars—Kaczmarek's comic force of will, Cranston's eagerness to poke fun at himself (even if it meant disco-dancing in roller skates to "Funkytown")—were immune to the passage of time.

Cranston gave a performance without vanity, as a man fighting a perpetually losing battle against his tendency to panic. Foreshadowing his acclaimed work on *Breaking Bad*, Cranston appeared frequently in saggy white jockey shorts and similarly ludicrous outfits. In season 4's "Malcolm Holds His Tongue," Hal takes up speed-walking, eventually appearing in a red body stocking covered in fire drawings, plus a yellow helmet that makes him resemble H. R. Giger's xenomorph from *Alien*. Besides the underwear, Hal and Walter White share a knack for having their plans go awry. But where Walt tends to improvise violently, Hal sobs or shrieks. In another piece of *Breaking Bad* foreshadowing that's still uniquely *Malcolm*, season 3's "Health Scare," Hal becomes convinced he has cancer and worries he'll die before his children can grow up. At night, he slips into the boys' room—not realizing that Malcolm and Reese have snuck out to a party—and delivers a quiet, heartfelt speech ("You kids are the best thing I've ever done. You'll never know how much I love you. Maybe you're not supposed to.") to what he thinks are his three sleeping boys, only to scream in horror when a kiss he gives to Reese's balloon stand-in makes his "son" pop and deflate.

Malcolm's dark streak complicates what might otherwise have been an exhausting weekly display of high-octane shtick. Tender, serious scenes often flip over into comedy, but the reverse happens, too—and when it does, the effect can be unexpectedly piercing. "Look at that sky, Malcolm," Hal tells his son, sitting in the yard in a scene from "Malcolm Babysits." "Just think. Somewhere out there, in all those stars and planets, there might be at this very moment a space dad who just got kicked out of his space trailer, who's looking down on us. Or would it be *up* at us? Or maybe sideways?" "Trust me, Dad," Malcolm replies, "they're all looking down on us."

—MZS & AS

BEST PILOTS

1. *Twin Peaks*
2. *Cheers*
3. *Police Squad!*
4. *Lost*
5. *The Sopranos*
6. *The Shield*
7. *The Wonder Years*
8. *My So-Called Life*
9. *Miami Vice*
10. *Hill Street Blues*
11. *The Larry Sanders Show*
12. *Kolchak: The Night Stalker*

13. *The West Wing*
14. *Arrested Development*
15. *Wonderland*
16. *Friday Night Lights*
17. *ER*
18. *Breaking Bad*
19. *Alias*
20. *The Walking Dead*
21. *Mad Men*
22. *The O.C.*
23. *WKRP in Cincinnati*
24. *Night Gallery*
25. *Modern Family*

BEST SERIES FINALES

1. *The Shield*
2. *The Fugitive*
3. *The Sopranos*
4. *Six Feet Under*
5. *Cheers*
6. *M*A*S*H*
7. *St. Elsewhere*
8. *Angel*
9. *Newhart*
10. *The Mary Tyler Moore Show*

Groundbreakers and Workhorses

Miami Vice (NBC, 1984–1990)
Total score: 84

Legend has it that *Miami Vice* was born when Brandon Tartikoff, NBC's entertainment president in the early '80s, scribbled "MTV cops" on a cocktail napkin and asked *Hill Street Blues* producer Anthony Yerkovich to turn it into a show. The phrase reads like a glib marketing label, and at the time it probably was. But Yerkovich and executive producer Michael Mann (a student of both documentary cinema and advertising who worked on *Starsky & Hutch*, *Vega$*, and other edgy prime-time cop shows) took it further.

Owing more to 1960s European art cinema than to any TV dramas being made at the time, *Miami Vice* superimposed ripped-from-the-headlines details about drug smuggling, arms dealing, and covert war onto a pastel-noir dreamscape. It gave American TV its first visionary existential drama: a cop show starring a team of salt-and-pepper badasses, James "Sonny" Crockett (Don Johnson) and Ricardo Tubbs (Philip Michael Thomas), lit by sunshine and neon, wreathed in cigarette smoke, and scored to chart-topping hits. Like all series, it was a team effort, enlisting such resourceful filmmakers as Thomas Carter, Rob Cohen, and Abel Ferrara as well as actor-directors Paul Michael Glaser and David Soul—stars of *Starsky & Hutch*—and *Vice* cast members Don Johnson and Edward James Olmos. But the guiding aesthetics belonged to Yerkovich, who oversaw the scriptwriting, and Mann, whose sensibility as both dramatist and visual stylist gave *Vice* its creative foundation. Taking most of its cues from Mann's midnight-slick 1981 thriller *Thief*, *Vice* was the most aggressively cinematic drama made up until that time—a visually musical show where style, mood, and imagery were more important than plot; a place where actors and filmmakers could play around like musicians, noodling and jamming.

The series' frank fascination with street life marked it as the rare network show not suitable for kids (which of course made it catnip for many young viewers). It was one of the most frankly sexual series in commercial TV history, notable not just for the frequency of Crockett's and Tubbs's hookups but for the varying degrees of intensity they invested in them. On *Miami Vice*, as in life, sex could be currency, recreation, or a real means of connection depending on the circumstances. But it was always, by network standards, hot—sometimes too hot for television. Johnson's first directorial outing, season 3's "By Hooker by Crook," juxtaposed the murder of a prostitute with a tryst between Johnson and his real-life ex-wife, Melanie Griffith, that included multiple positions, plus cunnilingus. NBC yanked the episode from repeats after viewers called affiliates to ask why the network was airing pornography.

Mann and Yerkovich consulted experts on both sides of the law,

to accurately depict street slang, SWAT team tactics, legal statutes, and the fine points of drug distribution. But in the end, the show was more daydream than news report. *Miami Vice* flaunted its movie-ness every chance it got. The visuals referenced everything from Jean-Luc Godard's *Contempt* and Jean-Pierre Melville's *Le Samouraï* to Brian De Palma's *Scarface* and every Sam Peckinpah gunfight ever filmed. A wide shot in the pilot shows Crockett in a phone booth beneath a neon sign that appears to be floating in space, an astonishing image that is but the prelude to a long night drive toward a dockside shoot-out, all scored to Phil Collins's "In the Air Tonight." A leisurely crane shot in season 1's "Milk Run" frames cops and their prisoners in a motel room window, then pans to reveal a nightclub on the corner—a real locale lit with such ludicrously rich colors that you wouldn't be surprised if Nathan Detroit crashed through the front doors belting, "Sit Down, You're Rockin' the Boat."

This Miami was ultimately no more "real" than the title locale of *Casablanca*, a film that *Vice*, in its glamorously grubby way, invoked—a global way station; a port city where people came to make a fortune and remake their identities; and where the CIA, the FBI, the Medellín Cartel, the IRA, and the Japanese yakuza wrought havoc with individual lives. The weekly body count made real-world, mid-'80s Beirut or El Salvador seem like Club Med. Crockett, Tubbs, and their fellow officers rarely went a week without shooting several people and having several more killed on their watch—often innocents too naive to realize their dreams were unattainable. The show's depiction of violence mixed artistry with hucksterism; even at its cruelest and coldest, it felt like an ad for itself. The bloodshed was grotesque yet gorgeous. It meant everything and nothing. And by the following week, it was usually forgotten.

The advertising part of Mann's sensibility is encoded in the show's brooding slickness. It treats clothes, cars, boats, buildings, and bodies as objects worth contemplating apart from their narrative function. Mann—who is said to have reshot a whole scene in his 1999 film *The Insider* because he didn't like the color of an actor's tie—pushed hard for an innovative feel. Rather than using traditionally orchestrated music, he insisted that much of the show be scored with Jan Hammer's pulsing synth work, and with

then-current, often expensive-to-license pop, rock, and soul. He micromanaged the color palette, issuing a now-legendary edict: "No earth tones." And he urged each episode's writers and directors to let compositions, cuts, and music bear the weight of the tale's emotions. The series' visceral inclinations are powerfully illustrated in a sequence from episode 5 of season 1, "Calderone's Return: Part 2"—a dialogue-free, four-minute montage scored to Russ Ballard's "Voices," showing Crockett and Tubbs headed to the Bahamas on a mission of revenge, their grudges illustrated only in flashback snippets of outrages perpetrated in earlier episodes.

The front-and-center fashion parade was too much at times—Crockett's sockless topsiders, linen jackets, pastel T-shirts, and stubble soon became shorthand for "clichéd '80s dude"—and the glib banter, often thin scripts, and contrived musical guest stars—and cutesy touches such as having Crockett live on a boat with a pet alligator named Elvis early in season 1—took some of the gritty edge off. By season 3, when the series largely abandoned pastels and blew up Crockett's Ferrari (only to replace it with a Lamborghini), *Vice* already seemed to have exhausted its cultural cachet, but it could still stage knockout episodes like "Out Where the Buses Don't Run," guest-starring the brilliant character actor Bruce McGill as an ex–vice officer obsessed with bringing down the drug lord who drove him mad.

Mann's comfort with racially diverse casts, evident from his TV movie *The Jericho Mile* onward, served as coolness insurance throughout, and has dated better than any of the show's style choices. The underused Tubbs never got as many meaty story lines (or as expensive a car) as Crockett; the blogger Lance Mannion once likened him to Tonto. But he was still a rare African American lead who displayed cutting wit, righteous anger, and moral intelligence—a tough, sensual black man moving through a multicultural universe in which ethnic and language barriers fell before the lure of sex and money. The show's artistic love-children are everywhere.

—MZS

The Office (NBC, 2005–2013)
Total score: 84

Which is the greater achievement: the twelve perfect episodes (plus a Christmas special) of the UK *Office* starring Ricky Gervais, or the decidedly imperfect, wildly uneven, but often brilliant two hundred-odd episodes of its American remake starring Steve Carell?

If you're being a purist, you go with the UK. Not only did Gervais and Stephen Merchant create the world and characters—particularly socially inept, painfully unfunny paper company branch manager David Brent—that would be faithfully adapted in America by Greg Daniels, but they were able to get on and off the stage before anyone got sick of the show.

On the other hand, you can not only find twelve episodes of the American show that match the UK version in laughs (if anything, the Mindy Kaling–scripted "The Injury," where Carell's Michael Scott accidentally cooks his foot on a George Foreman grill, is funnier than any single Brit installment) and exquisite discomfort, but dozens upon dozens more that are in the ballpark.

Of course, you have to wade through some dire episodes to get to all the gems, even if you're willing to pretend that most of the two post-Carell seasons didn't happen.

Start with the word-for-word remake of the UK pilot episode, where lines that sounded harmless and cheeky from Gervais seemed menacing from Carell. Within a few episodes (and with the guidance of having seen Carell achieve a perfect balance of awkward but sympathetic in *The 40-Year-Old Virgin*), Daniels adjusted, changing Michael's base motivation—he wanted a family, where David had craved an audience—to something more benign, even if the end result was just as off-putting to his coworkers.

Even with those tweaks, though, Michael's personality could shift wildly: a petulant fourth grader in a man's suit one week, someone with moderate to severe Asperger's the next, and simply an awkward but reasonably clever guy the one after that. Everyone in the audience (and perhaps on *The Office* writing staff) had their own favorite flavor of Michael—and of his beet-loving henchman Dwight Schrute (Rainn Wilson)—and no one was guaranteed their preferred version of him, or the show, each time out.

But Carell was versatile enough to make all the Michaels seem more or less like the same person, and to be believable as both the idiot who had to buy himself a World's Best Boss mug and the savant whose sales genius kept his branch afloat in a struggling company in a dying industry. He could, within the space of one episode, be convincingly astute enough to win over the coworkers at his moonlighting job by breaking down the problem with the later *Die Hard* films, and naive enough to believe that all he needed to do to declare bankruptcy was to literally walk into the Dunder Mifflin bullpen and yell, "I declare…BANKRUPTCY!" He could horrify the entire staff by assuming the best way to apologize for outing closeted accountant Oscar Martinez (Oscar Nuñez) would be to kiss him full on the mouth in the conference room, but also rope them in for pet projects like producing a local TV ad (with the problematic tagline "Limitless paper in a paperless world") or starring in his zero-budget action movie *Threat Level Midnight*.

Michael's and Dwight's idiocy—which reached its apex in the heart attack–inducing fire drill that began the show's post–Super Bowl episode "Stress Relief"—also provided a comic anchor as the show went in a more serious and romantic direction with the slow-burning love story of Jim Halpert (John Krasinski) and Pam Beesly (Jenna Fischer). That romance was one example of Daniels's turning the greater number of episodes to fill to his advantage, as he got far more mileage out of it (traveling each step of it inch by agonizing inch) than the original could with Tim and Dawn. Similarly, the show had to expand the roles of background characters like cranky Stanley Hudson (Leslie David Baker), cold Angela Martin (Angela Kinsey), sweet Phyllis Lapin (Phyllis Smith), drunk Meredith Palmer (Kate Flannery), and chili lover Kevin Malone (Brian Baumgartner), making the workplace a richer and more complete world.

Sometimes less is more, and the UK version gets all the credit in the world for originality and consistency. But if sent to a desert island and told I could bring twelve episodes of only one *Office*, I'd be inclined to grab the incredibly rewatchable cream of the American crop.

—AS

St. Elsewhere (NBC, 1982–1988)
Total score: 84

To understand *St. Elsewhere*, you have to begin at the ending:

Dr. Donald Westphall stands in the office of his late friend Dr. Daniel Auschlander, grieving the recent loss and listening to one of Auschlander's opera records to find a connection between the world where Daniel used to be and the one he's in now. Westphall's autistic son Tommy stares out the window at the falling snow outside St. Eligius Hospital…

And suddenly the familiar St. Eligius exterior doesn't look quite right, and now we're in a shabby apartment where Tommy is holding a snow globe, and Auschlander is somehow alive, well, and father to Westphall, who is not a hospital's chief of medicine but a construction worker. St. Eligius isn't a real place, but the building inside the snow globe, whose doctors, nurses, and patients exist only inside the imagination of a boy who can't interact with the world around him, and who places the globe atop the family TV set in the series' final shot to make sure we get the message.

Many *St. Elsewhere* fans felt the twist, dreamed up by writer Tom Fontana, was mocking their love for the show by equating it with this autistic child's fantasy. But Fontana had a point: Westphall (Ed Flanders), Auschlander (Norman Lloyd), Mark Craig (William Daniels), Jack Morrison (David Morse), Wayne Fiscus (Howie Mandel), and the rest of the St. Eligius staff were no more real to the show's viewers than they were to Tommy Westphall (Chad Allen), even if we invested dozens of hours and a whole lot of our emotional lives in them.

The snow globe scene delivered

that point more coldly than Fontana may have intended. But in reminding us that this was a world that existed only in our collective imaginations, he also underlined the many ways that the rules of an imagined world aren't so strict as in a physical one—an understanding that *St. Elsewhere* frequently took advantage of to brilliant effect.

Introduced a couple of seasons after *Hill Street Blues, St. Elsewhere* initially seemed like an attempt to replicate that show's controlled chaos within the context of another classic TV profession. In Flanders, Lloyd, and Daniels, the show had a marvelous trio of wise old character actors to provide mentorship to promising young actors like Morse, Denzel Washington, and Mark Harmon. Stories tackled what were at the time cutting-edge issues in the world of medicine: Dr. Craig experimented with organ transplants and artificial hearts, while head nurse Helen Rosenthal (Christina Pickles) got a mastectomy, and Harmon's charming plastic surgeon Bobby Caldwell became one of the first notable TV characters to contract AIDS.

But the series was most special whenever it tested the boundaries of its constructed reality.

St. Eligius staffers and patients sometimes confuse people with characters those actors had played on other TV shows, and in one strange outing, the three senior doctors stop by Cheers to drink and banter with Cliff, Norm, and Carla. The classic "Time Heals" two-parter covers fifty years in the hospital's history, with each jump in time signified by a shift in the filming style to resemble movies of that era. In a later episode, Wayne Fiscus gets shot by a patient's angry wife and spends the rest of the hour bouncing between purgatory (presented as a depressing vacation spot populated by NFL referees and other people who didn't do enough with their lives), heaven (a beautiful garden party), and hell (a desolate lake where serial rapist Dr. Peter White, played by Terence Knox, is condemned to spend all eternity trying to catch fish that aren't there), before having a conversation with God, who turns out to look and sound exactly like Wayne Fiscus. ("I created you in my own image, didn't I?" he tells a puzzled Wayne.)

The show could be pretty spectacular even when it kept things relatively grounded. An early story arc finds Dr. Craig hoping to perform a heart transplant, at once advancing modern surgery and saving the life of a sweet patient. In a cruel twist of fate, the donor is Jack Morrison's young wife, and the episode ends with him slipping into the patient's ICU room to listen to his wife's heart keep beating inside another woman's chest. Even Fiscus's trip to the afterlife is contrasted with the desperate struggle to save him in surgery, with an anxious Dr. Craig performing his first major operation since a potentially career-ending hand injury.

Even before the snow globe revelation, the finale offered up a cracked-mirror view of TV history, with homages to *The Fugitive* (a one-armed man flees the attentions of a Dr. Kimble), *M*A*S*H* (morgue patient #4077 is Henry Blake, who died in a helicopter crash), *The Mary Tyler Moore Show* (a group hug similar to the last one at the WJM newsroom), and more. On some level, *St. Elsewhere* had always been aware it was a TV hospital show; the finale just removed any doubt.

During Fiscus's trip through the afterlife, God tells Fiscus that He doesn't manipulate every aspect of life on earth: "I just create possibilities." And if the writers of a TV show are the deities of their fictional universes, while they don't always have a master plan, they exercise far tighter control than the Almighty describes to Wayne.

As Fontana recalls, he and the other top *St. Elsewhere* writers jokingly discussed putting the St. Eligius snow globe next to ones representing the settings of other shows from the MTM production company, including *The Mary Tyler Moore Show* and *The White Shadow*, but decided that "would be overkill, even for us!" As it turned out, enough characters from past shows had already wandered through St. Eligius, just as they and some of the doctors would link up to characters on so many future series (Alfre Woodard reprised her role as OB/GYN Roxanne Turner on *Homicide*, which thus joined *St. Elsewhere* to every other show where Richard Belzer has played John Munch), that a website called "The Tommy Westphall Universe" currently lists more than four hundred shows—including *The X-Files*, *The Dick Van Dyke Show*, *Seinfeld*, and even *The Wire*—that occupy the same fictional continuity as *St. Elsewhere*, and thus also must exist inside Tommy's imagination.

And ours, too, thankfully.

—AS

Community (NBC, 2009–2014; Yahoo!, 2015) Total score: 83

The essay begins like this, with an acknowledgment that you are reading an essay; it contains five phrases, separated by commas and one semicolon, and ends with a colon:

Dan Harmon's sitcom *Community* is set on a community college campus populated by adult learners whose adultness and ability to learn are never sure things. The core set of characters—a "study group" that often has to force itself to study—consists of a wiseass, womanizing, disbarred lawyer named Jeff Winger (Joel McHale); his on-again, off-again squeeze Britta Perry (Gillian Jacobs), a high school dropout and self-styled activist; the anal-retentive but supermotivated Annie Edison (Alison Brie), who has a crush on Jeff; crabby racist millionaire Pierce Hawthorne (Chevy Chase); Christian single mother Shirley Bennett (Yvette Nicole Brown), who keeps getting pulled into the group's asinine schemes and destructive misadventures no matter how stridently she questions them; former star athlete Troy Barnes (Donald Glover), whose macho facade soon melts to reveal a geeky side; and Troy's best friend, Abed Nadir (Danny Pudi), a half-Polish, half-Palestinian film student whose pop culture–saturated ramblings, imaginative leaps, and symptoms of spectrum disorder mark him as Harmon's go-to stand-in and mouthpiece.

"Are you staying for the party?" Jeff asks Abed (dressed at the time as Batman for a Halloween party) in season 1's "Introduction to Statistics." "If I stay," he replies, "there can be no party. I must be out there in the night, staying vigilant. Wherever a party needs to be saved, I'm there. Wherever there are masks, or if there's tomfoolery in joy, I'm there. But sometimes I'm not, because I'm out there in the night staying vigilant, watching, lurking, running, jumping, hurdling, sleeping. No, I can't sleep. You sleep. I'm awake. I don't sleep. I don't blink. Am I a bird? No. I'm a bat. I am Batman. Or am I? Yes, I am Batman."

The title of each *Community* episode hints at the story's main concerns in language that suggests the title of a course that the characters (and we) are about to take (e.g., "Remedial Chaos Theory," "Herstory of Dance," "Intermediate Documentary Filmmaking"). But the show is about college the same way that *Gilligan's Island* is about surviving on an island and

Waiting for Godot is about a couple of friends waiting for a third to show up; which is to say it is that, and it isn't, and is and isn't, and it's a lot of other things besides. It is the most meta-textual live-action half-hour comedy of all time. More so than any network show besides *The Simpsons*, it *is* television, and almost anything that might appear on television. It is typical sitcom tomfoolery, built on misperceptions, wacky schemes, shenanigans, overheard and misunderstood remarks, petty ego battles, pranks, love affairs and breakups and reconciliations and dates gone horribly wrong. It is satire and parody. It can be an action film (the classic paintball episode "Modern Warfare") or a Western or a paranoid thriller or a musical. It spoofs documentarian Ken Burns, mockumentary sitcoms, daytime and nighttime soaps and timeline-twisting science fiction, and cartoons, and puppetoons. It deals with hallucinations, fantasies, parables, and parallel timelines (one of which, as Abed explains with awe and fear, is "the darkest timeline").

The stories are sometimes just stories, but more often they are stories about storytelling, or stories about stories about storytelling. It is a snake that seems to be swallowing its own tail but often turns out to be swallowing the tail of a snake that swallowed the tail of yet another snake. Even its parenthetical asides have asides. Some dialogue is straightforward, but much more is italicized, as if the characters are aware of being characters (and indeed, much of the time they are). "Abed, it makes the group uncomfortable when you talk about us like we're characters in a show you're watching," warns Jeff in season 1's "Football, Feminism and You." "Well, that's sort of my gimmick," Abed replies. "But we did lean on it pretty hard last week. I can lay low for an episode."

Some of the most sublime moments contemplate the ridiculousness of being human, or thinking of ourselves as substantially removed from an animal state. "Conversation was invented by humans to conceal reality," Jeff says in season 2's "Critical Film Studies," a meditation on art, friendship, being, nothingness, *Pulp Fiction*, *Cougar Town*, and *My Dinner with Andre*. "We use it to sweet-talk our way around natural selection. You know who has real conversations? Ants. They talk by vomiting chemicals into each other's mouths." And yet even when it's mocking the very idea of civilization and human dignity, it cares about its characters. The Jehovah's Witness Troy's religiously sensitive birthday cake inscription reads, "Hello during a random dessert, the month and day of which coincide numerically from your expulsion from a uterus," but he's still touched by it. The school's pansexual dean, Craig Pelton (Jim Rash), is often used as a sight gag, parading in front of the study group in an array of ridiculous (and usually feminine) costumes, but he will occasionally pause to acknowledge that he's being too defined by that gimmick, and is far more complex, and lonely.

Even when a scene or sequence or episode isn't quite working, you can appreciate the complexity, the ambition, the fervor of each situation, image, and joke, as well as the baked-in (maybe just baked) tension between the show and the "show." Harmon and his writing staff seem engaged in some mysterious ongoing contest to see how many pop culture footnotes they can hang on a conversation and still have you care about the story as a story and the characters as people, or "people." It is certainly the only series in network TV history equally inspired by *Gilligan's Island*, *Our Town*, *Taxi*, and the holodeck on *Star Trek: The Next Generation*. Not only did it seem too smart and ostentatiously self-aware for network TV, but few cable series could match its ingenuity. So of course it struggled merely to exist, clinging to NBC's schedule by its fingernails for five seasons—the fourth produced without Harmon's involvement, and dismissed as "the gas leak season" the moment he returned—then landing a sixth courtesy of Yahoo!, which wanted to go the Amazon or Netflix route but couldn't get the hang of it and nearly allowed Harmon's creation to play out in a pop culture void.

Ah, well: The world is filled with millions of Abeds; they have memorized every syllable spoken on *Community*, and they will recite it to you at the drop of a hat, whether you want to hear it or not, because its incantatory strangeness speaks to them, quote marks and parentheses and semicolons and all, period, the end.

—MZS

The Golden Girls (NBC, 1985–1992) Total score: 83

Friends (NBC, 1994–2004) Total score: 77

The Golden Girls concluded two years before *Friends* premiered (though the gap shrinks to only a year if you count the short-lived *Golden Palace* spin-off), and it's a good thing, because the former show would have never gotten on the air in a universe that already included the latter.

Before *Friends*, one of the unwritten rules of television was that young, pretty people couldn't be at the center of a sitcom. Not only was it hard to find attractive actors who could also deliver a joke, but the business's conventional wisdom suggested the audience wouldn't relate enough to them or their struggles to find them funny. Dramas were for the young and blemish-free; comedies for faces that had some character, and preferably some age lines as well. There might be one or two token young and/or hot people (say, Woody on *Cheers*), but that was it. If you study publicity stills of sitcom casts from even a couple of years before *Friends* debuted, it looks like the earlier shows were dipping into not just a different casting pool but a different gene pool.

Then, somehow, everyone doing casting on *Friends* caught lightning in six bottles in a row, with a sextet of actors—Jennifer Aniston, Courteney Cox, Lisa Kudrow, Matt LeBlanc, Matthew Perry, and David Schwimmer—who were young, good-looking, likable, and, most important, could deliver the quippy dialogue of cocreators Marta Kauffman and David Crane with their own amusing inflections.

At first, NBC didn't realize what it had with *Friends*, scheduling it on Thursday nights, but in the less plum time slot after *Mad About You* (which it would forever displace the next fall), while *Madman of the People* (starring Dabney Coleman and a much more traditional-looking sitcom ensemble) was on after *Seinfeld*. That changed in a hurry, as *Friends* became a phenomenon, and fundamentally altered the very DNA of sitcom casts.

This was around the time that the broadcast networks began truly obsessing over shows that could attract young adult viewers, and *Friends* suggested an obvious way to get that audience: Give them shows with characters who were around their age. Imitation is the sincerest form of television, and few shows have ever been as imitated—almost always badly—as *Friends*. Suddenly, every other new sitcom out there featured a cast of would-be models, were often produced by second- and third-tier *Friends* writers (and, on occasions like CBS's short-lived *Can't Hurry Love* with Nancy McKeon, featured actors who were runners-up to be in the *Friends* cast), and usually struggled to come anywhere close to the alchemical level of talent, wit, heart, and silliness of *Friends*. The industry had watched *Friends* hit on 17 a bunch of times in a row and get blackjack every time, and foolishly assumed the strategy would keep working for everyone else.

As a result, it's hard to imagine the NBC of the mid- to late '90s, or most of its rivals (save maybe CBS, which aired *The Golden Palace* and was still building sitcoms around veteran performers like Bill Cosby, Bob Newhart, and Judd Hirsch), seriously considering a show about a quartet of senior citizens sharing a house in Miami as they try to find meaning in their final decades. It wouldn't matter that it featured, in Bea Arthur and Betty White, two of the most gifted and indelible sitcom actresses of all time; a pair of outstanding foils in Rue McClanahan and Estelle Getty; and dazzling joke writing from creator Susan Harris and others (including a bunch of future series creators like *Desperate Housewives*' Marc Cherry, *Modern Family*'s Christopher Lloyd, and *Arrested Development*'s Mitchell Hurwitz). *Friends* had made sitcoms into something cool, which they had never really been before, and a show about women in their sixties (or in the case of Getty's Sophia Petrillo, eighties) would

have seemed the exact opposite of cool in that moment.

But *The Golden Girls* was made in a time before the expectation that viewers would or should watch shows about people their own age, which is why there was a generation of kids who grew up watching the show and can still recall all of Rose Nylund's weird stories about her childhood in St. Olaf just as easily as they'd eventually grow into *Friends* viewers who understood that Joey's favorite food was sandwiches and would quote Ross screaming "PIVOT!" whenever asked to move a piece of furniture.

Because once you get past the superficiality of the age and appearance of the two casts, *Golden Girls* and *Friends* are fundamentally the same show: a group of people, brought together by a mix of circumstance and the odd familial relationship, moving through a distinct time in adulthood with minimal responsibility and many questions about what the future holds, tossing around razor-sharp punch lines and occasionally pausing to hug. It's not hard to imagine Rose and Phoebe getting along, or Blanche trying to put the moves on Joey (and, given his openness to sleeping with older women, him agreeing), or Dorothy and Chandler trying to figure out who has a higher degree of withering disdain for the world around them.

Friends didn't render sitcoms about older people extinct. The explosion of original content across cable and streaming in time created a demand for every niche, including comedy geared to a more mature audience, whether TV Land's *Hot in Cleveland* (essentially a next-gen, slightly more glammed-up *Golden Girls*, but with Betty White now in the Estelle Getty slot) or Netflix's *Grace and Frankie*. Nor has the failure of nearly all the '90s *Friends* clones scared the business away from trying to make shows about hot young singles, occasionally finding ones like *How I Met Your Mother* that can be pretty great in their own right.

For a long time, the sitcom trade discriminated against younger performers. More recently, the scales tipped the other way. The moral of the story (and these were two shows that, if they didn't always moralize, were at least deeply comfortable with sentiment) is that the goal shouldn't be to find only comedies featuring characters in a specific age bracket, but to find comedies featuring the funniest actors you can possibly get, regardless of demographic.

—AS

Police Squad! (ABC, 1982) Total score: 83

You know the old comedy axiom about a movie having a laugh a minute? The Zucker brothers—aka the filmmaking team of Jim Abrahams and actual brothers David and Jerry Zucker—scoff at that. In films like *The Kentucky Fried Movie*, *Airplane!*, and *Top Secret!*, no joke is too crude, too silly, or too old to be deployed. If they aren't getting laughs every ten to fifteen seconds, surely something has gone awry.

And stop calling me Shirley.

Police Squad! was team ZAZ's only foray into television, and ended so abruptly that you can't blame them for never making another show. ABC aired four episodes and postponed the other two for months, and the creators would later claim the head of the network said he was canceling the series because "the viewer had to watch it to appreciate it."

This sounds insane, yet it also summed up the downside to the show's frantic, anything-for-a-yuk ethos on TV in 1982. In a darkened theater, audiences were conditioned to pay attention to every last detail so that they could appreciate all the visual gags and throwaway details that filled a movie like *Airplane!* But sitcom audiences were used to being passive, if not outright distracted, and so it was easy to miss so many of the details, like the way that each episode's announced title was different from its displayed title, or the amount of inappropriate background action taking place while the actors stood awkwardly still at the end of each episode in a spoof of TV freeze-frames.

ZAZ and company took their act to the movies, where the feature spin-off *The Naked Gun: From the Files of Police Squad!* was a huge hit with the same approach, spawning two sequels in which Leslie Nielsen reprised his role as stoically bumbling cop Frank Drebin. But the six episodes that preceded it were comic marvels, packed with jokes from the first moments (including the on-camera murder of that week's very special guest star) to the last (those wonderful fake freeze-frames, which were disrupted by a rogue chimp and an overflowing mug of coffee, among other things). They used wordplay, like a "Who's on first?"–style interrogation that would have impressed Abbott and Costello, slapstick, and spot-on parody of the kind of self-serious police dramas that would have employed Nielsen in a different context even a few years earlier.

With recent shows like *Arrested Development* and *30 Rock*, TV finally made room for the kind of relentless, dense joke-telling style that *Police Squad!* deployed so well, if not for long. One running gag involved Johnny the shoeshine man, who played dumb about any query until slipped a couple of bucks, after which he could tell Frank everything about the chief suspect in his case, or explain the Cinderella complex to Dr. Joyce Brothers, or teach Dick Clark about ska. If the head of ABC had slipped Johnny a fiver, he might have explained there was a lot of money to be made off of Frank Drebin, if he could just be patient.

—AS

24 (Fox, 2001–2010) Total score: 82

If *The West Wing* was the defining network drama of the Bill Clinton era, *24* was the defining drama of the George W. Bush years. Debuting just a few weeks after the terrorist attacks of 9/11, the series was in the wrong place at the right time, not unlike its stalwart hero, Jack Bauer (Kiefer Sutherland), a counterterrorist agent tasked with foiling attacks on major cities while continuing to fret over personal relationships with his daughter, wife, and friends. Created by Joel Surnow and Robert Cochran (TV's *La Femme Nikita*), the show was conceived as a cross between a James Bond adventure and a *Die Hard* film, piling temporal constraints (every story took place in twenty-four consecutive hours) on top of geographical ones (most seasons were confined to major metropolitan areas, including Los Angeles, New York, London, and Washington, DC). But it soon became a warped mirror of then-current political tensions. Jack represented both the desire to abandon civil liberties and the Geneva Conventions in the name of fighting terrorism, and the left-wing horror at the moral ruin that such behavior brings to people (and nations). Soon Vice President Dick Cheney was citing Bauer to justify the legality of torture, and media outlets were writing think pieces asking if, in presenting Jack's gruesome handwork as the unavoidable response to ticking-clock threats, the show wasn't exploiting humankind's ugliest impulses for ratings. There were also not-unjustified charges that the show's regular images of murderously fanatical Persian and Arab men were inherently racist, and that by depicting a pulpy United States constantly beset by terrorist threats, the series was rubber-stamping the worst excesses of the War on Terror, even as some of its Pentagon and Washington subplots made corrupt generals, politicians, and CEOs out to be secret architects of much of the mayhem.

Even as critics argued about the show's sensationalist tendencies, there was no denying its effectiveness as entertainment. Like such civil liberties–averse 1970s cop thrillers as *The French Connection* and *Dirty Harry*, *24* was at least partly a Western at heart, with Jack as a snarling commando cousin of *The Searchers'* Ethan Edwards: a military-industrial complex attack dog who keeps turning on his masters, uniquely equipped to lead civilization out of the darkness yet unfit to live in it. The best seasons were probably season 1, which featured Dennis Hopper as the Serbian arms-dealer bad guy, and that had one of the biggest out-of-nowhere shocker endings of the aughts; season 2, which eerily anticipated the Bush administration's WMDs-in-Iraq gambit (but also suffered from silly scenes in which a cougar menaces Jack's daughter, Kim, played by Elisha Cuthbert); and season 4, which amounts to a collection of mini-seasons built around individual terrorist threats by a single bad guy. Memorable characters strut in and out as needed, played by actors including Leslie Hope, Sarah Clarke, Carlos Bernard, Xander Berkeley, Penny Johnson Jerald, Jean Smart, Mary Lynn Rajskub, James Badge Dale, Gregory Itzin, Regina King, Cherry Jones, and Dennis Haysbert (whose weekly appearances as a fictional African American president might've helped pave the way for the first real one). There were no small moments, only big and bigger. Sean Callery's alternately bombastic and mournful score made the show seem even more expensive than it was, and the split-screen montages and ticking-clock graphics ratcheted up the tension to thumbscrew levels. Torture rarely works in real life, but the version practiced by *24* got results.

—MZS

The Defenders (CBS, 1961–1965)
Total score: 82

The tradition of the ripped-from-the-headlines TV show begins with *The Defenders*, starring E. G. Marshall and Robert Reed as father-son defense attorneys in New York; it continues with *East Side/West Side* and keeps going and going, through Norman Lear's blunt-spoken 1970s sitcoms, plus *Soap* and *Hill Street*

Blues, and *L.A. Law* and pretty much every drama David E. Kelley was ever associated with, plus every incarnation of *Law & Order*. Today it is as durable a genre (or, when merged with the cop or detective show, subgenre) as the Western, the domestic comedy, and the science-fiction anthology. This is remarkable enough when you consider that prior to *The Defenders*, network TV tried to avoid political or social controversies for fear of angering viewers on one side of an issue or another, or else retreated into "We're just raising questions here" equivocations. This institutional resistance is the reason why writer-producers like Rod Serling got tired of having their ideas for socially conscious live plays rejected by network suits and migrated to places like *The Twilight Zone*, where they could traffic in metaphor and fable.

The Defenders came out of the same TV-theater era that eventually broke Serling's spirit. Series creator Reginald Rose, author of the TV and then film classic *Twelve Angry Men*, introduced his basic concept to audiences on *Studio One* in a 1957 two-part production titled *The Defender*, starring Ralph Bellamy and William Shatner in the father and son roles. Like its progenitor, the series (which partnered Rose with Herbert Brodkin, his *Studio One* writing partner) addressed its hot-button issues in a straightforward way. "The law is the subject of our programs: not crime, not mystery, not the courtroom for its own sake," he wrote in a 1964 article, rebuking legal series like CBS's *Perry Mason*, which concentrated on courtroom tactics and often resolved their stories through coincidence, contrivance, or the sudden appearance of a surprise witness. Episodes of *The Defenders* examined the morality and legality of capital punishment, the insanity defense, the Cold War blacklist and the denial of visas to suspected Communists, jury tampering, the ethics of using illegally obtained evidence, and, most notoriously, abortion. The latter—examined in a 1962 episode titled "The Benefactor," in which the lawyers defend a doctor who performs abortions—caused sponsors to desert; it would have been spiked had another sponsor not stepped in at the eleventh hour, a development that would be cleverly folded into a same-titled episode of *Mad Men*.

Showtime briefly revived the series in 1997, with Beau Bridges and Martha Plimpton playing Marshall's son and granddaughter, and Marshall, then eighty-four, backing them up in a supporting role as mentor and sounding board. After he died two episodes into the first season, Showtime ended production; the remaining episode aired in 1998 as a TV-movie titled *Taking the First*. Beyond its success at infusing drama with news and politics, its glamorization of professional problem solvers who did not carry guns or scalpels, and its invigoration of New York–based location shooting, *The Defenders* was a drama in which nothing happened that could not happen in life. Rose felt free to show his lawyers losing cases sometimes, maybe because every week, *The Defenders* won a greater victory by existing.

—MZS

Gunsmoke (CBS, 1955–1975)
Total score: 82

This Western drama was the longest-running continuously aired dramatic series in the history of American TV; its only competition was the original flagship edition of NBC's *Law & Order*, which tied it for number of seasons (20) but aired fewer episodes (452 versus *Gunsmoke*'s 635). It was also one of the most influential series, demonstrating that the Western format, once the province of self-contained escapist adventures and morality plays, could be used to tell human-scaled stories about psychologically credible individuals who just happened to live in a nineteenth-century rural environment, and who aged and changed over time.

James Arness starred as Matt Dillon, the marshal of Dodge City, Kansas, a crossroads of regional commerce so teeming with ambitious and troubled residents and visitors that violent conflicts were inevitable. (An apocryphal story insists that CBS offered the lead role to John Wayne, who was actually too big a star to have accepted, but Wayne did recommend Arness and introduced the pilot.) Although Arness was onscreen throughout the show's two-decade run, the supporting and recurring cast turned over many times. Like *Law & Order*, *Gunsmoke* provided employment to generations of character actors and future stars (some of whom showed up in more than one role, sometimes in the same year). The lineup of deputies included Dennis Weaver as the cranky but reliable Chester B. Goode, whose limp was never explained; Buck Taylor as gunsmith Newly O'Brien; Ken Curtis as the drawling hillbilly Festus Haggen; Roger Ewing as part-timer Clayton

Thaddeus "Thad" Greenwood; and Burt Reynolds as a half Native American, half white blacksmith named Quint Asper. Amanda Blake played saloon owner Kathleen "Kitty" Russell, who was clearly the love of Matt's life, even though they never married and the show was mostly circumspect about what, exactly, they were about. (Curiously, their interactions became more chaste as the series moved through the '60s and into the '70s.)

The show began as a CBS radio series in 1952, with roughly the same mission statement: CBS president William Paley tasked his programming chief with creating a Western drama more temperamentally aligned with hard-boiled detective fiction, and populated by characters with some depth, to set the story apart from escapist fare like *The Lone Ranger* and *The Cisco Kid* (both of which migrated to TV and became beloved CBS series). William Conrad, future star of TV's *Cannon*, voiced the marshal for radio. The TV version continued in the same ambitious vein, giving viewers the two-fisted action they craved, but in service of stories about lawmen, government employees, bankers, farmers, ranchers, schoolteachers, and other members of the community, all of whom were struggling to carve out peaceful and productive lives for themselves despite being beset by outlaws, maniacs, con men, rapacious capitalists, and other external threats. *Gunsmoke* regularly dealt with what would later be considered hot-button issues, including bigotry against African Americans and immigrants, the mistreatment of Native Americans, domestic violence, alcoholism, governmental corruption, and economic exploitation in all of its forms. But these subjects were folded into the fabric of life in Dodge City, and rarely came off as sermons delivered by men in Stetsons and women in petticoats.

Gunsmoke was so brutal that "family values" activists cited it as one of the most offensive series of the early 1960s, along with ABC's weekly tommy-gun festival *The Untouchables*; it dialed back the bloodshed during the second half of its run and became more about other kinds of personal conflict. The show's consistently high quality drew high-profile guest stars, including Bette Davis, who played a vengeful woman who blamed Matt for her husband's death in 1966's "The Jailer." As the show wore on, the sight of the main characters aging lent the weekly stories of emotional or physical conflict a poignant quality. We were constantly made aware of the cost of violence, as manifested in the characters' scars and wounds and in their increasing willingness to talk instead of shoot. In more than one sense, television grew up with *Gunsmoke*.

—MZS

Sex and the City (HBO, 1998–2004) Total score: 82

"I'm dating a guy with the funkiest tasting spunk," Samantha Jones (Kim Cattrall) announces over brunch to her three best friends during the season 3 *Sex and the City* episode "Easy Come, Easy Go."

The women trade stunned looks, and Charlotte York (Kristin Davis)—who fancies herself the most prim and proper of the group, even if her list of sexual partners contains more kinky weirdos than the others combined—simply walks out of the restaurant. Though the other two express their own dismay at the topic—when Samantha asks with whom she can discuss this if not with her girlfriends, *SATC*'s chief heroine and narrator Carrie Bradshaw (Sarah Jessica Parker) replies, "Might I suggest *no one*?"— they eventually try to offer some practical solutions, then laugh wearily while imagining how willing men would be to perform oral sex if some of the physical conditions were reversed.

The funky spunk debate was far from the first time that *Sex and the City*—adapted by Darren Star from sex columnist Candace Bushnell's same-titled anthology—had invited its heroines to discuss the social mores and physical complications of sex in such explicit fashion. One of the series' earliest episodes featured the women piling into the back of a cab to give Charlotte advice on whether to accede to her boyfriend's desire for anal sex, with Samantha blithely suggesting, "A hole is a hole," and Miranda Hobbes (Cynthia Nixon) warning her that doing so would fundamentally alter the relationship's power dynamics. But by the time of "Easy Come, Easy Go," the show had become such a phenomenon that it was hard not to imagine writer Michael Patrick King (who succeeded Star as *SATC* showrunner early on) using Charlotte's walkout as a meta comment on the viewers who objected to the series' candor not just on sex, but female desire in general—for emotional as well as orgasmic satisfaction. That the other three keep talking about it after Charlotte's exit was King making clear that he didn't care who disapproved; if you sat at the table with these women,

uncomfortable topics were going to be discussed early and often, and why shouldn't they be?

Although it was viewed as a light alternative to such frequently grim HBO dramas as *The Sopranos*, *The Wire*, and *Deadwood*, *Sex* was an integral part of the cable channel's success in the '90s and early aughts, earning big ratings and sparking op-ed page arguments about whether its main characters were truly feminist and independent or merely materialistic, entitled, and shoe-obsessed, as well as whether they were even women at all, much less "ladies," as opposed to coded gay men. The latter theory, which was both homophobic and sexist, was advanced under the assumption that women didn't talk about men sexually the way men often talked about women—that giving sexual partners nicknames like "Mr. Pussy" and "Skidmarks Guy" was unbelievable as well as inappropriate. This was an astonishing notion given the content that routinely appeared on male-driven HBO shows, and how comparatively mild, even sweet, *Sex* could be. (Miranda: "What's the big mystery? It's my clitoris, not the sphinx." Carrie: "I think you just found the title of your autobiography.")

No matter: The show's fans were

as loyal to it as the heroines were to one another, treating *Sex* as a dear friend who deserved unconditional support. They took fashion advice from the characters (frequent images of the women's bare legs nearly killed the panty-hose industry), argued over who in their own group was the Carrie and/or the Samantha, and tuned in each week to follow the women's romantic and professional adventures: corporate lawyer Miranda's difficult single motherhood and her troubles with boyfriend-then-husband Steve Brady, played by David Eigenberg; Samantha's moving, late-series struggle with cancer; the failure of Charlotte's marriage to a guy who was perfect on paper but sexually and temperamentally all wrong.

Carrie spent much of the series falling in and out of lust with Chris Noth's emotionally distant businessman Mr. Big, who simultaneously represented everything romantic comedies had taught women to dream of, and everything self-help books warned them against. But *SATC* wasn't interested in hewing to those rules, nor with making Carrie into a victimized good girl. She made her own choices, even if they were often as damaging to herself and others as those of the more celebrated male HBO protagonists of the period.

Midway through the show, Carrie dates saintly furniture maker Aidan Shaw (John Corbett), only to ruin things by cheating on him with Big. Later, they reconcile and even get engaged, but things end ugly a second time when she realizes he still doesn't trust her not to go back to Big, and Aidan realizes that Carrie simply doesn't want to marry him.

"People fall in love, they get married," he insists. "That's what they do."

"Not necessarily," she replies, choosing to follow a different path from what societal or narrative convention expected of her.

Carrie and Big eventually do get married in the first of the two *Sex and the City* films, which in their excesses of plot, conspicuous consumption, and promiscuous punning seemed determined to prove the series' harshest critics right. But the show itself was never as frothy or superficial as its detractors claimed. It dealt with sexism, relationships (and was often at its strongest when just dealing with the platonic bonds between the four leads), body-image tyranny, mortality, failure, and the lure of fleeing regrets by blowing up your life and starting all over (a favorite *Mad Men* topic). Other shows, some of them from *SATC* writers, tried and failed to copy its formula, proving that there was a lot more to it than coy narration, double entendres, and smash cuts to Samantha having orgasms.

Sex and the City's peak was probably the end of season 5, which aired nine months after the attacks of 9/11 and felt like a bittersweet farewell not just to the pre–War on Terror New York (represented by the Twin Towers glimpsed in Carrie's snow globe) but the realization that Carrie and her friends were growing out of their extended "single girl" phase. Still, they would entertain *Breakfast at Tiffany's* fantasies for the rest of their lives, even after making peace with the fact that they might not come true. The final shot of that season's finale would have made a perfect series closer: Carrie walking down a West Village street at dawn while the *Tiffany's* theme "Moon River" plays. "We're after the same rainbow's end," it sings, "my huckleberry friend."

—AS & MZS

Star Trek (NBC, 1966–1969)
Total score: 81

"To boldly go where no man has gone before." That's what *Star Trek*'s star, William Shatner, promised in the opening narration of Gene Roddenberry's science-fiction series, and the show delivered. Even though it really had only one great season, the first, and its liberal-for-1966 situations and attitudes seem, on closer inspection, not too radical by modern standards, or even the standards of the 1980s, its innovations lay in its willingness to depart from TV norms of the time rather than in any particular attitude or position that its characters espoused. This was plenty radical on its own, though, and without the show's determination to mix intergalactic derring-do with *Twilight Zone*–type morality plays about civilization and human nature, much of what we think of as adult mainstream science fiction either would not exist or might have come down the pike much later.

Star Trek was set in the twenty-third century, during an era of intergalactic peace maintained by the Federation's exploratory/military Starfleet with occasional Cold War–type incidents involving Klingons and Romulans. The series had a fairly hawkish attitude about the merits of interfering in other cultures—*Starship Enterprise*'s captain James T. Kirk (Shatner) always had intense discussions with his half-human, half-Vulcan first mate, Mr. Spock (Leonard Nimoy), and the ship's doctor, Leonard "Bones" McCoy (DeForest Kelley), about the integrity of the Prime

Directive, which mandates that Starfleet not intervene in cultures in ways that might change them. They always intervened anyway, phaser-blasting and in some cases personally karate-kicking the stuffing out of space Nazis or ghostly gunfighters or gladiators or one of the seemingly endless array of godlike creatures that were eventually revealed to be a child, a con artist, or both. The only notable instance of the *Enterprise* crew declining to intervene was in season 1's Harlan Ellison–scripted time-travel episode "The City on the Edge of Forever," which finds Kirk learning that a 1930s labor activist (Joan Collins) whom he's fallen in love with is fated to die in a car accident, and accepting that he cannot save her because doing so would profoundly alter the future. It seems strangely fitting, given the show's schizoid Cold War eagerness to intervene, that the impossibility of changing history is treated here as unambiguously tragic, only because of the loss of a single human who matters personally to Kirk. David Gerrold, who wrote the series' most purely charming episode, "The Trouble with Tribbles," said Roddenberry was enamored of President John F. Kennedy, whose mix of socially liberal and antiracist attitudes was leavened by his compulsive

womanizing and his determination to show that he wasn't scared by the Soviet threat. Indeed, there were times when Kirk seemed like the two-fisted, sci-fi action figure version of JFK, beaming down to planetary surfaces to negotiate treaties, beat the crap out of anyone who stepped to him, and bed women in foil bikinis.

If Kirk was Roddenberry's leading man, Mr. Spock was the series' soul. Roddenberry wanted the *Enterprise* to have an alien crew member, and pushed against NBC executives wary of what one of them described as "the guy with the ears." Even Roddenberry would later acknowledge that many of the character's most famous traits— the formal posture and elocution, the Vulcan nerve pinch, the split-fingered "Live long and prosper" salute (modeled on the Jewish priestly blessing)—came more from Nimoy than from him or any other *Trek* writer. Without Spock, *Star Trek* might have become another half-forgotten space opera from that period, rather than the unofficial fan religion that it still is today. The character simultaneously offered an outsider's and an insider's perspective, coolly reacting to situations that made Mr. Chekov panic or Dr. McCoy sputter with rage, yet never feeling wholly a part of either the *Enterprise* crew or his own species, which ended an ancient legacy of war-making by suppressing emotion and replacing it with logic. There was still passion, and even distemper, in Spock's people, though; viewers got a taste of it in the season 2 episode "Amok Time," which revealed that every seven years, Vulcans suffer a blood fever that could kill them unless they undergo a "Pon Farr" ritual in which they either mate with someone empathically connected to them or take part in hand-to-hand combat. Spock's conflicted status as a "half-breed"—a term used by the speciesist McCoy, who needled Spock every chance he got—was at the center of many episodes. Spock's nonviolent characteristics—epitomized by his Socratic dialogues with other characters, his egoless, empathetic mind-melds with every manner of creature, and his "nerve pinch," which could incapacitate foes without resorting to weapons—aligned him with countercultural forces that reshaped US life in the '60s. Multiple episodes saw Spock stating an affinity for hippie-friendly societies or beliefs: "This Side of Paradise," "Shore Leave," "The Apple," "The Naked Time," "The Way to Eden," among others. There were moments throughout the show's run when Spock's stoicism, isolation, and devotion to service evoked two of Shakespeare's greatest outsider characters, Shylock and Othello.

It wasn't hard for sci-fi fans to see their own sense of otherness reflected in Spock. Their love inspired not only the initial letter-writing campaigns to NBC to keep the show on the air after the first and second seasons, but *Star Trek* conventions, essays, and fan fiction (some of it depicting Spock as the one true love of Kirk's life) in the years after its cancellation. In a way, though, Spock's popularity served as a political deflector shield, focusing so much media attention on a metaphor-rich character that the show's more direct engagement with social change could fly under the radar at warp factor 5. *Star Trek*'s milestones include TV's first interracial kiss, between Kirk and Nichelle Nichols's Bantu communications officer Uhura (in season 3's "Plato's Stepchildren"—under duress by alien captors, but still!), and an ethnically and internationally diverse bridge crew that included George Takei's Japanese Sulu, Walter Koenig's Russian Pavel Chekov, and James Doohan's bluff Scotsman Scotty, who regularly told Kirk, "The engines canna take much more!" but then proved otherwise. "Leave any bigotry in your quarters," Kirk tells a Vulcan-hater in season 1's "Balance of Terror." "There's no room for it on the bridge. Do I make myself clear?" After season 2, when Nichols considered leaving the show because Uhura wasn't being given enough to do, the Reverend Martin Luther King Jr. talked her out of it.

After *Star Trek* entered syndication in the 1970s, it became such a success that NBC bankrolled an animated Saturday morning spin-off. A 1979 feature film followed, motivated in large part by the success of 1977's *Star Wars*. The show's direct descendants include three discrete film series; five prime-time TV spin-offs (*The Next Generation, Voyager, Deep Space Nine, Enterprise*, and a new program, produced by longtime *Trek* movie producer Alex Kurtzman and *Hannibal*'s Bryan Fuller, that was announced as this book was going to press); novelizations; board games; video games; and comics. But it also influenced everything from *The X-Files* and both versions of *Battlestar Galactica* to *Firefly, Andromeda*, and the *Alien* franchise, as well as any film or TV series that tries to combine action with ideas. "One man cannot summon the future," an alternate-universe version of Spock tells Kirk in season 2's "Mirror, Mirror." "But one man can change the present," Kirk counters. By changing TV's present, *Star Trek* summoned its future.

—MZS & AS

Firefly (Fox, 2002–2003) Total score: 80

There is inspiration, there is hubris, and there is whatever divine madness gripped Joss Whedon when he decided to create *Firefly*. After years of running *Buffy* and *Angel* over at the WB, he finally had his shot at the network big leagues, and chose to make a mash-up of Western and science-fiction tropes, combining one genre that TV had left for dead in the early '70s with another that had a wildly mixed commercial-TV track record. This wasn't putting your chocolate in my peanut butter; this was putting your goulash in my chicken à la king and expecting the world at large to want to eat it.

It was, of course, doomed from the start. Even if Fox executives hadn't sabotaged the show by shelving the two-hour pilot—which not only introduced the large cast of characters but explained the show's elaborate universe, where a human exodus to a new solar system had created a stratified class system with elements of both the Wild West and the Reconstruction-era South—it was never going to be a big commercial hit. Still, it struck such a chord with its small but fiercely loyal audience that Whedon was able to leverage their passion into a sequel feature film, *Serenity*, released three years after *Firefly*'s cancellation.

It was an underdog show full of underdog heroes. Roguish ship captain Mal Reynolds (Nathan Fillion, as charming and funny as he is on *Castle*, but in a role that allowed him to show off a much greater range) and his second-in-command, Zoë (Gina Torres), had both been on the losing end of a civil war, and now had to make a living as smugglers on the outer planetary rim. Traveling with them on their beat-up little smuggling ship was a wagon train's worth of Western archetypes given a shiny new gloss: the whore with the heart of gold (Morena Baccarin's Inara), the preacher with a dark past (Ron Glass's Book), the brute who's good with a gun but not always reliable (Adam Baldwin's Jayne), the sweet tomboy (Jewel Staite's Kaylee), the wisecracking sidekick (Alan Tudyk's Wash), and the fugitives (Sean Maher and Summer Glau as Simon and River). They had sharp dialogue, moments of great heroism and greater comedy, and adventures in a fully realized world made up of equal parts *Stagecoach*, *The Professionals*, and *Blade Runner*.

At fourteen episodes, *Firefly* is the shortest-lived of the five shows Whedon has created (or, in the case of *Agents of S.H.I.E.L.D.*, cocreated). It's also the one that came into focus most quickly—where *Buffy* needed most of a season, and *Angel* needed parts of several, to figure out what they were, *Firefly* was thrilling and clever and entirely itself from the jump—which made it even more maddening that viewers didn't get to see the beginning until the very end.

But what did Whedon expect? Like his hero, he had thrown his heart and soul into a noble cause that was guaranteed to fail—even if it failed most gloriously.

—AS

Law & Order (NBC, 1990–2010)
Total score: 80

We often talk about formula in television as if it's a cardinal sin, or a relic of a dumbed-down era best forgotten. But formula doesn't automatically equal laziness or lowest common denominator programming. There can be enormous pleasure in reliability (who wouldn't want the gang at *Cheers* to yell "NORM!" when Mr. Peterson came in?), and it can be a greater storytelling challenge to find subtle and clever variations on a formula the audience knows so well they can set their watches to it.

Few shows in TV history have been as formulaic from episode to episode as the original *Law & Order*, but that was always a feature, not a bug.

Over twenty seasons, viewers became so conditioned to the rhythms of each hour that they became fodder for stand-up comedians, like John Mulaney's routine about how the victim's coworkers are always so unmoved by the murder of a colleague that they insist on going about work as usual while the cops interview them. But the show understood which recurring elements were comforting and necessary—say, the gallows humor of Jerry Orbach's character, Detective Lennie Briscoe, taking us into the opening credits every week for twelve seasons—and which could be turned upside down to keep the audience guessing.

Some weeks, for instance, the cops would land on the killer almost immediately, and the drama of the courtroom half was in whether the district attorneys could get a conviction; in others, the lawyers would either figure out that the cops didn't get the right man, or decide

that another party was more at fault than whoever technically pulled the trigger. Sometimes, the prosecutors won, and sometimes they lost, but senior DA Adam Schiff (Steven Hill) always (at least for the first ten seasons) had a world-weary bon mot to toss out before the final credits rolled.

For that matter, the show's oft-promoted habit of crafting stories that were "ripped from the headlines" worked not because viewers could recognize a plot's tabloid inspiration but because the episode would almost immediately pivot away from the true story to tell a twisty parallel-reality version of it. So an early episode from the first season might be a riff on the Bernie Goetz vigilante case, but here the shooter would be a woman (a young Cynthia Nixon, the first of many future stars to wander through an *L&O* courtroom) turning subway avenger as a coping mechanism after an earlier rape.

And even the show's revolving-door cast was arranged to simultaneously reassure and confound the audience. There were six regular positions—a senior detective, his partner, and their boss, plus a lead prosecutor, his assistant, and the head of the DA's office—and the casting of each role often fell into a narrow type, yet the characters themselves varied wildly in personality (and, on occasion, quality). All of the assistant district attorneys after Richard Brooks's Paul Robinette were played by willowy supermodel types, but you could switch from Carey Lowell's reserved former defense attorney Jamie Ross in one season to Angie Harmon's cutthroat staunch conservative Abbie Carmichael in the next.

The basic cops-and-lawyers *Law & Order* formula didn't come out of creative inspiration but financial desperation. It was the late '80s, and hour-long dramas had stopped selling into syndication, which is where the real money was in TV at the time. So producer Dick Wolf came up with a way to make a show that would air as an hour on the network but could be split into half-hour episodes down the line. As it turned out, A&E and later TNT were perfectly happy shelling out a fortune to air the episodes as they were, at all hours of the day and night, but it took a while to get to that point.

The young Fox network ordered thirteen episodes sight unseen, then backed out the next day, telling Wolf that it wasn't a Fox show. (This was surely correct.) CBS made a pilot (with most of the season 1 cast, but a different DA, which always makes it jarring when it turns up in reruns) but didn't order it to series. And though it was never in danger for most of its NBC run—the only time it came close to cancellation before the end was after season 3, when Wolf was told he had to add some women to the cast to keep it on the air—it didn't become a bona fide phenomenon, which would in time launch several spin-offs (the most successful of which, *Law & Order: Special Victims Unit*, is still on the air, and could run longer than the mother ship when all is said and done), until the network aired a handful of episodes in the *ER* time slot on Thursdays. (Not coincidentally, that higher-profile season earned the show its only best-drama Emmy.)

But if making enormous sums of money was the inspiration for—and end result of—*Law & Order*, the show was a classic reminder of how commerce and creativity can go hand in hand just as easily as formula and surprise.

—AS

ALL THE *LAW & ORDER* CAST COMBINATIONS RANKED, FROM EASY BEST TO ABSOLUTE WORST:

1. **Season 5:** Briscoe/Logan/Van Buren/McCoy/Kincaid/Schiff
Note: The '27 Yankees of *L&O* casts, featuring not only Hall of Famers at every position but the very best example of each respective role in the franchise's history.

2. **Season 10:** Briscoe/Green/Van Buren/McCoy/Carmichael/Schiff
Note: Schiff's last year, and the first for the very satisfying partnership between Briscoe and Green.

3. **Season 4:** Briscoe/Logan/Van Buren/Stone/Kincaid/Schiff
Note: Almost identical to the perfect season 5 cast, and Ben Stone was no slouch in that lead prosecutor position.

4. **Seasons 18 (midway through)–20:** Lupo/Bernard/Van Buren/Cutter/Rubirosa/McCoy
Note: The series' final cast was one where the whole was greater than the sum of its parts: no weak links, great chemistry among the whole group, and the fun dynamic of Jack McCoy having to boss around a younger version of himself.

5. **Season 3 (episode 9 on):** Briscoe/Logan/Cragen/Stone/Robinette/Schiff

Note: Some deeper overall casts came later (both Cragen and Robinette were much more interesting when they returned to the franchise down the road), but any group with the Briscoe/Logan partnership is going to score very highly.

6. **Season 6:** Briscoe/Curtis/Van Buren/McCoy/Kincaid/Schiff
Note: Curtis was a significant step-down from Logan, but the rest of the lineup could carry him.

7. **Season 9:** Briscoe/Curtis/Van Buren/McCoy/Carmichael/Schiff
Note: Abbie Carmichael's first season, and the other year where the talent around him allows me to overlook the sleepy presence of Curtis.

8. **Season 18 (through episode 14):** Green/Lupo/Van Buren/Cutter/Rubirosa/McCoy
Note: A badly needed stabilizer after a lot of years with one or two utter head-scratchers in the cast at all times.

9. **Season 11:** Briscoe/Green/Van Buren/McCoy/Carmichael/Lewin
Note: The first season without an original cast member, and the first of two puzzling instances of a great actor—in this case, two-time Oscar winner Dianne Wiest as new DA Nora Lewin—joining the show late and utterly failing to fit in.

10. **Seasons 7–8:** Briscoe/Curtis/Van Buren/McCoy/Ross/Schiff
    Note: The first time the show made it through two full seasons without any cast changes (though semi-official seventh regular Elizabeth Olivet was replaced for a while by Emil Skoda as the resident shrink).

11. **Season 1:** Greevey/Logan/Cragen/Stone/Robinette/Schiff
    Note: The show was still finding its way, but the original group had Stone and Logan, and George Dzundza's Max Greevey was a good early foil for Logan.

12. **Season 2–early season 3:** Cerreta/Logan/Cragen/Stone/Robinette/Schiff
    Note: I slightly prefer Greevey's dour personality to the more laid-back Cerreta, but both partnerships were being carried by Logan anyway.

13. **Seasons 13–14:** Briscoe/Green/Van Buren/McCoy/Southerlyn/Branch
    Note: The writers at least knew what to do with Fred Dalton Thompson as Branch, whose conservative ideology put him in frequent conflict with McCoy.

14. **Season 12:** Briscoe/Green/Van Buren/McCoy/Southerlyn/Lewin
    Note: The show's worst DA and its worst deputy DA together in the same cast! And yet the cops were so good that it still keeps this bunch out of last place.

15. **Season 17:** Green/Cassady/Van Buren/McCoy/Rubirosa/Branch
    Note: Cassady (the show's only regular female detective) was forgettable, but Rubirosa was one of the better ADAs.

16. **Season 16:** Fontana/Green/Van Buren/McCoy/Borgia/Branch
    Note: As Jerry Orbach's replacement, Dennis Farina was another piece of casting that surprisingly didn't work, while Borgia's most memorable contribution to the franchise was dying by choking on her own vomit, almost *Spinal Tap*-style.

17. **Season 15:** Fontana/Green (and briefly Falco)/Van Buren/McCoy/Southerlyn (and then Borgia)/Branch
    Note: When you put Joe Fontana and Serena Southerlyn in the same cast for thirteen episodes, then fire Serena and have her ask Branch, in a hilarious non sequitur with no foreshadowing in any previous episode, "Is this because I'm a lesbian?" you've pretty well screwed the pooch in terms of figuring out your cast for the year.

—AS

Maude (CBS, 1972–1978) Total score: 80

The best of the many spin-offs descended from Norman Lear's *All in the Family*, *Maude* focused on the brash, imperious Maude Findlay (Bea Arthur), the cousin of *Family*'s Edith Bunker. It was nearly as controversial as its progenitor because it dealt with the day's political and social controversies in a more head-on way. Sexism, gay rights, abortion, draconian drug laws, racism, class anxiety, and the hypocrisies of white liberalism were all subjects of spirited argument in Maude's house. Those last three were combined via conversations between Maude and her domestics, starting with Florida Evans (future *Good Times* star Esther Rolle), whom Maude urged to enter through the front door even though the back was more convenient for her, and Florida's second replacement, Victoria Butterfield (Marlene Wakefield), whom Maude falsely accused of stealing. (In one episode, Maude introduced Florida as "My dear, dear friend, probably the best friend I have in the whole world," and Florida clarifies: "I'm the maid.")

Like a more educated and liberal mirror of Archie Bunker, Maude bickered with everybody in earshot, including her third husband, Walter (Bill Macy). The show made space for plotlines revolving around Carol Traynor (played by Adrienne Barbeau, followed by Marcia Rodd), Maude's daughter by her second husband; her staunchly Republican neighbor Dr. Arthur Harmon (future *Diff'rent Strokes* star Conrad Bain); and other recurring characters. Some scripts departed from the usual ensemble format, concentrating exclusively on Arthur and Maude or spending the entire half hour with Maude in therapy.

The show often went darker than even the darkest *All in the Family*s. Maude was dependent on tranquilizers. Walter's evening drinking devolved into alcoholism in season 2, leading to an incident where he struck Maude for trying to stop him from reaching for the bottle again, then a nervous breakdown. In season 5, Walter had a second breakdown, lost his business, and tried to kill himself. A legendary two-part episode found Maude deciding to abort an unexpected pregnancy after consulting with Walter about it. The episode was scheduled to air in November 1972, two months before *Roe vs. Wade* declared state-level antiabortion laws unconstitutional; CBS delayed broadcast until the dead months of August.

—MZS

The Rockford Files (NBC, 1974–1980) Total score: 80

Created by Roy Huggins (*The Fugitive*) and Stephen J. Cannell, then a writer on cop and mystery shows like *Adam-12* and *Columbo*, this series about Los Angeles private eye Jim Rockford gave its star, James Garner, the role he was put on earth to play. Rockford, a former Seabee and wrongfully convicted ex-convict, fused bits of three of Garner's best early roles: the scrounger from *The Great Escape*, the eloquent coward from *The Americanization of Emily*, and one-half of the fast-talking, poker-playing brothers from *Maverick* (also created by Huggins). The character was a principled antihero who would rather talk than fight. When a magazine writer (Joan Van Ark) in season 2's "Resurrection in Black and White" sees him loading a gun and says, "I thought you didn't shoot people," he replies, "I don't shoot it, I just point it!" The most memorable scenes hung back and watched Rockford as he chatted up eccentrics, crawled through weeds and into windows in search of evidence, and begged for his life.

The show's directors luxuriated in seedy but sun-drenched Southern California vistas and doted on the endlessly enjoyable supporting cast. Stuart Margolin played Rockford's old prison cellmate, Angel Martin, who never stopped scheming even when it got Rockford in trouble. Noah Beery Jr. played the hero's father, Rocky, a retired truck driver and sometime partner in investigations who wished his son would get a respectable job like truck driving. Vividly etched guest characters floated in and out, including would-be private eye Richie Brockelman (Dennis Dugan), an overconfident, patronizing young college graduate who thought he could talk his way to success. "Look, this guy actually lives in a trailer," says Richie in season 4's "The House on Willis Avenue," trash-talking a dead detective's living quarters. "It just seems to me that living in a trailer is at the bottom." "*I* live in a trailer!" Rockford whines. Much of Cannell's subsequent career drew on *The Rockford Files: Hardcastle and McCormick, The Greatest American Hero, Baretta, Baa Baa Black Sheep*, and the superb but very short-lived *Tenspeed and Brown Shoe* (starring Ben Vereen and Jeff Goldblum as chatterbox detectives who seemed to get beaten up every ten minutes) all had that Garner-esque mix of battered idealism and been-there exasperation. *Rockford*'s writing staff included future *Sopranos* creator David Chase; he wrote sixteen episodes, two of which concerned mobsters: His characters included a couple of wiseguys who did business from the back of a deli, and characters named Artie, Carmela, Tony, and Anthony Jr.

The cold opening of each episode was a slow pan that moved across Rockford's cluttered office while his answering machine played messages that drove home the poignant smallness of his life: "Jimmy, this is Manny down at Ralph's and Marla's. Some guy named Angel Martin just ran up a fifty-buck bar tab, and now he wants to charge it to you. You gonna pay?" The opening credits, scored to Mike Post and Pete Carpenter's harmonica-driven, faintly Western theme music, consisted of a series of slightly blurry photographs that looked as if they'd been taken by a private eye who had the hero under surveillance. The unseen watcher stood in for viewers who never tired of following Jim Rockford.

—MZS

China Beach (ABC, 1988–1991)
Total score: 79

An Army nurse, ordered to recall the night a particular soldier died, weaves a tapestry filled with gruesome details—of sticks and Zippo lighters embedded into the skin of the wounded, of floors covered with detached limbs that she hopes she placed next to the correct bodies, of the way she's grown accustomed to the smell of burned flesh but still pukes at the scent of maggots found in wounds—before admitting that she remembers absolutely nothing about the soldier in question.

"You seem to remember that night pretty well," the officer in charge tells Lt. Colleen McMurphy.

"I don't," she confesses. "They're all like that. I just picked one at random."

I didn't have to choose that scene from *China Beach* to help illustrate why it's the greatest forgotten drama of its era. They're all like that. But pick pretty much any episode at random and you'll find gorgeous acting, evocative writing, and an enormous sense of empathy for every man, woman, and child—many of that last group handed a rifle and helmet and asked to grow up much too quickly—whose life was forever changed by their time in Vietnam.

China Beach arrived in the midst of a Vietnam drama boom in the movies and on TV, and a general boomer fascination with the '60s. For much of its run, it overlapped at ABC with *The Wonder Years*, which covered the same years and had a sound track from the same record collections. But if *China Beach*'s period was familiar, its approach was anything but.

Its Army base was dominated by women, none more than Dana Delany's laconic McMurphy, who somehow carried herself like the hero of a Clint Eastwood movie while also plausibly (and without it ever feeling annoying or like star-flattery, because Delany was that jaw-droppingly great) making every man on the show fall in love with her. Over the years, it learned to weave remembrances of real combat nurses in with its scripted stories—and in so doing, to make clear how little needed to be embellished for the demands of a fictional drama. It played around with structure (an episode that moved backward to explain why a character got an abortion) and location (finding just as much discomfort for characters who returned home as those who stayed). It had little use for the antihero types who were so prevalent in Vietnam movies of the era (and would become de rigueur on TV a decade later), with only Marg Helgenberger's calculating prostitute K.C. remotely qualifying, but it was unflinching in the way it showed how war causes even the best-intentioned people to do things they would have once found unimaginable.

And in its spectacular final season, it cut loose the shackles of conventional TV narrative altogether, bouncing back and forth through the decades to show what happened to McMurphy and friends for the rest of their time in country, as well as their difficult readjustments to civilian life.

In the series finale, McMurphy—middle-aged, a recovering alcoholic, never having been as sure of herself back in the real world as she was over there—attends a China Beach reunion, where she's interviewed by K.C.'s teenage daughter, Karen (Christine Elise). Again, she's asked to recall the death of a soldier, and again the details are too horrible for anyone to have to hear, let alone actually experience.

"I couldn't save them all," she says, smiling through tears. "But I saved some."

—AS

Enlightened (HBO, 2011–2013)
Total score: 79

Cocreated and executive-produced by Laura Dern and actor-writer Mike White, *Enlightened* is about an office drone named Amy Jellicoe (Dern) who suffered a nervous breakdown, went away to a New Age detox and spiritual healing colony in Hawaii, then returned home to try to put her life back together. It ran just two seasons and was canceled before audiences got a chance to see whether its story could sustain over the long haul, but the eighteen episodes it did produce were close to perfect, demonstrating an appreciation of human complexity and a mastery of narrative voice rarely seen outside of the best short fiction. On top of all that, *Enlightened* might be the sharpest satire of modern white-collar work since the original British version of *The Office*; its skewering of that world intertwines with its portrait of individual personalities so deftly that you can't really separate them.

Amy is our heroine and surrogate. She narrates parts of the show in voice-over often accompanied by subjective camerawork, including first-person point-of-view shots and Expressionist slow motion that draws out her perceptions and amplifies her feelings. The bits that Amy narrates are first-person subjective: They're colored by her experience at the colony and by the supplemental reading she's been doing since she returned to Los Angeles, went back to work with a demotion, and moved in with her aging mom, Helen (Diane Ladd, Dern's real-life mother). The rest of the show, though, could be described as third-person limited.

We're seeing Amy—and all the other characters, including her mother; her still-drug-addled ex, Levi Callow (Luke Wilson); and her new boss, the socially inept, profane, hot-tempered Dougie Daniels (Timm Sharp)—from a more detached point of view, one that conveys the fullness of the characters' self-flattering delusions even as it looks through them and sees something like the truth about them.

White and Dern have a social satirist's keen ear and eye. They capture the unsettling blandness of office protocol, politics, and jargon, from the chill that workers feel when Human Resources calls them out of the blue to the impressive-sounding word-salad labels that the company gives to its projects. (The experimental department to which the newly demoted Amy is assigned goes by the hopeful and curious name "Cogentiva," but it's pushing the dehumanizing aspects of work to new depths.) At the end of the first season, executives invite Amy to present evidence of the company's misdeeds at a board meeting, then mock her as a nutcase Pollyanna; she overhears them and becomes so enraged that she fantasizes about burning the place to the ground. In season 2, she attempts to lure a hunky journalist (Dermot Mulroney) into writing a muckraking piece about her employer. He tells her the company's behavior is "unethical, it's immoral, I know that, but it's not illegal." He won't write about Abaddon because its heinousness is sadly typical. It's a scene more chilling than any of Walter White's mustache-twirling antics on *Breaking Bad* because it depicts a banal kind of evil, born of moral exhaustion.

There's an opportunistic spaciness to Amy that's appalling at times. You understand why her former assistant Krista Jacobs (Sarah Burns) wouldn't want to have anything to do with her, why Dougie finds her exasperating, and why most of her coworkers look slightly panicked when she tries to talk to them. Amy always wants something. As far as she's concerned, other people exist to make her life easier and bail her out when she fails; when other characters call her on this, she seems baffled, as if they've begun describing someone Amy's never met. But the show never reduces Amy to a caricature. She's hard to hate because she means well. As irritating and often clueless as she is, she really is trying to be a better person—and her self-serving tirades about her workplace contain germs of truth. *Enlightened* doesn't adopt a morally superior tone to any of this. Things

are never either-or. They're always both-and. Amy is a deeply damaged and irritating woman. Her voice-over reveries are filled with rehab platitudes and portentous images that suggest a Los Angeles tourism ad directed by Terrence Malick. She's so narcissistic that when she grins at the targets of her goodness, she seems to be admiring her reflection in their pupils. But she's right about Abaddon, and she's right to be mad that no one cares. "I'm just tired of feeling small," she says. Isn't everyone?

—MZS

Everybody Loves Raymond (CBS, 1996–2005) Total score: 79

The first few years of *Raymond* overlapped with the last few of *Seinfeld*, and the two shows built around comedians with skimpy acting résumés—and that grew into huge hits from humble, low-rated beginnings—often felt like funhouse-mirror versions of each other.

Seinfeld was pointing the way forward in sitcom storytelling, with its interwoven plot threads and loathing of sentiment; *Raymond* was a throwback that proudly told only one story per episode and found a way for the absurdity and yelling to lead to a sincere moment between the characters.

Jerry Seinfeld never showed much interest in growing as an actor; Ray Romano won an Emmy for this show and later did acclaimed dramatic work on other series. Larry David wound up at HBO, while *Raymond* creator Phil Rosenthal liked to brag that while they were making *Raymond* for CBS, "in the back of my mind, it's for Nick at Nite."

Both were, superficially, shows about nothing, but *Raymond* used its minutiae—Ray Barone buying the wrong brand of tissues, or wife, Debra (Patricia Heaton), waging a cold war with Ray over putting away a suitcase from a trip, or Ray's overbearing mother, Marie (Doris Roberts), refusing to divulge the recipe for her famous meatballs—in service of greater emotional truths about the characters. It was loud and broad, bordering on vaudevillian at times, yet again and again, Romano, Heaton, Roberts, Peter Boyle, and Brad Garrett switched effortlessly from farce to pathos.

Not every show needs hugging and learning, but this one sure did well with it.

—AS

The Wonder Years (ABC, 1988– 1993) Total score: 79

It's funny, if unsurprising, how nostalgic TV shows can take on an added retro layer as they age. Seventies' sitcoms *Happy Days* and *M*A*S*H* both took place in the 1950s, but today Fonzie's thumbs-up and Hawkeye's sensitivity seem more evocative of the decade in which they were made than the one in which both were set.

The Wonder Years, though, doesn't so much evoke the late '80s as it does a time when baby boomer nostalgia hadn't turned into insufferably ubiquitous navel-gazing. In 1988, it still seemed novel, and powerful, to open a show set twenty years earlier with a montage of Bobby Kennedy, Martin Luther King Jr., urban riots, soldiers in Vietnam, and Apollo astronauts in orbit, all scored to the Byrds' version of "Turn! Turn! Turn!" There was still a freshness and innocence to looking at one of the most tumultuous periods in American history through the eyes of rising middle schooler Kevin Arnold (Fred Savage) and his best friends Paul Pfeiffer (Josh Saviano) and Winnie Cooper (Danica McKellar). When Winnie's brother was killed in combat or when Kevin's sister horrified her parents by moving in with her boyfriend without marrying him, the emotions still felt fresh and raw, rather than boxes to be checked in our obligatory journey through pop culture's favorite decade.

The series' greatness wasn't just a result of timing but of the way that creators Neal Marlens and Carol Black, and later writers like Bob Brush, made Kevin's coming-of-age feel simultaneously so rich and universal that it could have been set in many different eras. He was Everykid in Everytown, and the specificity came as much from the natural, appealing performances of Savage and his costars (including Dan Lauria and Alley Mills as Kevin's parents, who came from the same generation but saw the new one very differently) as it did from the classic-rock sound track and references to Nixon and the moon landing.

Unsurprisingly, the Kevin who seemed so sweet and adorably awkward in junior high became much more complicated, and at times unlikable, as he got old enough to drive, and his relationships with his parents and his closest friends grew strained, or worse. But that was a truth that stretched well past the '60s and '70s. And ABC executives—protective of what had been a relatively wholesome show for the whole family when it began—seemed more uncomfortable than any viewer as Kevin started edging into adult behavior. The show's end was both abrupt and bittersweet, with the narration of Daniel Stern's middle-aged Kevin having to fill us in on the many triumphs (Kevin becomes a writer, his mom an executive, etc.), tragedies (Kevin's father, whose stutter-step relationship with his son would become the series' heart, dies while Kevin is still in college), and everything in between (Kevin and Winnie remain friends, though their romantic destinies lie elsewhere) that we would never get to see.

In a closing monologue that speaks to both the era in which Kevin Arnold became a man and almost any coming-of-age story, the adult Kevin tells us, "Growing up happens in a heartbeat. One day you're in diapers, next day you're gone. But the memories of childhood stay with you for the long haul. I remember a place, a town, a house, like a lot of houses. A yard, like a lot of other yards. On a street like a lot of other streets. And the thing is, after all these years, I still look back...with wonder."

—AS

BEST TEACHERS

1. Gabe Kotter, *Welcome Back, Kotter*
2. George Feeny, *Boy Meets World*
3. Valerie Frizzle, *The Magic School Bus*

4. Ken Reeves, *The White Shadow*
5. Mr. Bergstrom, *The Simpsons*
6. Charlie Moore, *Head of the Class*
7. Eric Taylor, *Friday Night Lights*
8. Marla Hendricks, *Boston Public*
9. Richard Katimski, *My So-Called Life*
10. Mr. Collins, *The Wonder Years*

Barney Miller (ABC, 1974–1982)
Total score: 78

Ask a lawyer to name the most realistic legal TV drama, and they'll likely roll their eyes and say, "None of them." Chances are you'll get a similar response asking doctors about hospital shows, reporters about newspaper shows (and/or season 5 of *The Wire*), or any other profession whose details have been bent and exaggerated for dramatic effect over the years on TV.

But ask a cop—particularly a cop above a certain age—and they may tell you that of the eight million stories in the naked city, the most accurate was told on a '70s sitcom called *Barney Miller.*

The show debuted at a time when New York City had come to be viewed by the rest of the country as a hell on earth, with the *Daily News*'s infamous "FORD TO CITY: DROP DEAD"

headline, and gritty crime films like *Dog Day Afternoon*. *Barney Miller* didn't sugarcoat or present a fantasy version of the city or its police department. The show's NYPD was perpetually broke (Steve Landesberg's spacey intellectual Arthur Dietrich transfers in only because his own precinct was closed due to budget cuts), while crime in the Greenwich Village neighborhood policed by Barney (Hal Linden) and his detectives was more abundant—and, in the case of vice, more public—than ever.

But if the series, created by Danny Arnold, didn't try to clean up the harsh realities of life in the NYPD at the time, it also didn't try to glam up the very mundane realities that came with it. Its cops didn't look like action heroes, whether the ancient Phil Fish (Abe Vigoda, who would live forty-two years past the series' debut, even though it was a running gag that Fish looked too old to still be breathing, let alone working as a cop), deadpan brewer of awful coffee Nick Yemana (Jack Soo), or even musclebound but sweet Vietnam vet Wojo (Max Gail). Even the relatively hip Ron Harris (Ron Glass) was only so cool: His goal in life was to parlay his time on the force into a career as a crime novelist.

And there, Harris struggled for source material, because *Barney*

Miller's cops spent most of their time doing paperwork and locking up low-level offenders. After splitting early episodes between Barney's work and home lives, the series quickly turned the detectives' squad room and Barney's office into the only sets that we saw. If exciting things happened away from the precinct, we heard about them later, usually with a lament from the ones who had missed all the fun.

It was, then, the workplace comedy as hangout show, with the plots mainly excuses to let this diverse collection of brilliant comic voices bounce off one another, whether Fish struggling to conceal his contempt for the much younger Dietrich; Harris or Barney trying to educate the well-meaning but impulsive Wojo; or everyone failing to get Yemana to change his affect even slightly (other than in the episode where he unwittingly eats a pile of hash brownies, the series' best contribution to the sitcom canon).

It wasn't fancy, but in the banter, the boredom, and the bureaucracy, real cops could finally see something resembling their own work, and viewers groomed on more exotic police stories could appreciate the sharpness of the writing and performances.

—AS

Frank's Place (CBS, 1987–1988)
Total score: 78

One of the great ancillary benefits of *WKRP in Cincinnati* was this one-and-done series from its creator, Hugh Wilson, and one of its stars, Tim Reid, aka Venus Flytrap. No viewer knew quite what to make of this half-hour scripted program about an African American professor at Brown University who ends up running his late father's restaurant and bar in New Orleans, Chez Louisiane. Frank Parrish travels to the Big Easy in the opening episode intending to sell the place; then Miss Marie (Frances E. Williams) puts a voodoo curse on him fating him to stay, and he does. Of course we immediately wonder if this isn't just a secret wish being fulfilled, and the show continues to keep us guessing.

Nearly thirty years after its brief run, *Frank's Place* now seems apocryphal. The sound track's expertly chosen mix of blues, jazz, rock, and prewar standards made it too expensive to relicense for DVD and online streaming platforms; today it can be seen only at the Paley Centers in New York and Los Angeles and in fragments on YouTube, often by way of blurry VHS uploads that reduce the show's feature film–quality lighting, composition, and camera movement to mush. The show's unavailability might be the greatest tragedy in this book's Pantheon. *Frank's Place* was so advanced in every way that network television still hasn't caught up with it. Shot on film and devoid of a laugh track, every episode is preternaturally unafraid to be not-funny; to just let characters be, and think; to savor the pauses and silent looks that pass between them; and to observe the differences between cultures, races, religions, and genders with curiosity and tenderness. It is equally comfortable with situations that aren't so much amusing as awkward, sexy, even mournful (as in the episode where Frank is pressured by a local gangster to assume responsibility for his father's gambling debts). Imagine an African American *Cheers* by way of *A Confederacy of Dunces*, then mix in astute commentary on New Orleans culture (including a spirited discussion of the difference between Cajun and Creole), and you've got a one-of-a-kind experience—so unique, in fact, that *Frank's Place* languished in the ratings even though pretty much every TV critic with a byline begged viewers to check it out.

—MZS

Justified (FX, 2010–2015) Total score: 78

Throughout its six seasons, *Justified* made an art of being underestimated, weaving intricate stories and creating vivid characters within a context that strove to entertain above all else. The rope-a-dope strategy was embedded in the series' identity before it even hit FX's airwaves. One of the finest adaptations of Elmore Leonard's writing is rooted in a work so minor that even a lot of fans hadn't heard of it: a short story titled "Fire in the Hole," set in Harlan County, Kentucky, about a lawman and a criminal whose animosity is complicated by the fact that they once dug coal together.

As overseen by screenwriter and producer Graham Yost (*Speed*), the first half of *Justified*'s first season was clever and affable and occasionally (expectedly) violent, but not necessarily the sort of thing you'd want to go up on a ridge and crow about. While the ensemble acting and cultural details were unusual for American TV (which is prejudiced toward big cities and suburbs), and the whole thing was anchored to strong lead performances by former *Deadwood* star Timothy Olyphant (as Stetson-wearing US marshal Raylan Givens) and *The Shield*'s

Walton Goggins (as Raylan's grinning, loquacious nemesis Boyd Crowder), on the whole it felt like a throwback to the 1970s and '80s way of making episodic crime dramas, where cocky or eccentric heroes (McCloud, Columbo, Jessica Fletcher, or whomever) solved a mystery or neutralized a threat to the community and then the narrative needle reset to zero.

Then something happened, probably somewhere toward the middle of season 1—maybe between "Blowback," the episode with *Deadwood* regular W. Earl Brown as an escaped inmate taking hostages in the US marshal's office until Raylan defused him by ordering him some spicy fried chicken; and "Hatless," which saw Raylan lose his hat in a stupid bar fight and spend the rest of the episode trying to prevent his ex-wife's doofus husband from getting killed over a real-estate debt. Both episodes forced Raylan to try to resolve situations without violence, not for pacifist reasons (Raylan has an Old Testament mind-set and a simple code—"You make me pull, I put you down"—hence the series' title) but for practical ones: He was starting to figure out that his hot temper and itchy trigger finger were ruining his chances for happiness.

And at that point the show began seriously looking at why that was; the investigation led the writers into Raylan's past, and Harlan County's past, including the family feuds that had been going on since the nineteenth century. We realized that the macho cowboy code of doing what a man's gotta do was baked into the marrow of this coal mining community, and the former Confederate States, and perhaps America itself, and that at some point every character would have to reckon with it.

Justified kept teasing this notion out, examining new facets, discovering new ways into it, through Raylan and Boyd, but also through their significant others: Raylan's ex-wife, Winona Hawkins (Natalie Zea), and Boyd's main squeeze, Ava Crowder (Joelle Carter), who was Boyd's brother's wife until she shot him for abusing her, and briefly Raylan's gal, too. Yost and his core group of writers and directors were fascinated by what sociologists have taken to calling "toxic masculinity"—the psychic as well as physical damage the macho code inflicts; but also the allure of it, as depicted on series like *Justified*, which, like most of Clint Eastwood's films, managed the neat trick of making audiences groove on smart-ass quips and pissing contests and bursts of savagery even as the dialogue and more mournful, quiet moments suggested that it wasn't good for people, or society, to be enamored of such behavior. So when Raylan threatens local mob fixer Wynn Duffy (Jere Burns) by dropping a bullet on his supine chest and promising, "Next one's comin' faster," it's presented as an ultracool moment, but within a few episodes, the stunt helps Duffy's boss, the sociopath carpetbagger Robert Quarles (Neal McDonough), temporarily frame Raylan for murder. Raylan once explains to a criminal, "You run into an asshole in the morning, you ran into an asshole; you run into assholes all day, *you're* the asshole." In the moment, that applies to the criminal, but when you look back on all the trouble Raylan gets into over the course of the series, and the number of people on both sides of the law whom he manages to annoy, it's hard not to admit that *he's* the asshole.

Throughout, *Justified* remained at least three-quarters a comedy, often of a bantering sort, but it still made space for moments of suffering (and transcendence) as well as filmmaking touches, which confirmed that the show's directors were never content merely to photograph actors talking. There was evident thought put into the relationships between characters and their environments. Sometimes those environments seemed to reflect their interior states (lots of shots of an about-to-explode Raylan partly shrouded in shadow or etched by the pulse of red police lights) or comment upon the show's dual allegiance to film noir (the show is more comfortable with silhouettes than most) and the Western (when Boyd confronts a group of Harlan power brokers in season 4, he's framed from behind like a gunfighter about to draw, even though he has no guns on his hips).

Some of the series' seasons were, to put it mildly, better than others, and for some reason they were the even-numbered ones. (The peak was season 2, with Margo Martindale as backwoods crime lord Mags Bennett, whose offer of moonshine should never be accepted.) The only superfluous season was the fifth, where a show that was usually so impeccable in its casting for some reason thought quintessential New York guy Michael Rapaport would make a convincing Florida swamp rat; but at least it set the stage for the magnificent final season, which focused tightly on the central trio of Ava, Boyd, and Raylan, characters bonded by love and wary respect as well as rivalry and resentment.

The key question for the three

of them—indeed, for most of the major characters—is whether they can let go of old pains, grudges, and fantasies long enough to make a peaceful future for themselves. Turns out it's harder than even the wisest among them imagined. Raylan tries to unload the family home that's represented nothing but misery, fear, and loss to him, where he had to grow up eyeing the future burial plots not only for his parents but for himself. At one point, an undertaker tells him, "What you are moving is not your mother's remains, but the idea of her remains." The more you turn that sentence over in your mind, the more it seems like the key to Raylan's stop-and-start progress toward controlling his pride and temper and becoming something other than the adult version of an angry, abused, helpless child, a hateful criminal's son. Everything's a ritual, everything's a symbol, is the point: Once you accept that, you don't feel as beholden to the idea of being "true" to your family, your home, your town, or your county, and you can make tough decisions that are ultimately good for your development.

—MZS & AS

Outlier Classics

thirtysomething (ABC, 1987–1991) Total score: 78

The gentrification of prime time didn't begin with *thirtysomething*, Ed Zwick and Marshall Herskovitz's drama about the lives of white, upper-middle-class, once-radical baby boomers in Philadelphia; but this mostly low-key, tenderhearted drama does feel like a milestone in retrospect, in that it proved that this milieu could be fertile ground for intelligent popular art.

thirtysomething was the first critically acclaimed drama built around the life choices, moral struggles, and self-doubts of characters who could have been classmates of the core cast of *Return of the Secaucus Seven* or *The Big Chill*. The main characters were advertising agency partners Michael Steadman (Ken Olin) and Elliot Weston (Timothy Busfield), their wives, Hope Steadman (Mel Harris) and Nancy Weston (Patricia Wettig), Michael's single photographer cousin, Melissa (Melanie Mayron), Hope's best friend, Ellyn Warren (Polly Draper), Michael's bestie, Gary Shepherd (Peter Horton), and Gary's eventual wife, Susannah Hart (Patricia Kalember).

The show mined much of its drama from the sorts of predicaments that successful people in the entertainment industry dealt with all the time: remodeling a house; dealing with the demands of their children, coworkers, and clients; preparing to face their parents' decline and death (Eddie Albert was brilliant in a supporting role as Elliot's dad, Charlie, who got divorced and moved to California). The situations were so mundane, compared to what the characters on legal and cop and hospital dramas went through, that when *thirtysomething* introduced a more overtly grim or traumatic arc, such as Nancy's struggle with ovarian cancer or the wave of despair unleashed on the group by Gary's freakish death in a car wreck, it hit audiences with hammer-blow force.

As was the case with Zwick and Herskovitz's other ABC dramas, *My So-Called Life*, *Relativity*, and *Once and Again*, there were complaints that the story lines occurred deep inside the collective navel of the Yuppie; therefore, there was no reason for anyone of a less-fortunate class to care what happened. The show overcame such objections by portraying the characters' world with anthropological exactness, conceiving every episode and scene in cinematic rather than purely theatrical terms, and creating conditions that allowed great lead and supporting performances (including David Clennon's scene-stealing work as Michael and Elliot's smug, opportunistic boss, Miles Drentell, so memorable that the producers brought him back for *Once and Again*) to flower.

—MZS

Columbo (NBC, 1971–1978; ABC, 1989–2003) Total score: 77

Right now, we're in the midst of a boom in TV detective geniuses that somehow requires two different contemporary Sherlock Holmes series, and that was recently home to Gil Grissom on *CSI*, Adrian Monk on *Monk*, Robert Goren on *Law & Order: Criminal Intent*, and Patrick Jane on *The Mentalist*, among many other crime-fighting savants who need little help to figure out whodunit, and usually are happy to let everyone know how brilliant they are.

It's funny, then, to look back to Lieutenant Columbo (no first name given, though if you squinted at his badge, it read "Frank"), who initially presented as the slovenly, inarticulate, blue-collar antithesis of all those Holmesian heroes, yet who time and again proved to be the smartest TV sleuth of them all.

Columbo was introduced in "Enough Rope," a 1960 episode of the anthology series *The Chevy Mystery Show*, written by Richard Levinson and William Link. It pitted Columbo (then played by Bert Freed) against a psychologist who has seemingly committed the perfect crime in killing his wife so he can be with his lover. The killer thinks little of the detective assigned to the case, but as the title suggests, Columbo's modus operandi is already in place: Play dumb, keep asking questions, and eventually give the bad guy enough rope to hang himself with his own statements.

Link and Levinson later adapted

the script into a play called *Prescription: Murder*, which they then readapted for a 1968 TV-movie starring Gene Barry as the killer and Peter Falk as Columbo. Four years later (after another successful TV-movie, *Ransom for a Dead Man*), *Columbo* began a long and acclaimed run as part of a "wheel" of NBC murder mystery series, sharing its time slot with the likes of *McCloud* and *McMillan & Wife*.

By the time of the first regular *Columbo* installment, "Murder by the Book"—featuring as great a writer/director combo as you'll ever find for an episode of television: Steven Bochco and Steven Spielberg—the formula for the character was already well-established, and completely irresistible.

Rather than leaving the audience in the dark until the final act about the killer's identity, *Columbo* stories opened with the killing, usually committed by a wealthy, powerful individual who appeared to have expertly covered his or her tracks. But we knew whodunit, and so, it seemed, did Lieutenant Columbo. He would shuffle onto the murder scene in his worn shoes and rumpled trench coat, acting completely befuddled by this whole business, even as he locked in on the killer with laser precision. The murderers would, of course, assume they were smarter than this buffoon, and thus indulge his endless queries, confident they were handily winning the battle of wits until Columbo would pause at the doorway, mutter, "Oh, just one more thing…," and smack them about with an interrogatory two-by-four.

No clue was too minor to elude Columbo's canny eye: that a victim's shoelaces were tied in a manner that only his killer could have done, or that an old movie's running time invalidated the alibi of his chief suspect. He just dug in and kept right on digging, always acting apologetic for being such a pest.

"I can't help myself!" he told one of his earliest foes. "It's a habit."

Some of these smug, aristocratic killers with whom Columbo was so often matched seemed irritated by him, some simply amused, but so many more were almost charmed by him—understandable given the enormous appeal of Peter Falk in the role. Levinson and Link had wanted an older actor for *Prescription: Murder*—legend has it that Bing Crosby turned down the role because he feared it would interfere with his golf game—but Falk was one of those actors who was just born old. (As a result, the *Columbo* formula required almost no tinkering when ABC revived it a decade after the last NBC episode, and kept it going, on and off, until Falk was in his seventies.) Columbo's deconstructions of the killers' alibis were often so bogged down in detail that they evoked the old saw about an actor whom you'd gladly watch read from the phone book; Falk was so relaxed and verbally nimble that he probably could have recited passages from the tax code for an encore and gotten a standing ovation.

Columbo never called attention to his own brilliance in the manner of his many TV descendants, but it was impossible for even his most arrogant foes to miss. One of the series' best installments, "The Bye-Bye Sky High I.Q. Murder Case," puts the highbrow snobbery of so many *Columbo* villains front and center. The killer is Oliver Brandt (Theodore Bikel), an aloof member of a Mensa-like secret society. Brandt thinks he's indulging Columbo the way a parent does a sweet but slow child, even as the lieutenant is casually picking apart his seemingly foolproof plan to get away with murder. In fact, it's Brandt's own superiority complex, and Columbo's ability to play it like a violin, that elicits the confession, and Brandt's only way of accepting his defeat is to administer an intelligence test as they wait for other officers to arrive.

Before we get there, Columbo recalls, in his usual humble manner, how he's done so well for so long against people who seem so obviously his intellectual betters.

"You know, sir," he says, "it's a funny thing. All my life I kept running into smart people. I don't just mean smart like you and the people in this house. You know what I mean. In school, there were lots of smarter kids. And when I first joined the force, sir, they had some very clever people there. And I could tell right away that it wasn't gonna be easy making detective as long as they were around. But I figured, if I worked harder than they did, put in more time, read the books, kept my eyes open, maybe I could make it happen. And I did.

"And," he adds, "I really love my work, sir."

—AS

Futurama (Fox, 1999–2003; Comedy Central, 2008–2013; various direct-to-video movies)
Total score: 77

"Detecting trace amounts of mental activity, possibly a dead weasel or a cartoon viewer." That's a quote from Big Brain, mastermind of the Brain Spawn invasion of Earth in *Futurama*, and it is characteristic of the show's self-deprecating humor. But Matt Groening and David X. Cohen's animated series about the crew of an interstellar courier ship has nothing to be modest about. Pitched by its original network, Fox, as a companion to their already-long-running hit *The Simpsons*, *Futurama* quickly proved to have its own personality, rhythm, and visual style. It also showed great affection for the quirks, obsessions, hang-ups, and dreams of its main characters: a dim-witted twentieth-century time traveler named Philip Fry (voiced by Billy West); a one-eyed mutant pilot and space adventurer, Turanga Leela (Katey Sagal); ancient eccentric professor and Planet Express company owner Professor Hubert J. Farnsworth (West again); Amy Wong (Lauren Tom), the intern and spoiled daughter of a buggalo rancher; the socially maladjusted, grotesque, deeply insecure crustacean Dr. Zoidberg (West yet again); Hermes Conrad (Phil LaMarr), a sweet-souled and easily flustered accountant; an alcoholic, sexaholic, kleptomaniac, sociopathic robot named Bender (John DiMaggio); the pantsless space captain Zapp Brannigan (West yet again); Brannigan's Amphibiosian fourth lieutenant Kif Kroker (Maurice LaMarche); and a galaxy's worth of recurring characters and guest stars (including every then-surviving member of the original *Enterprise* crew, which reunited for a *Star Trek*–themed episode).

The show meandered across media platforms like Farnsworth's *Planet Express* ship spelunking the galaxy. It debuted in 1999 on the Fox network, got canceled four seasons later owing to low ratings, reinvented itself as a series of direct-to-DVD movies, landed on Comedy Central in 2008, and stayed there through 2015 (with some interruptions). Despite its chaotic production history, if you could chart wit on a longitudinal graph, *Futurama*'s line would be robust. It blends genre parody, social satire, raised-eyebrow postgrad cleverness, and fifth-grade-lunchroom spit-take humor. As a bonus, it showcases flat-out beautiful visuals: collapsing galaxies, elaborately choreographed space battles and hovercraft races, time-lapse terra-forming worlds, ravenous space beasts, formless sentient beings. In the season 6 Herman Melville parody "Möbius Dick" (an episode whose very title is a sci-fi-geek pleaser: Note the umlaut), the *Planet Express* crew tries to escape an interdimensional whale beast in an outer-space version of the Bermuda Triangle by zipping through a graveyard of iconic vessels, including the shuttle from *Space: 1999*, the monolith and the *Discovery One* from *2001: A Space Odyssey*, the *Satellite of Love* from *Mystery Science Theater 3000*, and the UFO from the cover of Boston's debut album.

Futurama has nearly as many dandy running gags as Groening's other classic. Among the best are the severed celebrity heads suspended in tanks of preservative fluid (a setup that allows Richard Nixon to serve as galactic president while being borne aloft on headless Spiro Agnew's shoulders) and Fry's dumber-than-dumber-than-dumb comebacks to simple statements (Rock creature: "Tomorrow morning, this planet makes its closest pass to the sun. You will all be boiled alive like retired circus animals unless you somehow can cross the great alkaline planes and reach shelter in the cave of harmony." Fry: "But that sounds hard!").

As in most sitcoms that are basically farcical, the characters always revert to type. But the writing keeps uncovering new shadings and surprising textures within those types. One can imagine many a smitten time traveler contriving to spend the rest of his life gazing into Leela's eye, as Fry does, but not many who would have endured as many brutal beatdowns at her hands, or been so moved by her beauty that he'd contrive to write her name in space or sell his soul to the Robot Devil in exchange for metal mitts that would let him serenade her on the holophonor. In various episodes, Bender becomes a pharaoh, a ghost, a god, a clone army, and the breakout star of the long-running soap opera *All My Circuits*. And the show is capable of poignant moments, too, none more devastating than Fry's dog in "Jurassic Bark," stuck in 1999 after his master's disappearance, waiting and waiting and waiting outside the pizzeria. His whiskers go gray, his spine slumps, and the neighborhood changes around him as Connie Francis sings, "If it takes forever / I will wait for you."

—MZS

The Outer Limits (ABC, 1963–1965) Total score: 76

"There is nothing wrong with your television set," the opening narration of *The Outer Limits* promised. "Do not attempt to adjust the picture. We are controlling transmission. If we wish to make it louder, we will bring up the volume. If we wish to make it softer, we will tune it to a whisper. We will control the horizontal. We will control the vertical. We can roll the image, make it flutter. We can change the focus to a soft blur or sharpen it to crystal clarity. For the next hour, sit quietly and we will control all that you see and hear. We repeat: There is nothing wrong with your television set. You are about to participate in a great adventure. You are about to experience the awe and mystery which reaches from the inner mind to... The Outer Limits."

Created by Leslie Stevens, a film and TV producer who also wrote an influential New Age philosophy book, *Est: The Steersman Handbook*, *The Outer Limits* was an anthology series strongly modeled on *The Twilight Zone*; the affinities were so obvious that it will probably always be thought of as an inferior imitation, or a second choice, a perception that disappears once you watch its often resonant and frightening episodes. Episodes dealt with time travel, extraterrestrial possession, and a rogues' gallery of monsters, mutants, and space creatures. The series drew high-profile science-fiction writers (including Harlan Ellison, whose *Outer Limits* episode "Soldier" was partly plagiarized, by James Cameron's own admission, for *The Terminator*, and resulted in a settlement and an onscreen acknowledgment). It was also a major influence on *Star Trek*, a series that mimicked its

merger of straightforward action and suspense with moral tales and brainteasers.

Where *The Twilight Zone* placed more of an emphasis on psychology, many of the episodes of *The Outer Limits* had a more existential feel. The series was mainly concerned with what happens when you're suddenly placed in a situation entirely beyond your control, much like the audience moved to inaction when the narrator warned visitors not to adjust their sets.

—MZS

Northern Exposure (CBS, 1990– 1995) Total score: 76

Fish, say good-bye to water. Joel Fleischman, say good-bye to Manhattan.

In the summer of 1990—at the dawn of a decade where the TV landscape would come to resemble that famous *New Yorker* cover, "View of the World from 9th Avenue," presenting a map of America where everything west of the Hudson may as well not exist—*St. Elsewhere* creators Joshua Brand and John Falsey opted for a different sort of medical drama, one that celebrated the mystery and wonder of one of the smallest, most remote communities in TV history.

Northern Exposure was the

whimsical, at times magical story of an obnoxious urban doctor (Rob Morrow as Fleischman) who, due to crippling student loans, was pressed into indentured servitude to the one-moose town of Cicely, Alaska. In the pilot, Joel is assured his new community is as sophisticated as it gets in these parts, but is horrified by how small and slow it feels: When he orders a bagel and cream cheese at the general store, the clerk asks, "What's a bagel?"

In time, though, Joel comes to recognize that Cicely is a haven for expatriates—including Maggie O'Connell (Janine Turner), a former debutante from Grosse Pointe who prefers a life as a bush pilot; Maurice Minnifield (Barry Corbin), a retired astronaut who owns much of the town and its businesses; Chris Stevens (John Corbett), ex-con and oracular DJ of the local radio station; and Holling Vincoeur (John Cullum), a bar owner who claims to be a direct descendant of Louis XIV—and that native-born Alaskans, like film buff Ed Chigliak (Darren E. Burrows), offer their own charms as well.

It's a town where everyone is in everybody's business, but in the best possible way. When Joel's fiancée, Elaine, calls off their long-distance engagement with a Dear John letter, the townsfolk go to elaborate lengths to afford him closure, including simulating a date between Joel and "Elaine" (actually Maggie, who will become the new love of his life for a time) so that he can explain how he really felt about the whole relationship. As the seasons went along, the town took on an air of the supernatural, sometimes benefiting from local phenomena like the aurora borealis, sometimes simply from the sparks generated by the eclectic cast of characters. The third season concluded with a flashback to the town's foundation in 1908 by a lesbian couple looking for a place where they wouldn't be condemned for their differences, when it briefly took on a reputation as "the Paris of the North," where Franz Kafka might come in search of a cure for writer's block. This seemed about right, based on what we had seen of the modern version.

When Morrow got into a contract dispute in later seasons, the show wrote him out by having the good doctor go native, falling so in love with a region he was once desperate to escape that he leaves the relatively sophisticated confines of Cicely to provide medical care to people in more remote parts of Alaska. By that point, it was easy to understand how he had become so seduced.

—AS

Batman (ABC, 1966–1968) Total score: 75

Thwack! Pow! Crash! Whenever a fight broke out on ABC's *Batman*, and the camera tilted to even more extreme angles than before, these onomatopoeic words splashed across the screen in brash block letters, their exclamation points and asterisks and "splat" graphics flashing like bits of defective neon signage while a funk-jazz brass section blatted and wailed.

This gimmick gave journalists an easy set of clichés to lean on whenever comics were discussed. But even in 1966, the year that this knowingly ludicrous series premiered, comics were already moving away from the naive aesthetic that formed the core of *Batman*'s style. They had to, really, after gallery artist Roy Lichtenstein blew up comic-strip panels to poster size as part of the Pop Art movement a few years earlier. Still, this was no one-joke show. The handwritten fight "sounds" were one part of a more complex and supple nostalgia act, one that included the black-and-white morality espoused by the Caped Crusader (Adam West) and his Boy Wonder ward, sidekick, and surrogate son, Robin (Burt Ward).

The year 1966 was pivotal in the development of the US counterculture. The Beatles took rock and roll a step closer to psychedelia with *Revolver*; and movies such as *Blow-Up, Masculin Féminin, The Battle of Algiers, Seconds,* and *Who's Afraid of Virginia Woolf?* expressed a cynical or depressive attitude toward bourgeois morality that was about to go mainstream. White middle-class college students were protesting the Vietnam War in increasing numbers, smoking pot and dropping out and burning draft cards and expressing sympathies with African Americans protesting police brutality and systemic discrimination. Snipers and mass murderers claimed headlines along with political prisoners and self-immolating monks. In this context, Batman's square jaw, cough-syrup monotone, and delicate hand gestures seemed hilarious to young viewers lit up on nonregulation ciggies; West's performance, the brilliance of which has required decades to be properly recognized, played as if series creator William Dozier and chief "developer" Lorenzo Semple Jr. had taken the establishment's fantasy of itself and dolled it up in tights and a cape.

West's Batman was the superhero as daddy-in-control, *Dragnet*'s Joe Friday in black rubber and gray spandex; Robin and Yvonne Craig's

Batgirl and all their allies were part of the 'Man's extended family. The anarchic gangs of supervillains and henchmen that kept trying to capture or destroy Gotham City stood in for the forces of chaos that kept threatening to engulf "civilized" America throughout the '60s, only made colorfully grotesque and knowingly silly. The show's bad-guy Hall of Fame included Cesar Romero as the Joker; Burgess Meredith as the Penguin; Frank Gorshin and John Astin as the Riddler; Catwoman, played variously by Julie Newmar, Lee Meriwether (in a spin-off film made between seasons), and Eartha Kitt; and numerous baddies created specifically for the series, including Joan Collins as the Siren, Milton Berle as Louie the Lilac, and Liberace as blackmailing twins Chandell and Harry. The puns were so bad that supervillains didn't so much speak them as lob them like grenades ("I'm not just pussyfooting around this time, Batman!" Catwoman exclaims). The heroes gave as good as they got, with Batman's imperviousness to humor becoming a bedrock of hilarity itself. He was the immovable object to the irresistible force of the show's bad guys, who gloried in their supposed audacity and wit, but were always undone by hubris. "It's obvious," Batman says, in a typical deductive epiphany. "Only a criminal would disguise himself as a licensed, bonded guard yet callously park in front of a fire hydrant."

If you doubt that every jagged bit of sociologically pungent camp swirling through this maelstrom was intentional, check out any of Semple's subsequent screenwriting credits, but especially 1974's *The Parallax View*, the most paranoid of paranoid thrillers, starring a long-haired reporter who loved mocking rednecks and authority figures; the 1976 *King Kong* remake, which turned the big gorilla into a serpent-slaying Christ figure caught in a love triangle between a hippie primatologist and a ditzy actress who asked Kong what his sign was; and of course the spin-off *Batman* movie, which showed the Caped Crusader trying to throw a lit bomb off a pier and being thwarted by the inopportune appearance of two nuns, a mother and child, a polka band, and ducklings. Like those cheeky movies, the weekly adventures of Batman and Robin were a funhouse mirror that turned real-world anxieties inside out and sock-puppeted them with goofy voices. The sets and costumes were boldly designed and garishly painted but still cheap-looking (every villain's lair seemed to have been built on the same medium-sized soundstage) and the repetitiousness of the fight scenes killed their in-jokiness after a while (though stray lines brought them back to life, like, "Batgirl's being frozen in that caviar!").

But it's still hard to revisit this series without seeing its hipster facetiousness as a roundabout kind of sincerity. The joke was ultimately on people who saw the show *only* as a joke: Batman's concern for Gotham was as sincere as the worrywart goodness of Christopher Reeve's Superman in the post-Watergate '70s, and there are moments when Batman/Bruce's easygoing patriarchal warmth toward Robin/Dick Grayson seems a harbinger of the Reagan '80s, which saw some of the same boomers who found the 'Man so absurd or menacing in the '60s acquiring $100 sneakers, stock portfolios, and Republican Party memberships. (Other times Batman seems like a toasted hippie fantasy of law enforcement; though he tends to lecture rather than talk, he's nicer than Joe Friday, and he often sticks up for the kids.)

Historical resonances aside, the '60s *Batman* is still a breath of fresh air if you grew up on the default, post–Frank Miller "Dark Knight" incarnation of Batman, who wore "armor" rather than a costume and snarled rather than spoke. Think about that for more than five seconds and then ask which image of a superhero is sillier.

—MZS

King of the Hill (Fox, 1997–2010)
Total score: 75

Mike Judge created *Beavis and Butt-Head*, and Greg Daniels wrote for *The Simpsons* at its peak. Both shows were once accused of heralding the end of Western civilization as we knew it, and though civilization has done just fine, it's not too surprising that when the two men teamed up to create a show, it would be one about a man convinced everything was better in the good old days.

But what made *King of the Hill* so special was that it chose Hank Hill's side of the argument most of the time. Yes, he was uptight, had trouble expressing his emotions, and worried far too much about son Bobby's (Pamela Segall Adlon) love of prop comedy. "That boy ain't right," Hank always said with both amazement and concern. But the series shared his dismay about things like the rise of big-box stores and the resulting loss of pride in craftsmanship and customer service. Hank could be a clown, but he knew how to take care of his lawn and his propane grill, dangit, and *King of the Hill* made it clear that it also admired those traits and many more.

Judge and Daniels are such great, gifted writers that they could have made a very funny show where Hank was a target of mockery (much like Tom Anderson, his *Beavis and Butt-Head* doppelgänger), but it's hard to imagine it lasting nearly as long, nor being as emotionally rich, as what we got from a version where Hank was the sane man in an increasingly insane world, in a series that wound up feeling not like a mash-up of *The Simpsons* and *Beavis*, but the best elements of *The Simpsons* and *The Andy Griffith Show.*

—AS

Veronica Mars (UPN, 2004–2006; CW, 2006–2007) Total score: 75

One show can't justify an entire network's existence, but *Veronica Mars* came close.

UPN spent eleven years locked in a pointless battle with the WB to see who could be TV's fifth-place broadcaster, shuffling through multiple identities—*We're the* Star Trek *network! We're the* Homeboys in Outer Space *network! We're UPS for UPN, here to pander to middle America!*—before both merged into the CW, whose combined DNA far more closely resembles the WB's than it does UPN's.

But UPN also gave us the unexpected delight that was *Veronica Mars*, Rob Thomas's high school noir about a former popular girl who, in the wake of a tragedy, reinvents herself as a teenage private eye apprenticing under her disgraced ex-cop father, Keith (Enrico Colantoni). A ridiculous idea on paper, it came to vivid life through the crackling dialogue of Thomas, Diane Ruggiero, and others, and through the tart, tough, vulnerable title performance by Kristen Bell.

Season-long mystery arcs have proved historically tricky for almost every TV show, with the resolution being either something the audience had long since predicted or something so out of left field that it felt like a cheat. But the first-season *Veronica Mars* arc—involving the murder of Veronica's best friend, Veronica's unexpected romance with bad boy Logan (Jason Dohring), and the reopening of many old wounds in a beach town that's home to only the superrich and their blue-collar servants—is a master class in how to do it right.

The next couple of seasons were uneven in their attempt to catch lightning in a bottle again, but for one year, *Veronica Mars* was so great it made UPN jokes feel like old news, and filled the show's fans with such love that, years later, they dipped into their own pockets to fund a Kickstarter campaign for a reunion movie.

—AS

Cagney & Lacey (CBS, 1981–1988) Total score: 74

It took a long time for TV to build a cop show around partners who were both women; the template was usually two or more men, a man and a woman (*Hunter*), or a glamorous loner (*Police Woman*). *Cagney & Lacey* got the memo, then threw it out. Despite widespread indifference from male viewers and weak ratings, this character-driven procedural survived for six seasons, injecting estrogen into a genre that had been tediously macho.

Created by feminist activist Barbara Avedon and TV executive Barbara Corday, the show started out as a riff on the mismatched-partners template, pairing two spirited, quirky female "types," the married mother Mary Beth Lacey (Tyne Daly) and the single, career-oriented Christine Cagney (Sharon Gless). The working title was *Newman and Redford* (as in Paul and Robert, stars of the classic buddy films *Butch Cassidy and the Sundance Kid* and *The Sting*); the network changed it for fear of getting sued, but as Cagney and Lacey worked their fictional Manhattan neighborhood of Midtown South, they became a more harmonious and mutually supportive duo than Newman and Redford had ever played, their jocular banter enriched by knowledge of how hard it was to be women doing what was thought to be men's work.

It was equally hard for a female-focused drama to survive in a male-dominated medium. *Cagney & Lacey* was originally a TV-movie, with *M*A*S*H* star Loretta Swit as Cagney. It was canceled after its initial, low-rated six-episode run in 1981 (featuring Meg Foster as Cagney), and returned for a regular series run in 1982–1983 (with Gless as Cagney). But it wasn't out of the woods yet. Cagney was deemed too déclassé, so her backstory was revised to make her the daughter of an upper-middle-class professional woman who had married a working-class cop. Even then, CBS pushed the producers to make Cagney "softer" and more stereotypically girlish—which was also the reason behind the switch from Foster to Gless—so that casual viewers wouldn't assume she was a lesbian.

The writers addressed the network's demands without damaging the partners' dramatic integrity, charting their workplace battles (and Cagney's many relationships) with sharp humor, and building memorable stories around workplace misogny, sexual harassment, the callous treatment of rape survivors by police, and reproductive rights. The latter was the focus of 1985's "The Clinic," which finds the partners investigating an abortion clinic bombing that claimed the life of a homeless man; Lacey reveals that she once terminated a pregnancy in Puerto Rico rather than seek illegal and possibly dangerous treatment in the United States, while Cagney expresses ambivalence due to her Catholic upbringing but ultimately supports a woman's right "to make up her mind about her own body." Antiabortion activists lobbied CBS to spike the episode and pressured affiliates not to show it, but it aired as scheduled, becoming the first installment of a regular series since CBS's *Maude* to put pro-choice sentiments in the mouths of central characters.

—MZS

EZ Streets (CBS, 1996–1997)
Total score: 74

Wiseguy (CBS, 1987–1990) Total score: 74

In the era of *The Sopranos*, *The Wire*, and *Breaking Bad*, CBS was the network of *CSI*, *Without a Trace*, and *NCIS*. Yet, despite its reputation for comfort-food crime procedurals, CBS was home to two incredible, intensely serialized cable-type dramas years before there even were dramas on cable.

The first of those, *Wiseguy*, came from perhaps the last producer you'd expect to be involved in something like it. Stephen J. Cannell wasn't a hack, but nor did he carry himself like an artist. He was a master craftsman, who could assemble works both exceedingly simple (*The A-Team*) and those aspiring to something more adult (*The Rockford Files*). Cannell always made sure the product was put together with care, in a way that felt comforting but fresh, and where everything would be neatly wrapped up by the hour's end.

But just because a man prefers to keep things simple doesn't mean he can't do complex, as Cannell and his *A-Team* partner Frank Lupo would demonstrate with *Wiseguy*, a show that proved they could make filet mignon just as easily as hamburger.

Better than any cop show before it, *Wiseguy* understood that the greatest asset of TV for storytelling purposes was time. The show's hero, federal agent Vinnie Terranova (Ken Wahl), was unremarkable, which made him ideally suited to infiltrate criminal organizations. Other cop shows had sent their heroes undercover, and/or given them recurring outlaw foes, but none had been willing to park themselves in one story line for a long stretch and let their hero and audience alike really get to know the bad guys.

It wasn't hard to understand why Vinnie's enduring conflict of the series was guilt over betraying the trust of each of the villains. The writers and the guest actors brought each of these bad guys to such vivid life that it was like we were all being seduced by them. For some of the guests, like Jerry Lewis or Glenn Frey, *Wiseguy* was a chance to reinvent an image, or to prove dramatic chops after becoming famous for other reasons. For others, this was simply the role—and opportunity—of a lifetime.

Wiseguy's first two villains were its best. We were introduced to Vinnie's world as he bonded with Atlantic City mob boss Sonny Steelgrave, played by journeyman actor Ray Sharkey. Sonny would die of self-inflicted electrocution, but Sharkey played the entire run as if he had been shot through with a few thousand volts right before the director called "Action!" After a career on the margins, Sharkey tore into the part for everything it was worth.

After that came Mel Profitt: a silky, incestuous, drug-addicted crime lord who had a knack for keeping all his darkest secrets well-hidden from the world (shooting up in his feet, for instance, because "the toes knows"), but not from Vinnie. The man playing him in such mesmerizing fashion? A young, unknown Kevin Spacey.

Later seasons kept shortening the arcs, and the last one did away with Vinnie altogether. But it's not hard to imagine the great showrunners of the twenty-first century looking at the Steelgrave and Profitt stories and asking themselves, "What if?"

Then there was *EZ Streets*, which starred Ken Olin as Cameron Quinn, a detective in an unnamed Rust Belt city; Joe Pantoliano as his gangster target, Jimmy Murtha (five years before Joey Pants popped up on *The Sopranos*, and with an even better performance than the one that won him the Emmy there); and Jason Gedrick as Danny Rooney, the parolee caught in the middle of their game. The series, created by Paul Haggis, featured storytelling so unabashedly dense and serialized that you not only had to watch every episode to have a prayer of understanding it, if you looked away from the screen at the wrong moment, you could become hopelessly lost. (I swear, one of the season's most important plot points was conveyed by a split-second nod delivered by a minor character to someone off-screen.) CBS's audience unsurprisingly ran screaming from it, and the show was effectively canceled after only two episodes had aired.

While the series was in limbo, Haggis took it to HBO, which was starting to get into the drama business, and claims he was told they'd love to buy it, but only after they held a meeting on another show—which turned out to be *The Sopranos*.

A few years too early, and half a dial away from being a phenomenon, *EZ Streets* instead had to settle for being something so rich and engrossing that it made its handful of viewers ravenous for other things like it. They would soon get it, in great abundance, far from CBS.

—AS

6. Bob Belcher, *Bob's Burgers*
7. Lucas McCain, *The Rifleman*
8. Howard Cunningham, *Happy Days*
9. Rocky Rockford, *The Rockford Files*
10. Jim Anderson, *Father Knows Best*

BEST MOMS

1. June Cleaver, *Leave It to Beaver*
2. Clair Huxtable, *The Cosby Show*
3. Tami Taylor, *Friday Night Lights*
4. Cookie Lyon, *Empire*
5. Marion Cunningham, *Happy Days*
6. Molly Goldberg, *The Goldbergs* (1949)
7. Marta Hanson, *I Remember Mama*
8. Elyse Keaton, *Family Ties*
9. Florida Evans, *Good Times*
10. Patty Chase, *My So-Called Life*
11. Jean Weir, *Freaks and Geeks*

BEST DADS

1. Charles Ingalls, *Little House on the Prairie*
2. Andy Taylor, *The Andy Griffith Show*
3. Mike Brady, *The Brady Bunch*
4. Cliff Huxtable, *The Cosby Show*
5. Eric Taylor, *Friday Night Lights*

Gilmore Girls (WB/CW, 2000–2007) Total score: 74

So many elements of the life of Lorelai Gilmore (Lauren Graham) are sheer fantasy: that she and teen daughter Rory (Alexis Bledel) could eat obscene amounts of unhealthy food at all times yet remain supermodel-thin, that the sleepy Connecticut town of Stars Hollow would have come together to help Lorelai raise Rory after she gave birth at sixteen, and that both Gilmore girls would always have the perfect pop culture bon mot ready to comment on the occasion, and delivered as warp-speed banter.

But as created by Amy Sherman-Palladino, the fantasy of *Gilmore Girls* was an intoxicating one. Stars Hollow was at times a parody of a caricature of small-town Americana, but who wouldn't want to live there? And perhaps no human other than Sherman-Palladino herself is able to speak that quickly and cleverly at every second, but Graham, Kelly Bishop (as Emily, Lorelai's disapproving aristocrat of a mother), and the rest of the cast delivered those lines with such panache that who would have preferred they speak more naturally?

And the show smartly laced the fantasy with some harsh realities, like the decades-old hurt between Emily and Lorelai over Lorelai's decision to raise a daughter on her own, or Lorelai's self-destructive romantic life, or the conflict between the two leads as Rory grew from perfect little daughter into a young woman making many of the same mistakes her mother once did.

Sherman-Palladino left before its final season, but is working on a *Gilmore* miniseries for Netflix that will revisit the family years later, and will presumably reveal the mysterious four final words she'd always promised to end the series on. Whatever they wind up being, I'm sure they'll be somehow funny and sweet, feature an obscure reference, and be delivered *very* quickly.

—AS

Six Feet Under (HBO, 2001–2005)
Total score: 74

The first thing we see on Alan Ball's creation is a series of images redolent of death and decay: a raven flying through an azure sky; a tilt-down to a lone tree rooted in a meadow, followed by a pair of tightly clasped hands rushing into the foreground and then letting go; another pair of hands, probably a mortician's, being washed in water; a pair of bare feet on a slab, marked with a toe tag; a pivoting point of view of clouds from a supine person's viewpoint; a single gurney wheel tracking across a slick floor. Thomas Newman's credits music chimes and chimes. The bell tolls. The bell tolls again. It never stops.

The first character we meet is the patriarch of the mortuary-owning Fisher family, Nathaniel Sr. (Richard Jenkins), a mortuary owner who becomes his own customer when a bus crash claims his life in the pilot's opening moments. Other Fishers soon enter the picture: the grieving widow, Ruth (Frances Conroy), who's not quite as loyal to her husband as her family might think; a hard-living, cynical older brother named Nate (Peter Krause of *Sports Night*), who's fallen for a stranger named Brenda Chenowith (Rachel Griffiths), who shared an anonymous tryst with him in an airport; a levelheaded middle brother, David (Michael C. Hall), who seems a logical candidate to take over the family business but is tied up in knots over his inability to admit that he's gay; and a troubled kid sister, Claire (Lauren Ambrose), who anesthetizes the pain of her empty life with drugs.

It sounds like an awfully depressing bunch, yet *Six Feet* manages to maintain a relatively upbeat tone. Much of this stems from the sheer energy of the performers. Ball, writer of *American Beauty* and future adapter of HBO's *True Blood*, mapped out the series and wrote much of it, pulling off some nice bits of playwriting craftsmanship. When it's not saddling its players with too-expositional dialogue ("My whole life I've been a tourist," Nate admits—a comment rendered unnecessary by his evident comfort with airports), *Six Feet* cleverly suggests parallels between the family mortuary business, which labors to make the dead look almost alive, and American society, which spiritually embalms its citizens with materialism, unrealistic life expectations, and meaningless pop culture dreck.

The series also indirectly honors the craft of acting, which raises abstract characters from death on the page and allows them to live onscreen. Jenkins appears repeatedly throughout the series, conversing with his wife and sons like a Shakepearean specter; the living characters are often seen talking with the dead. The deceased are portrayed not as literal apparitions but as shards of the living character's self-image, influences that haunt every major decision they make until death claims them, too. Vivid supporting characters drift in and out over the seasons, including Brenda's bipolar brother Billy (Jeremy Sisto); geologist George Sibley (James Cromwell), who becomes Ruth's second husband; Freddy Rodriguez as Nate and David's mortician and business partner, Federico Diaz; and Mathew St. Patrick as Keith Charles, David's tough but kindhearted life mate, a policeman who resents David's inability to be open about his sexuality, and who later becomes traumatized by the unceasing violence of his job.

Ball and his writers moved through five seasons with some difficulty, often resorting to seemingly arbitrary and sometimes violent or perverse plot twists to goose the audience's flagging interest (the most notorious of these is a season 4 episode that spends most of an hour on David getting kidnapped by a crackhead). But in retrospect these flourishes seem consistent with the show's central conceit, established not just in Nate Sr.'s sudden death but in the regular prologues showing how the mortuary's subjects died: Life can turn on you at any moment, for no reason. The opening expirations were sometimes darkly comical, sometimes horrendous or weird, sometimes sadly mundane. Many times you assumed the cameo character you'd been following would get offed, only to be shocked when the victim turned out to be someone tangentially connected to them. *Six Feet* paid off this recurring bit in its brilliant finale, the last few minutes of which jump into the future to show how and when all of the show's major characters will die. *Six Feet*'s opening credits, which are filled with resonant images of doom and decay, merge here in the mind with those how-they-died prologues, and as we see all of the characters growing old and gray, sickening and shrinking,

and finally succumbing to the inevitable, the sprightly chimes of Newman's theme resonate on a poetic level. The bells toll for everyone.

—MZS

BEST CARS

(American shows only, so no Mach 5 from Speed Racer*)*

1. KITT, *Knight Rider*
2. General Lee, *The Dukes of Hazzard*
3. Robin Masters's Ferrari, *Magnum, P.I.*
4. Batmobile, *Batman*
5. Mystery Machine, *Scooby-Doo*
6. B. A. Baracus's van, *The A-Team*
7. Gran Torino, *Starsky & Hutch*
8. Bluth Company stair car, *Arrested Development*
9. Black Beauty, *Green Hornet*
10. Crockett's Ferrari Spyder and Tubbs's Cadillac convertible, *Miami Vice*
11. El Camino, *My Name Is Earl*
12. Pontiac Firebird, *The Rockford Files*
13. Fred's foot-powered car, *The Flintstones*
14. The Munster Koach, *The Munsters*
15. Jed's roadster, *The Beverly Hillbillies*

BEST SPIES

1. Sydney Bristow, *Alias*
2. Jack Bauer, *24*
3. (tie) Philip and Elizabeth Jennings, *The Americans*
4. Napoleon Solo, *The Man from U.N.C.L.E.*
5. Sarah Walker, *Chuck*
6. Michael Westen, *Burn Notice*
7. Angus MacGyver, *MacGyver*
8. Agent 99, *Get Smart*
9. Lana Kane, *Archer*
10. Rollin Hand, *Mission: Impossible*
11. Artemus Gordon, *The Wild Wild West*
12. Kale Ingram, *Rubicon*
13. Alexander Scott, *I Spy*
14. Saul "the Bear" Berenson, *Homeland*

Sports Night (ABC, 1998–2000)
Total score: 74

Television, meet Aaron Sorkin.

The medium didn't know what to make of the playwright and screenwriter (*A Few Good Men*, *Malice*) when he first made the move to TV. And Sorkin was clearly still finding his way in the early days of *Sports Night*, a dramedy set backstage at a cable sports network. The jokes—what there were of them—tended to lean too much on repeated dialogue (to the constant befuddlement of ABC executives, who forced a laugh track on the show for much of its first season), and the romantic comedy beats already showed signs of the uncomfortable gender politics that would bloom into enormous problems on later Sorkin shows-about-shows *Studio 60 on the Sunset Strip* and *The Newsroom*.

Some Sorkin fans might argue that the most important thing about *Sports Night* was the way it prepped Sorkin and director Thomas Schlamme for their Emmy-winning collaboration the following season on *The West Wing*, but that would sell this show very short. Even with those early bumps, *Sports Night* had Sorkin's crackling dialogue and those gorgeous speeches. (The on-air apology Josh Charles's Dan Rydell delivers to his late brother in the show's second episode remains one of the best bits of oratory Sorkin— or anyone else, for that matter— has written for the small screen.) It had a cast of actors (also including Peter Krause, Felicity Huffman, Robert Guillaume, Joshua Malina, and Sabrina Lloyd) who seemed born to deliver Sorkin's words, plus Schlamme's gliding camerawork, a Capraesque sense of optimism and fun, and, in time, a superb balance between comedy and pathos.

In the series finale, a white-knight investor buys the network, insisting, "Anybody who can't make money on *Sports Night* should get out of the moneymaking business." *Sports Night* was unlikely to ever be a big hit (Sorkin has had much greater commercial success in movies than television), and it had its flaws from beginning to end, but each time Sorkin returned to the inside-TV well, it was hard not to wish he could just get the original band back together.

—AS

Star Trek: Deep Space Nine (Syndicated, 1993–1999) Total score: 73

Deep Space Nine was often the unloved stepchild of the latter-day *Trek* empire. For most of its run, it overlapped with either *Star Trek: The Next Generation* or *Star Trek: Voyager*, both of which had familiar franchise trappings like starships and visits to strange new worlds, while *DS9* took place on a space station in an unglamorous corner of the galaxy, and its main character, troubled widower Benjamin Sisko (Avery Brooks), didn't even attain the traditional rank of captain until the end of season 3.

But that unusually fixed position in space had its advantages. At its absolute strongest, *Next Generation* is the best of the spin-offs, as you might expect from a show employing the wildly overqualified Patrick Stewart as its star. But *DS9* was more consistently excellent, dug deeper with its characters, and took advantage of its also-ran position to break franchise rules against interpersonal conflict, serialization, and other fundamental elements of modern TV drama. It boldly stayed where no *Star Trek* show had stayed before, building an ever-richer world involving politics, religion, genocide, and the brutality of war.

It could have fun when it wanted to—say, dropping Sisko and friends into the middle of classic *Trek*'s "The Trouble with Tribbles"—but was rightly content with being the most serious, mature, and cohesive of all TV *Treks*.

—AS

Batman: The Animated Series (Fox, 1992–1995) Total score: 72

Animation is often thought of as a more natural fit for superhero movies and TV shows not simply because comic books physically resemble cartoons much more than they do live action but because animation has an unlimited special-effects budget, rendering the entire medium into something like

Green Lantern's power ring: If you can imagine it, you can make it real.

Outside of occasional appearances by superpowered villains like Clayface and Mr. Freeze, *Batman: The Animated Series* (sometimes known as *The Adventures of Batman & Robin*) didn't often have to depict things that wouldn't have looked convincing in the *Batman* films of the '90s. Instead, the series—developed by Bruce Timm and Eric Radomski—used the power of animation in a counterintuitive way: to make Batman and his rogues' gallery seem more real than they ever could in live action.

Even when Batman and his adventures are taken as seriously as they were in the Christopher Nolan films, there's still an inherent ludicrousness to the image of a man fighting crime in a batlike costume. *Batman: The Animated Series* never had that problem, using stylized designs for Batman (Kevin Conroy), the Joker (Mark Hamill), and everyone else—including Joker's lovestruck sidekick Harley Quinn (Arleen Sorkin), a creation of Timm and writer Paul Dini who proved so popular, the comic books had no choice but to incorporate her—but placing them in a film noir world where the many tragedies of Bruce Wayne and Gotham City never felt ironic or campy.

To many Batman purists, the show (along with spin-off film *Batman: Mask of the Phantasm*) is the best screen adaptation the character has ever had. But even if you prefer a different flavor of the Caped Crusader, these eighty-five episodes are hard to knock as a thrilling, emotionally resonant take on a Dark Knight unfettered by a need to make him seem plausible. In this format, Batman needed no justification or defense, and this creative team could just let him loose on the biggest monsters Gotham had to offer.

—AS

Boardwalk Empire (HBO, 2010– 2014) Total score: 72

Created by *Sopranos* writer Terence Winter, starring *Sopranos* alum Steve Buscemi, and set in the Garden State—albeit seventy-nine years before our first meeting with Tony—the Prohibition gangster drama was inevitably compared to its Jersey predecessor. The more apt HBO analogue, though, is *The Wire*, which favored a similar novelistic structure that tied together all the stories by season's end to make the whole feel greater than the sum of its parts.

Those impressive parts included stunning direction (by Martin Scorsese, Tim Van Patten, and others) and an incredible collection of supporting players: Michael Shannon as a fallen Treasury agent, Michael Pitt and Jack Huston as WWI vets damaged in very different ways, Kelly Macdonald as a deceptively canny widow, Stephen Graham as a volcanic but sympathetic Al Capone, Michael Stuhlbarg as the calculating Arnold Rothstein, Jeffrey Wright as a hypnotic Harlem crime lord, and so many more.

At the center of all these great performances and all this attention to narrative and visual detail was Buscemi as fixer Nucky Thompson, whose careful, inscrutable style didn't always serve the show well in elevating him above the more colorful gangsters. It's not a coincidence that the best *Boardwalk* season, the fourth, temporarily makes Michael Kenneth Williams's fiery Chalky White into Nucky's narrative equal.

Which is another thing it has more in common with *The Wire* than *The Sopranos*. Anyone at any time could be *The Wire* lead; put Tony on the sidelines for long and *The Sopranos* doesn't work. *Boardwalk* was at its best when Nucky was just one character among many. Pitt's Jimmy Darmody once warned Nucky that he couldn't be "half a gangster" anymore, but *Boardwalk* surrounded him with so many full-on gangsters that it got by just fine.

—AS

NewsRadio (NBC, 1995–1999)
Total score: 72

Emboldened by the success of *Friends*, and convinced that Ross and Rachel's slow-burning relationship was at the heart of that success, NBC tried turning itself into the romantic comedy network in the mid- to late '90s. No coupling was too implausible to become fodder for sappy promos, and no obstacle was too stupid to put in the path of true love so that it wouldn't arrive until at least the February sweeps period of season 3.

NewsRadio, however, very clearly missed that memo, and as a result wound up the great, unloved child of the Must-See TV era.

In only the show's second episode, with virtually no buildup, station manager Dave Nelson (Dave Foley) has sex with reporter Lisa Miller (Maura Tierney). *NewsRadio* creator Paul Simms did this over the objections of his bosses at NBC, robbing the show of a marketing hook, but giving it something more creatively useful: a rich and abundant source of humor as those two continually broke up, reunited, and were constantly mocked by their coworkers for it.

It was one of many elements of this weird but hilarious show that NBC execs didn't appreciate; perhaps not coincidentally, *NewsRadio* was one of the few sitcoms of the era to never once air on Thursdays after *Friends* or *Seinfeld*. NBC put a lot of sitcoms on Thursday in the '90s, many of them utter garbage like *Veronica's Closet* and *Union Square*, but this gem—with Foley as the best kind of exasperated straight man, Phil Hartman finally finding a normal(ish) role to fit his vast comic gifts as the pompous news anchor Bill McNeal, and Stephen Root having a ball as the station's eccentric owner, Jimmy James, among other pleasures—kept being assigned to obscure nights and times. (If NBC could invent a day of the week no one would ever hear of, they'd have scheduled *NewsRadio* there.) While nobody was looking, *NewsRadio* did amazing work, including a scene—from season 4's "Super Karate Monkey Death Car," where Jimmy reads aloud from a memoir that's been translated from English to Japanese, and then back to English as gibberish ("But Jimmy has fancy plans, and pants to match!")—that's as worthy of a sitcom time capsule as Lucy at the chocolate factory or Reverend Jim taking his driving test.

—AS

Picket Fences (CBS, 1992–1996)
Total score: 72

Picket Fences creator David E. Kelley had bigger commercial successes:

He ran *L.A. Law* during its mid-'80s peak, and his law-office romantic comedy *Ally McBeal* struck such a chord—for good and for ill—that the title character appeared on the cover of *Time* alongside Susan B. Anthony, Betty Friedan, and Gloria Steinem, with the headline "IS FEMINISM DEAD?"

But *Picket Fences* was Kelley's signature work. It combined the former lawyer's love of courtroom theatrics with his love of soliloquies about the way we live now, balanced with the kind of kinky, quirky touches that would eventually swallow later shows like *Ally* and *Boston Legal* whole.

Set in a small Wisconsin town where strange and dramatic events took place with improbable regularity, *Picket Fences* was a volatile blend of comedy, family drama, cop drama, political drama, and legal drama. It presented utterly ridiculous characters like hammy lawyer Douglas Wambaugh (played by Yiddish theater vet Fyvush Finkel) alongside serious ones like cop Jimmy Brock (Tom Skerritt) and his doctor wife, Jill (Kathy Baker), and successfully demanded that you view them all as equals, and it found a way to wrap up almost every story with a powerful oratory from Judge Henry Bone (Ray Walston from *My Favorite Martian*, of all people).

Kelley's among the most gifted

wordsmiths TV has ever employed, and his skill at crafting monologues has helped earn his actors (including Baker, Skerritt, Finkel, and Walston here) more than three dozen Emmys across multiple series. His shows tend to combine so many incompatible elements, though, that they rarely stay in balance for long. Over its four-season run, *Picket Fences* not only covered more of what fascinated Kelley than the other series did before or after, but somehow held itself together for longer than the others could.

—AS

Scrubs (NBC, 2001–2008; ABC, 2009–2010) Total score: 72

In the late '80s, TV gave birth to a new hybrid form called the dramedy. The name suggested an even blend between drama and comedy, but more often than not these shows have been dramas that simply run for a half hour, or hour-long shows that are a shade lighter in tone than *Breaking Bad*.

Scrubs, though, was equally comfortable on either side of that blurred line. Following the residencies of young doctors J. D. Dorian (Zach Braff), Elliot Reid (Sarah Chalke), and Christopher Turk (Donald Faison), it laughed in the face of death—or, at least, had J.D. lose a game of Connect Four with the Grim Reaper—cried at

the complexities of life, and was frequently overtaken by J.D.'s hyperactive imagination, which could transform the doctor/surgeon rivalry into a musical number out of *West Side Story*, or merge Elliot and Turk into his ideal roommate. (The show grew more creatively uneven in its later years as the line blurred between the real world and J.D.'s imagination—even if some of the oddball "real" sequences, like Turk expertly performing the choreography from Bell Biv Devoe's "Poison" video, were delightful—before reining itself in for the final season with the original cast.)

Patients died often at Sacred Heart Hospital, and those deaths were treated with the utmost seriousness. Yet *Scrubs* was able to quickly pivot from tragedy to absurdity and back again, allowing J.D. to embarrass himself in front of sarcastic Dr. Perry Cox (John C. McGinley) in one moment, then help counsel his mentor through the aftermath of a fatal mistake in the next.

It was silly, it was stupid, it was lovely, and it was often great.

—AS

WKRP in Cincinnati (CBS, 1978–1982) Total score: 72

Hugh Wilson's series about a struggling Cincinnati, Ohio, radio station came from Mary Tyler Moore's production company MTM, which also produced such intelligent, assured, fundamentally kind-hearted programs as *The Mary Tyler Moore Show, The Bob Newhart Show, Hill Street Blues,* and *St. Elsewhere.* The main character was station manager Andy Travis (Gary Sandy), who kept trying to find new ways to boost WKRP's weak ratings, including switching its format in the pilot from easy listening to rock and roll and R & B. Station owner Arthur Carlson (Gordon Jump), an amiable but befuddled and easily cowed man, kowtowed to his dragon-lady mama, Mrs. Carlson (Sylvia Sidney in the pilot, Carol Bruce later), the not-so-secret power behind his throne, and avoided conflict by hiding in his office with his golf putter. The supporting cast included the loud-mouthed, unctuous, white-shoed advertising director Herb Tarlek (Frank Bonner), whose suits seemed patterned after Scottish kilts; late-night soul show DJ Venus Flytrap (future *Frank's Place* star Tim Reid), the station's lone African American and a consummate ladies' man; burned-out ex-hippie Dr. Johnny Fever (Howard Hesseman); Mr. Carlson's secretary, Jennifer Marlowe (Loni Anderson), who was every inch the stereotypical buxom blonde but performed

intellectual jujitsu against men who condescended to her; the station's news director Les Nessman (Richard Sanders), a bespectacled twit in a bow tie who was awful at his job but carried on as if he were the second coming of Edward R. Murrow; and Bailey Quarters (Jan Smithers), a Jill-of-all-trades who would put her journalism-school-trained mind to work in Les's job if management would only see her talent.

The dominant mode of the show was relaxed, personality-based buffoonery, along the lines of *The Bob Newhart Show* or *Barney Miller,* but with a hip sound track. In one great episode, Andy hires a consultant to study the station and recommend changes, and everyone acts as outrageously as possible to reinforce stereotypes and foul up his data; Venus even pretends to threaten Johnny with a switchblade. In another classic, the station's Thanksgiving Day promotional turkey drop becomes a massacre, with Les narrating the carnage à la the *Hindenburg* disaster ("Oh, the humanity!") and Mr. Carlson concluding, "As God is my witness, I thought turkeys could fly."

But mixed amid the slapstick and the often surprisingly complex relationships (including Johnny's late-season hookups with Bailey, and Jennifer and Andy's ongoing chemistry, which was driven by mutual respect), the show often segued into rather dark drama without breaking a sweat. One powerful episode climaxed with Venus Flytrap, a Vietnam veteran, telling the World War II veteran Mr. Carlson about the atrocities that made him go AWOL. Another responded to the real-life deaths of eleven fans who were crushed to death during a 1980 Who concert at Riverfront Stadium in Cincinnati. Titled "In Concert," the episode was produced just eleven weeks after the tragedy, which led large venues to ban general admission seating.

Every episode offered a new tidbit of information about the characters that deepened our view of them or set the stage for another inventive comic set piece, as in season 3's "Venus and the Man," which finds Venus, a graduate of a state teacher's college, convincing a street-tough black teenager not to drop out of school. He explains the atom in two minutes, using the young man's knowledge of local gangs to draw a "territory map" on a storeroom wall with a Sharpie.

The show's use of then-current pop (including Blondie's "Heart of Glass" and Foreigner's "Hot Blooded") was witty, sometimes moving, and always imaginative. Unfortunately, this aspect of the show's legacy was rendered nearly incomprehensible when *WKRP*'s syndication run ended and its music licenses expired. When DVDs finally became available for sale three decades after the finale, perfectly chosen songs had been replaced with generic sound-alikes, and accompanying citations of song titles and artists had been deleted from dialogue, in ways that mangled jokes and plot points. The draconian reality of music licensing being what it is, it seems unlikely that the *WKRP* that '70s and '80s viewers loved will be seen and heard again. A similar fate has befallen more series than can be cited in this book; considering the deft way that this gem of a sitcom wove music into the fabric of its comic tapestry, the loss is keenly felt.

—MZS

How I Met Your Mother (CBS, 2005–2014) Total score: 70

In TV, the journey is virtually always more important than the destination. It's insane to devote dozens of hours to a show over years without deciding if you liked it or not until the very end. A terrible ending can sour how you look back on a series, but it can't travel through time to erase the enjoyment you felt in the moment.

I know this to be true because the end of *How I Met Your Mother*—which killed off the mother in the future so sensitive hero Ted Mosby (Josh Radnor) could get back together with ex Robin Scherbatsky (Cobie Smulders), even though the show had long since salted the earth on which their romance once stood—angered me as much as any series finale ever has, yet I'd still argue vehemently for its placement here.

That's how great *HIMYM* was at its best: a smart, romantic, funny show that had as many clever ideas about friendship (with the core group also including Neil Patrick Harris as inveterate hound Barney Stinson, and Jason Segel and Alyson Hannigan as giddy soul mates Marshall Eriksen and Lily Aldrin) as it did about relationships, and that used its time-bent structure to play with our perceptions (in flashbacks, smoking pot becomes "eating a sandwich," or a girlfriend whose name the older Ted can't recall is referred to as "Blah-Blah"), to terrific comic and even dramatic effect.

The finale was ultimately one piece of cleverness too many—an idea hatched early in the run that should have been abandoned once the characters had evolved beyond it—but put episodes like "Slap Bet" or "Ten Sessions" in front of me, and I will still laugh, and be touched, and marvel at just how inventive a traditional-looking sitcom can be.

—AS

Terriers (FX, 2010) Total score: 70

There are high-concept shows, where you can explain both the premise and the appeal in a single sentence, like "Federal agent battles terrorist threats in a thriller that takes place in real time." And there are low-concept shows that are often more about the characters and how they interact than about the premise, setting, or plot.

Terriers is, if anything, lower than low-concept. There is almost nothing I can tell you about the show that won't make it sound like something very old and creaky. It's a private detective show. With two wisecracking partners. Who are perpetually underestimated because of their present circumstance and past history. And they take on the wealthiest, most powerful, most dangerous players in their very SoCal noir community, bantering just to forget how scared they are the whole time.

You've seen all this a thousand times before. But you haven't seen it with Donal Logue (as alcoholic ex-cop Hank Dolworth) and Michael Raymond-James (as reformed thief Britt Pollack) as the detectives with a level of raw honesty and comic alchemy between them that most TV shows would pray to get at half-strength. You haven't heard the irresistible rhythms of Ted Griffin's dialogue, nor seen how Griffin and Shawn Ryan weaved a complex yet comprehensible and satisfying mystery story over their only thirteen episodes.

Some blamed the death of *Terriers* on the name, and/or an ad campaign that hid the two stars behind the image of a snarling little dog. But *Terriers* by any other name would have been just as hard to sell, because the idea of it wasn't special, even if the execution was. You had to see it to believe in it.

—AS

TOP 40: TV'S BEST THEME SONGS EVER

1. *The Twilight Zone*
2. *The Rockford Files*
3. *The Wire*
4. *Hawaii Five-0*
5. *The Muppet Show*
6. *All in the Family*
7. *Cheers*
8. *The Simpsons*
9. *Star Trek*
10. *Miami Vice*
11. *The Bob Newhart Show*
12. *Mission: Impossible*
13. *Peter Gunn*
14. *Sanford and Son*
15. *Gilligan's Island*
16. *It's Garry Shandling's Show*
17. *Hill Street Blues*
18. *Twin Peaks*
19. *The Andy Griffith Show*
20. *The Fresh Prince of Bel-Air*
21. *The Brady Bunch*
22. *The Beverly Hillbillies*
23. *The Jeffersons*
24. *Friends*
25. *The Dukes of Hazzard*
26. *Magnum, P.I.*
27. *Law & Order*
28. *The X-Files*
29. *Sex and the City*
30. *The Greatest American Hero*
31. *Taxi*
32. *Starsky & Hutch*
33. *The Mary Tyler Moore Show*
34. *Good Times*
35. *The Addams Family*
36. *The Sopranos*
37. *The Wonder Years*
38. *Dragnet*
39. *M*A*S*H*
40. *The Odd Couple*

■ WORKS IN PROGRESS ■

(Current series that could be Pantheon-worthy when all is said and done; all these entries were completed by June 2016, and thus may be missing current developments, including whether certain series concluded after our deadline.)

Adventure Time (Cartoon Network, 2010–present)

Lots of animated series could be said to appeal equally to children and adults, but not many appeal to the potential adult in children and the eternal child in grown-ups. *Adventure Time*, created by Pendleton Ward, is such a show. Set in the postapocalyptic land of Ooo, it's mainly about the adventures of Finn the Human (Jeremy Shada) and his best friend and adoptive brother, Jake (John DiMaggio, Bender from *Futurama*), a squat orange dog who can change shape à la Plastic Man. They are joined by Princess Bubblegum (Hynden Walch), the Ice King (Tom Kenny, the voice of SpongeBob), and Marceline the Vampire Queen (Olivia Olson), a thousand-year-old immortal who loves rock and roll. The gentleness of the series belies its consistently dazzling visuals as well as its sure grasp of dream logic. Drawing on role-playing games, underground comics, anime, and the cartoon fantasies of Hayao Miyazaki (*Spirited Away*), the show has an almost sketch-comedy vibe; episodes run about eleven minutes each and tend to be built around free-associative conversations rather than plot, and the distinctive timbre of the actors' voice performances at times suggests how adults sound when they're imitating children without changing the pitch of their voices.

—MZS

American Crime (ABC, 2015–present)

John Ridley's *American Crime* is another anthology series in which a recurring cast plays different characters and the unit of measure is the season rather than the episode. But unlike its gridmates *True Detective*, *American Horror Story*, and *Fargo*, it has no easy-to-peg genre hook, unless you consider the kind of storytelling that film scholar David Bordwell dubbed a "network narrative" to be a genre unto itself. Like most cinematic examples of the form, *American Crime* gives us several ongoing, subtly interlaced but essentially parallel stories in which unsuspecting average citizens' lives are bound together by a seismic event.

American Crime is written, directed, and acted in an unadorned, at times punishingly austere style that sometimes lets whole scenes play out in one long take while focusing on a single character and letting others (including some leads) remain out of focus or off-screen. Other times, we might see characters wading into some of the most intense arguments of their lives while the camera observes them from across the street or from the other side of an apartment, until finally it cuts to a tight close-up that lets the heart of the scene play out through an actor's face or, occasionally, hand gestures. Like Ryan Murphy (*American Horror Story*, *American Crime Story*) and Noah Hawley (*Fargo*)—and Orson Welles in his Mercury Theater days—Ridley has put together a formidable repertory company of actors (including Felicity Huffman, Timothy Hutton, Regina King, Elvis Nolasco, and Johnny Ortiz)

and slotted them into different lead roles depending on the story.

Ridley, who adapted the Oscar-winning *12 Years a Slave* and oversees *American Crime*, has a lot of issues on his mind, but the series never feels entirely issue-driven. Season 1 is about the effects of a rape-murder case on the families of the victims and the accused and the surrounding community. It deals with racism, xenophobia, secular versus religious mind-sets, class bias, the incompetence of the criminal justice system, the socially destructive effects of the War on Drugs, and the ways in which prison tends to breed criminals rather than show them the error of their ways. Season 2 revisits all these issues, plus the tribal mentality that pits, say, Hispanics, blacks, and whites against one another within the same school, or the same community, and the coach of a winning basketball team (Hutton) against the headmistress (Huffman) who's trying to be sensitive to the pain of a gay teen (Connor Jessup) who says he was sexually assaulted by basketball teammates. The boy's mother (Lili Taylor) wants justice for her son but keeps slamming against the concrete wall of bureaucratic self-protection.

Though certainly not the most enjoyable of the new anthology dramas, *American Crime* might be the most politically and socially relevant; artistically it's the nerviest, because it insists on doing a lot with a little, making artistic choices and building scenes, episodes, and seasons around them, and sticking with a notion or a theme until every facet of it has been explored.

—MZS

The Americans (FX, 2013–present)

The lesson that many TV creators and executives took from *The Sopranos* was that the audience was ready for antiheroes. And we got some wonderful shows like *The Shield* and *Breaking Bad* out of that. But the lesson that a few smart people took was that you can use a familiar commercial genre as a Trojan horse to smuggle in something more ambitious and thematically complex: *Come for the whacking! Stay for the social commentary!*

So *The Americans* is on paper a spy thriller set in the Cold War's final decade, following a pair of Soviet sleeper agents posing as all-American couple Philip (Matthew Rhys) and Elizabeth (Keri Russell) Jennings, performing covert missions for the KGB right in the heart of the Reagan presidency. And it functions perfectly on that level, with a collection of tense and thought-provoking espionage

missions that offer a sense of what representatives of the "Evil Empire" were thinking (particularly after Ronald Reagan hung that nickname on them, to their shock and amazement).

But really, what *The Americans* is about is marriage: the compromises we make when we decide to permanently join our life with someone else's, the way the years and the relationship can turn us into completely different people from when we started, the debates about kids and careers and everything else. And it's extraordinary at that.

The Jenningses' "marriage" was designed as mere camouflage by their superiors in Moscow, but when you spend decades sharing a bed, and a life, with someone else, and when you have children together (even if just to help maintain the cover), it's hard for it to not morph into something resembling the real thing. As the series begins, Philip has begun to have genuine feelings for his fake spouse, and in time Elizabeth learns to reciprocate. They still regularly have sex with assets as part of the job—one of the few times it gives either of them real pause is when Philip is ordered to seduce a CIA section chief's teenage daughter, who's not much older than their own Paige (Holly Taylor)—and when they gather in the laundry room to divvy up the weekly chores, the list is as likely to include a honeypot or assassination attempt as it is figuring out the carpool schedule.

And just as the realities of Tony Soprano's career in the mob significantly raised the stakes of his relationships with his wife, mother, and uncle, everything that happens in the Jennings house gets filtered through the unforgiving lens of what Mom and Dad really do for a living. On another show, atheist parents discovering that their daughter wants to go to church would create some mild tension; here, Paige's interest in getting baptized becomes a threat to her parents' entire way of life, and makes Elizabeth (always the more hard-core Communist of the two) much more willing when the KGB asks them to recruit Paige to be an asset. (Philip, who's become accustomed to their softer American lives and cares only about protecting his family, is horrified by the request, and does everything he can to fight it.)

History tells us that Philip and Elizabeth's side will lose the Cold War, and at times it feels like *The Americans* has been losing the battle for relevance in the age of Peak TV. Its ratings are low and awards recognition for the staggering work being done by Rhys, Russell, and

Noah Emmerich (as the FBI agent who doesn't realize his neighbors are in the KGB) has been few and far between. But when histories of this era of television are written, all will have to acknowledge that this was one of the very best shows in it.

—AS

Better Call Saul (AMC, 2015–present)

Why?

Why did we need any kind of *Breaking Bad* spin-off?

And if we had to get one, why did it have to be about Saul Goodman, a character who was there predominantly as comic relief, but who was virtually never the funniest person on *Breaking Bad*? Why not give us *The Chicken Man Cometh*, about the rise to power of Gustavo Fring? Or why make unflappable fixer Mike Ehrmantraut into a supporting character when it would be so easy to let Jonathan Banks's world-weary charm carry the whole thing?

Mainly, though, why? With all due respect to star Bob Odenkirk, *Breaking Bad* creator Vince Gilligan, and Saul Goodman's own creator, Peter Gould, why mess with perfection to do any kind of prequel, let alone this one?

Those questions were easy to ask

in the run-up to *Better Call Saul*, which even Gilligan and Gould admitted took much longer to gestate than either had expected. Within a few episodes of the new show, there was only one question worth asking:

Why the hell not?

In traveling back in time to roughly six years before Walter White's cancer diagnosis, *Saul* is somewhat bound by the facts of the original series, but not a lot. Saul is so far away from the character we met on *Breaking Bad* that he literally isn't even Saul Goodman at the start of the new show. Instead, he's using his real name, Jimmy McGill—better known to con artists and cops alike in his native Cicero as Slippin' Jimmy for his flair for slip-and-fall hustles, but here doing his best to be an honest lawyer and impress mentally ill older brother Chuck (Michael McKean) and Kim Wexler (Rhea Seehorn), a fellow lawyer who gets turned on by participating in Jimmy's low-level cons, even as she pushes for him to stay clean overall.

By starting there, Gilligan and Gould turned the conceit of *Breaking Bad* on its head. Instead of a story about a man everyone thinks is good turning out to be evil, they were telling a story of a man struggling to be good in a universe that

has no faith or interest in this version of him. Odenkirk, a wonderful comic actor with a limited dramatic résumé, has been a revelation as Jimmy: endearing and vulnerable and so sympathetic that his inevitable slide down into Saul-dom feels like it's going to somehow hurt more than when Walt fully embraced his inner Heisenberg.

While the show also makes excellent use of Banks as a Mike who isn't quite the superhuman killer he'd be as Gus's right-hand man, perhaps its most impressive feat is how quickly it silenced all the fan speculation about when and how Walt, Jesse, Gus, or anyone else from the parent series might turn up. Before *Better Call Saul* debuted, fans looked at it as a way to cling to some vestige of the *Breaking Bad* universe. Once people actually saw it, the last thing most of them wanted was for Jimmy McGill to turn into the man who could one day be a drug lord's consigliere.

—AS

Black-ish (ABC, 2014–present)

In the second decade of the twenty-first century, broadcast networks and cable channels rushed to air shows that asked general audiences to look at life through something other than a straight, white, middle-class lens; this yielded such gateway series as *Modern Family, Empire, Scandal,* and *How to Get Away with Murder* (multiracial, plus gay characters) and more focused works like *Fresh Off the Boat* (Asian American), *Jane the Virgin* (Latino), *The Goldbergs* (specifically suburban-Jewish in a way that few sitcoms had dared to be), and *Looking* (young, gay Yuppies). The most buoyantly confident comedy in this wave is *Black-ish,* which had the audacity to carry itself like an American institution from its very first week on the air.

Set in the leafy Los Angeles suburbs, and cocreated by Kenya Barris, *Black-ish* is a laugh track–free, heavily narrated sitcom about an upper-middle-class African American family whose patriarch Andre "Dre" Johnson (Anthony Anderson) worries that they're moving up in the world at the expense of their cultural identity. By turns evoking *The Wonder Years, Malcolm in the Middle, The Cosby Show,* and *The Honeymooners* (the latter due mainly to Anderson's hair-trigger, Jackie Gleason–esque physicality), the show's observations often circle back to issues of race, class, religion, and tradition. The scripts are specifically and unapologetically black in a way that very few network sitcoms had previously been

allowed to be. Even the socially aware Norman Lear sitcoms of the 1970s (many of which are discussed in this book) felt it necessary to frame every story in terms that a hypothetical white viewer could understand. But here the attitude is always warm, embracing, and familiar: not, "Let me be a cultural ambassador and tell you about my people, white viewers," but rather, "Don't you hate it when..." and "Have you ever noticed that..." This holds true whether a given episode is about gun control, the rituals of street "authenticity," distress over racially motivated police brutality, racist micro-aggressions in the workplace, the politics of black hair and hair care, Dre's panic over interracial dating, or the fascination with the Harlem renaissance (memorably depicted in a season 1 memory/fantasy).

The peerless cast includes Yara Shahidi as Dre's eye-rolling daughter, Zoey; Marcus Scribner as his teenage son Andre Jr., who begins the show by asking if he can be bar mitzvahed; Miles Brown and Marsai Martin as the precious youngest Johnsons, Jack and Diane; Tracee Ellis Ross as Dre's biracial wife, Rainbow, a beautiful kook in a Diane Keaton vein ("If I'm not 'really' black, could somebody please tell my hair and my ass?" she

286 ■ ■ ■ TV (The Book)

says); co–executive producer Laurence Fishburne as Dre's old-school father, Pops; and Jenifer Lewis as Pops's ex-wife and sometimes hookup Ruby, aka Rosy, a deeply religious firebrand of a woman.

At the core of every story is fear of change, followed by grudging acceptance that change is inevitable, and that as long as you have the love of friends and family, things will be fine. When Dre says he wants his kids to be "black, not black-ish," he's trying to get at something very culturally specific, and yet—and this is the beautiful part—as soon as he names exactly what's eating him, he (and we) realizes that it's not as specific as he thinks, and that, in fact, he's on a quixotic quest. How much of Dre's anxiety comes from race and culture, and how much is midlife crisis in disguise? We wonder, and *Black-ish* seems to wonder along with us. In its own sweet way, this is a landmark show, finding the universal in the specific and vice versa.

—MZS

BoJack Horseman (Netflix, 2014–present)

A nearly perfect merger of high and low humor, this series from Raphael Bob-Waksberg would be totally uncategorizable even if it were a straight-up live-action Hollywood satire, rather than what it is: an animated series in which humans and anthropomorphized animals (led by the titular ex–sitcom star, a fiftyish half-horse voiced by Will Arnett) coexist. It's very funny and yet somehow not funny at all; the reserves of loneliness and misery that these characters tap into have few equivalents on current or recent TV, though if you imagine something along the lines of an early Albert Brooks film, or maybe *The Larry Sanders Show*, you'd be in the ballpark. BoJack dictates a tell-all autobiography to his ghostwriter, Diane Nguyen (Alison Brie), while the publishing house (headed by Patton Oswalt's emperor penguin Pinky) frets over its commerciality. He squabbles with his agent and girlfriend Princess Carolyn (Amy Sedaris), and competes with his chief professional rival, the narcissistic and passive-aggressive yellow lab Mr. Peanutbutter (Paul F. Tompkins). He tries to land a career-reinvigorating part in a great movie but has to settle for crap. And like most of the characters, he stumbles through life, making nearly catastrophic professional and personal mistakes, alienating and winning back allies, and (in the magnificent second season) getting involved with an ex-girlfriend's daughter. The filmmaking veers into flights of fancy, dreams and drug trips, and picaresque journeys through American panoramas that would make lovely velvet paintings. If *Mad Men* were populated by animals, this is what it might have felt like; though, of course, you'd have had to cut ear-holes into BoJack's fedora.

—MZS

Broad City (Comedy Central, 2014–present)

One of the most exciting things about the current TV landscape isn't just the ever-expanding number of outlets in need of original series but the ever-expanding number of ways for talent to be discovered.

Once upon a time, *Broad City* creators and stars Ilana Glazer and Abbi Jacobson would have had to spend years paying their dues at Second City, then either get lucky in an *SNL* audition or else land a minor role on someone else's sitcom as the heroine's weird best friend, and good luck convincing anyone that they wanted to make a show where they were the heroines.

Instead, after stagnating at the lower levels of Upright Citizens Brigade, they just made *Broad City*— a stoner comedy about two best friends in a city that's simultaneously the most exciting and scariest in the world—on their own, as a series of YouTube shorts, honing their craft and building up a passionate fan base that eventually included Amy Poehler, who invited them to bring the show, largely as-is, to television.

That kind of journey wouldn't have been impossible in the good old days, but it would have been very hard. And where there are plenty of YouTube comedy stars today who can't sustain any story that lasts longer than five minutes, Glazer and Jacobson had spent their time on the *Broad City* web series fine-tuning their craft as storytellers so that the Comedy Central version arrived fully formed: surreal, sexually frank in unexpected ways, and with a wicked flair for slapstick. At a time when many of TV's most acclaimed "comedies" are really half-hour art films, it's balls-out funny, and clearly made by women who are much more focused and driven in real life than the characters they play.

—AS

Fargo (FX, 2014–present)

It had no business working.

None.

Its very existence should have been considered a joke.

Who in his right mind would

think to take the Coen brothers' *Fargo*—the most acclaimed movie by two of the most idiosyncratic filmmakers in a generation—and turn it into a TV show? It had already been tried in the late '90s with a pre-*Sopranos* Edie Falco as Marge in a straightforward adaptation of the film; it was terrible, and CBS never aired it.

Writer Noah Hawley saw that approach as folly, and found a way to create a series that exists in the movie's universe, with a familiar tone—along with frequent nods to other Coen projects—and even a brief intersection between the two plots (where a character on the show discovers the satchel of money that Steve Buscemi buried in the snow in the film), but tells its own stories with its own characters in the same anthology miniseries format popularized by *American Horror Story* and *True Detective*. The show isn't a Coen brothers cover band but a tribute act whose original material not only evokes the original but frequently lives up to it.

The first season weaved in and out of *Fargo* archetypes, giving us Martin Freeman as a far more loathsome take on the hapless salesman who gets mixed up in crime, and Allison Tolman as a cop with an uncanny knack for piecing together an impossible puzzle. To

that, it added Billy Bob Thornton as a remorseless, seemingly unstoppable hit man with his own moral code—like Chigurh from *No Country for Old Men*, but with more curiosity about people—Colin Hanks as another cop looking for redemption after a moment of cowardice, Oliver Platt as a businessman with tangible proof that God is real, and too many other colorful characters to list here. It captured the film's chilly look, and the humor that ensues when upper-Midwestern politeness comes up against multiple homicides, and even managed to work in the Coens' love of parables, as cops, crooks, and innocent bystanders shared folk tales that had powerful bearing on all the carnage being laid out before us.

It was a delight, and season 2 proved it to be no fluke, boogying back to 1979 to show us the full version of a mob-war story that season 1 had only hinted at. This time around, Patrick Wilson was our hero as a younger version of Tolman's father, and played the role as if it were a rebuttal to Tony Soprano's frequent questions about whatever happened to Gary Cooper. Around him, Hawley placed a dazzling array of vivid characters, played spectacularly by, among many others, Bokeem Woodbine (a loquacious gangster),

Zahn McClarnon (a Native American killer with his own agenda and a lifetime of pain behind it), Jean Smart (the cold matriarch of the Fargo syndicate), Ted Danson (Wilson's father-in-law, himself a quietly brave cop), Nick Offerman (a conspiracy-obsessed local lawyer), Bruce Campbell (Ronald Reagan, campaigning for the presidency), and Kirsten Dunst and Jesse Plemons (the mismatched civilian couple who inadvertently become the center of all the violence).

The Coen references became more frequent and varied, with bits of *Miller's Crossing*, *The Man Who Wasn't There*, and even *Raising Arizona* intermingling with the riffs on the original *Fargo*, yet the show somehow felt more like its own thing than ever before. At this point, the series could plausibly run for years, bouncing around different corners of the upper Midwest, without feeling like it's just repeating itself or what the Coens have done before.

So, you betcha, *Fargo* had no business working. But then it did.

—AS

Game of Thrones (HBO, 2011–present)

If *The Sopranos* and *Mad Men* were *The Godfather* and *Mean Streets* of early twenty-first-century TV drama—deeply personal works that elevated what was artistically possible in the medium, without initial worry about commerce—then perhaps *Game of Thrones* is the *Jaws*: a thrilling blockbuster that's often on creative par with its predecessors but successful on such a scale that it makes what came before seem like quaint little boutique hits. (That probably makes *The Walking Dead* the *Star Wars* of this analogy, though more in terms of its enormous popularity than its uneven quality.)

Game of Thrones is first and foremost a triumph of logistics. Writers David Benioff and D. B. Weiss have somehow managed to adapt ten hours of television per season from George R. R. Martin's increasingly long (and increasingly late) series of fantasy novels, *A Song of Ice and Fire*, featuring dozens of significant characters—like the Hydra of myth, if you cut off the head of one key player, three more will pop up to take his place—spread out across thousands of miles over a parallel world where a version of the War of the Roses now involves dragons, zombies, and other forms of magic. The production spans a large swath of Europe, including Northern Ireland, Croatia, Spain, and Iceland, with the crew filming in blocks based on location, so that all the scenes of a particular episode may take five months or more to film, compared to a couple of weeks at most for any other TV drama.

And when filming's done, somehow all these patchwork pieces of story and production come together to form a bracing mosaic about power and the terrible things men (and sometimes women) do to either get or keep it. The series vividly brings to life many of Martin's creations: noble, doomed Ned Stark (Sean Bean); verbally dextrous imp Tyrion Lannister (Peter Dinklage); Tyrion's smugly cruel sister, Cersei (Lena Headey); and far too many more to list, especially since the series has a nasty habit of killing off the characters we like the most, while rewarding the most despicable with longer lives and reigns.

The series can suffer from Martin's nihilist streak, which also manifests itself in the frequency, creativity, and duration of the physical torture depicted. And though it has a few strong female characters, it also relies too much on rape for shock value, and too often pairs monologues with shots of naked women. (Media scholar Myles McNutt dubbed the practice "sexposition.") But at its best—whether mounting an epic battle between zombies and humans in a frozen wasteland, or letting Tyrion match wits with the Mother of Dragons herself, Daenerys Targaryen (Emilia Clarke)—*Game of Thrones* does for fantasy what many of its HBO predecessors did for similarly disreputable genre fiction.

—AS

Girls (HBO, 2012–present)

The season 2 premiere of *Girls* opens with the show's heroine, Hannah (creator-star Lena Dunham), waking up in the narrow bed that she shares with her ex-boyfriend Elijah (Andrew Rannells), who realized he was gay after breaking up with her. "I'm sorry I have a boner," he says. "It's not for you." Then they laugh at the awkwardness of sharing a cramped and cluttered apartment. It's a funny, honest scene. But it might also remind the viewer that your twenties seem a lot less fun once you've moved beyond them.

The twenty-something, college-educated, white American urbanite's blissful unawareness of how little he and she actually know, including what a drag being young can sometimes be, has always been the main subject of *Girls*. Dunham, a young independent filmmaker raised among gallery artists, had no idea what a hornet's nest she would stir by having the audacity to put a sexually frank, often aggressively discomfiting comedy (or more often "comedy") on pay cable, give it an all-encompassing title, and skewer the girls' arrogance and cluelessness at every turn while also insisting that they and their often equally insufferable friends, lovers, and relatives were still worthy of empathy. And the sex. The sex! It's *Sex and the City* sex, raw but awkward and often deliberately mortifying.

Hannah starts out close friends with the blandly ambitious wannabe singer Marnie (Allison Williams), the acidic but free-spirited Brit Jessa (Jemima Kirke), and the initially meek but soon spirited Shoshanna (Zosia Mamet), then drifts apart from them. She bounces from one nonjob to another before landing a magazine internship and then going off to the Iowa Writers' Workshop, even though for long stretches of the show she seems to be more interested in telling people she's a writer than in perfecting her craft. She tries to keep a relationship going with her (maybe) soul mate Adam (Adam Driver), a muscular actor and recovering alcoholic who comes on like the gene-spliced offspring of Marlon Brando and Dustin Hoffman, but they seem to have nothing in common but

sex and conversation, and in the long haul, that's not enough. Actor-filmmaker Alex Karpovsky's character, Ray, flits around the margins of the show, managing the coffee shop where Hannah briefly works, pining for Shoshanna, and becoming a neighborhood organizer. His mix of exasperation, incredulity, and disdain makes him the closest thing to an audience surrogate on *Girls*. There are times when he seems disgusted with himself for caring so much about people he considers basically trivial.

Every now and then there's a lyrical moment, like Hannah eating a slice of cake on the Coney Island beach at dawn, or a formal experiment, like the parenthetical episode where Hannah hooks up with a married doctor (Patrick Wilson) in his brownstone and experiences the ups and downs of a long-term relationship in eighteen hours. The very specific milieu—pasty Williamsburg and Greenpoint, Brooklyn; Ground Zero for US hipster culture—is so spot-on that it's no wonder the residents tend to despise the show. It seems unlikely that *Girls* can sustain itself for much longer, because it's getting harder to believe that these characters would still want to keep tabs on one another now that their lives are so different. But it was—well, perhaps not *fun* while it lasted, but real. Sometimes beautiful.

—MZS

Jessica Jones (Netflix, 2015–present)

Jessica Jones is a pretty faithful adaptation (by writer Melissa Rosenberg) of Brian Michael Bendis and Michael Gaydos's early '00s comic series *Alias*, which was part of Marvel's new imprint for adult readers. It's set in a world with its own distinctive aesthetic, gathering tropes from film noir, hardboiled detective fiction, and David Cronenberg–style psychological horror, and uniting them beneath a jagged modern feminist sensibility.

Krysten Ritter (*Breaking Bad*, *Don't Trust the B---- in Apartment 23*) stars and narrates as Jessica, owner and sole employee of the Alias detective agency, who is hired by a Nebraska couple to find their missing daughter. Employing a storytelling style driven by submerged flashbacks and obliquely remembered incidents, it plunges the heroine into a *Chinatown*-deep conspiracy tale, fleshing out a past that was lost to Jessica after suffering a psychically invasive trauma at the hands of a serial abuser of women (David Tennant's Kilgrave) who's still wandering free. Her experience

is analogous to rape even though the show is never so blatant as to hang a simple label on it. Jessica's cool-tender affair with bartender and super-badass Luke Cage (Mike Colter) highlights cultural differences, frank sexuality, and a love of solitude rather than prurience and exoticism. (The camera worships Luke; this is a rare series that could be said to have a female gaze.)

Few superhero adaptations have tried harder to build a modern, multicultural, woman-centered universe not chained to dude nostalgia for burly men saving the world. One of Jessica's clients, Carrie-Ann Moss's attorney Jeri Hogarth (who was a man in the comics), is a lesbian, and the series does her the favor of treating her sexuality as different from but equal to all the other flavors of love and lust showcased on the series.

—MZS

The Leftovers (HBO, 2014–present)

In a second-season episode of Damon Lindelof and Tom Perrotta's drama set three years after an event known as the Sudden Departure, where 2 percent of the world's population suddenly disappeared without rhyme or reason as to who vanished and who didn't, a character tries to sell a memoir about her own troubled post-Departure life to a big publishing house. The publisher acknowledges that the material—involving families being torn apart, the many religious cults that sprang up in the wake of a cosmic tragedy that defied both scientific explanation and everything traditional religion had to say on the subject of the Rapture, death, destruction, and more—is inherently powerful, but complains that the writing is too dry.

"If you want them to connect with it," he tells his prospective author, "you have to *tell them how it felt.*"

Telling its audience how things feel has never been a problem for *The Leftovers*, an engrossing, devastating meditation on grief that's enraged some viewers and delighted others but never failed to capture the sense of loss, alienation, existential despair, and even madness pervading its intricately detailed, broken fictional world. In its first season, the series was an overwhelming experience for believers and deniers alike, even as it sometimes struggled to craft stories for each episode that went much beyond "Everyone still feels terrible. The end." In its second, it became more tonally and narratively diverse, but still tended to make its

viewers feel like they were trapped in the post-Departure world.

Though the series revolves around a supernatural event, it's hard not to find parallels to 9/11, the Sandy Hook massacre, and so many of the unfathomable catastrophes that have come to define our own lives. Time and again, the show asks, *How do you go on? How do you act like everything is still normal? How do you find meaning in a world where terrible things happen without warning or cause or pattern?* And it conveys that struggle through characters taking a wide variety of approaches to post-Departure life, played wonderfully by a cast that includes Justin Theroux (a cop who's either talking to angels or slowly being driven insane by it all); Amy Brenneman (his ex-wife, who for a time joined the show's chief cult, the Guilty Remnant, whose members wear white, don't speak, and chain-smoke, all to remind themselves and those around them that the world ended on Departure Day); Carrie Coon (a woman drawing on extraordinary reserves of strength after her husband and two small children vanished in the Departure); Ann Dowd (the smug leader of the local Guilty Remnant chapter, who later becomes an inescapable voice in Theroux's head); Liv Tyler (Dowd's spiritual successor, and in some ways an even more frightening villain); Christopher Eccleston (a minister whose personal struggles also blur the lines between divinity and madness); and, starting in the second season, Regina King and Kevin Carroll as a couple living in the one place on earth completely untouched by the Departure.

Like the members of the Guilty Remnant, the series is uncompromising in its commitment to making its audience uncomfortable. This is a bleak, difficult show to get through, and one with enough unsolved mysteries that it's hard to blame former *Lost* fans, or humans in general, for wanting nothing to do with it. But it's not misery porn, or a wallow; it's cathartic. There's genuine thought and artistry behind it all, masterful performances, immersive direction (by Peter Berg, Mimi Leder, and others), and the kind of casual, detailed world-building to which most TV science fiction aspires, but rarely achieves on this level.

Ultimately, trying to sing the praises of a show whose main character has apparently been to the afterlife and back twice (both times discovering that it's an upscale hotel with a karaoke bar) is a bit like trying to discuss religion with an atheist: You either believe or you don't.

For those who believe in *The Leftovers*, few modern TV series have ever struck as powerful a chord week after week.

—AS

Mr. Robot (USA, 2015–present)

"Hello, friend," Elliot Alderson tells us, before questioning the phrase. "'Hello, friend'? That's lame. Maybe I should give you a name. But that's a slippery slope. You're only in my head. We have to remember that. Shit. It's actually happening. I'm talking to an imaginary person."

We haven't seen Elliot at this point. He's just a disembodied voice, narrating his tale to an audience he has no idea is very real. He continues: "What I'm about to tell you is top secret, a conspiracy bigger than all of us. There's a powerful group of people out there that are secretly running the world. I'm talking about the guys no one knows about, the guys that are invisible. The top 1 percent of the top 1 percent. The guys that play God without permission.

"And now I think they're following me."

And with that, the bait is hooked, and *Mr. Robot* has us in its seductive, insidious clutches. It's a conspiracy thriller larded with pieces of other conspiracy thrillers, and gleefully mixes in other bits of pop culture iconography (*Fight Club* in particular is a huge influence) to become something that feels not like a rehash, but engrossingly new. It deploys a variety of devices that have become so overused on TV in recent years—in particular, that voice-over, which Elliot (Rami Malek, haunted, riveting) uses to tell us about his psyche, the world of computer security, his illegal drug regimen, his questionable mental health, his belief that the world's most powerful corporation is genuinely evil, and his involvement with a group of anarchist hackers called fsociety—that they should seem more played-out. But because Elliot is such an unreliable narrator—and aware of this fact, like the way he begins questioning the reality of the show's title character (Christian Slater) from the moment they meet—and has such difficulty interacting with others, it works.

Creator Sam Esmail gets Elliot's alienation across not only through writing, but directing. The show violates a half dozen rules of cinematic grammar in practically every shot, always finding a way to place Elliot or the other characters in a position too far to an edge of the frame, or too close to the camera, to convey that he and they feel overwhelmed by and disconnected from this great big scary modern world. When Elliot stages a prison break to help out a drug dealer who's kidnapped his girlfriend, only to discover that she's been dead for hours, the escaping inmates recede into the distant background, so that all we're paying attention to—all that matters—is Elliot's pain and disbelief. We become Elliot's "friend," whether we want to be or not.

—AS

Orange Is the New Black (Netflix, 2013–present)

Based on Piper Kerman's 2010 memoir, *Orange Is the New Black* is a comedy-drama about a clueless Yuppie named Piper Chapman (Taylor Schilling) who gets sent to a women's prison in Litchfield, Connecticut, for her long-ago and one-time-only participation in drug smuggling. She learns that her old sense of self means nothing there, if it was even solid to begin with. We meet her on the cusp of her prison stint and learn that she's a bisexual woman who had an intense postcollege affair with the woman who roped her into drug smuggling (Laura Prepon's Alex Vause), and that she settled down with a barely employed writer named Larry Bloom (Jason Biggs) and started a small business selling artisanal bath products. There's also a transgender character, Sophia Burset (played by African American transgender actress Laverne Cox), who enters the story with the eccentric definition of every other character and is never once presented as inherently comical or strange. The prison staff includes Michael Harney, Matt Peters, and Pablo Schreiber; all have been given actual characters to play rather than being reduced to mere foils for the inmates. An early scene involving Harney's character, a prison counselor named Sam Healy, hints at yet another of the show's agendas: to give American TV viewers a sense of the surreal inequities in the criminal justice system. "I've got a crack dealer who's doing nine months, and then I've got a lady who accidentally backed into a mailman who's doing four years," he tells Piper.

Orange is astute in showing how individuals struggle to maintain their individuality not just in the psychic cauldron of prison but in institutions of all kinds; the show's quilt of adjacent and interlocking subplots is mostly a bleak comedy with elements of satire, more reminiscent of *M*A*S*H* than *Prison Break* or *Oz*. The cast is packed with lively character actresses. Some could be called "names" (including former *Star Trek: Voyager* captain Kate Mulgrew as Red Reznikov, a Russian American who battles to control the kitchen), but most are unknowns who've landed their first breakthrough role (up-and-comers who've never had a recurring role on a series before, and likely wouldn't fit into an ensemble at a broadcast network, where the bandwidth of acceptable look/sound is much narrower). The series is adamant that the only barrier preventing us from feeling empathy for most strangers is the fact that they're strangers; even the most eccentric, off-putting, or scary characters on *Orange Is the New Black* are illuminated through flashbacks or startling twists of fate, disclosing new layers and drawing us closer than we could have imagined. Uzo Aduba's Suzanne "Crazy Eyes" Warren seems to skirt the edge of menacing racial stereotype until we learn that she was adopted and raised by white parents and struggles with mental illness; later she becomes an ambitious genre-fiction writer, penning a science-fiction erotica series titled *The Time-Hump Chronicles*. Taryn Manning's scheming, transphobic Tiffany "Pennsatucky" Doggett is a redneck—literally a snaggle-toothed one at first, owing to the effects of crystal meth use—who killed an abortion clinic nurse who made fun of her for having five abortions; but when Pennsatucky gets raped in season 3 by a prison guard, we feel sympathy for her, too, because nobody deserves that, no matter how ruthless or dishonest they are. ("Men being in charge has never done me any good," she admits.)

Many episodes are explorations of difference—black versus white versus brown, straight versus lesbian, male versus female, privileged versus poor—and how it affects whom we decide to befriend, oppose, sleep with, and betray. The inmates, the guards, the administrators, and their families are united by the knowledge that the penal system is broken and its gears grind up all who pass through them. The show's attention to the daily indignities of institutional life links it not to any other series about prisons or convicts, but to M*A*S*H, another story set in a real-life purgatory where survival is the goal and individuality is constantly being threatened by the demand for conformity or the threat of punishment. "Hey!" a guard shouts at Piper after she angrily pounds on a wall full of pay phones. "That's federal property." "You're federal property!" she replies. And she's right.

—MZS

Rectify (Sundance, 2013–present)

This series from writer-actor Ray McKinnon (*Deadwood*, *Sons of Anarchy*) examines the life of Daniel Holden (Aden Young), a convicted rapist and killer suddenly sprung from prison on a technicality, but it does so in a way that takes advantage of TV's endless capacity to extend and even pull apart time. Much of the action in the first season took place over six days, and there were many flashbacks and dream sequences; subsequent seasons have been nearly as compact. Any flourishes after that were mainly about pace and tone—slowing things down even more; zeroing in on a detail; lingering on a reaction.

Not once does the series tell us whether Daniel did or did not commit the crimes of which he was accused. Of course we get the sense that a lot of people believe he's innocent, especially his loyal sister and staunchest advocate, Amantha (Abigail Spencer, whose ability to project wary, cynical intelligence is unmatched). And we know that other characters can't be sure but still want to believe the best, such as Tawney Talbot (Adelaide Clemens), the wife of Daniel's stepbrother Teddy (Clayne Crawford). And there were people in law enforcement and government who either truly believe Daniel did it or convince themselves that they believe it because their careers are invested in that narrative: Sheriff Carl Daggett (J. D. Evermore) and former-prosecutor-turned-senator Roland Foulkes (Michael O'Neill), to name two. The second season's end brought new revelations (and an act of violence by Daniel) that complicated viewers' sympathies.

There's always a sense of a world beyond what we can see— not merely heaven or hell but an inscrutable clockwork machine somewhere high above that rains blessings and misfortunes on the just and the unjust alike. The characters' attempts to grasp these forces set *Rectify* apart from every other TV drama. Its monologues ring out with the cadences of scripture, and its ellipses hum with promise.

—MZS

Review (Comedy Central, 2014–present)

There's a downside to being any kind of pop culture critic. Movie reviewers have to annually grapple with Adam Sandler's latest, music critics have to listen to more Nickelback than should be legally allowed, and a TV critic may be ordered to write a *Keeping Up with the Kardashians* think piece at a moment's notice.

Still, we all have it much easier than *Review* protagonist Forrest MacNeil (Andy Daly), who fancies himself "a reviewer of life," tasked to experience whatever life events— drug addiction, road rage, participating in an orgy—his viewers assign him, then review them on a five-star scale. (There is no such thing as a zero-star review in Forrest's mind, so racism gets half a star.)

It's a bizarre concept to which Forrest and the show outside the show are spectacularly committed. Though Forrest occasionally wavers in fulfilling his assignments—he understandably tries to avoid eating fifteen pancakes ("an upsetting number of pancakes," as he puts it) in one sitting, until his malevolent producer Grant (James Urbaniak) compares it to the discovery of penicillin—he ultimately lets the job destroy every last good thing about his life. He gets divorced because a viewer asks him to, burns down his father's house because the fire extinguisher is too high to reach while he's reviewing what it's like to be a little person, starts a cult whose members are ultimately massacred by law enforcement, and winds up in jail after shooting a man while reviewing what it's like to murder someone.

Adapted from an Australian series by Daly, Jeffrey Blitz, and other writers, *Review* could have simply been a collection of goofy sketches that played off of Daly's innate good cheer: the world's blandest, least self-aware WASP putting himself through one humiliation after another because it's his duty. But the way the damage of each review piles on the one before it, both within each episode and across the series, renders it among the darkest shows ever put on television, yet in a way where the biggest laughs come out of the most horrific moments (the death of Forrest's father-in-law on a brief voyage into space), while the most profound emotion can come from the most ridiculous concepts (Forrest's imaginary friend Clovers being imaginarily shivved to death in prison).

Forrest hurts himself time and again by pushing his job past the limits of reason and good taste, but his show—the real one that we get to watch, at least—benefits enormously from always taking things that far.

—AS

Scandal (ABC, 2012–present)

On this electrifying, very busy melodrama, Washington power broker Olivia Pope (Kerry Washington) runs a PR operation with warehouse headquarters whose huge windows serve as a makeshift data-display wall. She and her colleagues spit out series creator Shonda Rhimes's (*Grey's Anatomy*) trademark "Aaron Sorkin ain't got nothin' on me" patter like machine-gun bullets. But, Olivia's big secret: She's had an affair with President Fitzgerald "Fitz" Thomas Grant (Tony Goldwyn). Vestiges of their love connection keep bobbing up and down in the show like rotten apples. It's an enjoyable, nutty series, set in a two-degrees-removed-from-reality world that might have reminded some viewers of *Dallas* and *Dynasty*. *Scandal* provides entertainment, and ups the ante with its military-industrial-political conspiracy that give the proceedings an unusual feel.

Still, this is far from a mere time waster. For all its knowingly ludicrous plotting, *Scandal* is smarter about race, class, gender, and sexual orientation, and how each of those elements factors into love and work, than almost any series that fancies itself deeper. And yet its gasp-inducing moments—such as Olivia likening her and Fitz's affair to Sally Hemings and Thomas Jefferson, or the flashbacks pointing out that Fitz is hung up on Olivia partly because she looks out for him in a way that his own parents never did, or the many scenes of the former Black Ops fixer Huck (Guillermo Diaz) enduring *24*-level torture and peeping through windows at the family he lost—are never set apart from the show's one-damned-thing-after-another plotlines. By season 4 the series had become more exhausting than exhilarating, leaving almost no taboo broken and no twist untwisted, but even a bad episode of *Scandal* is more engrossing than a lot of series with more pretensions.

—MZS

Transparent (Amazon, 2014–present)

"Are you saying you're going to start dressing up like a lady all the time?" Sarah asks her father, who stands before her in full feminine dress, hair, and makeup.

"My whole life, I've been *dressing up like a man*," her father explains. "*This* is me!"

This is the key conversation at the heart of *Transparent*, a series that couldn't be more timely in subject matter, form, or distribution. To Sarah Pfefferman (Amy Landecker), this is her father, Mort (Jeffrey Tambor), standing before her in drag; to Maura—as she now prefers to be called—Mort Pfefferman was always the disguise.

Transparent arrived at a tipping point for social awareness of transgender issues—the Kardashians would tell the show's creator, Jill Soloway, that

they watched it to better understand Caitlyn Jenner's transition. Soloway had firsthand knowledge of the subject, having witnessed one of her own parents come out as trans late in life, and she had a background as both a cable-drama writer (*Six Feet Under, United States of Tara*) and independent filmmaker (*Afternoon Delight*) that made her well-qualified personally and professionally to depict the specific, wildly dysfunctional rhythms of the Pfefferman clan, turning Maura and her adult kids—wealthy stay-at-home mom (and semi-closeted bisexual) Sarah, music industry player Josh (Jay Duplass), and chronic screwup Ali (Gaby Hoffmann)—into three-dimensional characters with a rich shared history that's conveyed with a few careful brushstrokes. The show is a triumph not only of nuanced writing but of intimate direction, which only became more beautiful over the course of the second season, which included flashbacks to Maura's mother, grandmother, and trans aunt in 1930s Berlin.

The show digs deep into the minutiae of the trans community and Maura's particular transition—proper pronoun usage, the difficulties of using a public restroom, which hormones to take and which surgeries to consider—but also into the way that Maura's long-held secret had ripple effects on her kids, which the entire family (including Judith Light—embracing her inner Jewish grandmother—as Maura's ex-wife) is only now starting to realize.

Tambor's mainly known as a comic actor, and while the show is laced with wry, dark humor, Maura herself is a very serious and sad character—she didn't grow up in a world of trans awareness, and thus is only coming out now to better enjoy what time she has left—and he captures every poignant nuance of her transformation. (What an amazing past three decades Tambor has had, with *The Larry Sanders Show* in the '90s, *Arrested Development* in the '00s, and his first Emmy ever coming for *Transparent* in 2015.)

The television business is going through its own remarkable transition now, exemplified by a show of this quality debuting on a streaming video service. Once upon a time, the idea of a show this nuanced, this complicated, and simply this great debuting outside of a more traditional means of TV distribution (say, on Showtime or FX) would have seemed ridiculous. But that kind of thinking feels almost as outmoded as the prejudice Maura and her trans friends are going through, both from the outside world and the family members who aren't prepared for how quickly the world, and their own lives, are changing.

—AS

Unbreakable Kimmy Schmidt (Netflix, 2015–present)

Tina Fey was head writer and a big star on *SNL*. She created and starred in *30 Rock*, which was nominated for more than a hundred Emmys during its run. It's not hard to understand why NBC would have wanted to be in business with Fey again on *Unbreakable Kimmy Schmidt*, which she cocreated with *30 Rock* vet Robert Carlock. But nor is it hard to understand why the Peacock ultimately backed out and sold the show to Netflix after the first season was produced.

This is a weird show, even by Fey standards, with as dark a backstory for its main character as any sitcom has ever tried. Kimmy (Ellie Kemper) was in the eighth grade when the Reverend Richard Wayne Gary Wayne (Jon Hamm) abducted her and placed her in an underground bunker with a handful of other women, all of them believing the Apocalypse had come and they were the only survivors. After fifteen years of captivity—and, as she reluctantly acknowledges later, "weird sex stuff"—she and the other "Indiana mole women" are rescued, and Kimmy attempts to start over by moving to New York.

The series deals mostly with Kimmy's new life in the Big Apple, where she becomes roommate to flamboyant unemployed actor Titus Andromedon (Tituss Burgess) and nanny to the children of vapid socialite Jacqueline Voorhees (Jane Krakowski), a Lakota woman passing for white. But Kimmy's time in the bunker is never far behind, and you can imagine NBC executives getting very uncomfortable at the thought of having to market the show, or deal with complaints from survivors of kidnapping and/or sexual abuse who might feel Fey and Carlock are making light of the whole subject.

Thanks to Fey's and Carlock's deftness as writers who can wring laughs out of taboo subjects, and especially thanks to the joy radiating from Ellie Kemper every minute she's onscreen, the series never feels bogged down by, or even disrespectful of, the ordeal that made Kimmy the woman she is today.

Instead, it's a ridiculous cracked-mirror view of every wide-eyed-girl-in-the-big-city story ever told, loaded with the same kinds of bizarre jokes, unexpectedly pointed social commentary (Titus is treated better dressed as a werewolf than as a gay black man), and irresistible song parodies (including that earworm of a theme—*They alive, dammit!*) that made *30 Rock* so great—only now in a place where Fey never has to apologize for the low ratings, because

nobody outside Netflix corporate knows what they are.

—AS

UnREAL (Lifetime, 2015–present)

The rise of the cable antihero drama and that of reality TV began around the same time, but the two seemed like matter and antimatter, destined to explode if they ever came into contact. Instead, the two opposites fused together perfectly with *UnREAL*, a scathing drama about the producers of a dating show very much like *The Bachelor* (where Sarah Gertrude Shapiro, who created *UnREAL* with Marti Noxon, used to work).

Quinn (Constance Zimmer), who has thrown her whole life into running shows like this, is unapologetic about the way she and her colleagues manipulate contestants into degrading themselves and how they contrive situations and edit footage to turn complicated human beings into two-dimensional TV characters. (Defending the casting of a woman with PTSD whom they will portray as "the crazy one," Quinn shrugs and says, "She knew what she was signing on for.") Her top lieutenant, Rachel (Shiri Appleby), acts like she regrets ever descending into this pit of lies (she's fond of wearing a "This Is What a Feminist Looks Like" T-shirt), yet she's even better—and more ruthless—at getting the contestants to act against their own best interests.

The dialogue is cutting, the performances layered and charismatic, and the writing has as much to say about gender norms in the twenty-first century as it does about the way dating shows help shape or reinforce them. And somehow, *UnREAL* threads the needle so that it's just as addictive to reality TV obsessives as to those who view series like *The Bachelor* as a blight on our culture.

—AS

Veep (HBO, 2012–present)

If Hollywood is high school with money, Washington is high school with power; or so it seems in *Veep*, the HBO comedy starring Julia Louis-Dreyfus as Selina Meyer, the vice president of the United States, from Scottish writer-producer Armando Iannucci. All of the characters are overgrown adolescents—bitchy, pouty, and narcissistic. And as it happens, they're employed in a field that equals showbiz in its immaturity, treachery, and obsession with surfaces. *Arrested Development*'s Tony Hale plays Gary, the vice president's "body man" and chief assistant, a lovable wretch whose foot is permanently lodged in his mouth. Anna Chlumsky is Amy, the veep's chief of staff, who always has one eye on her smartphone. Reid Scott's Dan is a sadistic but resourceful political fixer whom Selina ends up hiring because he's "a shit" and "I *need* a shit." Mike (Matt Walsh) is the world-weary press spokesman who pretends to have a beloved dog so that he can use it as an excuse to escape unpleasant social obligations (his officemates call the imaginary canine a "bull-shitsu"). The insufferably smug White House liaison Jonah (Timothy Simons) wields his West Wing access like a cudgel and tries to leverage his proximity to power to score dates with interns, as well as with Amy, who loathes him. Despite the hopeful *West Wing*–style credits music, the series feels like a live-action version of *Doonesbury* with baroque profanity and metaphors. "If you can get a Senate reform bill through the place it's designed to reform," a senator says, "that would be like persuading a guy to fist himself!"

As Selina, a former senator, Louis-Dreyfus draws on her loopy, self-involved *Seinfeld* persona but adds hints of cynicism and brittleness. Everyone around Selina is likewise selfish and image-obsessed. This is a shark-tank world of a type that HBO specializes in; the ego-warring over perks, loyalty, and respect might remind you of the cable channel's other classic half-hour studies in bad behavior: *The Larry Sanders Show*, *Curb Your Enthusiasm*, and the brilliant, short-lived Lisa Kudrow vehicle *The Comeback*.

—MZS

ETC....

American Crime Story (FX, 2016–present) The addictive first season of this anthology drama, about the O.J. trial, set an incredibly high bar that we hope future installments can clear...*Archer* (FX, 2010–present) What if Inspector Clouseau were as hypersexual and unerringly lethal as James Bond, and every time he opened his mouth, a frat bro's voice came out? The humor is so scabrous and weird, the cocktail-cool graphic designs are so pleasing, and the action is so inventively choreographed (better than most live-action spy film violence, honestly) that it's the closest thing to brain candy on cable right now...*Bob's Burgers* (Fox, 2011–present) Warm, weird animated comedy about a family as off-kilter as the ingredients in the title character's Burger of the Day, featuring some of the wildest musical numbers this side of *Crazy Ex-Girlfriend*...*Brooklyn Nine-Nine* (Fox, 2013–present) Crackerjack ensemble comedy from several *Parks and Rec* alums, in

which Andre Braugher proves his talents can be just as powerful when applied to the silliest of humor as when he was being deadly serious on *Homicide* and elsewhere...*The Carmichael Show* (NBC, 2015–present) Thought-provoking and funny in equal measure, comedian Jerrod Carmichael's multi-cam sitcom is a worthy descendant of Norman Lear...*Casual* (Hulu, 2015–present) Part of the rising tide of TV shows with the tone and artistry of independent films, this dramedy about profoundly damaged siblings who hurt as much as help each other's chances at happiness features a remarkably layered performance from Michaela Watkins...*Crazy Ex-Girlfriend* (CW, 2015–present) Former YouTube star Rachel Bloom's musical-comedy-romance raised hackles with its title, but the series is considerably deeper and more complex than the name, something akin to *Seinfeld* or *BoJack Horseman* with Broadway-style song-and-dance numbers, about the human tendency to see one's own desires and problems as the most important things in life and everyone else's as a distraction...*Empire* (Fox, 2014–present) *Dallas* with hip-hop and a predominantly black cast, it surges relentlessly forward, packing enough plot twists for a whole season of other shows into single episodes, always cranking the emotional volume to 11... *Fresh Off the Boat* (**ABC, 2015–present**) Comedy about an Asian American family in '90s Orlando is a fine, funny example of why TV benefits as much creatively as socially from diversifying the kind of people and stories that we see... *Halt and Catch Fire* (**AMC, 2014–present**) and *Silicon Valley* (**HBO, 2014–present**) Two excellent shows set in different eras, and wildly different genres, about how goddamn hard it is to find both fortune and happiness in the tech field... *It's Always Sunny in Philadelphia* (**FX/FXX, 2005–present**) DIY sitcom about a quintet of grubby sociopaths has run forever without losing its rough edges or ability to inspire howling laughter... *iZombie* (**CW, 2015–present**) Supernatural/procedural mash-up from the *Veronica Mars* team, it abandons nearly everything from the comic book on which it's based, but is so sharp and fun, it serves as a reminder that adaptations don't have to be faithful to be good... *Jane the Virgin* (**CW, 2014–present**) That rare, magical beast: a spot-on parody (of telenovelas) that simultaneously functions as a sincere, well-crafted version of the thing it's parodying... *Master of None* (**Netflix, 2015–present**) Half romcom, half anthropology, made special by cocreator/star Aziz Ansari's irrepressible curiosity about the world around him... *The Mindy Project* (**Fox, 2012–2015; Hulu, 2015–present**) Creator and star Mindy Kaling segued seamless from *The Office* to this romantic comedy that's also a meditation on the allure of the romantic comedy, as well as a look at the complexities of modern dating and (to a lesser extent) what it's like to be an Indian American woman in a culture and a profession (medicine) that's still very white... *New Girl* (**Fox, 2011–present**) Profoundly uneven but explosively funny hangout comedy that's at its best when it forgets about pesky things like story and logic and just lets things get weird... *Rick and Morty* (**Adult Swim, 2013–present**) Inventive animated sci-fi comedy that crosses barriers of good taste at least as often as its characters cross dimensions... *You're the Worst* (**FX/FXX, 2014–present**) A dark, touching, raucous romantic comedy about two people who would be horrified to discover they're the leads in a romantic comedy.

▪ A CERTAIN REGARD ▪

(Shows we love for one strange reason or another)

American Family (PBS, 2002–2004)

Showtime's *Resurrection Blvd.* (2000–2002) was the first dramatic series about a Latino family on US TV: a multigenerational saga about the Santiagos of East Los Angeles, a clan whose identity is built as much around boxing as the experience of being Mexican American. *American Family*, which debuted in 2002, was a more ambitious and arresting work, aiming to be something like a Latino *Rich Man, Poor Man* with magical realist touches. Created by director Gregory Nava, who'd been refining the idea since the 1995 feature film *Mi Familia* (*My Family*), the program was originally intended for CBS, but the network bumped it after deeming the pilot insufficiently commercial. To be fair, it was: Nava, his regular cinematographer Reynaldo Villalobos, and his star and coproducer Edward James Olmos (who also acted in *Mi Familia*) rooted the story in current political reality, to an extent not seen since Norman Lear's 1970s sitcoms. The second season went several steps beyond that, telling a serialized, thirteen-episode story that jumped between the present day and the Mexican Revolution, the event that sent the Gonzalez family from Mexico to the United States. It also confronted the divisiveness of the Iraq War (which had started only a year earlier) head-on: Olmos's character, Jess Gonzalez, a politically conservative barber and Korean War veteran, fights about it with his liberal lawyer daughter (Constance Marie), believing that they're obligated to support the war because his son (Yancey Arias) is an Army doctor. The opening of season 2 is the most dazzling technical achievement of its TV decade: a thirty-eight-minute tracking shot that moves through and around the Gonzalez household during a party, weaving in ghostly visitations by ancestors from another century.

—MZS

American Horror Story (FX, 2011–present)

Ryan Murphy and Bradley Falchuk's horror series was the first
blockbuster prime-time series to
reinvent the anthology, changing
the unit of measure from the
episode to the season. (See also
ABC's unrelated but incredible
American Crime, which may have
been canceled by the time you
read this, but whose second season you should hunt down by any
means necessary.) Cast members
(including Sarah Paulson, Jessica
Lange, Zachary Quinto, Kathy
Bates, and Angela Bassett) reappear in consecutive seasons as
new characters in new story
lines, nearly always a Frankenstein hybrid of several touchstone
series, films, or horror genres. Seasons 1 (*Murder House*) and 2 (*Asy-
lum*) are the best, marrying the
show's trademark baroque visuals,
gross-out violence, pervy sex, and
anything-for-a-jump-scare aesthetic to social criticism and historical muckraking; subsequent
installments are skippable, unless
you're a Lange or Paulson completist, or can't get enough of endless Steadicam shots and Dutch
angles.

—MZS

Beavis and Butt-Head (MTV, 1993–1997, 2011)

Daria (MTV, 1997–2002)

"*Huh-huh, huh-huh, huh-huh.*" That
hoarse, cretinous laugh was also
the sound of cash registers ringing
at MTV, where Mike Judge's *Beavis
and Butt-Head* improbably became
a ratings powerhouse. The characters began life as characters in
Judge's 1992 short "Frog Baseball,"
which single-handedly stole the
traveling theatrical anthology *Spike
& Mike's Sick and Twisted Festival
of Animation*; the duo are delin-
quent, obtuse, fire-obsessed best
friends who are never shown smoking pot but always seem stoned to
the point of numbness. They're such
badly behaved and incompetent
students that in one episode they
briefly get demoted to kindergar-
ten; at home (in Highland, Texas, or
so we're told) they seem to exist in
a world without parents. Although
they wander around the neighborhood getting into trouble (at one
point they become convinced that
a homeless man is a werewolf),
they spend most of their afternoons
fused to a couch, scarfing sodas
and junk food and commenting
on trash talk shows, infomercials,
and (especially) MTV videos. Their
guttural witticisms, showcased in

stand-alone shorts ranging from five to eleven minutes in length, were a suburban waste-case's answer to *Mystery Science Theater 3000*, written and performed by Judge (as both characters) with unhinged enthusiasm. (Beavis frequently imagines himself as the Great Cornholio, who "needs TP for my bunghole.")

The TV-watching segments were the show's big draw, putting a snarky postmodern wrapper around MTV's already self-consciously artificial music programming. Some of the boys' offhand remarks were clever, in their way ("These guys are pretty cool, even though they're sixty," Beavis says of Aerosmith), and they qualified as cultural commentary: They were dispatches from two fools live-casting a slow-motion apocalypse that was consuming them as well, even though they didn't know it. Although the show's dependence on then-recent pop culture references makes it almost incomprehensible to anyone who wasn't actively watching it in the '90s, its satire of American dunderheadedness hasn't aged a day; Beavis and Butt-Head are entitlement personified, sexist and classist, arrogant and dense, proudly unteachable in every subject, including life lessons. *South Park* creators Trey Parker and Matt Stone consider *Beavis and Butt-Head* a primary influence; the

show paved the way for Judge's superior and much sweeter *King of the Hill*, the 1997 feature film *Beavis and Butt-Head Do America*, and Judge's *Idiocracy*, a nightmarish slapstick comedy set in a postapocalyptic world in which the boys might be considered wise men.

The power of seeing yourself represented onscreen should not be underestimated; it kept the animated sitcom *Daria* on MTV for five seasons. Spun-off from Judge's *Beavis and Butt-Head*, the show was executive-produced by two of Judge's writers, Glenn Eichler and Susie Lewis, but otherwise had little in the way of continuity. Previously a foil for Beavis and Butt-Head who showed up to harsh their buzz and remind audiences that they weren't hero-worship material, Daria Morgendorffer was a sprightly-cranky beacon of hope to every woman who had ever felt marginalized by her education, her wit, her cynicism, and her reluctance to give in to sexist messages that urged teenage girls to act peppy and harmless, obsess over clothes and makeup, and hide their eccentric specialness to make boys like them. (Appropriately, the theme song was "Standing on My Neck," by Splendora.) The supporting cast included Daria's mother, Helen, her father, Jake, her younger sister, Quinn, and her best friend, Jane Lane; her suburban town of Lawndale was just as vacuous as Beavis and Butt-Head's but more realistic and ultimately hopeful, if only because it allowed a character as rich as Daria to live in it without losing her marbles.

—MZS

The Bernie Mac Show (Fox, 2001–2006)

Stand-up legend Bernie Mac starred as his comic alter ego, Bernie "Mac" McCullough, a comedian who takes in his drug-addict sister's three kids and tries to raise them with help from his devoted wife, Wanda (Kellita Smith). The show's lovingly directed, single-camera format evoked *Malcolm in the Middle*, but the tone, language, and worldview were unapologetically and innovatively black, in a way that channeled Tim Reid's CBS art-object *Frank's Place*, and prefigured the arrival of *Black-ish* and *Empire* a decade-plus later. (*Black-ish* star Anthony Anderson showed up near the end of the run as the children's previously AWOL father, giving this sitcom and his own an accidental sense of artistic continuity.) Mac's gruff demeanor and defiant, direct-address monologues marked him as a different kind of sitcom dad, working-class in his outlook

and Jackie Gleason–esque in his tendency to go ballistic. The series was distinguished by its cultural details, knockabout humor, and corner-barbershop worldview (Mac caused a minor outcry in the pilot when he pledged to bust disobedient children's heads "until the white meat shows"), and by its impressive array of guest stars, which included Don Rickles, Angela Bassett, Parker Posey, Stone Cold Steve Austin, Wesley Snipes, Charles Barkley, and, of all people, Hugh Hefner.

—MZS

The Bold Ones: The Senator (NBC, 1970–1971)

Shown as part of an "umbrella" program of series that rotated in and out of the same lineup, *The Senator* started out as a TV movie (*A Clear and Present Danger*, not to be confused with the Jack Ryan adventure) and aired seven regular episodes; it stars Hal Holbrook as Senator Hays Stowe, who tries to implement idealism and work out political impasses within the system, which isn't easy considering how inert and corrupt it can be. Most of the program is shot in a documentary style, letting complex arguments play out in real time, like a town meeting scene in a Frederick Wiseman documentary or an argument over protest strategy in a Ken Loach film. It has such immediacy that when you watch it, you feel as though you're in the room with these characters, in the early '70s, getting a sense of what life was actually like.

—MZS

A Charlie Brown Christmas and It's the Great Pumpkin, Charlie Brown! (CBS, 1965 and 1966)

Based on Charles Schulz's comic strip, directed by Bill Melendez, and scored by Vince Guaraldi, these two *Peanuts* specials represent the creative peak for the trio and rank among the finest single episodes of anything to air on American television. The first, a melancholy examination of the true meaning of Christmas, has been referenced in everything from the early films of Wes Anderson to *South Park* and *Arrested Development*; the latter was spoofed in a *Simpsons'* "Treehouse of Horror" episode and is never far from the minds of children on Halloween who would really rather get candy in their goodie bag than a rock.

—MZS

Chuck season 2 (NBC, 2008–2009)

Sometimes, TV shows peak in their first seasons, either because the idea has been rolling around in the creator's head for years until it's just right, because the concept is inherently limited, or because the show simply burns through too much story up front.

Sometimes, though, shows are thrown together in relative haste, and need time to sort the wheat from the chaff, and don't really come into their own until season 2. Case in point: *Chuck*, a goofy action comedy about Chuck Bartowski (Zachary Levi), a geek at a big-box store who unwittingly uploads an entire government intelligence database into his brain. Created by Chris Fedak and Josh Schwartz (whose *The O.C.* is a classic case of peaking in season 1 and not having enough plot left after), *Chuck* went through a lot of trial and error in its abbreviated first season as it tried to figure out the right balance between spy adventure and wacky store hijinks, and how to get the tone quite right so that one minute you'd take Chuck's peril seriously, or his feelings for his gorgeous handler, Sarah Walker (Yvonne Strahovski), and then the next laugh at Chuck and best friend, Morgan Grimes (Josh Gomez), swapping nerd references at the store.

When *Chuck* returned for year two, it was a more confident, more cohesive, and simply more fun show, having made small but crucial improvements up and down the board. Morgan was a lot more entertaining once he stopped being an obstacle to Chuck's secret identity, for instance, and the spy missions (also involving Adam Baldwin as the sadistically proficient John Casey) became more satisfying once the show started stunt-casting the bad guys and assets, allowing the mere presence of a John Larroquette or Chevy Chase to fill in characterization there wasn't time to otherwise craft on a show with lots of moving pieces. The action, the comedy, and the romance all began working in perfect harmony.

It didn't become great art, but it wasn't trying to be. It was just pleasurable genre television being done exceptionally well, giving its fans such weekly joy that they became involved in one of the more famous Save Our Show campaigns ever, buying Subway sandwiches in droves to encourage the sponsor to get involved in keeping the show alive.

Chuck actually stuck around for three more seasons, produced on a lower budget and living perpetually on the edge of cancellation, never again quite recapturing that perfect balance of season 2. But for that one year, *Chuck* was everything a young Chuck Bartowski might have fantasized a show about his life could one day look like.

—AS

The Comeback (HBO, 2005 and 2014)

This dark sitcom from producer Michael Patrick King (*Sex and the City*) and producer-star Lisa Kudrow is about a washed-up TV comedy star who tries to revive her career by hiring a camera crew to shoot her latest gig on a sitcom. It's cringe TV at its finest—a comic acid bath few viewers were brave enough (or masochistic enough) to dip into when it first aired in 2005, although during the intervening decade its reputation grew to the point where HBO brought King and Kudrow back for another go-round. Every week *The Comeback* forced viewers to ask what, exactly, they want from their protagonists: hard truth or audience-coddling fantasy. It divided viewers' sympathies, encouraging them to root for Kudrow's character, the ditsy, aging sitcom starlet Valerie Cherish, then having her scheme, overreach, and self-destruct so horribly that it was hard to look at the screen. The 2014 series was even more punishing because Valerie, already considered too old to be bankable in 2005, was a decade older but just as desperate and deluded. Like *The Larry Sanders Show*, the classic Canadian media satire *More Tears*, and Steve Coogan's various Alan Partridge programs for English TV, *The Comeback* reminded us that comedy is often tragedy that's happening to someone else, and that behind each joke, there's a grievance.

—MZS

Cop Rock (ABC, 1990)

Was Steven Bochco's musical police drama *Cop Rock* the most ridiculous show ever to air on an American broadcast network or one of the boldest? The latter—which is not to say that everything in it worked, but that its full-throated belief in its vision was unique, and it deserves a reappraisal. Bochco somehow convinced ABC to green-light this chimera of a show after his critically acclaimed one-two punch of *Hill Street Blues* and *L.A. Law*, and he spent his creative capital by envisioning a musical melodrama about the intersection of law enforcement, the criminal courtroom, city hall, and the private lives of citizens with original songs by Randy Newman (who appeared with a band in the opening credits) and characters segueing from spoken dialogue to rock, blues, and rap songs and back again. The pilot featured gang members rapping about the racism and brutality of police while being rousted, and a jury returning a verdict by bursting into a gospel number titled "Guilty."

Main characters included Peter Onorati as Vincent LaRusso, a corrupt detective in the vein of *Hill Street Blues'* Sal Benedetto, who eventually ends up in prison surrounded by criminals he'd hounded, abused, or framed; Ronny Cox as the harried police chief; and *Blues* costar Barbara Bosson (Bochco's then-wife) as the mayor. Some of the actors were not really what you'd call singers, but others (notably Onorati) were terrific; the supporting cast included Vondie Curtis-Hall, Paul McCrane, and Anne Bobby, as well as Kathleen Wilhoite as a manipulative addict who, in the pilot's chilling final scene, sings a Newman-penned love song to her infant before selling it to black marketers for drug money.

English playwright Dennis Potter had been working in this vein in England for years to great acclaim, in such miniseries as 1978's *Pennies from Heaven* and 1986's *The Singing Detective* (Bochco cited the latter as a primary influence), but American network TV was inhospitable to the very idea of *Cop Rock*, despite inroads made by such formally playful predecessors as *Moonlighting* and *St. Elsewhere*. The series ended up on nearly every TV critic's year-end Worst list, and the ratings cratered a bit more each week, until ABC finally canceled it after its eleventh episode. Viewed in succession, though, its lone season holds together well, despite lumpy storytelling and some songs that feel like placeholders; the middle section has the lurid power of a telenovela and the shamelessness of an Andrew Lloyd Webber musical. *Glee* is *Cop Rock*'s hormonal daughter.

—MZS

Crime Story season 1 (NBC, 1986–1987)

One of the lesser known but more fondly remembered Michael Mann productions is *Crime Story*. Although it was packaged and sold as a period cousin of *Miami Vice*, the shows had little in common besides cops-and-robbers scripts, a fondness for reflective surfaces, and a deft sense of how to use pop music to enhance the mood. Where *Vice* was an internalized, at times abstract series set in a kind of dream space, *Crime Story* was more concrete—an epic cat-and-mouse chase pitting Major Crimes Unit detective Mike Torello (Dennis Farina) and his crew against an up-and-coming mobster named Ray Luca (Anthony Denison), who wanted to conquer the world of organized crime overnight and was talented and ruthless enough to pull it off. Set in early 1960s Chicago and Las Vegas and shot on location in both cities, the series was cocreated by screenwriter Gustave Reininger and Chuck Adamson, a former Chicago police detective turned producer who was a close friend of Mann's.

Set on the brink of mass revolt against the status quo, *Crime Story* showed the American city's tribal mentality fading, and the melting-pot ideal being replaced by Jesse Jackson's patchwork-quilt metaphor. The principal cast included actors who had originally been policemen or crooks and had worked with Mann on his 1981 feature *Thief*, in which the director perversely cast cops as criminals and criminals as cops. (Farina, who had a bit part as a gangster's henchman in *Thief*, was a former Chicago police detective before he turned to acting, while John Santucci, who played Luca's dumb but loyal right-hand man, Pauli Taglia, was an infamous jewel thief who had been arrested by Adamson.) Torello's Major Crimes Unit included the cigar-chomping, shotgun-toting Walter Clemmons (Paul Butler), a black detective whose pioneering presence went largely unremarked by perps because they didn't want to get their heads busted. The criminals' ranks included Italians, Irish, blacks, and Jews (played by Jon Polito, Andrew Dice Clay, David Caruso, Ted Levine, and Michael Madsen, among others) who set aside ethnic hatred in the name of filthy lucre.

The Sopranos, Lost, Deadwood, The Wire, The Shield, Mad Men, and *Breaking Bad* walked a wide-open road that *Crime Story* had done much to pave. The series was a densely plotted serialized drama: Imagine *The Godfather: Part II* flattened into a comic strip. Each episode began with a recap of the plot up to then, but after a few episodes, there was so much to summarize that the recaps themselves became confusing; this, coupled with the show's brutal violence and period ambience, probably sealed its fate. Although *Crime Story* did okay in its original time slot, Fridays after *Miami Vice*, NBC moved the show to Tuesdays to counterprogram ABC's *Moonlighting*, which had a similarly retro flavor but more comedy and sex appeal. With its ratings in free fall, *Crime Story* got a surprise second-season order from the network. But that wasn't the end of its troubles. It had reached a natural

endpoint in a literally explosive season 1 finale, which wrapped up every loose end; it took a mighty display of pretzel logic to continue the tale. Add in the crippling effect of the 1987–1988 writers' strike, and the result was a sophomore season so inferior to the first that even some die-hard fans would rather pretend it never happened.

—MZS

Dallas (CBS, 1978–1991; TNT, 2012–2014)

"Like my daddy always said: If you can't get in the front door, just go around to the back." That's one cold pearl of wisdom from J. R. Ewing (Larry Hagman), the drawling Richard III of nighttime soaps, the rapacious engine that powered through every episode of *Dallas*, making deals and bedding women and pitting fellow members of the Ewing clan against one another to control their family estate, Southfork, and their family-owned petroleum empire.

The Ewings were like a lusty cartoon version of the Texas oil clan in the novel and movie *Giant*; the bad guy even had the same initials as James Dean's antihero Jett Rink, and was one step up on the capitalist evolutionary ladder; he was less interested in drawing crude oil out of the ground than in processing and shipping it all over the world, and building Ewing Oil into a megacorporation to rival Exxon or Mobil. Well—that and getting laid with every big-haired vixen in North Texas. His moral counterweight, Bobby Ewing (Patrick Duffy), was as decent and compassionate as J.R. was ruthless, though he had his moments of weakness. The supporting cast included Barbara Bel Geddes as the family matriarch, Miss Ellie (replaced for one season by It's a Wonderful Life star Donna Reed when Bel Geddes briefly "retired" from acting); Jim Davis as Miss Ellie's rock-solid husband, Jock Ewing, the company's founder; Victoria Principal as Bobby's wife, Pamela, daughter of the rival Barnes family; Linda Gray as J.R.'s tormented alcoholic wife, Sue Ellen; Charlene Tilton as Lucy Ewing, J.R. and Bobby's scheming, sensual teenage niece; and Steve Kanaly as ranch hand Ray Krebbs, Jock's bastard son.

Their weekly melodramas made Dallas the highest rated and most influential of the nighttime soaps that were all the rage in the 1970s and '80s, thanks in large part to the success of this series. It inspired one official spin-off, Knots Landing (CBS, 1979–1993), and two ABC imitators: Dynasty (1981–1989), basically Dallas Goes to Denver; and its own proprietary spin-off, The Colbys (1985–1987), which followed members of the Dynasty clan to Los Angeles. Viewed through the lens of today's more jaded viewers, the show seems exuberant but artless—a brightly lit, indifferently directed, and obvious potboiler. But those qualities were always the key to its success; you were never in doubt as to who any of these people were, and the only mystery was what treachery J.R. would pull off next. He dominated every scene, even ones he wasn't in, because, like a Shakespearean villain, he was the only character who seemed aware that he was in a play.

The show perfected the art of the audience-torturing cliff-hanger when, at the end of its third season, J.R. got shot by an unseen assailant (later revealed to be Mary Crosby's Kristin Shepard, Sue Ellen's sister); fans and the media went wild speculating on how the story would resolve, and the producers spent the rest of the show's run trying to top themselves, leading to escalating series of absurdities, including an assassination attempt on Bobby, Bobby's death in a car wreck, and Bobby's mysterious return in a shower scene, which revealed that the preceding season had been a dream.

Dallas returned to TV in 2012 via cable channel TNT, with Hagman reprising his role, and seeming all the more malevolent having survived so long; with his Heat-Miser eyebrows and avowed preference for money over sex, he seemed as agelessly malevolent as *The Simpsons'* Mr. Burns, who got shot in a cliff-hanger that itself spoofed *Dallas*. Hagman finally died in 2013 of the cancer he'd battled for twenty years; both *Dallas* and the tradition of the middlebrow network prime-time soap died with him, although traces of its DNA can be found in everything from *The Sopranos* and *Boardwalk Empire* to *Revenge* and *Scandal*—and, of course, *Empire* and *Nashville*.

—MZS

Dexter season 4 (Showtime, 2009)

Showtime has this unfortunate ongoing habit of airing shows with limited premises that run forever because they're too popular not to. *Homeland* is a recent victim of this phenomenon (see page 326), but never was it more obvious than with *Dexter*, a drama about a serial killer trained by his late cop father to channel his psychopathic instincts in a socially useful way, by killing only other killers. Early on, the show had a great lead performance by Michael C. Hall, a sharp visual sense, and a cheeky sense of humor. It just stayed on the air much too long, until the creative team first developed Stockholm syndrome with the eponymous character and began treating him as a hero, then ran out of ideas entirely and ended the series with Dexter randomly becoming a lumberjack. (And not the fun, cross-dressing, Monty Python kind.)

There's a version of the series that could have gone down as a classic, where it ran only three years. Leave the first season intact so the audience can get to know Dexter, his methods, and the people around him. Then keep season 2's arc where the police get wise to Dexter's activities, if not his secret identity as one of their own forensic analysts, but don't wimp out at the end by having Dexter's crazy girlfriend murder an innocent police officer, rather than letting him do it. Then skip over the misconceived third season with Jimmy Smits as a DA trying to apprentice under Dexter, and go straight to the show's best year, featuring the cat-and-mouse game between Dexter and Arthur Mitchell (John Lithgow), aka the infamous Trinity Killer.

Structurally, the Trinity season was a rehash of the first, but Lithgow was mesmerizing as a kindly old man who was so cruel underneath. And the climax, where Dexter kills Arthur, then comes home to find that Arthur had already murdered Dexter's wife, Rita (Julie Benz), and left their baby son, Harrison, crying in a pool of her blood—repeating the cycle of violence that began when young Dexter found himself covered in his own dead mother's blood—was such a perfect ending not only to that season, but to *Dexter* as a whole, that continuing the series felt redundant.

All stories come to an end. But the economics of the TV business mean some shows stick around long after their stories essentially ended, and eventually turn their protagonists into lumberjacks.

—AS

Dragnet (NBC, 1951–1959, 1967–1970)

"This is the city: Los Angeles, California. I work here. I'm a cop." "Just the facts, ma'am." "Ladies and gentlemen, the story you are about to see is true. The names have been changed to protect the innocent." These oft-repeated phrases defined Sgt. Joe Friday (Jack Webb), a poker-faced bulldog of an L.A. cop who investigated all manner of crimes, from murder, racketeering, and armed robbery to grifting, prostitution, and petty drug dealing. He dragged the truth out of liars by tricking, needling, threatening, cajoling, and outsmarting them, always stopping short of evidence planting, torture, and other extralegal methods. Friday's interrogations alongside his more easygoing partners formed the template for all buddy-cop stories, and most buddy stories, period.

Film noir and the hard-boiled detective novel strongly influenced Webb, the show's creator, coproducer, head writer, and star. Webb was a World War II washout who reinvented himself as a radio announcer and actor, penning *Dragnet* in a purplish macho style modeled on Raymond Chandler. ("You got nice eyes, for a cop," an overconfident dame tells Friday in season 1's "The Hammer." "And I bet your mother had a loud bark," he replies.) The success of *Dragnet* made Webb a star on radio (where a version of the program ran from 1949 to 1957) and then on TV. The fat-free storytelling, which leaned on Friday's voice-over narration (a holdover from radio), was influential as well. It is hard to imagine such plot-and-character-driven, stubbornly non-arty crime series as *Columbo*, the various *Law & Orders* and *CSIs*, or *Monk* existing without its example. Webb treated each case like a terse short story, front-loading the partners' approach to crime scene investigations and interrogations with background details and using the walk-aways to set up the next scene or foreshadow complications. It also gave worldwide positive publicity to the LAPD, and made the city seem like a fascinating setting in its own right, rather than a real-world back lot that could double for other places. The wide streets, ranch-style homes and palm trees, and the actors and models and screenwriters who mixed with machinists and nurses and short-order cooks, all strengthened a seedy-glamorous vibe that would become intrinsic to L.A.-genre tales over the next eight decades.

Dragnet's super-square attitude toward the underground economy and countercultural attitudes was another factor in its success; it let fans enjoy the thrill of visiting taboo terrain, coupled with the assurance that there was no chance of being seduced by anything they saw there, because the righteous, incorruptible Friday, their surrogate and guide, would never allow it. The series returned for a second go-round in the '60s, adding color and replacing Ben Alexander's Officer Frank Smith with Harry Morgan as Officer Bill

Gannon (a talented cook who made great barbecue sauce and garlic nut-butter sandwiches). The '60s version seemed even more of a sociocultural relic than its predecessor, although the scenes of Friday lecturing hippies and other layabouts hit the Nixon-era silent majority's sweet spot, and the special pleading on behalf of police officers made Webb such a hero in the eyes of working cops that when he died, he was given an honor guard by the LAPD, and his character's badge number, 714, was retired.

—MZS

Flight of the Conchords (HBO, 2007–2009)

TV shows end for all sorts of reasons: The ratings are too low. The budget is too high. One of the stars wants out. The new network president isn't a fan. The writers have run out of stories.

Flight of the Conchords may be the first show to end because it ran out of songs.

Comedy-musicians Bret McKenzie and Jemaine Clement toured for years as Flight of the Conchords, aka "the fourth-most-popular folk duo in New Zealand," and had built up a decent-sized back catalog of song pastiches from multiple genres, including hip-hop, glam rock, and funk, as well as folk. Then the Conchords teamed up with writer/director James Bobin to create an HBO comedy where they played dumber, wildly less successful versions of themselves, barely subsisting on the pathetic gigs scored by their aggressively formal manager Murray (Rhys Darby)—a New Zealand consulate worker in New York who views the band as his true life's work, even though he understands nothing of the music business, or really business of any kind—and trying to avoid the creepy attentions of their lone fan, Mel (Kristen Schaal).

As a buddy comedy with very specific cultural references (particularly the guys' hatred and resentment of all things Australian) and an absurd sense of logic (Bret purchasing a second cup for the apartment so throws their finances out of whack that Jemaine eventually becomes a prostitute), it would have been amusing enough. But the two or three songs featured per episode elevated it into something truly special, whether the guys were failing to scare off a couple of muggers with their rap tune "Hiphopopotamus vs. Rhymenoceros" ("There ain't no party like my nana's tea party! Hey! Ho!") or Jemaine was purring the lyrics to the decidedly unsexy "Business Time" ("Girl, tonight we're gonna make love. You know how I know? Because it's Wednesday. And Wednesday night is the night that we usually make love.").

The problem was, the show burned through the duo's preexisting song list very quickly, and McKenzie and Clement were exhausting themselves writing new tunes on top of co-writing many of the scripts with Bobin. Making a TV series with wholly new songs can be done (*Crazy Ex-Girlfriend* has already produced nearly as many episodes as *Conchords*, and didn't have a stack of old tunes lying around to be used first), but it's damn hard, and thus understandable why the duo decided to go out on a high note after only two seasons, including a closing number that condensed the entire series into a bad Broadway musical, and a public statement that captured the show's deadpan humor and blurring of the lines between the real and fake versions of its stars: "While the characters Bret and Jemaine will no longer be around, the real Bret and Jemaine will continue to exist."

—AS

The Fugitive (ABC, 1963–1967)

The Fugitive was, like *Route 66* before it and other series like *The*

Incredible Hulk and *Quantum Leap* after it, a kind of stealth anthology, following the same main character week after week, but with an ever-changing setting and style. Our hero was Dr. Richard Kimble (David Janssen), wrongly convicted of the murder of his wife, trying to stay free—and just out of the outstretched arm of lawman Philip Gerard (Barry Morse)—while searching for the one-armed man who really committed the crime.

Created by Roy Huggins (in between *Maverick* and *The Rockford Files*), it was sober, well-crafted, and engrossing, even though—like most dramas from TV's early decades—it largely occupied a perpetual present, where Kimble could never really change or get any closer to proving his innocence without invalidating the premise of the show. Series in that era were thought of by the executives who green-lit them as disposable: When they stopped being successful, you just tossed them aside, because who could possibly care about getting closure for a silly TV show?

But when the decision came down to end *The Fugitive*, the show's producers pleaded with ABC for one more episode to bring Dr. Kimble's story to a proper conclusion—an idea so foreign in the era that the network's executives dismissed it as unnecessary. So producers went directly to advertisers to scrounge up the necessary money to pay for the finale, where Kimble finally caught up with the one-armed man and was set free. (As narrator William Conrad intoned, "Tuesday, August 29: the day the running stopped.") The episode was the most-watched episode of television at the time, with more than seventy-eight million people watching, and nearly three-quarters of all televisions in use at the time tuned to ABC.

And still it took the business another couple of decades to fully receive the wisdom that audiences like definitive endings.

—AS

Gilligan's Island (CBS, 1964–1967)

Has any show in TV history benefited more from its theme song than *Gilligan's Island*? Without that catchy, expository tune, cowritten by series creator Sherwood Schwartz and composer George Wyle, *Gilligan's* might well be another goofy, high-concept '60s sitcom remembered only as a punch line, like *My Mother the Car*. With the song, which lays out how an eclectic band of castaways got stranded on an uncharted desert isle, the show became encoded in the DNA of every Gen Xer and many late boomers, who can not only quote the theme song's lyrics but cite the many ways that the bumbling Gilligan (Bob Denver) screwed up escape attempts. (Schwartz understood the power of his lyric-writing skills well enough to use them again for his other camp classic, *The Brady Bunch*.)

Schwartz intended the show to be a social satire along the lines of *Ship of Fools* or *Lord of the Flies* but with Abbott and Costello slapstick, a laugh track, and a never-ending array of castaways who would appear on the island for one episode and then leave the original SS *Minnow* travelers stuck in jungle purgatory. The notion of *Gilligan's Island* as prime-time fable never stuck (though Dan Harmon cites it as an influence on *Community*); its nearly three-decade run as a syndication powerhouse was due to its clever placement on independent stations on weekday afternoons, where children starved for the live-action equivalent of a cartoon could bask in its ritualized silliness. Viewers could always rest assured that B-movie bombshell Ginger Grant (Tina Louise) would do a Marilyn Monroe boop-boop-de-doo number; that wholesome Mary Ann Summers (Dawn Wells)

would improbably play the role of the "homely" one despite looking smashing in bared-midriff outfits; that the Skipper (Alan Hale Jr.) would tire of Gilligan's idiocy and bash him over the head with his yachtsman's cap; that the Professor (Russell Johnson) would MacGyver a miraculous homemade gadget that Gilligan would then destroy; and that millionaire couple Thurston Howell III (Jim Backus) and his wife, Lovey (Natalie Schafer), would continue to act like millionaires at a country club even though they'd been wearing the same clothes for years and eating coconut with every meal.

—AS & MZS

Good Times (CBS, 1974–1979)

Good Times, about a working-class African American family living in an inner-city Chicago neighborhood, was a third-generation spin-off from Norman Lear's sitcom factory, derived from *Maude*, which in turn was spun off from *All in the Family*. It was one of the most audacious sitcoms of the 1970s and one of the most problematic and ultimately frustrating. Its virtues and faults are woven so tightly together that watching any episode (but especially earlier ones) can give you whiplash, but its vitality eclipses most of the trouble spots, especially when you know how relentlessly CBS pressured the show's producers to make an inherently raw premise as light and goofy as possible. The main character was Florida Evans (Esther Rolle), wife of the occasionally employed but always hardworking and responsible James Evans (John Amos), and the mother of three children: the "militant midget" Michael (Ralph Carter), Thelma (Bern Nadette Stanis), and James "J.J." Jr. (Jimmie Walker). Florida was last seen working as a domestic for the title character of *Maude*, but the show erased nearly all of her backstory, moved her from Maude's stomping ground of Tuckahoe, New York, to Chicago, Illinois, and started over, even renaming her husband (who was originally called Henry).

The show kept racism, deprivation, class snobbery, and financial distress on the front burner to an extent that was unusual even for a 1970s sitcom; the Bunker family struggled, too, but series creators Eric Monte and Mike Evans and their writers always made sure to point out that it was harder for African Americans to survive, let alone thrive, in a historically unequal society, especially when they had trouble "keeping our heads above water," to quote the show's earworm of a theme song. In season 2's "The I.Q. Test," Michael interrogates a test question: "'A mother, father, and two children live in a residence with five bedrooms. The mother and father sleep in one bed and the two children each have their own bedroom. How many guest bedrooms are there?' How many kids in the ghetto are going to know what a guest bedroom is?" "Yeah, the only time we get a guest room around here is when somebody puts a sleeping bag in the bathtub," J.J. says. "And a lot of kids in the ghetto don't have their own bedrooms either," Florida adds. The dialogue was often this bluntly explanatory, and the fact that it seemed intended for white viewers to affirm the shared experience of black ones could rankle; but it was still refreshing to see a lot of the same issues that were hashed out on *All in the Family* and another one of its predominantly African American spin-offs, the upper-middle-class *The Jeffersons*, examined in a rougher context. Every Lear sitcom was distinguished by its willingness to jump between broad comedy and dark drama; *Good Times* pushed that tendency far indeed, especially in season 5's two-parter "The Evans Get Involved," which introduced Janet Jackson as Penny Gordon Woods, a girl whose mother beat her and burned her with an iron.

Unfortunately, the same breakout supporting performance that made the show a hit—Walker's wisecracking, loudly attired J.J.—doomed its creative potential. CBS wanted to turn him into another de facto lead, like Fonzie from *Happy Days*, the better to goose the ratings and sell lunchboxes and other merchandise to kids. John Amos worried that J.J.'s clowning crossed the line into what black arts scholars called "coonery," and chastised Lear and other producers over stereotypical touches that kept creeping into the scripts; after one too many disagreements, his contract was not renewed and his character was killed off in the season 4 two-parter "The Big Move." Rolle left the show the following year, with the writers marrying off the now-widowed Florida to her new love, Carl Dixon (Moses Gunn). Rolle was back on the show again a year after that (minus Carl, who had died of cancer offscreen), but *Good Times*' structural integrity had been so abused that the best it could do was limp toward the finish line.

—MZS

The Good Wife (CBS, 2009–2016)

If you saw Chicago attorney Alicia Florrick (Julianna Margulies), the heroine of *The Good Wife*, in a crowd and didn't recognize her as the embattled wife of disgraced Cook County state's attorney Peter Florrick (Chris Noth), you might not form any immediate impression beyond the fact that she was attractive, elegant, and watchful. She's the sort of person who never speaks just for the sake of speaking; she reads the room first, and probably makes a mental flowchart to remind herself of who's powerful and who's not and what consequences might accrue if she's too familiar with this person or that person. Alicia acquired this skill from being a politician's wife, a lawyer, and a woman—but perhaps not in that order. Whether Alicia is bantering with the firm's chief investigator, Kalinda Sharma (Archie Panjabi), flirting with her old college classmate turned mentor Will Gardner (Josh Charles), or trying to please and impress Will's fellow senior partner Diane Lockhart (Christine Baranski), you can sense the calculations beneath the easygoing facade—the resentment at Peter for derailing her professional life and decimating her personal life, then trapping her into supporting him; her annoyance at herself for feeling attracted to Peter anyway; her fear that that the wrong word, the wrong move, could set her back again.

Individual episodes stuck to the crime-and-legal-show template, following Alicia and her colleagues at a prestigious law firm as they represented clients in class-action lawsuits against polluters and negligent railway companies, private citizens accused of felony offenses, whistle-blowers calling foul on corrupt businesses and government agencies, and murder suspects. But at its core, this was a bleeding heart of the big-city show, continuing a lineage that stretches from *The Defenders*, *Naked City*, and *East Side/West Side* through *Hill Street Blues* and *The Wire*. The show often felt like *The Bonfire of the Vanities* transferred to the Windy City, but with better female characters and more compassion: a borderline-screwball comedy filled with quotable lines. ("If you go nuclear, don't leave missiles in your silo," Diane advises.)

The series understood how news organizations can be used as weapons, and how they knowingly *allow* themselves to be used as weapons. (The chief exponent of this principle was Alan Cumming's Eli Gold, Peter's campaign manager, a ruthlessly expedient PR manipulator whose machinations could have powered quite a spin-off had the producers decided to make one.) There were scandals, scandals within scandals, double crosses, triple crosses, sweet victories and bitter defeats, and sudden, horrendous deaths (including one so tragic that fans still feel its sting).

In time, Alicia evolved from a humiliated spouse and lowly associate to become a coolheaded leader, public figure, and founder of her own law firm, the First Lady to the governor of Illinois (alongside her once-estranged, still-untrustworthy husband), and, briefly, Cook County state's attorney (a position taken from her after an ethics scandal). It flagged somewhat in its final seasons, perhaps because Alicia had come so far since the pilot that it seemed as if her journey, in drama if not life, was done. "Men can be lazy, women can't, and I think that goes double for you," Diane once told Alicia. Lesson learned.

—MZS

Grey's Anatomy (ABC, 2005–present)

The most remarkable part of the *Grey's Anatomy* story isn't that it's been a hit for more than a decade, nor that it inspired ABC to devote an entire night of programming to shows produced by *Grey's* creator Shonda Rhimes, nor even that Rhimes had never so much as written for another TV series, let alone created one that got on the air, prior to *Grey's*.

No, the most remarkable part of the story is how little use ABC had for *Grey's* when it debuted.

In the spring of 2005, ABC executives were feeling pretty damn pleased about themselves, and with good reason. A network is lucky if it debuts one giant hit every couple of years, but ABC had just launched two of them in one season with the fall premieres of *Desperate Housewives* and *Lost*. That duo dragged the network out of irrelevance and made it a viewer destination again.

It was a destination without many vacancies, particularly on Sunday nights, where *Desperate* and *Boston Legal* looked like a pairing that could run together for a long time. A year before, ABC had bought an absurd number of new series because the network was so starved for hits over the past few seasons. Winning the lottery twice with *Desperate* and *Lost* meant most of those shows were no longer necessary, and came and went quickly. (Hang your heads in memory of *Blind Justice*, a show about a blind, gun-toting NYPD detective that was somehow cocreated by Steven Bochco.) Those other shows were at least being placed in open time slots where they could, in success, remain; *Grey's* was being squeezed into a four-week window on Sundays when *Boston Legal* would otherwise have been airing repeats, and there was no plan for what to do with the remaining episodes once Denny Crane and friends reclaimed the hour.

Instead, *Grey's* was such an instant smash that it was the Lou Gehrig to *Boston Legal's* Wally Pipp, becoming the backbone of ABC's entire lineup for the next decade.

In hindsight, it seems improbable that anyone wouldn't have expected *Grey's* to be a big hit. In telling the story of five attractive young surgeons beginning their internships at a Seattle hospital, Rhimes had spliced together the most appealing parts of *ER* (high-stakes, fast-moving medical drama) and *Friends* (good-looking twenty-somethings bonding together during their first real taste of adulthood), with a dash of *Sex and the City* (the on-again, off-again, frequently self-destructive relationship between Meredith Grey and Derek Shepherd), and combined that with her own flair for melodrama and oratory to make it feel like something wholly new.

Grey's could be erratic, sometimes due to forces beyond Rhimes's control (actors bad-mouthing the show or one another in the press, or leaving the series abruptly), sometimes from her reaching too far for a big idea (the fifth-season story arc where Izzie Stevens had sex with the ghost of her dead lover Denny Duquette, later revealed to be a hallucination caused by cancer that had spread to her brain). But when the show clicked in its depiction of romance, friendship, or the incredibly violent stakes of working at Seattle Grace (like the two-parter where Meredith had her hands on a piece of unexploded ordnance stuck inside a patient's body), it could be extraordinary. Even relatively recently, after churning through so many different iterations of the cast, an episode like Derek's death—injured in a car crash (only minutes after saving the survivors of a *different* car crash) and rendered unable to talk, he's helpless to do anything but watch as the underqualified staff at a regional hospital misses an easy diagnosis—can work spectacularly well, because Rhimes still has precision aim for her viewers' tear ducts.

While Rhimes's other series were designed with finite creative life spans, it's conceivable *Grey's* could be around for fifteen seasons, maybe even twenty. Not bad for a show whose own network had no plans for it past its first month.

—AS

Homeland season 1 (Showtime, 2011)

In the fourth episode of the first season of Showtime's military thriller series *Homeland*, CIA analyst Carrie Mathison (Claire Danes) and her quarry, returned Marine POW and possible terrorist Nicholas Brody (Damian Lewis)—who'd been orbiting each other since the pilot—get drunk at a pub and have impulse-sex in a parked car. It was the biggest of many pull-the-rug-out-from-under-you moments in the first leg of *Homeland*, a series that was created by *24* producers Alex Gansa and Howard Gordon (adapting the Israeli series *Prisoners of War*) and that often played like its slowed-down, more psychologically oriented cousin.

Nobody who'd become engrossed in the show by that point expected it to become a doomed love story: a cat-and-mouse story where the cat and the mouse are secretly crazy about each other, and this might have been a credibility-destroying gambit in any other ostensibly realistic series; but because *Homeland* had prepped the moment—carefully detailing Brody's alienation, depression, and troubled marriage and Carrie's antipsychotic drug regimen and lifelong history of flouting rules and courting danger—it felt psycho-logically credible and hilariously right. And it turned the show into a unique television event: a sexy, sad, sometimes emotionally dev-astating *amour fou* superimposed upon a *Manchurian Candidate*-like story of a brainwashed war hero who may or may not be helping Islamic terrorists plan another 9/11.

The season finale found Brody, now the beloved mascot of the US executive branch, preparing to detonate an explosive-laden vest inside a bunker in order to kill the vice president and his advisers. Had the story ended there, with a bloody detonation or Brody being killed or arrested, *Homeland* might have been acclaimed as one of the great, wild miniseries in TV history. Instead, both Brody and his targets lived so as not to kill the source of the show's unexpectedly huge rat-ings; the machinations required to hide Brody's murderous plan as well as his last-minute change of heart (brought about by a cell-phone call from his teenage daughter) were absurd even by *Homeland*'s increas-ingly lax standards of credibility, and they tipped the series over into cartoonland, where it wandered for two more years.

Seasons 2 and 3 were all about digging the plot and characters out from under the rubble left by the producers' expedient deci-sion; Brody, who had been elected to Congress, found himself doing nasty but menial errands for his handlers (such as strangling a fel-low plotter in the woods) and then murdering the vice presi-dent in his own office and getting away with it; by season 3 he was a fugitive, and by the end Carrie watched from afar as he was pub-licly hanged as a traitor by Irani-ans. Seasons 4 and 5 managed to recover a bit of the show's luster, but the stench of opportunism contin-ued to contaminate the good work of *Homeland*'s writers, actors, and filmmakers.

—MZS

I'll Fly Away (NBC, 1991–1993)

The only US dramatic series to deal primarily with the meaning and impact of the civil rights move-ment, and another example of a brilliant but low-rated program that was kept alive by fan adoration and critical praise, *I'll Fly Away* was the brainchild of *Northern Expo-sure* cocreators Joshua Brand and John Falsey. Set in an unspecified Southern state in the late 1950s and '60s, it was sold as a counterpart of *To Kill a Mockingbird*, and featured an appealing lead performance by Sam Waterston as Forrest Bedford, an Atticus Finch–like district attorney who struggles to raise his three children (played by John Aaron Bennett, Ashlee Levitch, and twins Jeremy and Jason London) after his wife's death. More daringly, though, the show gave equal time to the life of Forrest's housekeeper, Lily Harper (Regina Taylor), who served as an unofficial adoptive mom to Forrest's kids as well as a biological mother to her own, yet still found time to get involved in the civil rights struggle, sparking an evolution that helped radicalize her earnest but politically calculating boss. An honest, affectionate, and evenhanded portrait of a tumultuous time and place, *I'll Fly Away* rose beyond the clichés of liberal humanist history, presenting the former Confederate States as a vibrant, complex place where familial, romantic, and racial allegiances were at odds. NBC's cancellation of the show left plot threads dangling; PBS helped the cast and crew tie them up with a powerful 1993 movie that borrowed on the real-life lynching of Emmett Till. The movie, more so than the regular series, is Lily's story, built around her return home thirty years later; its climax, a moment of rapprochement between Lily and Forrest, is quietly devastating.

—MZS

Julia (NBC, 1968–1971)

It would be wonderful to report that *Julia*, one of the most important series in TV's early political and racial development, was also a great show. It's actually so pleasantly inoffensive as to be nearly unwatchable, but its milestone status is still guaranteed by virtue of its central casting: Diahann Carroll's performance in the title role of widowed nurse and single mother Julia Baker marked the first time in network TV history that a woman of color had been given the lead role in a situation comedy, without having to play a domestic of some kind. Series creator Hal Kanter and his writers were never quite able to balance social relevance with involving comedy; Julia's defining traits were indomitable patience and niceness. But the show did give her an active romantic life (her boyfriends were played by Fred Williamson and Paul Winfield), and there were plotlines that somewhat gingerly plugged into hot-button topics that viewers could read about in the newspaper (in season 2, the clinic where Julia worked had to tighten its belt, and nonwhite staffers got laid off first). Carroll was proud of her game-changing performance on the show but clearly had a lot more fun as the scheming Dominique

Deveraux on ABC's *Dynasty* (1981–1989), an African American counterpart to that show's resident bitch queen Alexis Carrington (Joan Collins).

—MZS

K Street and *Unscripted* (HBO, 2003 and 2005)

Producers Steven Soderbergh and Grant Heslov created these two heavily improvised series, which are temperamentally and stylistically unlike anything ever aired on American TV. The former is a comedy about lobbyists (including *Mad Men*'s John Slattery) working in Washington shortly after the US invasion of Iraq; it was shot newsmagazine-style, with every episode written, shot, edited, and aired in the span of a week. The result was necessarily rough but has an undeniable energy, and the cameos by real politicians and celebrities (à la Robert Altman's *Tanner '88* and *Tanner on Tanner*) add to the credibility even when the plotting is fuzzy or patently absurd. The latter, a drama about struggling Los Angeles actors under the sway of a guru-type acting coach (Frank Langella), is one of the more penetrating psychological dramas about performance in both art and life.

—MZS

Kolchak: The Night Stalker (ABC, 1974–1975)

Along with *Freaks and Geeks*, *My So-Called Life*, *Firefly*, and a handful of other one-and-done series, this single-season horror-thriller series had an impact far beyond its brief run on network television. Created by Jeff Rice, it started out as a stand-alone TV-movie, 1972's *The Night Stalker*, starring Darren McGavin as Fox Mulder's pop culture forefather, Chicago newspaper reporter Carl Kolchak, who realizes that a serial killer terrorizing Las Vegas is actually a bloodsucking vampire. That twist was startling to viewers because screenwriter Richard Matheson, adapting Rice's then-unpublished novel, wraps Kolchak's investigation in *X-Files*-style uncertainty and official obfuscation. The film was such a ratings success that a sequel, 1973's *The Night Strangler* (also scripted by Matheson), inevitably followed; this time the killer was a non-bloodsucking immortal that had been preying on innocents since the Civil War.

The regular series, which ran just twenty episodes, pitted Kolchak against a series of monsters drawn from folklore and horror literature, including a succubus, witches, a doppelgänger, a thawed-out caveman, an android, a headless motorcycle rider modeled on the horseman who tormented Ichabod Crane, a possessed suit of knight's armor, and an immortal Helen of Troy. McGavin soon became disillusioned by the series, which he found repetitious and formulaic, but its format influenced *The X-Files*, *Supernatural*, *Buffy the Vampire Slayer*, and other shows that merged the police procedural and horror-movie situations. *X-Files* creator Chris Carter failed to convince Gavin to reprise Kolchak on his '90s series but managed to get him to appear as retired FBI agent Arthur Dales, a character described, appropriately, as "the father of *The X-Files*."

—MZS

The Knick (Cinemax, 2014–2016)

"A servant doesn't talk back to his master," a loan shark tells a debtor in the early twentieth-century period drama *The Knick*. It's just a throwaway line, but it comes close to summing up this series from creators Jack Amiel and Michael Begler and executive producer Steven Soderbergh, who directed every episode. Power dynamics are in the foreground of each scene. The show's title is a nickname for New York's Knickerbocker

Hospital, where Dr. John Thackery (Clive Owen), a cocaine addict and casual racist, has just been installed as chief of surgery following a sudden staff upheaval. John butts heads with Cornelia Robertson (Juliet Rylance), who runs the for-profit hospital on behalf of her social-reform-minded new-money dad, as well as with pretty much everyone else on staff, including Dr. Algernon Edwards (André Holland), an African American surgeon with European hospital experience who's been made the deputy chief of surgery, against John's wishes, as a precondition of getting the place wired for electricity.

As on all hospital shows, the building serves as a crossroads for the city and becomes a microcosm of the larger society, a petri dish in which social malaise can be treated and reforms incubated. Representatives of every class, race, and ethnicity pass through the Knick's doors at one point or another, and the world's issues are given an old-fashioned dramatic (often melodramatic) workout. Not since *Deadwood* has a period-drama production designed to a fare-thee-well and steeped in nasty atmosphere been so politically astute about who has power over whom and why—although the subtler brand of gallows humor and

Soderbergh's fondness for intricately choreographed long takes aligns *The Knick* with a different TV classic that *Deadwood* creator David Milch worked on, *Hill Street Blues*.

—MZS

Lace (ABC, 1984)

Adapted by Shirley Conran from her same-named novel, this miniseries follows a young film siren named Lili (Phoebe Cates) as she travels the world hoping to learn the identity of the mother who gave her up for adoption, a woman known only under the pseudonym Linda Lace. Brooke Adams, Bess Armstrong, and Arielle Dombasle play the three likely candidates, all of whom went through failed relationships, one of whom got pregnant; a sacred pact to protect the identity of Lili's birth mom. Flashback and present-tense intrigue follows, none memorable, all lurid and dumb. The miniseries is hot garbage and tedious to boot, fun only if you watch it with bitchy friends emboldened by your intoxicant of choice; but it's worth enduring for the thrill of being able to say you witnessed the delivery of the greatest line in 1980s television: "Which one of you bitches is my mother?"

—MZS

Little House on the Prairie (NBC, 1978–1982)

Based on Laura Ingalls Wilder's beloved series of memoir-novels about growing up on the Kansas prairie in the late nineteenth century, this labor of love from producer-star Michael Landon (formerly of the so-called "adult Western" *Bonanza*) became one of the most beloved family series of the 1970s and beyond. Landon starred as Charles Ingalls, patriarch of a hardscrabble pioneer family in Walnut Grove that also included Karen Grassle as Charles's wife, Caroline; Melissa Gilbert as Laura; Melissa Sue Anderson as Laura's older sister, Mary; twins Lindsay and Sidney Greenbush as their kid sister, Carrie; Dean Butler as Laura's future husband, Almanzo Wilder; and Victor French as Charles's loyal best friend, Isaiah Edwards.

The show's title is now synonymous with a kinder and sweeter sort of entertainment, but anyone who watched it when it was on can tell you how bleak it often was. Mary went blind, and there were story lines about rape, extreme poverty, economic exploitation, racism, morphine addiction, and mob justice. Landon's Charles had the shaggy hair and gentle demeanor of a me-decade, post-hippie dad, but he had a streak of Old Testament toughness reminiscent of Chuck Connors's Lucas McCain on *The Rifleman*. The series eventually devolved into a prairie soap, more engaging than its equally successful CBS rival *The Waltons* but much less gentle in its methods. Landon personally directed 87 of the series' 203 episodes and took the lead in battling NBC to get some of the rougher story lines past censors. His thorny relationship with the network was most vividly expressed in one of several reunion movies, 1984's *Little House: The Last Farewell*, in which Charles and Caroline revisit Walnut Grove to discover that it's fallen into the clutches of a railroad baron; they blow up every building in town with dynamite.

—MZS

Luck (HBO, 2011–2012)

A dream project turned nightmare: Longtime racing fan David Milch got to make a drama set at the Santa Anita Park racetrack, then was barred from the set by fellow producer Michael Mann, then saw the series canceled abruptly after three different horses died following participation in one of the show's staged races. But the nine episodes that aired are a strong testament not only to its creator's love of the subject but of his ability to repackage that love into a series that could, for a brief, precious time, make his audience feel that same love, regardless of their prior interest.

The cast included movie stars like Dustin Hoffman (as a recently paroled gangster splitting his time between plotting revenge against his rivals and tending to the career of his beloved new horse) and Nick Nolte (a bitter, guarded old trainer taking one last shot at the big time), along with fine character actors like Dennis Farina (Hoffman's genial but deadly bodyguard) and John Ortiz (a brilliant, paranoid trainer). But the series' heart was with a quartet of degenerate gamblers (played by Kevin Dunn, Jason Gedrick, Ritchie Coster, and Ian Hart) riding the greatest hot streak of their lives. None can quite believe the way their fortunes keep rising, and all expect it to fall apart in an instant. As Dunn's wheelchair-bound Marcus puts it in the last completed episode, "You want to know how I feel? Today's the day they take it all away from us."

Milch, who had already seen HBO cancel *Deadwood* and the inscrutable *John from Cincinnati* out from under him (and who reportedly lost much of his TV fortune betting on the ponies), could empathize with Marcus. *Luck* wasn't perfect (the Hoffman revenge plot seemed to exist on another show entirely, and Ortiz's character spoke in a syntax that was impenetrable even by Milch standards), but nor did it feel like self-indulgence from a creator who finally had the money and (relative) power to make a show about his favorite subject. For those nine episodes, that track, and the people and horses who populated it, came to thrilling, poignant life. It's a shame the streak couldn't have gone on a little longer.

—AS

Maverick (ABC, 1957–1965)

James Garner's smart-mouthing, fast-dealing Wild West gambler Bret Maverick was the closest thing TV had to a pure antihero in its black-and-white days. But even he tended to do the right thing when the occasion called for it. This was the show that made Garner one of TV's best and most enduring stars—and led him to team up with Maverick creator Roy Huggins years later for The Rockford Files—even if he ultimately appeared in about half the episodes for the first few seasons, alternating with Jack Kelly as Bret's brother, Bart, when the workload got too tough, and then being replaced by Roger Moore and then Robert Colbert when he quit in a contract dispute. Bret may have been "the second-slowest gun in the West," according to Bart (who admitted to being the first-slowest), but TV in the '50s and '60s didn't lack for cowboys who were quick on the draw. None of them had the pure charm of wily Bret Maverick, though.

—AS

Mission: Impossible (NBC, 1966–1973)

Your mission, should you choose to accept it: to seek out episodes of the original Mission: Impossible, the lean, clever, irresistibly ritualized spy drama-caper adventure that aired each week on NBC for seven seasons; to appreciate the imagination and tenacity of the Impossible Missions Force, a team led by Jim Phelps (Peter Graves) and filled out by intrepid men and women who engaged in international espionage part-time, using skills honed in their civilian jobs; to admire the absurdity of hiring fashion model Cinnamon Carter (Barbara Bain), scientific genius and Collier Electronics founder Bernard "Barney" Collier (Greg Morris), iron-spined weight lifter William "Willy" Armitage (Peter Lupus), actor and escape artist and master of disguise Rollin Hand (Martin Landau) and his replacement, the Great Paris (*Star Trek*'s Leonard Nimoy), to do dangerous jobs more often assigned to flesh-and-blood superheroes like 007 and Napoleon Solo; to dig the '60s fashions, cars, and architecture showcased in the series' international adventures, most of which were faked on sets in and around Los Angeles and populated by actors whose accents were less than United Nations–credible; to think about how much more democratic this ensemble series feels in comparison to the Tom Cruise film spin-offs, which are spectacular and fun, but downplay teamwork in favor of steely-eyed, lone hero endurance; to try and fail not to bob your head in time to Lalo Schifrin's still-groovy opening credits music, which played out over almost subliminally brief flash-forward images of the episode you were about to watch; and to turn your rational mind off long enough to believe that no task is truly impossible if you hire good people and trust them to do their thing. This entry will self-destruct in five seconds.

—MZS

Murphy Brown (CBS, 1988–1998)

In the '80s and early '90s, *The Mary Tyler Moore Show* and *Maude* begat a whole bunch of tough,

complicated CBS sitcom heroines, particularly Dixie Carter as the eloquent shatterer of bullshit Julia Sugarbaker on *Designing Women* and five-time Emmy winner Candice Bergen as Murphy Brown: flinty, Motown-singing, recovering-alcoholic star of a prime-time network newsmagazine. An over-reliance on name-dropping and topical references have given *Murphy Brown* the shelf-life of a Stone Phillips bobble-head, but Murphy herself remains one of TV's great characters, and an important point on the continuum of fictional single women working in TV, even if she'd have little patience for Mary Richards's sentimentality or Liz Lemon's...everything. At its peak, the series was such a big deal that Vice President Dan Quayle objected to a story line about Murphy becoming a single mother, treating her as a real-life role model rather than a fictional one. Bergen, and the writing by Diane English and company, were so vivid that you can understand his confusion.

—AS

The Odd Couple (ABC, 1970–1975)

In the fifty-plus years since the first Broadway performance of Neil Simon's play about two divorced men sharing a New York apartment, *The Odd Couple* has been adapted into a feature film (with a decades-later sequel), three different TV sitcoms, and countless theatrical remakes. In some versions, the characters have changed races and even genders.

But of the many versions across stage and screen, the definitive one was the first made for television, adapted by Garry Marshall and Jerry Belson, and starring Tony Randall as clean-freak photographer Felix Unger and Jack Klugman as slovenly sportswriter Oscar Madison. It owes some of that to the ubiquity of its syndicated repeats—for about twenty years, it was all but impossible to channel surf in the late afternoon or early evening without stumbling across the episode where the guys competed on *Password*—but mainly to the sheer force of will of Randall as Felix.

Klugman made a fine Oscar, but there were excellent Oscars before and after him (including a few Olives in the gender-flipped play). Randall and his writers, on the other hand, made this Felix stand apart from any other take. He was a force of nature: dainty, uptight, and allergic, but so assertive in his convictions about cleanliness and culture that he could bend the entire world (including his spiritual opposite, Oscar) to his will

whenever necessary. (In that way, *The Big Bang Theory* is something of an unofficial remake, with Sheldon as a Felix with Asperger's.) He could be annoying, he could be insufferable, and yet you understood exactly why Oscar hadn't tossed him out an apartment window years ago.

On paper, Felix should've been so easy to hate, but Randall made him weirdly admirable. In perhaps the show's most famous moment (inspired by a teacher Belson had in typewriter repair class), Felix acts as his and Oscar's defense attorney when they're wrongly charged with ticket scalping, and gets the prosecution's key witness to admit she just assumed they were scalpers. Knowing he has the case won, Felix requests the use of a blackboard to loudly and boldly explain that "when you assume, you make an 'ass' out of 'u' and 'me'!" It's a smug, preening moment, but one that leaves even the judge smiling.

—AS

Phineas and Ferb (Disney, 2007–2015)

In television, formula often seems to come from a lack of imagination. It's simply easier to do the same thing every week when your audience doesn't mind. *Phineas and Ferb*, though, managed at the same time to be wildly imaginative and slavishly formulaic, using its repetitive structure not as a crutch but as a sturdy framework on which it could hang all kinds of fantastic new ideas.

The formula, as created by Dan Povenmire and Jeff "Swampy" Marsh: On each day of summer vacation, stepbrothers Phineas and Ferb dream up and execute an impossible task—building the world's largest roller coaster, traveling through time, or otherwise bending the laws of physics—all while their older sister, Candace, tries in vain to bust them for their antics in front of their mom, only to have their latest incredible invention disappear as the result of each episode's B story, where Perry the Platypus (the kids' pet, but really a spy for a government agency that employs cute animals in fedoras) foils evil scientist Heinz Doofenshmirtz's latest attempt to conquer the Tri-State Area.

These things happen in every episode with such predictability that the characters' awareness of that formula—and any deviations from it—quickly became one of the show's most fertile sources of humor. While the basic structure stayed the same (even in episodes set in feudal Japan or caveman times), that familiarity made it easier

to focus on the audacity of what the kids were doing in every episode, or on the ever more absurdly tragic backstory of Doofenshmirtz, whose sole friend during his lonely childhood in the backward European country of Drusselstein was a helium balloon.

Pretty much everything the kids do defies the rules of nature—up to and including the fact that their summer vacation is 104 days long—yet they, and the series, always made it look easy.

—AS

Quantum Leap (NBC, 1989–1993)

By the late '80s, the original form of the anthology drama—new people and stories every episode—had gone more or less the way of the dodo, because audiences wanted continuing characters they could invest in, while networks wanted those familiar characters to make each show easier to promote from week to week. With Quantum Leap, Donald P. Bellisario (who earlier created Magnum P.I. and would later give CBS the NCIS franchise) borrowed the stealth anthology format of The Fugitive and Route 66, but with a science-fiction twist: Each week, polymath scientist Sam Becket (Scott Bakula) would travel to some period in the past, temporarily occupying the body of a person who needed his help improving his or her future. The audience would see Sam—always scrambling to figure out who he was and what he came here to do and muttering a nervous "Oh, boy" upon realizing the nature of his latest identity—while the people he met would see him as a blind concert pianist, a gorgeous *Mad Men*–era secretary, a young man with Down syndrome, or even a NASA chimpanzee.

It was an ingenious idea that invited all kinds of crossover viewing: sci-fi fans interested in the nature of Sam's time travel device and the brief glimpses of future tech via his best friend, Al Calavicci (Dean Stockwell), who appeared in the past as a hologram only Sam could see; history fans who enjoyed the re-creations of the '50s, '60s, and '70s the show offered; drama fans who appreciated the little short stories the show told each week about the life Sam had dropped into; and people who simply grew attached to Sam and Al and wanted to see Sam fix events in their own lives, and maybe make it home somehow.

Anyone rooting for the last thing came away disappointed—the series ended with a title card reading "Dr. Sam Becket never returned home"—but the nimble series satisfied the rest of its constituency throughout. None of it would have worked without an actor as versatile and game as Bakula—a beefy guy who could sing and dance and do light comedy and intense melodrama and who gave himself fully to this crazy idea and his ever-changing role. He may not have fully transformed into a woman or an African American chauffeur or (as part of a sketchy late-period grab for ratings that saw him interacting with famous historical figures) Lee Harvey Oswald, but as each episode moved on, you would see the lines begin to blur between Sam and the part he was playing. Bakula's passion, and his chemistry with Stockwell, elevated even the most run-of-the-mill relationship drama story, and when the personal stakes were higher—particularly during a two-parter where Sam was given a chance to rewrite his own timeline, including the death of his brother in Vietnam—*Quantum Leap* went from a fun genre mash-up to an incredibly powerful drama.

The Vietnam episode featured the kind of story that couldn't have been told as well in a conventional anthology, because all of its impact came from the audience knowing and caring about Sam. We had watched him for years helping other people improve their lives, and just once, we wanted to see him get a win of his own.

—AS

Recess (ABC and UPN, 1997–2001)

Easily one of the smartest, most prankishly playful adult cartoons ever passed off as children's entertainment, this comedy from Paul Germain and Joe Ansolabehere was set mainly in and around a fourth-grade playground before, after, and during, ahem, recess. Although it had the setting of an afterschool special, the show's mentality was more attuned to 1960s social allegories in the vein of *Catch-22* and *One Flew Over the Cuckoo's Nest*, with nods to Kafka and the Marx Brothers. The resident Randle Patrick "Mac" McMurphy, T. J. Detweiler, leads a bomber crew of types that include hot-tempered tomboy Ashley Spinelli, military brat Gus Griswald, tenderhearted hulk Mikey Blumberg, brainiac Gretchen Grundler, and jock Vince LaSalle. When they aren't battling the shortsighted and arbitrary edicts of school administrators, teachers, and parents, the kids have to contend with the whims of King Bob, the self-appointed despot of the playground, who exerts his will through a never-ending series of schemes, tests, and epic tasks, including building a great pyramid and declaring himself pharaoh.

Like *Community*, which might have learned something from its tone and structure, *Recess* is a highly ritualized bit of entertainment that strikes the same notes over and over again, but always in infinite variation, and with a surprising eye for psychological grace notes, especially when characters you thought of as brusque and one-dimensional reveal their dreams and fears to one another.

—MZS

The Rifleman (CBS, 1958–1963)

In the 1950s and early '60s, Westerns were all over the airwaves, but very few of them held up as well as the smartest Western films being made during that period, because the ritualistic quality of the weekly stories seemed more repetitious than comforting. A curious exception is *The Rifleman*, a series about a widowed rancher named Lucas McCain (Chuck Connors), who struggles to raise his young son, Mark (Johnny Crawford), while helping the local sheriff, Micah Torrance (Paul Fix), stand tall against rustlers, stagecoach and bank robbers, duelists, and uncategorizable antiheroes (the most vivid of which was a tormented gunman, played by Sammy Davis Jr., sworn to avenge his lynched father).

Originally titled *The Sharpshooter*, *The Rifleman* was created by Arnold Laven, who brought *The Big Valley* to CBS and directed a number of theatrical Westerns, including *Geronimo*, and developed for television by Sam Peckinpah, who would go on to revolutionize the depiction of violence on film in *The Wild Bunch*. (He also created *The Westerner*, which receives its own citation in this section.) The gorgeous black-and-white imagery, contained stories (Lucas rarely left the county), stirring music (by Herschel Burke Gilbert), expected but always startling bursts of violence, and heart-to-heart father-son talks gave each episode the ritualistic quality of a parable or a heroic poem. The core theme was always the difficulty of being a moral person in an immoral world.

Lucas was hot-tempered, macho, and prideful, and the opening credits (which showed him rapid-firing sixteen shots from a Winchester carbine) promised gunplay that the show nearly always delivered. But despite this, Lucas usually advocated diplomacy and de-escalation. He killed mainly to save himself, his loved ones, or the integrity of the town's institutions, as represented by the beleaguered Micah. The deeper narrative of the series was about a man continuing to learn and grow and improve his character, even as an adult saddled with grave responsibilities.

—MZS

Robbery Homicide Division (CBS, 2002–2003)

Michael Mann's first TV series since *Crime Story* felt like a continuation of themes and images from his 1995 masterpiece *Heat*, but shot in the loose, documentary-inflected style that would increasingly become his trademark. It ran just thirteen episodes and was of no particular interest dramatically. *Heat* supporting player Tom Sizemore played a philosophically inclined motormouth of a detective, prowling the streets of Los Angeles, investigating gang activity, mass murders, robberies, and the like. *RHD* merits a citation here mainly because its technical innovations provided a glimpse of television's future.

At that point, most dramatic series were still shot on 35mm film, which required large crews, lots of lights, and a fair amount of preparation, especially when shooting took place in real locations, as was usually the case on *RHD*. Mann's most recent theatrical film, *Ali*, had used high-definition video to create some of its more impressionistic moments; this show used it throughout, and the smaller crews and lighter equipment gave the whole production a degree of spontaneity previously unheard of on broadcast network dramas as logistically complex as this one. Every subsequent Mann film would be shot digitally, in a manner that made no attempt to pass off video as celluloid; he was straightforward in telling interviewers that he did the show mainly to test out new equipment that he thought would revolutionize motion pictures, including his own. Large swaths of dialogue were improvised or rewritten on the fly, new scenes were invented en route from one location to another, and some of the locations were impulse decisions as well. Mann often served as his own camera operator, traveling in cars with Sizemore and other actors like a news cameraman. Mann made it a point of pride to shoot using available light whenever possible. Other series were experimenting with high-def video around this time, including Sidney Lumet's A&E city drama *100 Centre Street*, but they all took pains to disguise how they were made. *RHD* did not. It decided it would rather be comfortable in its own (digital) skin, an aesthetic decision that had an enormous impact. Within fifteen years, only a handful of TV dramas would be shot on film. The show's lone season now seems like a crucible in which TV's new digital reality was forged.

—MZS

Rubicon (AMC, 2010)

A one-and-done spy drama, set in a civilian think tank whose employees provide advice to US intelligence, *Rubicon* had a story arc that never made much sense. But the think tank's low-tech atmosphere was so richly evocative of paranoid '70s conspiracy thrillers, and the performances—by James Badge Dale as a hero perhaps too brilliant for his own good, by Arliss Howard as an ex-CIA operative without Dale's moral qualms, by Michael Cristofer as the think tank's hypnotic boss, and more—were so exciting that the plot was almost beside the point. Before the phrase "Peak TV" was coined, *Rubicon* was both an early example of the phenomenon (created as part of AMC's initial push into original programming) and one of its first victims (because it was hard to convince people to sample a wonky show with some clear flaws when more complete and commercial alternatives were abundant elsewhere on cable).

—AS

Samurai Jack (Cartoon Network, 2001–2004); and Star Wars: Clone Wars (Cartoon Network, 2003–2005)

Even the most cinematic TV series rarely approach what film buffs might call Pure Cinema. Genndy Tartakovsky achieved it every week with *Samurai Jack* and *Clone Wars*. These two half-hour Cartoon Network series used two-dimensional, cell-style animation and a bare minimum of dialogue, and often kept anything resembling plot to a minimum as well. But their low-tech action spectacles were so intricately designed, boldly staged, and gracefully executed that they made the most expensive contemporaneous Michael Bay blockbusters feel puny. Anybody who had been introduced to the Russian-born filmmaker through his animation direction on *Dexter's Laboratory* already knew that Tartakovsky went above and beyond when it came to staging action, but nothing in that show could have prepared them for his follow-ups, which took action cinema back to its roots in late-period silent cinema—the era that, along with anime, seems to have most strongly inspired his aesthetic sensibility, even though the music and sound effects on both shows were magnificently mixed, alternating eerie silence with all-hell-breaks-loose noise.

Samurai Jack, about a stoic swordsman battling creatures, robots, and an ancient demon in a postapocalyptic future, also owes a large debt to Frank Miller's purely action-driven comics, particularly *Ronin* and *300*; the *Lone Wolf and Cub* series; the paintings of Katsushika Hokusai; and the schlocky 1980s Saturday-morning adventure *Thundarr the Barbarian*. *Clone Wars* envisions the events that transpired between the second and third *Star Wars* prequels, but concentrates on military history: wins, losses, and quagmires for the republic that would later sour and become an· empire. But both series ultimately manage to fold and refold their influences with the concentration of a sword-maker hammering a katana in a forge, until they become as pure of mind as their heroes (respectively, a young Japanese prince and the Jedi Knights).

Both series feature borderless backdrops and characters drawn in a barely representational style reminiscent of ancient woodcuts or figurines, but they are photographed (or maybe we should say "shown") in the manner of an epic live-action movie. Every clash feels genuinely mythic—and not just the relentless showdowns between Jack and armies of mechanical spiders, or the large-scale military engagements pitting the Jedi and their storm-trooper underlings against armored columns on a desolate plain or snipers and urban infantry in a bombed-out city reminiscent of Hue in *Full Metal Jacket*; the more intimate contests—between, say, Jack and a doppelgängerlike swordsman who can merge with shadows, or the Sith assassin Asajj Ventress and Anakin Skywalker for possession of his soul—are no less tense, because Tartakovsky always makes sure that every act of violence and moment of hesitation has dramatic significance as well as a clear tactical purpose (one that we always understand eventually, if not in the moment).

These two series often attain a hypnotic power comparable to the final battle in *The Seven Samurai*, the mountaintop climax of *The Last of the Mohicans*, and the closing acts of *The Wild Bunch* and *Akira*: They are lethal dance routines composed with a painter's eye. Neither series offers much in the way of traditional storytelling pleasures (thus their absence from the Pantheon, where they'd score poorly in most major categories). They merit a citation here because they are unique among both TV series generally and animation specifically, and their finest segments rank with the greatest action cinema ever produced.

—MZS

Sons of Anarchy season 2 (FX, 2009)

Another outlier second season like *Chuck*, where everything came together perfectly for a year, suggesting a show that had taken a permanent leap up in class before things kept moving inexorably downward.

Conceived by writer Kurt Sutter as a kind of Hells Angels version of *Hamlet*, *Sons of Anarchy* followed Jax Teller (Charlie Hunnam), crown prince of a violent California motorcycle club unsure whether to support the gunrunning status quo or tear the whole thing down for desecrating the vision his late father had for the group.

After working out a few kinks in the first season, Sutter nailed everything in season 2, pitting the Sons against a gang of white supremacists looking to take over their territory and willing to do horrific things—like kidnap and rape Gemma (Katey Sagal), mother of Jax and wife of club president Clay Morrow (Ron Perlman)—to ensure victory. It was a great enemy, the best possible showcase for Sagal, and a story arc that kept twisting and turning, but always staying true to who the characters were and what they would do.

The show increasingly fell victim to its own excesses in later years, as more became less: so much gore (much of it visited on a character Sutter himself played, who at one point bit out his own tongue to avoid testifying against the club) that it became desensitizing, stories that became so knotty that the characters seemed to be acting less out of their own motivations than the Rube Goldberg needs of the plot, and eventually episodes that began running longer and longer to their own detriment, because who were the FX executives to say no to more of their biggest hit ever?

Sutter would defend the later seasons by insisting that *Sons* had no aspirations toward being an important drama for our times, describing it as "an adrenalized soap opera" and "bloody pulp fiction with highly complex characters."

He was selling the show short. For that one year, at least, *Sons* comfortably belonged in company with TV's most celebrated and thoughtful dramas.

—AS

Star Trek: The Next Generation (Syndicated, 1987–1994)

Patrick Stewart starred as Jean-Luc Picard, captain of the refurbished Starship *Enterprise*, in this reimagining of Gene Roddenberry's beloved science-fiction adventure series. The early seasons suffered somewhat from chintzy production values (including computer graphics that were crude even by late 1980s standards), as well as a tendency to fragment the original's all-purpose-outsider character, Mr. Spock, into a variety of somewhat similar types (including Brent Spiner's android Data, Marina Sirtis's empath Deanna Troi, LeVar Burton's blind helmsman Geordi La Forge, and Michael Dorn's Klingon junior officer Worf). But it soon found its own voice and became more expansive and ambitious by the season, mixing ferocious space battles with stories that tested the integrity and humanity of all the major characters. It also introduced a new adversary that eventually supplanted the old series' Klingons and Romulans as a fount of pure menace: the Borg, a race of cyborgs that obeys orders from a hive-mind and is bent on subjugating and absorbing all other sentient life. The series continued the original's legacy while deepening its multicultural vision and fleshing out every character with a novelistic attention to detail. The result was a milestone in televised science fiction.

—MZS

Tanner '88 (HBO, 1988) & Tanner on Tanner (Sundance, 2004)

Robert Altman (*Nashville, The Player*) teamed up with cartoonist Garry Trudeau (*Doonesbury*) to create *Tanner '88*, a stylistically unique political satire about an idealistic, blunt-talking, somewhat reticent Michigan congressman (Michael Murphy) who tries to win the 1988 Democratic presidential nomination. In the manner of some of Altman's early films, as well as novels like *Ragtime*, it blends fictional characters with real personages (making cameos as "themselves"). The entire thing is shot in what was described at the time as a documentary style by people who had never seen a Robert Altman movie: The camera zooms in and out and pans and glides, picking out individual characters in a panorama and then showing you the panorama again. The larger panorama depicts the American political process in all its hypocrisy and promise. Tanner, his campaign manager (Pamela Reed), his statistician (Jim Fyfe), and his political ad-maker (Matt Malloy) struggle to capture Tanner's passion and authenticity without going so far as to "sell" him, a prospect that gives Tanner hives. The cameo players included Kansas senator and future presidential candidate Bob Dole; Kitty Dukakis, wife of 1988 Democratic presidential nominee Michael Dukakis; 1988 Democratic presidential candidate Jesse Jackson; and conservative evangelist Pat Robertson. All interacted seamlessly with Altman and Trudeau's characters, and the direction is brilliant, particularly in a scene where Kevin J. O'Connor's cameraman surreptitiously captures an impromptu Tanner rant that becomes a campaign commercial.

A long-delayed follow-up, 2004's *Tanner on Tanner*, reunited much of the core cast in a story centered on Tanner's documentary filmmaker daughter Alexandra (Cynthia Nixon), whose illness was the reason Tanner originally left politics, as she made a nonfiction movie about her father, struggling with representatives of Democratic presidential nominee John Kerry over whether to excise footage that was critical of the U.S. invasion of Iraq. The result was an alternately poignant and acidic look at how much more shallow and image-driven politics had become since 1988 (not a year for idealists in the first place). A number of subsequent programs have drawn on either or both *Tanners*, including *The West Wing*, *Veep*, *K Street*, and Trudeau's own Amazon series *Alphas*.

—MZS

Tremé (HBO, 2010–2013)

David Simon's follow-up to his critically acclaimed but low-rated *The Wire* was as perversely uncommercial as it was intellectually rigorous and heartfelt: a racially diverse ensemble drama about a group of New Orleans residents struggling to rebuild their city in the aftermath of Hurricane Katrina's devastation. Season 1, set just three months after the flood, showed citizens of different social classes lifting one another up even as their personal lives collapsed into chaos and despair; season 2, which was set a year later, was considerably darker, showing how civic and police corruption, institutional failure, corporate greed, and national amnesia made nearly every character's life worse; season 3 and the truncated season 4 showed the characters starting to rebuild, or at least move on, even as they remembered loved ones who died of natural and unnatural causes (including suicide and murder).

Many of the players were familiar from past Simon productions, including *Homicide: Life on the Streets* and *The Wire*. As envisioned by Simon and his cocreator, Eric Overmyer, *Tremé* was notable for its ferociously democratic storytelling style, which insisted on giving nearly all of the major characters equal screen time in a given episode no matter what they were going through, and for the way that it wove detailed explanations of New Orleans civic life (including the politics of the local jazz and restaurant scenes and the traditions of Mardis Gras Indians and pedestrian funeral processions) into almost every subplot. The core cast included a police officer (David Morse's anticorruption crusader); a civil rights lawyer (Melissa Leo) and her blustering college professor husband (John Goodman); a drug-addicted piano player (Michiel Huisman) and his vastly more talented fiddle-playing girlfriend (Lucia Micarelli); a worldly-wise singer-songwriter (Steve Earle); a brilliant chef (Kim Dickens) and her sometime boyfriend (Steve Zahn), a community radio host who dreamed of becoming both a record industry bigwig and the mayor; a bar owner (Khandi Alexander) and her trombonist and band teacher ex-husband (Wendell Pierce); a Mardis Gras Indian chief (Clarke Peters); and his semifamous jazz trumpeter son (Rob Brown). Most of these characters were based on real people.

The show's key creative inspirations were Robert Altman's sprawling, anecdotally driven movies (*Nashville* and *Short Cuts* especially) and the epic documentaries of Frederick Wiseman (*High School*, *Jackson Heights*, et al.), both of which savored basic human interactions in real time, and weren't afraid to linger for a few minutes on a musical number. The Mardis Gras episodes were consistent highlights, drawing all of the disparate characters together in an organic way that made coincidental meetings seem inevitable rather than contrived. Simon and Overmyer's deliberately fragmented and decentralized storytelling was off-putting to viewers who were accustomed to more goal-directed, plot-driven series, and the mix of professional and nonprofessional actors didn't always work, but even at its least assured, *Tremé*'s mix of righteous anger and tenderhearted journalistic observation set it apart from every other series on the air at that time. And if you watch the whole thing again, you realize that, as in jazz, aspects that seemed to have been conjured on the fly were the product of considerable foresight and a lifetime of experience.

—MZS

"Julie" and "Millicent and Therese," are quite good (the former is about a college professor exacting brutal revenge on a student who spikes her drink and rapes her; the latter stars Black as twin sisters, one repressed, the other monstrous). But everybody remembers the final segment, "Amelia." That's the one with the Zuni fetish doll that chases the title character around the apartment with a miniature spear, shrieking a hideous, high-pitched "YI YI YI YI YI!" At one point, Amelia locks herself in her bathroom, screaming in mortal fear, and you can see the doll's tiny blade going *snicker-snick!* under the door. The entire segment has a pile-driving relentlessness that's still nerve-racking; the fact that the doll is clearly just a marionette with pointy teeth (essentially an evil Muppet) only adds to the creep factor. It's the scariest half hour in the history of US television; even Pennywise the Clown might think twice before watching it after dark.

—MZS

Trilogy of Terror (ABC, 1975)

The one, the only *Trilogy of Terror* was directed by *Dark Shadows* creator Dan Curtis from three stories by Richard Matheson, starring Karen Black as the heroine of all three tales. The first two segments,

True Detective season 1 (HBO, 2014)

The line from the first season of *True Detective* most often quoted by viewers is "Time is a flat circle." It's not originally spoken by the show's philosophizing hero Rust Cohle (Matthew McConaughey), but by a criminal he's in the process of arresting, and even that man is only paraphrasing Nietzsche. But Cohle incorporates the phrase into his own running monologue about time, death, string theory, alternate dimensions, and the painful, repetitive uselessness of human existence. As Cohle talks and talks and talks, the dazzling performance by McConaughey and the sheer tonnage of slippery words and phrases and concepts by writer Nic Pizzolatto are each so impressive in their own way that it's easy to ignore the reality of the show's signature phrase:

All circles are, by definition, flat.

But that was *True Detective* in a nutshell: compulsively watchable, mashing up strains of many different philosophies and TV shows and literary works, and seemingly laden with meaning, but not always as profound as it seemed at first glance.

Created by Pizzolatto, a novelist with minimal TV experience, *True Detective* was part of the new wave of anthology miniseries led by *American Horror Story*. With the short time commitment, Pizzolatto was able to land McConaughey and Woody Harrelson to play his Louisiana state cop heroes: Cohle, a hollowed-out wreck of a man who refers to his oft-tragic life as "a circle of violence and degradation," believes human consciousness to be a "misstep in evolution," and has an unsurprising knack for being able to think like the monsters he chases; and Harrelson's Marty Hart, who presents himself as a normal guy who has all of life's answers but is really a walking hard-on, barely able to control either his temper or his libido, both of which ultimately bring an end to his marriage.

Longtime friends McConaughey and Harrelson brought the characters to such crackling life, and were so hauntingly shot by director Cary Joji Fukunaga (who, in a rarity for TV drama, directed the entire season himself), that the triteness of their personal dilemmas (Hart's in particular) and their investigation (into TV's umpteenth serial killer of young women) scarcely mattered at times. Pizzolatto piled layer upon layer onto the story, which took place across seventeen years and was frequently narrated by older versions of Rust and Marty (whose accounts to two younger detectives didn't always match what we were seeing), with liberal quoting (in both snippets of dialogue and in casting of minor roles) from past HBO dramas like *The Wire* and *Deadwood*, and allusions to not only all of Rust's favorite philosophers but the Robert W. Chambers story collection *The King in Yellow*, which led many viewers to assume the killer was somehow supernatural in origin. Instead, the finale involves our heroes, now middle-aged ex-cops, pursuing a very earthbound bogeyman through a house whose haunting was only the figurative kind.

It was a story about the way we tell stories, and thus more interesting the more different ways that Pizzolatto and Fukunaga had to tell the story. (The season lost a bit of its spark, for instance, once the elder versions of Rust and Marty were part of the action, rather than commenting on it.) And it was aiming to do so many things, and alluding to so many more, that it was all but destined to disappoint some viewers—many of whom had experienced those performances, those haunting visuals, and the Möbius strip narrative structure and, for a few weeks, decided it was not only the next great thing but already the greatest drama ever. It was neither, particularly as the second season—done without Fukunaga or the original stars—tried too hard to correct for some of the first season's flaws (not enough well-defined characters, not enough interest in women), and in the process only cast a spotlight on more of them.

But even with its many borrowed parts, its weak spots and occasional bouts of overpromising, the original *True Detective* installment was riveting television. If it had been a traditional miniseries rather than the anthology kind, I expect we'd look back on it even more kindly.

—AS

The Westerner (NBC, 1960)

American viewers had never seen anything like the half-hour drama *The Westerner*, and after it was gone, it would be a long time before they saw its ilk again. Created by Sam Peckinpah, the series took the then-new tradition of the "adult Western"—exemplified by the likes of *Gunsmoke* and *The Rifleman*—to a new level of sensitivity and maturity, without stinting on the frontier brutality that genre fans expected. The pilot, which aired as part of the anthology series *Zane Grey Theater*, is a thirty-minute mini-movie that sends hero Dave Blassingame (Brian Keith) on a mission to "rescue" a former flame—a woman known as "Jeff" (Diana Millay). Problem is, she doesn't really want to be saved. She's a frontier barmaid who's a virtual slave to a bullying saloon owner and onetime bare-knuckles brawler from England, and although she recognizes the awfulness of her existence, it's the only life she knows. From the pilot's opening moments—which establish the saloon's grubby regulars (including future Peckinpah MVP Warren Oates as a drunk) and show Dave arriving in town and being greeted by a wild-eyed, probably deranged woman trying to sell him a Bible—Peckinpah makes it clear that he isn't interested in cartoon Western heroics. The hero wins the battle but loses the war. (Jeff can't bring herself to leave her captor, who says he'll fall apart without her—a typical abusive male strategy.) "Why should I worry about you?" Dave tells Jeff tenderly as he prepares to leave town, untying a ribbon from her hair. Peckinpah leaves us with a bittersweet message written on the saloon wall: "Tonight a soul is lost / He wanders the wide earth / But he finds only emptiness."

Future episodes refined the series' already distinctive vibe, which presented the hardness and cruelty of frontier life but also celebrated the resilience of people strong enough to live in it. As Dave wandered the show's lovely monochrome landscapes in the company of his dog Brown (and sometimes his best friend Burgundy Smith, played by John Dehner), *The Westerner* cast an empathetic but often merciless eye on all of its characters, including Dave, who often comes across as a forerunner of the antiheroes who

distinguished TV's post-*Sopranos* era. One of the better examples is the episode "Treasure," in which Dave finds a buried stash of coins only to be disputed by an old and feeble prospector (played by Arthur Hunnicutt, but unnamed and identified only as "Old Man"). Dave eventually has to kill the man in self-defense, but there's no glory in it; it's just sad. The genre's "do what a man's gotta do" ethos is constantly questioned and found lacking, never more so than in "Hand on the Gun," which finds Dave trying to persuade a young "greenhorn" cowhand (Ben Cooper) not to fetishize guns and gunfighting; the episode ends with Cooper being gunned down in the street by an older, meaner gunslinger whose dead expression testifies to what killing can do to the soul. Throughout, Keith's appealingly naturalistic performance makes Dave seem like a fundamentally decent man made hard and nearly unreachable by his environment and upbringing. (He's illiterate, too. "I know all the letters already, most of 'em, and I can mark some," he tells the doomed cowhand in "Hand on the Gun," "but I just don't know how to put them together to make words.")

The Westerner was canceled after thirteen episodes due to low ratings (it got crushed by *The Flintstones* on ABC and *Route 66* on CBS) and made little impression on the

■ MINISERIES ■

(TV's dominant prestige format from the mid-'70s through the early '90s, and still an exciting alternative to the ongoing narratives of traditional series)

1. Roots (ABC, 1977); and Roots: The Next Generations (ABC, 1979)

Roots is the most important scripted program in broadcast network history. It aired across eight consecutive nights in January 1977—a go-for-broke gesture by ABC, which made the miniseries out of a sense of social obligation and wanted to "burn off" the entire run quickly in a mostly dead programming month. The producer was David L. Wolper, who specialized in blockbuster documentaries and miniseries (including 1982's *The Thorn Birds*). The source was a book by Alex Haley, coauthor of *The Autobiography of Malcolm X*; it was described as nonfiction until the 1990s, when African American historians and genealogists checked Haley's account of his family's experiences as slaves in North Carolina and Virginia and decided that it was filled with conjecture, inaccuracies, and plagiarized material.

The revelations cast a pall over the program's reputation, which is a shame. Nearly forty years haven't dimmed its ability to illuminate one of the grimmest aspects of US history: its two-hundred-year participation in the transatlantic slave trade and the racism that became institutionalized throughout the country up until the 1960s, barely a decade before *Roots* aired. When you consider *Roots*' timeline proximity to the civil rights marches and riots of the sixties, the intraracial arguments about nonviolent-versus-violent resistance to oppression, and the overall whiteness of popular culture at that time, its very existence seems remarkable. Once you actually watch it, it seems still more remarkable. The episodes' scripts indict white viewers in a meticulous, unrelenting way, showing that the entire nation was complicit in this horror, which ripped indigenous people from one continent and transplanted them in another, taking away language and religion and ritual and replacing it with the practices of oppressors, then insisting that they graciously accept servitude as a fact of life, or worse, as the manifestation of an alien Christian God's will. Unknown or underappreciated black actors played slaves and former slaves. Famous, and in some cases beloved, white TV stars played plantation owners, slave traffickers, overseers, and the wives and children and hired hands who benefited from the slave-based economy even though they didn't think of themselves as active participants in it.

The face of the production was young LeVar Burton, who played the Mandinka tribesman Kunta Kinte, the earliest known descendant of the author. In an iconic opening sequence that was later appropriated by Disney's *The Lion King*, we see the newborn Kunta being held aloft by his father, an image of freedom and possibility that will be ground into dirt when the teenage version of the character is kidnapped by African slavers, carried across the ocean in the hold of a slave ship, and sold into bondage in Maryland, where a fellow slave named Fiddler (Louis Gossett Jr.) teaches him to speak English and advises him to accept his new "American" name, Toby, give up his Mandinka heritage, and accept his lot in life. Kunta tries to escape anyway—the first of several attempts—and is savagely whipped by an overseer. As a middle-aged slave (now played by John Amos), he tries to escape again and has part of his foot amputated with an ax as punishment. He was given a choice between that or castration. "What kind of man would do that to another man, Fiddler?" Kunta asks his friend. "Why they don't just kill me?"

The entire production is dotted with moments of savagery this extreme, including beatings, whippings, lynchings, forced sexual relationships between female slaves and their white bosses or owners, and the separation of families whose members have been sold off to different masters. Every one of these horrific moments is justified, because the intent of *Roots* is to affirm the shared trauma of generations of blacks and make whites who had never really contemplated the visceral reality of it feel at least some small part of its sting. Viewers who had read *Uncle Tom's Cabin* and were aware of the realities of slavery knew about the brutality, as well as the countless daily degradations, and the overall sense of despair that afflicted people who had been reduced to the status of glorified livestock to be worked, bred, sold, and put down.

As in a silent melodrama (a mode that might have inspired parts of *Roots*), every scene is conceived in very broad strokes, and there's no ambiguity about what's happening or what it means for the characters; but the bedrock of *Roots* is still a historical vision of considerable sophistication. It's showing us an inverted form of colonialism: Rather than going to another country to superimpose their culture, the miniseries' European-descended whites have brought Africans to North America, then systematically beaten and bred their indigenous culture out of them over the course of several generations. The casually doled-out whippings, the almost lordly indifference of the plantation owners, the repeated insistences that the slaves speak English and worship the Christian God, all testify to the mass brainwashing that was necessary to maintain the slave economy. As early as episode 2, the sound of fiddle-dependent European folk music, which replaced the Mandinka drums of the opening section, starts to seem psychically oppressive: aural shackles.

Roots brought it all into American living rooms, night after night, and dramatized it through well-written characters portrayed by actors with imagination and empathy. For many white viewers, the miniseries amounted to the first prolonged instance of not merely being asked to identify with cultural experiences that were alien to them but to actually feel them—by watching Kunta and his fellow slaves struggle to be free, either physically or emotionally, only to realize that in a country that had institutionalized white supremacy and had no compelling reason to change its ways, it just wasn't possible.

The bulk of *Roots'* messages and meanings were transmitted through its black actors: Burton; Gossett; Amos; Cicely Tyson (as Kunta's mother, Binta); Madge Sinclair (as Belle Reynolds, who falls in love with the middle-aged, maimed Kunta); Leslie Uggams (as Kizzy Reynolds, a slave secretly taught to read and write); Lawrence Hilton-Jacobs (as Kizzy's lover Noah, who tries to escape as Kunta did before him); and Ben Vereen (as the future cockfighting impresario "Chicken" George Moore, Kizzy's son by a white slaveholder). Many of the performances are as saddening as they are revelatory: Hilton-Jacobs, who was stuck playing a smooth-talking clown on *Welcome Back, Kotter*, is heroically righteous as Noah, and Amos and Sinclair's tenderness in love scenes reminds us of how rarely African American performers were allowed to play romantic, sexual beings on national TV in the '70s. (When Kunta and Belle meet secretly in a barn, she strokes his shoulders and cradles his face, then removes his shirt and caresses the whip scars on his back, and he speaks to her in their native language, home at last.)

But the show's casting masterstroke occurred in the white roles. They were filled by actors who had usually played sympathetic, adorable, or noble characters. Ed Asner, best known as the curmudgeonly but honorable Lou Grant on *The Mary Tyler Moore Show*, played the hired captain of the ship that brought Kunta and other kidnapped Africans to the United States. The moment when he's shown the blueprint of the ship and realizes what those cramped berths and shackles are for, then accepts the job anyway, might be the most damning statement TV had yet made about the white man's ability to compartmentalize revulsion when there is money to be made. The overseer on the voyage who assures the captain that the slaves aren't really human is played by Ralph Waite, the crinkly-eyed dad from *The Waltons*. Chuck Connors, the righteous widowered rancher from *The Rifleman*, plays Tom Moore, a planter who rapes

and impregnates Kizzy. Dr. William Reynolds, portrayed by Robert Reed, the father from *The Brady Bunch*, at first seems like a fairly benign master, at least compared to some of the openly sadistic characters we'd met up until that point; he assures his slaves that he won't splinter blood ties by selling any of them off. But when Noah tries to escape, he changes his mind and sells Noah and Kizzy to separate plantations. Kizzy turns to Missy Anne Reynolds (played by Broadway's Peter Pan, Sandy Duncan) for help because they've always been close; but when Kizzy's carted off, screaming, "No, no, I don't want to go!" Missy Anne watches through an upstairs window, her face a cold mask. The political and emotional reality of *Roots'* drama is still stunning. Nothing happens that would not have happened. There is no hand-holding of white viewers, no dog-whistle assurances that if they were in this situation, they would not have behaved abominably. Time and again, the white characters are faced with a stark choice: Do the morally right thing and set themselves in opposition to slave culture, or maintain the status quo and hold on to their privileges. They always go with the second option.

Roots was produced on the cheap, with blandly lit interior scenes, unconvincing old-age makeup, and scrub-dotted California locations standing in for the humid greenness of the former Confederate States, and the physical continuity in the casting is sometimes laughable (in no universe does LeVar Burton grow up to become John Amos). But for all its missteps and faults, and there are many, it is distinguished by its moral and political clarity about what slavery was and what it meant to US history and African and African American identity. A sequel, *Roots: The Next Generations*, followed in 1979, and was nearly as good, following the family's story through Reconstruction, the Northern migration, Prohibition, World War II, and the 1960s. It featured Marlon Brando in a cameo as Ku Klux Klan leader George Lincoln Rockwell, and culminated with Alex Haley (James Earl Jones) meeting his first great subject, Malcolm X (Al Freeman Jr.), then returning to his family's ancestral village in Jufureh, the Gambia, Africa. The saga ends with a griot telling Haley the story of a young man named Kunta Kinte. The power of this moment, like so many others in *Roots*, is overwhelming, and it renders the questions of historical accuracy largely moot. This is not the story of one man's family, but the story of a nation's secret history, a tale that hasn't yet been fully engaged with and understood, and that still lacks a satisfying ending.

—MZS

2. *Angels in America* (HBO, 2003)

The thesis of Tony Kushner's drama, brilliantly adapted by stage and screen director Mike Nichols, goes like this: Before AIDS, it was possible for straight Americans to either ignore homosexuals or accept them as personalities without dwelling on the one aspect of their lives that defined them as different—what they did in the bedroom. After AIDS, such a reaction became impossible, but the compassion demonstrated by many straight people was met with an equal or greater rise in public, virulent homophobia, which treated AIDS sufferers as pariahs and harbingers of death. *Angels* is acutely sensitive to this phenomenon, and captures it in both graceful language and simple but striking moments of observed behavior. The entire miniseries is filled with philosophically minded soliloquies. Nichols visualizes them by splitting the difference between theater and cinema—opening Kushner's adaptation out, but not so much that you lose sight of the fact that it derived from a play of ideas. The alternately sprightly and haunting score is by Thomas Newman, and the special effects by Richard Edlund, who worked on the original *Star Wars* trilogy. Meryl Streep plays four roles: AIDS researcher Hannah Pitt, convicted spy Ethel Rosenberg, a rabbi, and an angel.

"We're just a bad dream the real world's having," says Prior Walter (Justin Kirk), a gay man afflicted with HIV, the virus that causes AIDS. "The rest of the world is waking up." It's a key line because it summarizes two of Kushner's more provocative assertions: first, that a large section of American society was secretly or not-so-secretly thrilled that AIDS hit gays so hard; second, that if the spread of HIV hadn't slowed, it might have decimated entire demographic groups that the white, heterosexual middle class and upper class considers threatening—not just gay men, but drug users, people of color, the poor, and others who were disproportionately harmed by the plague.

Nobody embodies this intolerance like New York lawyer and Republican political fixer Roy Cohn (played with demented charisma by Al Pacino, who chews through Kushner's elaborate soliloquies with a chainsaw tongue). As a gay man diagnosed with HIV, Cohn could have used his famous name and his clout with the Reagan administration to help afflicted people gain access to experimental medicine—or at least be treated with dignity. Instead, he protected his own health and reputation; in *Angels*, he's shown bulldozing a government health official into giving him a stockpile of AZT, a then-experimental drug, while intimidating his own physician (James Cromwell) into treating his condition secretly so that his public image as a straight man wouldn't be damaged. "AIDS is what homosexuals have," Cohn instructs his doctor. "I have liver cancer." Cohn hates the word "homosexual" because, he says, it reduces the complexity of human life to a single characteristic.

In a roundabout way, *Angels* endorses Cohn's philosophy even as it condemns his treachery. In a scene that ironically echoes Cohn's rant about labels, Walter's boyfriend Louis Ironson (Ben Shenkman) insists that in human relationships, it is necessary to look beyond labels, beyond snap judgments, beyond absolutism of all sorts, because "it is the shape of a life, the total complexity, gathered, arranged, and considered in the end, that matters, not some stamp of salvation which disperses all the complexity in some unsatisfying decision. The balancing of the scales."

—MZS

3. *Lonesome Dove* (CBS, 1989)

Larry McMurtry wrote the novel *Lonesome Dove* at a time when he was fed up with the romanticization of the American West and the books and films inspired by it. It's an epic with a bleak, cynical tone, about a cattle drive from Texas to Montana where the heroes tend to die in the most stubborn or embarrassing ways possible, while the chief villain is captured offscreen by other characters.

What's impressive about the miniseries, directed by Simon Wincer and written by Bill Wittliff, is the way it changes almost nothing of McMurtry's story or dialogue, yet manages to find the sentimentality within it in a way that coexists with the despair, rather than undermining it.

So Robert Duvall's talkative old gunslinger Gus McCrae still comes to a grim end (refusing to let a poisoned leg be amputated out of vanity), but earlier moments when he's asked to deploy his Texas Ranger skills are genuinely thrilling; if anything, it makes his ignoble death hit even harder. And though finishing the cattle drive doesn't fill the chasm at the core of Gus's stoic

partner Woodrow F. Call (Tommy Lee Jones), the long journey north contains all the elements of a classic adventure story, even if Call is unmoved by most of it.

Maybe the trick is to read McMurtry's book—or the sequels and prequels that followed (and were later adapted for TV), each seemingly even bleaker in response to the audience's love of the first miniseries—while listening to Basil Poledouris's soaring score, which gives you the romanticism and revisionism all at once. But the miniseries itself does a great job of that.

—AS

4. *Band of Brothers* (HBO, 2001)

Just as *From the Earth to the Moon* allowed Tom Hanks to expand the micro story of Apollo 13 into the macro tale of the whole Apollo program, *Band of Brothers* let Hanks and Steven Spielberg tell a far more thorough accounting of the European theater in World War II than they got to do with *Saving Private Ryan*.

Following a single company of airborne infantrymen from basic training to V-day, the ten episodes are a sprawling affair, full of unknown, skinny actors—many of them, like leading man Damian Lewis as decent and inspiring Easy Company commander Dick Winters, Brits trying on American accents—with grimy faces and matching uniforms. As a result, it's not always easy to make out who's who in the early chapters, which compensate with impressive spectacle, particularly in the terrifying depiction of what it was like to parachute into Normandy the night before D-day.

It's in the miniseries' second half where the creative team (including *From the Earth to the Moon* holdover Graham Yost) really start landing haymakers, switching from the ensemble style of the opening to a single-POV structure that makes situations like the Battle of the Bulge or the liberation of a concentration camp feel even more harrowing from the personal touch.

With Lewis, Ron Livingston, Donnie Wahlberg, Neal McDonough, Michael Cudlitz, and the rest of the cast so committed and so likable as the men of Easy, it's among the most compulsively rewatchable miniseries ever made: a dark and soul-scarring journey, but also an epic and rousing adventure yarn.

—AS

5. Life with Judy Garland: Me and My Shadows (ABC, 2001)

Life with Judy Garland: Me and My Shadows was part of a wave of showbiz-centric historical movies and miniseries that aired on network TV in the '90s and early aughts; the deluge included the Marilyn Monroe biopics *Blonde* and *Norma Jean & Marilyn, Martin and Lewis, Lucy* (as in Lucille Ball), *Hendrix* (as in Jimi), *The Three Stooges*, and *The Beach Boys: An American Family*. This one and the TV-movie *James Dean* (located elsewhere in this book) were the best, matching superior writing and filmmaking to personalities that rose far beyond the level of celebrity impersonation, and managing to suggest something akin to a critic's or biographer's point of view on the material.

Me and My Shadows treated its title character with much empathy and intelligence. Directed by Robert Allan Ackerman, and adapted by Robert L. Freedman from the memoir by Garland's daughter Lorna Luft, this two-part miniseries is bracketed by Garland's first and last public performances, as a little girl singing "Jingle Bells" in a vaudeville theater and as a boozing, pill-addicted grown-up singing "Get Happy" for a sold-out crowd in Copenhagen. Tammy Blanchard plays the young Garland, then known as Frances Ethel Gumm; Judy Davis plays her from 1944 onward. All of the expected biographical highlights get touched upon (including Garland's career battles, substance-abuse issues, marriages, and children), but they're structured around specific musical and acting milestones, a simple but clever device that gives the story a crystalline linearity while validating the idea that performance was Garland's most potent and rewarding intoxicant. Davis's incarnation of the grown-up Garland ranks with her very best work. Blanchard, then a juvenile, is as strong as Davis, and does her own singing. As in the similarly lush *James Dean*, the re-creations of period Los Angeles—specifically the back lots, nightclubs, restaurants, and bungalows—amount to a show of their own. Anybody who's thinking of trying to pack an entire legendary career into two nights should study these two classics.

—MZS

6. *From the Earth to the Moon* (HBO, 1998)

Like many a boomer, Tom Hanks grew up dreaming of being an astronaut. Starring in *Apollo 13* didn't so much satisfy that old fantasy as rekindle it, to the point where he went to HBO to craft an even more elaborate love letter to the men (and, occasionally, women)

responsible for taking humankind to the surface of another heavenly body.

What's most impressive about the twelve-hour miniseries isn't the scope—though in re-creating both life on earth in the 1960s and in the void of space, the technical work is impeccable—but the variety. Most episodes are devoted to a single Apollo mission, and where the public unfortunately grew bored with what they felt was the sameness of them after Neil Armstrong's first footsteps, *From the Earth to the Moon* finds a different angle and narrative approach to each.

So the Apollo 9 episode is less about the astronauts who first tested the lunar module in space than it is about the nerds who devoted a decade of their lives to designing and building a spacecraft no one thought would work. The Apollo 12 episode is a buddy comedy about the three wisecracking pals assigned to history's greatest afterthought, the one about Apollo 15 deals with NASA's scientists teaching a bunch of test pilots how to be field geologists, and so on.

Overall, it's an even more persuasive argument for why we should someday go back to the moon than the beloved movie that inspired it.

—AS

7. *The Corner* (HBO, 2000)

This four-part miniseries about a year in the life of a drug-riddled Baltimore neighborhood is the ancestral inspiration for *The Wire*. Written by David Simon and David Mills from Simon and Ed Burns's same-titled nonfiction book, and directed by actor-filmmaker Charles S. Dutton (*Roc*), it has all of the characteristics of a Simon TV production, including scenes shot in real locations, a cast that mixes film industry veterans, local actors, and nonprofessionals, a determination to situate all of the action within a wider sociopolitical context, and an austere style that often feels like a twenty-first-century American cousin of Italian neorealism. The main characters are Gary McCullough (T. K. Carter), a junkie who lost a respectable middle-class life to heroin, scavenges for scrap metal, and lives in terror that his son DeAndre (Sean Nelson) will see what he's become; DeAndre, who suffers through a love-hate relationship with his dad while trying to live a legitimate life in a series of mostly humiliating jobs; and Fran Boyd (Khandi Alexander), mother of DeAndre and lover of Gary, who worries about respectability when she's not shooting up or getting embroiled in scams. Except for a shoot-out in episode 3 that's mainly notable for its clumsiness and sheer chaos, there's nothing in the way of traditional crime-film violence in *The Corner*. It focuses instead on the intractable realities of inner-city drugs, showing time and again that even if using is a matter of willpower, morality, and upbringing (the official conservative narrative, seen here as dubious), it's hard to get clean and stay clean when you have to wait eight weeks for a state-sponsored detox bed, and can't find a decent job anywhere near a neighborhood so poor that few of its residents own cars. The acting, writing, and direction are peerless, the material heartbreaking but never maudlin; despair is barely held at bay by knockabout humor.

—MZS

8. *Olive Kitteridge* (HBO, 2014)

Eyebrows understandably rise upon hearing of a miniseries about repressed small-town Maine residents described as "thrilling," but that's what *Olive Kitteridge* is. Its excitement originates in Frances McDormand's performance as the titular character, a schoolteacher whose sharp tongue wounds everyone, and who takes her kindhearted pharmacist husband, Henry (Richard Jenkins), and their son, Chris

(John Gallagher Jr.), for granted. The character would be purely comical, and perhaps insufferable, if her crankiness were all that we knew about her, and if *Olive Kitteridge* were only about what it's like to deal with a bullying prig who prefers to think of herself as a person of high standards.

Luckily, there's much more going on in this miniseries, which was directed by Lisa Cholodenko (who directed McDormand in *Laurel Canyon*) and adapted by Jane Anderson (*How to Make an American Quilt*) from Elizabeth Strout's novel. Throughout, the filmmakers give us quietly extraordinary moments of empathy and lyricism, such as the scene where Olive's former student Kevin Coulson (Cory Michael Smith) hallucinates plants growing out of a bar singer's baby grand piano as she sings the Carpenters' "Close to You," and the pathetic way Henry overdoes his smiles and laughs whenever he talks to the cute pharmacy employee (Zoe Kazan) that he's sweet on, and that Olive has cruelly nicknamed "the Mouse." The saltwater-abraded panoramas are by Frederick Elmes, who shot some of David Lynch's masterpieces, including *Blue Velvet* and *The Straight Story*.

Because the program works so well as curdled Americana, you might not be inclined to peel back its other layers, much less delve into what's happening at a storytelling level (which is even more impressive); but unobtrusive ambition is part of what makes *Olive Kitteridge* so pleasurable, along with its deep empathy for mentally or emotionally disturbed people who believe their problems are minor.

—MZS

9. *Generation Kill* (HBO, 2008)

Having already done plenty of disguised Iraq War commentary in their previous project, *Wire* creators David Simon and Ed Burns were able to dispense with metaphor entirely and tackle the harsh, ill-designed realities of the Iraq invasion head-on.

Adapted from Evan Wright's book about his time embedded with the First Recon Marines at the start of the invasion, *Generation Kill* is three parts black comedy to every one part military adventure. A pugnacious noncom fanatically enforces their commanding officer's grooming standard, bellowing, "POLICE THAT MOOSTASH!" at Marines who theoretically have better things to worry about. An officer the men derisively nickname "Captain America" takes a recovered enemy weapon as a trophy and likes to shoot it off in celebration, even though the sound of an AK-47 can invite friendly fire from other units who don't know who's wielding it. Rules of engagement are constantly changing, and while American forces easily dismantle the Iraqi military within three weeks, it becomes clear that no one in charge has thought through what to do next.

Yet even as its commentary on the overall experience is pointed, the miniseries is very much on the side of the Marines, and particularly the group traveling in the Humvee with Wright. They have off-key sing-alongs to "Tainted Love" and "Teenage Dirtbag," do unseemly things with a photo of Wright's girlfriend, and mock one another constantly, but they're also excellent at their jobs, even if those giving the orders don't know quite how to use them.

The overall commentary is chilling, even as the presentation is unapologetically entertaining.

—AS

10. *Show Me a Hero* (HBO, 2015)

Sometimes, you have to wonder if David Simon's entire career in television was based on a dare:

Okay, your first big cable project is going to be a miniseries about dope fiends. Then you're going to make a show where the average viewer will need to watch at least four episodes to understand or even decide if they like it. Then you're going to follow that up with another miniseries about the Iraq invasion at a time when the public has no interest in stories about that mess. Oh, and then you'll do a show about jazz and cooking with an even less traditional plot than all the others.

Hey, and while you're at it, you might as well try a third miniseries about municipal housing laws!

Working with a higher-profile cast (Oscar Isaac, Catherine Keener, Winona Ryder) and director (Paul Haggis) than he ever had before, Simon and cowriter William F. Zorzi made *Show Me a Hero* into a superb example of how Eat Your Vegetables TV can also be incredibly enjoyable. Adapting Lisa Belkin's book about the ugly late '80s attempt to integrate public housing in Yonkers, New York, it returns to Simon's pet themes about the difficulty institutions have in accepting and effecting change, and puts some profoundly human faces on it, from Isaac as the city's overwhelmed young mayor to Keener as an aging resident who starts out seeming like the intolerant face of the opposition and proves to be much more complicated over time.

The performances are great, Haggis does a superb job capturing the ugliness of the protests in and around city hall, and the concluding moments contain that usual dose of David Simon magic, where everyday occasions that the audience takes for granted suddenly become an invitation for the waterworks to fly.

—AS

11. Rich Man, Poor Man (ABC, 1976)

Although *Roots* is widely credited with starting the 1970s and '80s miniseries craze, this adaptation of Irwin Shaw's 1969 novel about the German American Jordache family got there first, becoming an unexpected smash and turning its principal cast (Peter Strauss, Nick Nolte, and Susan Blakely) into rising stars.

Strauss is the rich man, Rudy, who rises out of his working-class background to become a powerhouse in business and politics; Blakely is Rudy's childhood sweetheart, Julie Prescott, who eventually marries him; Nolte is Tom, the black-sheep (actually blond-haired) brother in the family, a handsome and charismatic but self-destructive man who eventually ekes out a living as a prizefighter; Edward Asner and Dorothy McGuire play the parents, Axel and Mary, who cling to old-world values as America remakes itself around them. The supporting cast is a veritable murderer's row of great character actors, including Kim Darby, Norman Fell, Fionnula Flanagan, Gloria Grahame, Murray Hamilton, Van Johnson, George Maharis, Dorothy Malone. Ray Milland, and Talia Shire. Semiscandalous at the time for its frank treatment of adult themes (including alcoholism, adultery, class bias, racism, and McCarthyism), *Rich Man, Poor Man* holds up well, thanks to its unfussy script (by Dean Riesner), its uniformly excellent performances (led by the irresistible Nolte), and its lush production values, which served notice to Hollywood studios that TV could feel big and important. The score, by Alex North (*Spartacus*), makes the whole thing feel exuberant yet wise. The final shot of Tom leaving town on a bus, contemplating a yo-yo that is this production's Rosebud, still stings. An inferior sequel, *Rich Man, Poor Man, Book Two*, followed in 1977, and was likewise a smash.

—MZS

12. *The Thorn Birds* (ABC, 1983)

Based on Colleen McCullough's 1977 best seller, this four-part, eight-hour miniseries spans fifty years in the lives of the Cleary family. Rachel Ward plays both the teenage and the adult versions of the heroine, Meggie Cleary, a poor girl who moves to the sheepshearing station of Drogheda in the Australian Outback to live with her rich cousin Mary Carson (Barbara Stanwyck). The local priest, Ralph de Bricassart (Richard Chamberlain, who's often stoic like an alabaster statue of a saint), befriends Mary, hoping to secure a large enough bequest from her to win a release from his purgatory. The hot-to-trot Mary wants to defrock Ralph, but he's not interested, tolerating her insistence because she's loaded, and because Meggie is so adorable; but once Meggie blossoms into a woman, you could cut the sexual tension with the blades used in episode 3's rightly celebrated sheepshearing sequence. There's more plot in *The Thorn Birds* than many of its synopses might suggest; most of it has to do with Meggie's two-steps-forward, one-step-back progress through a male-dominated world that has plenty of use for a beautiful woman but none for an independent one. But most of her major decisions are still informed by her tortured relationship with the priest, and this miniseries—much more so than the novel—keeps building toward the inevitable moment when Ralph doffs his turned-around collar and breaks at least three commandments.

The ultimate TV "will they or won't they," *The Thorn Birds* is the second-highest-rated miniseries ever to air on American TV, behind *Roots*. In terms of social impact, it couldn't compete, not that it seriously pretended to; it aspired to be more of a broadcast network's answer to a serious-but-not-really Hollywood epic like *Gone with the Wind* or *Giant* (which, like this miniseries, aged its cast with subtle latex eye wrinkles and gray hair dye rather than sagging skin and liver spots). Scored by Henry Mancini and photographed by Bill Butler (*Jaws*), it's a superior example of long-form melodrama, '70s-style; not a whole lot happens by twenty-first-century TV standards, yet the eight hours fly by. The supporting cast includes Christopher Plummer, Jean Simmons, Richard Kiley, and Bryan Brown, whose working-class magnetism briefly steals the spotlight away from Meggie and Ralph's pining and moping.

—MZS

13. *Top of the Lake* (Sundance, 2013)

This New Zealand–set crime thriller is highly recommended to fans of its cowriter, coproducer, and sometime director, Jane Campion (*The Piano, Portrait of a Lady*); its leading lady, *Mad Men*'s Elisabeth Moss, who stars as the heroine, a troubled police investigator; and, most of all, to anyone who's watched in dismay over the past twenty-one years as program after program tried to equal the great British anthology series *Prime Suspect* only to fail miserably. The main plot concerns the mysterious disappearance of Tui Mitcham (Jacqueline Joe), a twelve-year-old pregnant girl who's the daughter of the town bully and top criminal, Matt Mitcham (Peter Mullan). *Top of the Lake*'s heroine, Robin Griffin (Moss), leaves her fiancé in Sydney to return to her hometown— a verdant mountain town—to confront demons in her past and becomes swept up in Tui's story. Her behavior seems erratic, bordering on unprofessional and nonsensical, until you learn her secrets and study her interactions with the townspeople and with her mother, who's suffering from cancer.

And at that point, you start to figure out that *Top of the Lake* is as much a fable or cautionary tale as it is a detective story. It's packed with situations that play like archetypal showdowns between representatives of male and female psychology. As in Campion's movies, the images here are as palpably female in their textures and implications as Martin Scorsese's are male; the entire production seems as fecund as the Garden of Eden, and as symbol-laden. Mitcham is a bad daddy par excellence, a long-haired patriarch with macho criminal sons, always twisting the verbal knife to gain advantage, especially when dealing with women. His counterpart is GJ (Holly Hunter, star of *The Piano*), an American guru with flowing white hair who leads a colony of damaged-but-healing females who've taken up refuge in storage containers on land that Mitcham claims was sold out from under him. (That it was sold to women adds insult to injury; the man's a reflexive misogynist, and each time he enters GJ's camp, the story seems to shudder.) From the opening scene in which Tui wanders into water and seems inclined to drown herself, you know you're in the hands of a master storyteller working close to her subconscious.

—MZS

14. *John Adams* (HBO, 2008)

Based on David McCullough's biography, this HBO miniseries is the finest dramatization of the life of a founding father of the United States of America: gritty, scrupulously intelligent, wryly amusing, sometimes bawdy, and altogether uninterested in tedious Great Man posturing. Paul Giamatti, who at that stage of his career was known mainly as a comic character actor, proved a perfect if surprising choice to guide audiences through formative events in the nation's early history, including the Boston Massacre, the Second Continental Congress, the Declaration of Independence, the formation of alliances with countries hostile to Great Britain, the Revolutionary War, and the aftermath (which is when the hard part really started because the new nation had to figure out how to protect and pay for itself). This miniseries' vision of Adams paints him as a passionate, sometimes intemperate and resentful intellectual, but righteous and clever and altogether decent, even when he's being judgmental. (The scenes of Adams disagreeing with Tom Wilkinson's earthy, sensually oriented Benjamin Franklin in postwar France are especially memorable. "You are not a man for Paris," Franklin tells him. "Paris requires a certain amount of indecency.")

All seven chapters were shot in and around Colonial Williamsburg, Virginia, and in Hungarian locations that could pass for unspoiled North American wilderness. HBO's "go 'head, burn money" attitude is very much in evidence. The re-creations of colonial and postcolonial life have a nearly tactile realism, especially when depicting less pleasant aspects of that time such as tarring and feathering by vigilantes and the use of "bleeding" as a treatment for smallpox. Director Tom Hooper (*The King's Speech*) keeps the camera at ground level whenever possible, the better to create a "you are there" feeling. As written by Kirk Ellis (a TV-movie and miniseries specialist who adapted Truman Capote's *The Grass Harp* for TV and penned the underrated *The Beach Boys: An American Family*), *John Adams* looks for the recognizably, at times poignantly human element in every encounter. The spine of its sprawling narrative is the marriage of true minds between John and his wife, Abigail (Laura Linney), his constant companion and most trusted adviser for fifty-four years, proving that when she admonishes him, "You do not need to quote great men to show you are one."

—MZS

15. *Hatfields & McCoys* (History, 2012)

This three-part History Channel miniseries, starring Kevin Costner and Bill Paxton as heads of feuding Southern clans, is so grim and despairing that only a masochist or a Western completist would binge-watch the whole thing. The impulsive post–Civil War killing of a McCoy by a Hatfield touches off round after round of reprisals, stretching out over decades, and the slow-motion bloodbath is observed by director Kevin Reynolds (*Waterworld*) and screenwriter Ted Mann (*Deadwood*) with incredulity and lament. For every one of the participants, this feud became, in effect, their life's work, eclipsing their war experience, their domestic roles, and any legitimate business they transacted over the decades.

And *Hatfields & McCoys* turns the macho code inside out to show its revolting interior. Some of the most seemingly ridiculous twists are drawn from reality: Matt Barr's rakish young Johnse Hatfield's dallies with two McCoy women, Roseanna McCoy (Lindsay Pulsipher) and her cousin Nancy (Jena Malone). This triangle might feel a touch too *Romeo and Juliet* if Johnse weren't such an adorable little weasel. The miniseries features sterling work from mostly grime-covered actors, including Costner, whose Devil Anse Hatfield presents as a typical strong-silent type but quickly seems intractable and vicious; Paxton as Randall McCoy, whose wife, Sally (played by Mare Winningham), finds the same grotesque shadings in "stand by your man" as Costner does in "do what a man's gotta do"; and Tom Berenger as Devil's uncle, Jim Vance, who reflexively fans the flames of every outrage because if its embers die, his life will have no meaning.

—MZS

16. *Mildred Pierce* (HBO, 2011)

This Todd Haynes adaptation of James M. Cain's proto-feminist potboiler stars Kate Winslet as Mildred Pierce, a divorced single mother who splits from her distracted, cheating husband, Bert (Brian F. O'Byrne), takes a grueling job as a waitress, starts selling her delicious homemade pies on the side, works her way into the restaurant business, has a torrid and troubled affair with a penniless former playboy named Monty Beragon (Guy Pearce), and struggles to master her fate, understand herself, and raise her daughters (the eldest of whom, Evan Rachel Wood's Veda, becomes a brilliant opera singer and a sociopathic, manipulative monster). Strong as Winslet is in *Mildred Pierce*'s lengthy dialogue scenes, she's even more effective in silent close-ups, letting conflicting emotions play out on the heroine's face as she watches, listens, and thinks. Haynes, whose filmography includes such art-house touchstones as *Safe*, *Velvet Goldmine*, and *Carol*, does every actor that favor, favoring action and reaction equally, delivering the opulent costumes, sets, vintage cars, and period music that viewers expect from an HBO historical drama, but with a more intuitive touch than is common to programs funded on this scale. There are no villains (not even the hateful Veda), only blinkered, damaged people. You react to them as you might to valued people in your own life, alternating exasperation and affection.

The scene in episode 3 where Mildred and Bert eat at her seaside restaurant and hear Veda's voice coming through the radio is one of the great set pieces of the aughts, TV or film. The shot over Mildred's and Bert's shoulders of the radio broadcasting the music; the close-up of Mildred staring at the radio and listening to it with half the frame blocked out by the back of the radio: All have talismanic power. After the scene's closing profile shot of Mildred staring out at the sea at night, the camera tracks right, and the screen fills up with blackness that expresses the void Veda's absence created in her mother. There's a sense that Mildred's emotions are casting themselves out into the blackness, or onto the ocean, in a cosmic reaching-out.

—MZS

17. *Andersonville* (TNT, 1996)

Bankrolled by Turner Network honcho and Civil War enthusiast Ted Turner, this two-part miniseries about life in the hellish Confederate Civil War prison camp is one of the most grueling historical dramas ever aired on US television. One part documentary-frank re-creation, one part prison-escape picture, the production has a Kafkaesque feel for the nightmare anti-logic of life inside an institution where basic amenities are nonexistent, dignity is a dream, and both inmates and guards are so numbed by deprivation and the dread that the war will never end that they've descended to an animalistic level. Forty-five thousand soldiers were imprisoned at Andersonville; more than twelve thousand died there, of starvation, disease, violent crime, and bullets fired by guards at inmates who were only trying to procure food, water, or a jailer's attention. Directed by John Frankenheimer, a pioneering live-TV drama director who went on to helm such cinema classics as *The Manchurian Candidate* (1962) and *Seconds* (1966), *Andersonville* is a master class in camera placement and movement and the use of percussive editing to build and release tension. It's Frankenheimer's assurance behind the camera that makes this harrowing drama fascinating rather than punishing. You don't just see and hear a place that hadn't existed for 130 years prior to this miniseries' production; you can practically smell the gunpowder and sweat and feel the muck beneath your hobnailed boots. The stark black-and-white Civil War photos of Mathew Brady were an inspiration for the cinematography (by Walter Hill's regular lenser Ric Waite); that affinity comes through, even though the images are in muddy, bloody color.

—MZS

of using clowns as children's entertainers was either a fool, a sadist, or a psychologist doing an experiment that continued long after his death.

More than twenty-five years later, some aspects of *It* haven't aged well, particularly the way the climax, due to the limitations of special effects at the time, presents the embodiment of all evil as, essentially, a giant spider creature. But the miniseries (written by Lawrence D. Cohen and Tommy Lee Wallace, and directed by Wallace) is the best of the many Stephen King TV adaptations (over even *Salem's Lot* and *The Stand*) because of the way it brings the book's primary villain—sewer-dwelling, child-murdering clown Pennywise—to such terrifying life in the form of Tim Curry.

Tell an adult of a certain age, "They all float," and just watch them jump back in disturbed memory of Curry's performance and how effectively King and the filmmakers used Pennywise as a stand-in for so many different nightmares (real and imagined) of childhood.

—AS

18. *It* (ABC, 1990)

Clowns are creepy. This is not an opinion. This is scientific fact. Whoever first came up with the idea

19. *The Winds of War* (ABC, 1983)

Shot on location in the United States, United Kingdom, Italy, Austria, and the former Yugoslavia, and boasting a $35 million budget ($80 million by today's standards), this seven-part, nearly fifteen-hour ABC miniseries about the early years of World War II was the largest production ever attempted for broadcast TV up through its premiere date in 1983—a roll of the dice so grand that some worried its failure would sink the network. But the production, which was written by Herman Wouk from his same-named best seller and executive-produced and directed by Dan Curtis (*Dark Shadows*), was such a smash that it inspired networks to wager ever-larger sums on ever-more-immense productions (including 1988's *War and Remembrance*, an even longer sequel). The network miniseries arms race continued through the late 1990s, at which point the mass audience splintered and broadcast networks began ceding limited-run prestige projects to cable. *The Winds of War*, which interweaves subplots about the fortunes of the fictional Henry and Jastrow families with actual historical events and personages (including Adolf Hitler), is significant mainly for its scope and popularity. Much of it has the feeling of having been made, and on a Brobdingnagian scale, not because it urgently *needed* to exist, but because ABC had enjoyed six comfortable years after *Roots* and was walking with a swagger.

The Winds of War was considered not half-bad in its day, though not worth as many hours as ABC gave it. Time has been unkind to its miniaturized re-creations of World War II naval battles (which were unconvincing even in 1983) and its overreliance on documentary clips and footage from other productions (including *Tora! Tora! Tora!*, which supplied much of the Pearl Harbor attack footage). Its juxtaposition of Jewish suffering in Fascist-dominated Europe against opulent black-tie diplomatic receptions and full-dress military presentations is irksome as well. Many of the scenes involving the Jastrows fleeing the Nazi war machine are tense, despite their Saturday-morning-serial ludicrousness, but the Navy and diplomatic stuff feels obligatory, and some of it lies there gasping for breath. Robert Mitchum's lead performance as naval officer and FDR adviser Victor "Pug" Henry keeps things watchable, even though he seems too old and bored to play a character famed for his alertness and intuition (he predicts the Nazi invasion of Poland and the German-Russian nonaggression pact before either are announced). Ali MacGraw is terrible as Natalie Jastrow, a steel-spined Jewish woman trying to save her dad, Aaron (John Houseman), and the rest of her family; Jan-Michael Vincent is even worse as Pug's son Byron, who risks his life for Natalie and her family without ever changing his expression. There should have been a numeric graphic in the corner of the TV totaling the dollars spent per minute; *The Winds of War* is risible as drama, but as a window into an Atlantis-like era of broadcast network plenty, it's essential.

—MZS

20. *Horace and Pete* (LouisCK.net, 2016)

Louis C.K.'s first project after *Louie* was a slow and quiet (though profane) series of interconnected plays, self-distributed through his website. Set in a Brooklyn bar that had passed through generations of owners named Horace or Pete, and intertwining 2016 social upheavals with the characters' resistance to change, the program owed more to live TV plays and Norman Lear sitcoms than to any comedies being made at the time. Nobody knew it was a miniseries until the finale cauterized every dangling subplot. The formidable cast included C.K. and Steve Buscemi as the current owners (respectively, a divorced schlub and a man battling mental illness); Edie Falco as their sister, a cancer patient looking to sell the bar; and Alan Alda as Pete's biological dad, an Archie Bunker type. Ragged, tenderhearted, and insightful, it suggested the way toward America's (and TV's) future could be found by studying the past.

—MZS

▪ TV-MOVIES ▪

(Films made directly for television, which rivaled contemporaneous big-screen movies in artistry or scope. —MZS)

1. *Duel* (ABC, 1971)

The start of a great career: Steven Spielberg's. Dennis Weaver plays David Mann, a motorist who's targeted for death by a faceless trucker while driving through hilly desert terrain in the American Southwest. As adapted by Richard Matheson (*I Am Legend*) from a short story originally published in *Playboy*, and as directed by a then twenty-three-year-old Orson Welles–wannabe with an uncanny grasp of screen geography, the result feels a bit like a dry run for such future Spielberg classics as *Jaws* and *War of the Worlds*, wherein plucky individuals scramble to endure or defeat a faceless, implacable force; the vehicular mayhem also prefigures the chase sequences in the Indiana Jones films and in Spielberg's first theatrical feature, 1974's road drama *The Sugarland Express*. Extreme high and low angles emphasize the fearsomeness of the rusty, battered truck, the front grille of which is dotted with license plates that were presumably collected as trophies from the trucker's previous victims. The sound design amps up the truck's engine noise to the point where it seems to be roaring and howling like a demon. Almost fifty years after its initial broadcast, this stripped-down, subtly mythic action thriller retains a good deal of its power, even though the perception of it as a nearly wordless film is belied by all the scenes of Mann talking to himself and musing about his predicament in voice-over. Spielberg has said that he rewatches it twice a year "to remember what I did."

2. *The Positively True Adventures of the (Alleged) Texas Cheerleader-Murdering Mom* (HBO, 1993)

Directed by Michael Ritchie from a script by playwright and screenwriter Jane Anderson (*If These Walls Could Talk*), this is a serio-comic (emphasis on serio-) account of a real and bizarre crime, but also a satire on media ethics and the entertainment industry's insatiable tendency to turn real people's pain into entertainment. Holly Hunter stars as Wanda Holloway, a Channelview, Texas, mother who contemplated hiring a hit man to kill her daughter's chief cheerleading rival; Beau Bridges plays her brother-in-law, Terry Harper, whom she approached about setting up the hit. The story is told in the form of a series of interviews, presumably for a documentary; Holloway and other participants are forthright about their catastrophic errors in judgment even as they interrogate the unseen filmmakers who are in the process of dramatizing their story for the very film you're watching. It's all expertly handled by Ritchie, who dealt with similar material in the feature films *Smile* (about behind-the-scenes ego wars at a beauty contest) and *The Candidate* (starring Robert Redford as a would-be congressman who lets his beliefs be modified and diluted to get elected). The film is self-aware from start to finish, essentially critiquing its participants as well as itself as it goes along, yet it never loses track of the pathetic and tragic aspects of the story, and it never condescends to its small-town characters, even as it concedes the pettiness of their grievances and the stupidity of their mistakes.

3. The Execution of Private Slovik (NBC, 1974)

A project sixteen years in the making, this TV-movie started out as a theatrical adaptation of William Bradford Huie's book about the title character, a World War II Army soldier who became the first US serviceman executed for desertion since the Civil War; Frank Sinatra acquired the rights to the book in 1960 and intended for it to be adapted by blacklisted screenwriter Albert Maltz (*Broken Arrow*, *The Beguiled*), but was convinced by his friend, Senator John F. Kennedy, to cancel the project, out of fear that it might be perceived as antimilitary and could dent his hawkish credentials and cost Kennedy the presidency. It finally saw the light of day with Martin Sheen in the title role—one of his finest performances, right on the heels of his work in Terrence Malick's *Badlands*. Adapted by Richard Dubelman and directed by Lamont Johnson (*The Last American Hero*), it's as close to a perfect character study as network TV has produced, quietly outraged yet somehow resolutely unsentimental, which of course makes its inevitable outcome—Slovik's death by firing squad, pictured in a painterly long shot in the snowy courtyard of an Army base—all the more upsetting.

4. *The Day After* (ABC, 1983)

Written by Edward Hume (*Cannon*, *The Streets of San Francisco*), directed by Nicholas Meyer (*Time After Time*, *Star Trek II* and *VI*), and broadcast during an especially hot period toward the end of the Cold War, *The Day After* is a drama about the effects of nuclear fallout on a single city. It remains the highest-rated stand-alone TV-movie broadcast in network history, drawing an audience of more than 100 million people. Although the film provides a detailed geopolitical backstory explaining the origins of World War III—it starts with a rebellion by the East German army, then escalates into a Soviet blockade of West Germany—the film is mainly concerned with the immediate effects of atomic war on two communities, Lawrenceville, Kansas, and Kansas City, Missouri, as well as rural communities near area missile silos.

The story is broken into three acts: the lead-up to the attack, the attack itself, and the protracted, hideous aftermath. Very possibly the bleakest TV-movie ever broadcast, *The Day After* is an explicitly antiwar statement dedicated entirely to showing audiences what would happen if nuclear weapons were used on civilian populations in the United States. JoBeth Williams, Steve Guttenberg, Jason Robards, William Allen Young, and Bibi Besch head the ensemble cast of Midwestern characters who all respond to this nightmare scenario with varying degrees of denial, despair, and resourcefulness; in the end, though, there is no hope for any of them, only the certainty of sickness and death. The film's existence was greeted with howls of outrage by conservatives who thought it was liberal propaganda meant to compromise President Ronald Reagan's administration's hard-line stance against the Soviet Union's expansionist policies (the *New York Post* called Meyer "a traitor"). The movie's final form was compromised: ABC made the filmmakers cut a sequence that showed a child waking up from a nightmare about nuclear war for fear that it would traumatize young viewers (as if the rest of the film weren't traumatizing already, and as if young children should have been allowed to view it in the first place), as well as scenes that showed flesh being melted by nuclear fire, looters tearing apart cities, and the scene in which Williams dies from radiation poisoning after stating that the dead are much better off than the survivors.

5. *Brian's Song* (ABC, 1971)

For at least two generations, this TV-movie about the friendship between two football players, one of them terminally ill, spawned tens of thousands of gallons of male tears throughout North America. James Caan plays Brian Piccolo, a football player diagnosed with terminal cancer early in his pro career, who dies at age twenty-six; Billy Dee Williams plays Chicago Bears running back and future Hall of Famer Gale Sayers, who supported Piccolo throughout his medical struggles and dedicated a "most courageous player" award to his friend, saying that Brian's the one who really deserved it. "I love Brian Piccolo," he said, "and I'd like all of you to love him, too. And tonight, when you hit your knees, please ask God to love him." The dramatic and emotional template for a good number of sports films and male weepies (categories that tend to overlap quite a bit), *Brian's Song* was also an influential early example

of the interracial buddy movie. It was remade, admirably though without as much impact, as a 2001 TV-movie starring Sean Maher and Mekhi Phifer.

6. *Path to War* (HBO, 2002)

The final film by director John Frankenheimer (*The Manchurian Candidate*, *Ronin*), this nearly three-hour epic plays like the greatest political drama that Oliver Stone never made. Michael Gambon plays President Lyndon Baines Johnson, whose sincere attempts to improve civil rights and create a safety net through his Great Society initiative were damaged by the quagmire of US military involvement in Vietnam. Daniel Giat's script reconfigures a talk-heavy story into a kinetic play of ideas, filled with ping-pong-edited policy arguments in the Oval Office and the US Congress, and psychologically and visually intense scenes that transform history into a waking nightmare (as when Alec Baldwin's Secretary of Defense Robert S. McNamara watches a Vietnamese monk immolating himself in protest against US intervention in his country). This is easily the greatest of Frankenheimer's late-period TV work, which equals his finest work from the 1960s: the TNT miniseries *Andersonville* (1995) and *George Wallace* (1997) and the HBO films *The Burning Season* and *Against the Wall* (both 1994).

7. The Burning Bed (CBS, 1984)

Directed by Robert Greenwald (*Steal This Movie*) from a script by Rose Leiman Goldemberg, this harrowing film dramatizes the true story of homemaker Francine Hughes (Farrah Fawcett), who in 1977 ended the abuse she'd suffered at the hands of her controlling husband, Mickey (Paul LeMat), by burning him to death in his bed as he slept. Hughes was eventually found not guilty of murder by reason of insanity. The film was a landmark in terms of content, depicting domestic violence as an unambiguous horror and a human rights violation; this point of view might seem obvious from the supposedly enlightened perspective of present-day Western values, but at the time the film's broadcast hit viewers like a thunderbolt, prompting frank discussions about the law's inability to protect women and children trapped in a situation like Francine's. Fawcett's performance in the lead role is one of the finest in the history of TV-movies (she would play a somewhat similar role in the 1986 feature film *Extremities*, based on the stage play about a rape victim getting revenge on her attacker).

8. And the Band Played On (HBO, 1993)

Based on Randy Shilts's 1987 best seller, this sprawling ensemble drama shows how governmental incompetence and homophobia abetted the spread of the HIV virus; it doubles as a medical thriller, tracking the spread of the disease that causes AIDS from its presumed source, a sexually indiscriminate flight attendant named Gaetan Dugas (Jeffrey Nordling). Matthew Modine plays epidemiologist Don Francis, who wants to investigate the mysterious illness and deaths of gay men in San Francisco in the early '80s but is thwarted by fears of privacy invasion (not unfounded, the film admits) and competing medical experts (including Alan Alda as American biomedical researcher Robert Gallo), who have their own theories about the disease's origins and want to be the first to effectively deal with it and claim credit. Few American films, television or theatrical, have taken such a sweeping view of the ethical, political, and financial aspects of combating an epidemic.

9. James Dean (TNT, 2001)

James Dean started out as a feature film project in the 1990s, with Michael Mann slated to direct and Leonardo DiCaprio to star. It passed through several sets of hands before landing with director Mark Rydell (*The Rose*), a former actor who studied with Dean at the Actors Studio in New York and competed with him for live TV parts. The title role went to James Franco, who had an almost eerie physical resemblance to Dean but was unknown outside of his role as the dreamy burnout Daniel Desario on *Freaks and Geeks*. The result, scripted by playwright Israel Horovitz, was a cut above the typical "and then he went here, and then he did that" highlight reel mishmash that usually passes for a showbiz biopic.

It was with this project that Franco, the future autodidact and postmodern celebrity, first removed any doubt that he was more than a skinny, dark-haired hunk with the smile of an adorable mutt. He beat out five hundred actors for the role not just by capturing Dean's posture, voice, and mannerisms but by connecting with the chameleonic fluidity that defined his personal life as well as his all-too-brief screen career. Mightily assisted by Rydell, who knew Dean as something other than a poster image or screen dream, Franco plays Dean as a searching young man who constructed a volatile, needling, curious character for himself, the better to keep from facing his own pain. The script delves into Dean's flightiness and insecurity, his considerable power over young women, the partly playacted machismo that tamped down his bisexuality, and his resentment of the father (Michael Moriarty) who abandoned him; it also suggests that Dean suffered from undiagnosed mental illness. The result is a thoughtful portrait of a complicated young man who never got to experience the acclaim that greeted his only three films, *Rebel Without a Cause*, *East of Eden*, and *Giant*.

10. The Lathe of Heaven (PBS, 1980)

Directed by David Loxton and Fred Barzyk from a script by Diane English (*Murphy Brown*) and Roger Swaybill, this low-budget adaptation of Ursula K. Le Guin's novel is one of the few examples of a made-for-TV science-fiction movie demonstrating a genuine interest in exploring the ideas it presents. Bruce Davison plays George Orr, a young man whose dreams come true, though rarely in the way that he might wish. Kevin Conway plays Dr. William Haber, who promises to help George harness his power for the good of humanity but ends up manipulating him in order to play God-by-proxy. Margaret Avery, who would later play a memorable supporting role in the film version of *The Color Purple*, is George's lawyer and eventual lover, Heather LeLache, who tries to help him escape Haber's clutches. Set in Portland, Oregon, but shot mainly in Dallas, Texas (whose 1970s brutalist architecture stands in for a "futuristic" city), *The Lathe of Heaven* is a sterling example of how to substitute storytelling acumen and purity of feeling for production values. It packs a miniseries' worth of story into 120 minutes but never forgets to appreciate its characters as well-rounded individuals rather than plot-delivery devices (even the power-mad Haber ultimately seems more deluded and pitiful than evil), and throughout, there are surprising and marvelous lyrical touches, such as the use of the Beatles' "With a Little Help from My Friends" as the score for a dry ice–choked dream-sex scene that features a cameo appearance by a benevolent turtle-shelled extraterrestrial with a blinking lightbulb for a face. Le Guin's novel was adapted again for the A&E network in 2002 with Lukas Haas, James Caan, and Lisa Bonet in the lead roles, with more production values, a vastly larger special-effects budget, and a lovely score by Angelo Badalamenti (*Twin Peaks*), but not as much charm or soulfulness.

BOSSES YOU'D MOST WANT TO WORK FOR

1. Andy Taylor, *The Andy Griffith Show*
2. Frank Furillo, *Hill Street Blues*
3. Arnold Takahashi / Al Delvecchio, *Happy Days* (wisely let Fonzie set up office in the men's room)
4. Lorelai Gilmore, *Gilmore Girls*
5. Lou Grant, *The Mary Tyler Moore Show / Lou Grant*
6. Leslie Knope, *Parks and Recreation*
7. Jean-Luc Picard, *Star Trek: The Next Generation*
8. William Adama, *Battlestar Galactica*
9. Charlie Townsend, *Charlie's Angels*
10. Oscar Goldman, *The Six Million Dollar Man / The Bionic Woman*
11. Leo McGarry, *The West Wing*
12. Al Giardello, *Homicide: Life on the Street*
13. Angela Bower, *Who's the Boss?*

BOSSES YOU'D LEAST WANT TO WORK FOR

1. Montgomery Burns, *The Simpsons*
2. Don Draper, *Mad Men*
3. Ari Gold, *Entourage*
4. Amanda Woodward, *Melrose Place*
5. Michael Scott, *The Office*
6. J. Peterman, *Seinfeld*
7. Tony Soprano, *The Sopranos*
8. Miles Drentell, *thirtysomething / Once and Again*
9. Annalise Keating, *How to Get Away with Murder*
10. James T. Kirk, *Star Trek*
11. Skipper Jonas Grumby, *Gilligan's Island*
12. Leslie Stevens, *Black-ish*
13. Tony Micelli, *Who's the Boss?*

■ LIVE PLAYS MADE FOR TELEVISION ■

(Hundreds of live plays were produced during the 1950s and early 1960s, garnering large popular audiences and serious critical scrutiny. They aired on such anthology series as *The Philco-Goodyear Television Playhouse*, *The Kraft Television Theater*, *Robert Montgomery Presents*, *Westinghouse Studio One*, and *Playhouse 90*, and they served as valuable launching programs for significant American directors [including John Frankenheimer and Arthur Penn], writers [including Reginald Rose, Paddy Chayefsky, and Rod Serling], and pretty much every significant movie and TV actor of the next twenty years. Some of the most popular programs were remade as feature films, in some cases more than once.

Unfortunately, little of this output is readily available to the public now. Some were recorded on film via the kinescope process, and others [from the late 1950s] were produced on videotape, but many more do not exist in any conveniently viewable form. It's possible to track down some of the more obscure material through the Paley Centers in New York and Los Angeles and through assorted private collectors, but because most people don't have the time or money to do that, the following list is intended as a sampler, focusing on titles that were milestones in the genre and that [as of this book's publication] were viewable via streaming services, YouTube, and DVD collections. —MZS)

12 Angry Men (*Westinghouse Studio One*, CBS, 1954)

This single-set play about jurors deliberating a murder trial might be the single most durable production to come out of TV's live-play era. Reginald Rose scripted it for television (where it was directed by *Patton*'s Franklin Schaffner and starred Robert Cummings); it was adapted for the stage the following year and has been performed ever since, both in its original incarnation and in revisionist versions with all-black, Latino, or female casts. The 1957 film version, directed by Sidney Lumet and starring Henry Fonda, is a classic; William Friedkin (*The Exorcist*) directed a 1997 version for Showtime starring Jack Lemmon.

Bang the Drum Slowly (The US Steel Hour, ABC, 1956)

Novelist Mark Harris adapted his own same-titled novel to create this drama starring Paul Newman as a pitcher for the fictional New York Mammoths baseball team who is stricken with Hodgkin's disease. It's perhaps the earliest example of the sports weepie, a subgenre that reached its apotheosis in the 1971 TV-movie Brian's Song (see "TV-Movies" section). Remade as a 1971 film starring Robert De Niro.

The Comedian (Playhouse 90, CBS, 1957)

Adapted by Rod Serling from Ernest Lehman's novella, and directed by John Frankenheimer, this searing drama starred Mickey Rooney as a once-beloved but miserable and fading vaudeville comic taking out his frustrations on his younger brother/assistant (Mel Tormé) and a writer (Edmond O'Brien). Claustrophobic and ruthless.

Days of Wine and Roses (Playhouse 90, CBS, 1958)

Written by J. P. Miller and directed by John Frankenheimer, this drama about two alcoholics (Cliff Robertson and Piper Laurie) was remade as a 1962 Blake Edwards film starring Jack Lemmon and Lee Remick, but in a much softer and more likable incarnation that lost the desperate edge of the original.

Judgment at Nuremberg (Playhouse 90, CBS, 1959)

Written by Abby Mann, this account of the Nuremberg tribunals reopened some of the deepest wounds of World War II, examining bureaucratic and civilian complicity in the Holocaust. Remade as a theatrical film in 1961.

Marty (Philco TV Playhouse, NBC, 1953)

The earliest smash hit from the live TV era, this low-key urban drama about a couple of "losers" who gain dignity through love starred Rod Steiger (On the Waterfront) as the title character, a Bronx butcher, and Nancy Marchand (The Sopranos) as Clara, the object of his affection. Paddy Chayefsky (Network) wrote it, Delbert Mann (The Bachelor Party) directed. Mann and Chayefsky remade Marty as a 1955 film starring Ernest Borgnine (who won an Oscar in the part) and Betsy Blair. Its central relationship was an influence for many more screen couples, including Rocky and Adrian Balboa.

No Time for Sergeants (*The US Steel Hour*, ABC, 1955)

Based on Mac Hyman's 1954 best seller, this is one of the few notable live-TV productions that was essentially a comedy, and a farce at that. It made a star of Andy Griffith, who plays Will Stockdale, a free spirit who rebels against the constraints of Army life, inspires his comrades, and makes life hell for his superior officer (Robert Emhardt). Griffith reprised his role on Broadway (opposite his future *Andy Griffith Show* costar Don Knotts as Corporal Manual Dexterity), then again for a 1958 film.

Old Man (*Playhouse 90*, CBS, 1958)

Adapted by Horton Foote (*The Trip to Bountiful*) from a portion of William Faulkner's *If I Forget Thee, Jerusalem*, this drama about the effect of the 1927 flood on a small town is one of the most elaborately produced stories ever to air on a live theater program. Directed by John Frankenheimer, the production involved the construction of enormous sets with tanks containing thousands of gallons of water; when a crew member nearly drowned in one of them during rehearsals, the network decided it was too dangerous to do live,

which meant that *Old Man* became the first "live" production to actually be produced in advance and videotaped (although other supposedly live plays had used previously taped material before). Its ratings and critical success are ironically credited with hastening the end of the live theater production on network TV.

Patterns (*Kraft Television Theater*, NBC, 1955)

Rod Serling's breakthrough as a television writer, this bleak, somewhat satirical drama about executives jockeying to control a corporation and undermine one another's careers might be the origin point for what we now think of as "quality TV." Richard Kiley, Everett Sloane, and Ed Begley star. An uncharacteristically excoriating look at what capitalism does to human dignity, *Patterns* was so talked about that it became the first live drama to be performed a second time three weeks after its initial broadcast. Emboldened by this, Serling wrote more socially conscious teleplays, but encountered so much network resistance that he ultimately abandoned the genre in favor of allegorical horror and science fiction, including *The Twilight Zone*, *Night Gallery*, and the original 1968 film adaptation of *Planet of the Apes.*

Requiem for a Heavyweight (*Playhouse 90*, CBS, 1956)

Written by Rod Serling and directed by Ralph Nelson, this is an existential exercise about a boxer named Mountain McClintock (Jack Palance) contemplating the end of his career after being beaten by a younger opponent. Almost unbearably sad at times, the drama stars Keenan Wynn as the boxer's manager and his father, Ed Wynn, as the cutman. *Requiem* struck such a chord with audiences that it was made for English, Dutch, and Yugoslav TV and as a theatrical feature starring Anthony Quinn in Palance's role.

BEST CLIFF-HANGERS EVER

1. **Who shot J.R.?, *Dallas*:** Ground zero for the season-ending cliff-hanger craze, inspiring more than 83 million people to tune in that fall to find out what happened.
2. **"I, Ross, take thee Rachel...," *Friends*:** The Ross/Rachel romantic tempest at its most unexpected.
3. **"Kate...WE HAVE TO GO BACK!," *Lost*:** They were flash-forwards, not flashbacks!
4. **"Mr. Worf...fire," *Star Trek: The Next Generation*:** Captain Picard is a Borg now; will the *Enterprise* kill him?
5. **Kimberly blows up Melrose Place, *Melrose Place*:** The most talked-about cliff-hanger of the watercooler show of the '90s.
6. **The Moldavian Massacre, *Dynasty*:** Pretty much every major player got plugged; if nothing else, the greatest contract renegotiation ploy of all time.
7. **It's one year later, and the Cylons are invading, *Battlestar Galactica*:** Added time jumps to the TV writers' standard tool kit.
8. **Hank figures out Walt is Heisenberg, *Breaking Bad*:** A literal "oh, shit" moment.
9. **Sam and Diane kiss for the first time, *Cheers*:** Funny and sexy and inspired *The Office* and so many other imitators.
10. **President Bartlet is shot, *The West Wing*:** The POTUS is actually collateral damage as white supremacists target his African American body man.

APPENDIX

The Final Scores

(For a description of each category, see The Explanation on page xv.)

	Innovation Alan	Influence Alan	Consistency Alan	Performance Alan	Storytelling Alan	Peak Alan	Innovation Matt	Influence Matt	Consistency Matt	Performance Matt	Storytelling Matt	Peak Matt	Total Score
The Simpsons	10	10	8	10	10	10	10	10	6	9	9	10	112
The Sopranos	10	10	8	10	10	10	10	10	7	8	9	10	112
The Wire	10	7	9	10	10	10	10	8	9	9	10	10	112
Cheers	9	10	9	10	10	10	6	8	10	10	10	10	112
Breaking Bad	9	8	10	10	10	10	8	8	10	9	10	10	112
Mad Men	8	8	9	10	10	10	10	8	9	9	9	10	110
Seinfeld	10	10	7	8	9	10	10	10	7	9	10	10	110
I Love Lucy	10	10	8	9	8	9	10	10	8	9	8	10	109
Deadwood	8	6	9	10	10	10	10	7	8	10	9	10	107
All in the Family	10	9	8	9	8	8	10	10	8	9	8	9	106
M*A*S*H	9	10	7	8	9	8	10	10	8	8	8	10	105
Hill Street Blues	10	10	8	8	8	8	10	10	8	8	8	8	104
The Shield	8	9	10	9	9	9	7	8	8	9	9	7	102
The Twilight Zone	9	10	7	8	9	6	10	10	8	8	7	9	101
Arrested Development	7	6	7	9	9	10	10	7	8	10	9	8	100
The Larry Sanders Show	7	8	8	8	7	8	10	8	10	10	10	6	100

	Innovation Alan	Influence Alan	Consistency Alan	Performance Alan	Storytelling Alan	Peak Alan	Innovation Matt	Influence Matt	Consistency Matt	Performance Matt	Storytelling Matt	Peak Matt	Total Score
The Honeymooners	6	9	8	9	8	8	7	8	9	10	9	8	99
Louie	10	6	8	7	9	9	10	6	7	8	9	10	99
The Mary Tyler Moore Show	7	9	8	9	8	7	7	9	9	10	8	7	98
The X-Files	9	10	6	7	9	8	9	10	6	8	7	8	97
Curb Your Enthusiasm	6	5	9	9	10	10	7	6	9	9	8	8	96
SpongeBob SquarePants							16	14	16	18	18	14	96
Twin Peaks	10	9	5	6	8	7	10	10	5	9	7	10	96
Lost	9	10	6	8	9	9	10	10	5	7	6	6	95
Buffy the Vampire Slayer	8	7	7	8	9	8	8	9	7	8	7	8	94
Freaks and Geeks**	6	9	7	9	9	9	6	8	7	9	8	7	94
My So-Called Life**	7	9	6	9	8	8	6	9	7	9	8	8	94
Oz	10	7	6	9	7	6	10	7	8	8	8	7	93
The Dick Van Dyke Show	6	10	9	9	8	7	6	7	8	9	9	4	92
Friday Night Lights	7	6	6	10	9	9	7	7	6	9	8	8	92
NYPD Blue	8	8	6	9	8	8	7	9	6	8	7	7	91

	Innovation Alan	Influence Alan	Consistency Alan	Performance Alan	Storytelling Alan	Peak Alan	Innovation Matt	Influence Matt	Consistency Matt	Performance Matt	Storytelling Matt	Peak Matt	Total Score
Frasier	6	5	9	10	9	9	5	4	9	10	8	6	90
Homicide	7	6	6	9	9	8	8	7	6	8	8	8	90
Battlestar Galactica	8	5	7	9	8	8	8	7	6	9	7	7	89
In Treatment	9	1	7	9	8	10	10	3	7	8	9	8	89
South Park	8	8	6	7	7	7	8	9	7	9	8	5	89
The West Wing	7	8	6	9	8	9	6	6	6	8	7	9	89
Mary Hartman, Mary Hartman							18	10	14	18	14	14	88
The Andy Griffith Show	6	8	8	8	8	5	6	6	8	8	8	8	87
The Cosby Show	6	10	7	8	8	6	6	9	7	8	8	4	87
Moonlighting	8	8	6	8	8	5	9	7	4	9	7	8	87
Taxi	6	5	9	9	8	9	6	4	9	9	8	5	87
East Side/West Side**							16	16	14	16	12	12	86
Hannibal	8	2	6	9	8	8	8	3	8	9	8	9	86
ER	8	9	7	8	7	7	6	7	6	7	6	7	85
Parks and Recreation	4	4	9	10	9	10	3	5	8	9	8	6	85
Roseanne	7	7	6	9	8	8	7	8	6	7	6	6	85

	Innovation Alan	Influence Alan	Consistency Alan	Performance Alan	Storytelling Alan	Peak Alan	Innovation Matt	Influence Matt	Consistency Matt	Performance Matt	Storytelling Matt	Peak Matt	Total Score
30 Rock	6	5	6	8	9	10	7	5	8	9	7	4	84
The Bob Newhart Show							10	10	20	20	14	10	84
Malcolm in the Middle	6	7	7	8	7	6	7	7	8	8	9	4	84
Miami Vice	8	9	6	6	7	3	8	9	4	9	6	9	84
The Office	5	7	5	7	7	9	5	9	7	9	7	7	84
St. Elsewhere	7	6	7	7	9	6	8	6	7	10	7	4	84
Community	8	2	6	8	8	9	9	3	5	9	7	9	83
The Golden Girls	6	7	8	8	7	6	6	7	8	9	7	4	83
Police Squad!**	7	7	6	7	9	7	9	8	7	8	7	1	83
Twenty-Four (24)	9	9	5	7	6	3	9	10	5	7	6	6	82
The Defenders							16	18	14	14	12	8	82
Gunsmoke							18	16	12	12	12	12	82
Sex and the City	8	9	6	7	5	5	8	8	6	8	7	5	82
Star Trek	8	10	5	6	6	2	8	10	5	7	6	8	81
Firefly**	6	4	6	9	8	8	7	5	7	7	7	6	80
Law & Order	7	9	8	8	7	3	5	10	8	8	6	1	80
Maude							12	8	16	18	14	12	80
The Rockford Files	3	7	9	9	8	5	4	7	8	8	7	5	80
China Beach	7	5	7	9	8	8	6	4	7	8	7	3	79
Enlightened	7	1	7	8	9	8	7	1	9	9	8	5	79

	Innovation Alan	Influence Alan	Consistency Alan	Performance Alan	Storytelling Alan	Peak Alan	Innovation Matt	Influence Matt	Consistency Matt	Performance Matt	Storytelling Matt	Peak Matt	Total Score
Everybody Loves Raymond	3	5	8	8	8	9	2	4	10	9	8	5	79
The Wonder Years	6	8	5	7	7	6	7	9	6	7	7	4	79
Barney Miller	4	6	7	7	7	8	4	6	8	9	7	5	78
*Frank's Place***							18	4	14	16	12	14	78
It's Garry Shandling's Show							20	8	12	12	14	12	78
The Jack Benny Program							8	18	16	16	12	10	78
Justified	5	4	7	9	8	8	5	4	7	9	7	5	78
The Rocky and Bullwinkle Show							14	12	14	14	12	12	78
thirtysomething	7	6	6	7	8	5	8	7	6	8	7	3	78
Columbo	6	8	7	8	8	2	6	7	7	8	7	3	77
Friends	6	10	6	7	7	5	5	9	6	8	7	1	77
Futurama	6	4	7	7	7	3	7	4	8	10	8	6	77
The Outer Limits							12	10	14	12	16	12	76
Northern Exposure	7	6	6	7	7	5	6	6	7	8	8	3	76
Batman	7	9	6	6	4	1	10	10	7	8	6	1	75
King of the Hill	4	3	9	9	8	6	5	2	8	9	7	5	75
Veronica Mars	6	5	5	8	7	8	7	4	6	8	6	5	75

	Innovation Alan	Influence Alan	Consistency Alan	Performance Alan	Storytelling Alan	Peak Alan	Innovation Matt	Influence Matt	Consistency Matt	Performance Matt	Storytelling Matt	Peak Matt	Total Score
Cagney & Lacey	5	5	6	8	7	5	6	7	6	8	7	4	74
*EZ Streets***	14	2	14	16	16	12							74
Gilmore Girls	5	3	6	8	7	6	6	5	8	8	7	5	74
Six Feet Under	7	6	5	7	7	4	6	5	5	9	7	6	74
Sports Night	7	5	6	8	7	6	7	3	7	8	7	3	74
Wiseguy	7	7	6	7	7	3	7	5	6	9	6	4	74
Star Trek: Deep Space Nine	4	5	7	6	8	5	3	6	7	8	8	6	73
Batman: The Animated Series	5	3	7	6	7	3	5	5	8	9	8	6	72
Boardwalk Empire	4	4	8	7	7	7	3	3	6	9	6	8	72
NewsRadio	3	3	8	9	9	8	3	2	8	9	7	3	72
Picket Fences	6	5	5	8	7	5	6	5	7	8	6	4	72
Scrubs	6	4	6	6	7	6	6	4	8	9	7	3	72
WKRP in Cincinnati	3	5	8	7	6	4	4	3	8	9	8	7	72
How I Met Your Mother	7	6	4	6	7	6	6	6	6	8	7	1	70
Soap							16	8	12	12	12	10	70
*Terriers***	1	1	7	9	9	8	2	1	7	9	9	7	70

**Single-season shows where we artificially limited the scores. The most they could score in each category was a 9, except for consistency, where the highest possible score was a 7.

ACKNOWLEDGMENTS

Alan Sepinwall: When David Mamet came in to write a late-period *Hill Street Blues* episode, David Milch asked if he might want to just take the whole show off his hands, telling him, "Do you want it? We've been here for seven years; we're insane. If you want the show, we'll give it to you." Looking back on it, Mamet told me years later, "I kinda wish I'd taken him up on it."

My esteemed coauthor didn't use Milch's exact phrasing when he asked if I wanted to take over the *Sopranos* beat at the *Star-Ledger* starting with season 4—which, even for the series' second half, was the TV critic equivalent of covering music for the *Liverpool Daily Post* in the early '60s—but the sentiment was the same. And unlike Mamet, I was wise enough in the moment to say yes, which put me in position for nearly every great thing that's happened in my career since then. So when Matt asked if I wanted to do a TV book with him, I didn't even need a moment to think about it. When Matt Zoller Seitz suggests I write something, my life tends to improve enormously.

Of course, this book's roots start in those early *Ledger* days, to which I owe an enormous debt to Susan Olds (and Peggy McGlone, who walked my résumé into Susan's office when I was a twenty-two-year-old college grad with no non-internship experience) and Mark Di Ionno for teaming us up, to Wally Stroby, Anne-Marie Cottone, Steve Hedgpeth, Rosemary Parrillo, Jenifer Braun, and everybody else from that golden era of the paper's feature section who supported and/or indulged us.

Thanks also to all my bosses and colleagues at HitFix, past and present, for giving me the encouragement and flexibility to take on big projects like this even as I'm down in the recapping trenches with them. I also bounced many ideas off TV critic friends like Dan Fienberg, Linda Holmes, Todd VanDerWerff, Maureen Ryan, Rich Heldenfels, and Ed Bark, who provided advice and inspiration throughout the brainstorming and writing phases. I also did most of my writing with my copy of Tim Brooks and Earle Marsh's *The Complete Directory to Prime Time*

Network and Cable TV Shows handy, just in case I needed reminding on things like who replaced Roger Moore (who had already replaced James Garner) on *Maverick*.

Thanks to our agent, Amy Williams, for helping put this all together, and our editor, Maddie Caldwell. I apologize if any hairs were lost or recolored by our near-constant revisions very late in the game.

Mainly, though, thanks to my wife, Marian, and our amazing kids, Julia and Ben, for your never-ending love and support. You didn't see much of me while I was writing this book. I hope you're proud of the finished product, and not just because we put *SpongeBob* and *Phineas and Ferb* in there.

Matt Zoller Seitz: My first thank-you is to Alan. Even though he is, as I have joked too many times, an unstoppable critical machine wrapped around poly-metal alloy, and capable of writing things faster and better than pretty much anyone alive, he's a compassionate and fair man who carries himself with modesty, which is the only reason that his arrival in the *Star-Ledger* newsroom in 1996, one year into my own tenure as a twenty-seven-year-old kid-critic wunderkind, didn't throw me into a doom-spiral of insecurity. Since then, Alan has become a true friend and one of the best collaborators I've ever had. He's both challenging and sensible, inspiring me to work harder and do better and let things go when it's time. Rock-paper-scissors is our solution to most disagreements and hard choices, and it has always worked fine for us. I recommend it.

Thanks are due to Maddie Caldwell, our editor, who kept this massive project on track, made countless suggestions that improved it, and tolerated my last-minute requests, à la Columbo, to add *just one more thing*. Thanks are also due to my agent, Amy Williams, who always thinks beyond the next deal, and has had a profound impact on my career; Chaz Ebert of RogerEbert.com and Adam Moss of *New York* magazine, who made it possible for me to take on projects beyond the scope of my regular duties at their publications; Eric Klopfer, my regular editor at Abrams Books, who didn't blink when I told him that I would be finishing *TV (The Book)* at the same time as *The Oliver Stone Experience*; Stephen T. Neave, Trey Moynihan, Eric Albrecht, Howard and Jill Kirsch, Amy Cook, Leslie Klainberg, Jane Wheeler, and the rest of the circle that helped me out with child care when work moved into the foreground. Thanks also to the experts who let me pick their brains, including Todd VanDerWerff, Maureen Ryan, Margaret Lyons, Ian Grey, Max Winter, Ken Cancelosi, Gazelle Emami, Lane Brown, Gilbert Cruz, Ed Bark, Stephen Bowie, Wallace Stroby, Joe Adalian, and my Twitter followers, who have helped me out at critical junctures.

Thanks, finally, to the *Star-Ledger* crew, who made a journalist out of me: Susan Olds, Rosemary Parrillo, Wally Stroby, Anne-Marie Cottone, Steve Hedgpeth, Jenifer Braun, Richard Aregood, and editor Jim Willse, who I am convinced hired me mainly because I had the temerity to quote the book of Corinthians at him during my job interview. Thanks especially to Mark Di Ionno, who called me and Alan "Kid and Genius," paired us on our daily column, "All TV," and motivated us with a never-ending supply of maxims that I call The Tao of Mark. They include: "Don't mess around with that topic sentence crap, puke on the page first, then move the pieces around until you've got something that works," "If you write a sentence that you know is good, break it out into its own paragraph to put a spotlight on it," "Before you file, try cutting paragraphs from the top to see how deep into the piece you can get without losing anything important," "Push the button, send it in, and go home," and, "Not every piece has to have a brilliant ending. It's okay to just stop."

INDEX